G000291742

PLYMOUTH'S FORGOTTEN WAR
(The Great Rebellion, 1642-1646)

German bombs and English cannonballs — twice during its proud history the port of Plymouth has resolutely stood firm as the horror of war rained down upon its streets. The World War II Blitz has been well documented, however the same cannot be said of the city's siege, 300 years earlier, during the English Civil War — until now!

Plymouth's Forgotten War is the result of many years of painstaking research. The build-up to war, both locally and nationally; the major battles and skirmishes in the southwest; the political and social aspects of the conflict; biographies of many of the major participants during and after the hostilities; relics that can still be found today; maps and illustrations; a complete and precise record of Plymouth's stand in the great rebellion, when its brave citizens stood alone against the Royalist forces.

Philip Photiou lives and works in the city of Plymouth and has always been interested in the town's early history. For many years he has researched the story of the civil war in and around Plymouth. Philip has written a number of articles for the *Evening Herald*, and has scripted a video production on the same subject. He has spent many years walking the battlefields, visiting the churches and towns, and searching out the characters that are described in this book.

PLYMOUTH'S FORGOTTEN WAR
(The Great Rebellion, 1642-1646)

Philip Photiou

ARTHUR H. STOCKWELL LTD.
Torrs Park Ilfracombe Devon
Established 1898
www.ahstockwell.co.uk

First published in Great Britain, 2005

British Library Cataloguing-in-Publication Data.
A catalogue record for this book is available from the British Library.

Cover depicts King Charles I asking Plymouth to surrender, September 1644. Taken from a window by J. Fouracre in the Plymouth Club, which was destroyed in the Blitz.

ISBN 0 7223 3669-1
Printed in Great Britain by
Arthur H. Stockwell Ltd.
Torrs Park Ilfracombe
Devon

Dedication

This book is dedicated to my family who have been very patient awaiting this publication. I also wish to acknowledge a debt we owe to those soldiers and civilians who fought and died for Plymouth during the great rebellion.

Acknowledgement

I gratefully acknowledge the invaluable assistance of many people and organisations for their help in gathering information for this publication and I wish to list them separately: Lord St Levan and Mr James St Aubyn, Marizion, Cornwall; Mr Richard Carew Pole, Anthony House, Cornwall; Mr Norman Cowling, Boyton, Cornwall; Mr Richard Preston, Local Studies Library, Winchester; Mr Hardacre, Winchester Cathedral; Ms Christine Campbell, Miss Moira Goff and Mr Michael J. Boggan, The British Library; Mrs Sylvia Guthrig, Plympton, Plymouth; Mr Ken Doughty, Aveton Gifford, Devon; Mr Bill Best, Harris, Plymouth; Miss Liz Luck, National Trust, Cornwall; Mr Colin J. Squires, Saltash Heritage, Saltash, Cornwall; Miss Sarah Noble, Plymouth City Council; Rev Bob King, Weobley Church, Hereford; Mrs Mary Freeman, Tavistock, Devon; Mr Stuart Peachy, Historical Managements Ltd.; Mr Nicholas Coney and Mr Adrian Ailes, The National Archives, London; Mr M. F. Scoble, Plymouth Athenaeum; Mr John Draisey, Devon County Council, Exeter; Miss Anne Morgan and all the staff at the West Devon Record Office, Plymouth: Mr Michael Webb at the Bodleian Library, Oxford; Mr Ian Criddle and all the staff at the Plymouth City Library, and Mrs Barbara Doggrell, Sherborne Castle, Dorset; and Helen Photiou for her help in designing the cover. Due to the length of time accumulating the material for this publication I may have overlooked a number of people, if so please accept my apologies.

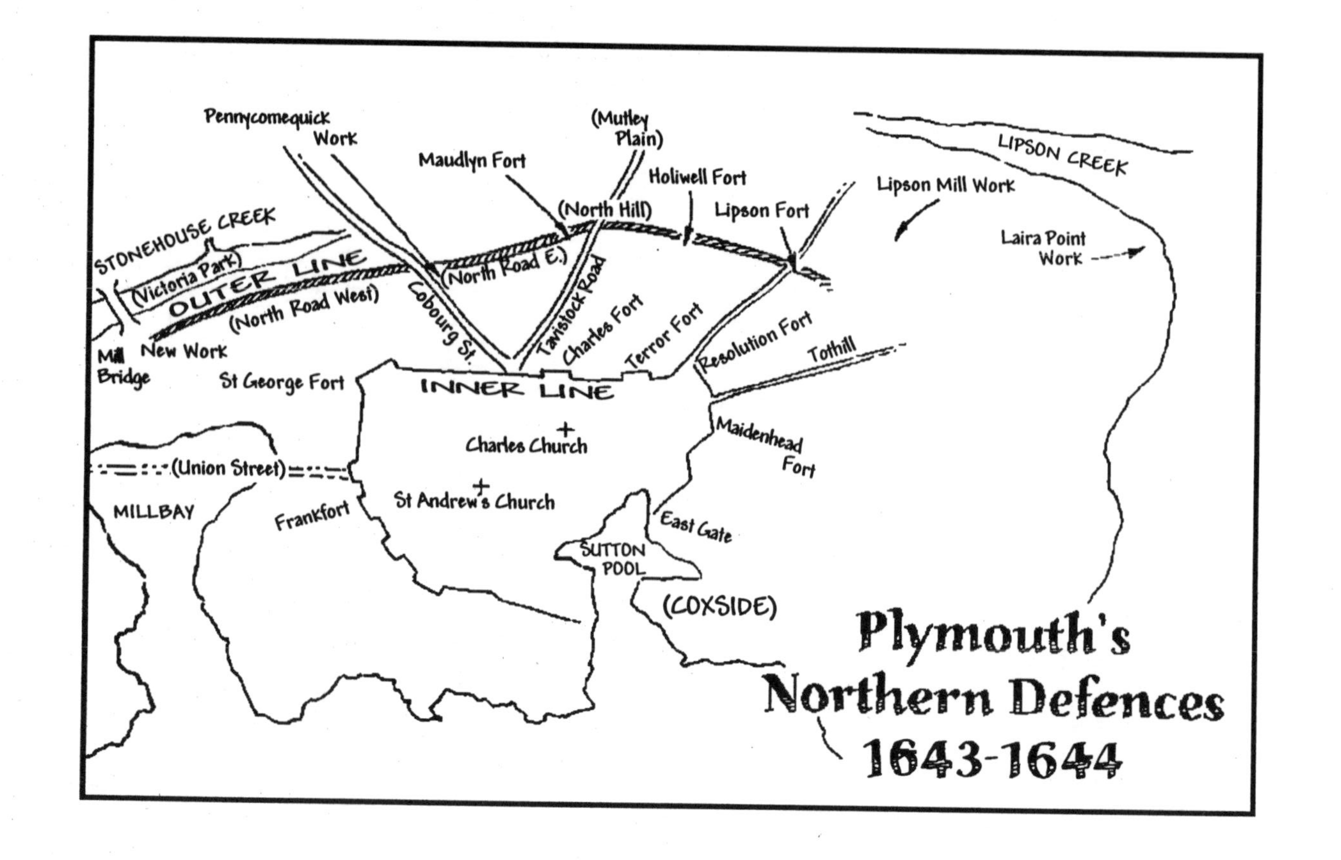
Pennycomequick Work
(Mutley Plain)
Maudlyn Fort
Holiwell Fort
LIPSON CREEK
Lipson Mill Work
(North Hill)
Lipson Fort
Laira Point Work
STONEHOUSE CREEK
(Victoria Park)
OUTER LINE
(North Road E.)
(North Road West)
Cobourg St.
Tavistock Road
Charles Fort
Terror Fort
Resolution Fort
Tothill
Mill Bridge
New Work
St George Fort
INNER LINE
Maidenhead Fort
Charles Church
(Union Street)
St Andrew's Church
MILLBAY
Frankfort
East Gate
SUTTON POOL
(COXSIDE)
Plymouth's Northern Defences 1643-1644

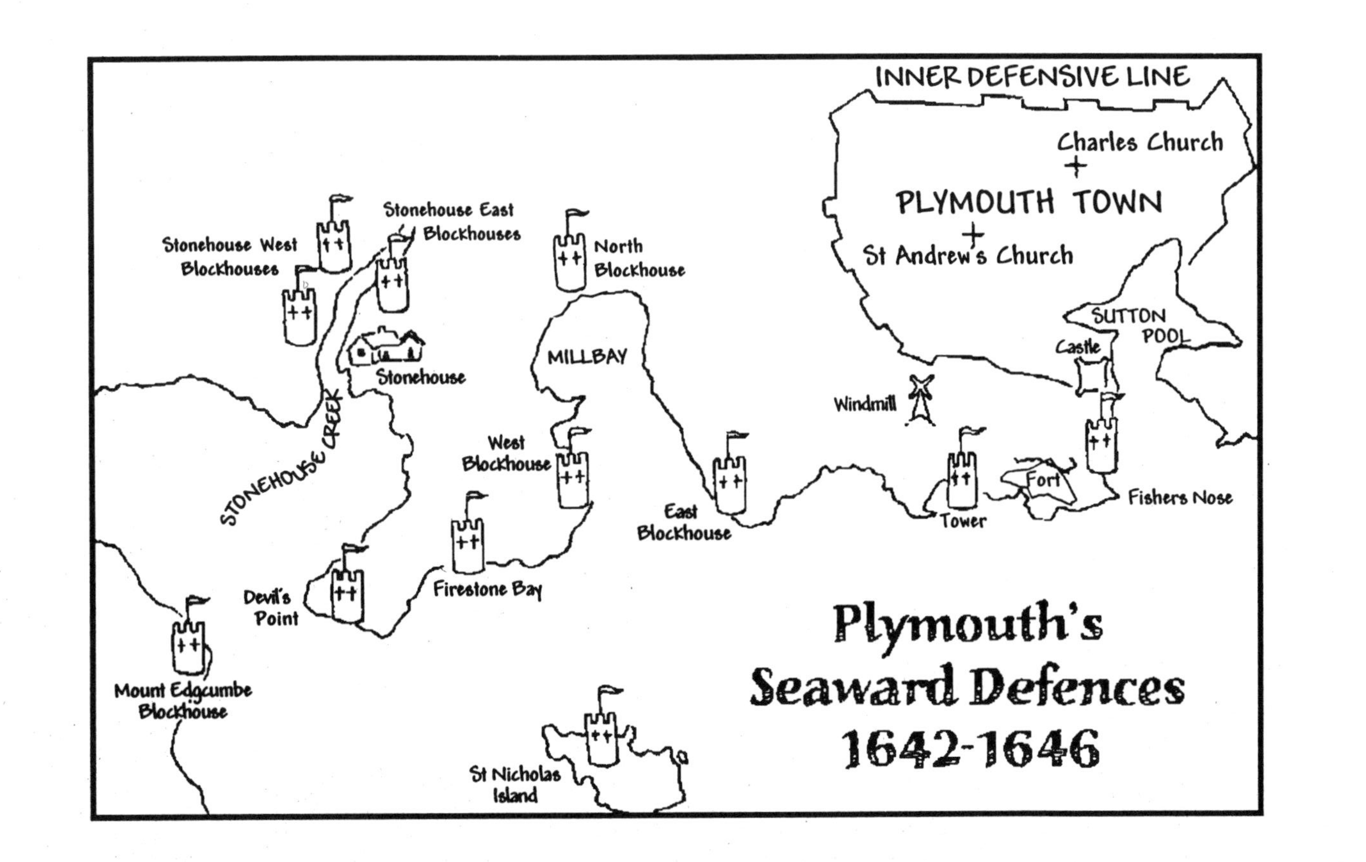
INNER DEFENSIVE LINE
Charles Church
PLYMOUTH TOWN
St Andrew's Church
SUTTON POOL
Castle
Windmill
Fort
Fishers Nose
Tower
East Blockhouse
MILLBAY
North Blockhouse
West Blockhouse
Firestone Bay
Stonehouse East Blockhouses
Stonehouse West Blockhouses
Stonehouse
STONEHOUSE CREEK
Devil's Point
Mount Edgcumbe Blockhouse
St Nicholas Island
Plymouth's
Seaward Defences
1642-1646

Mount Stamford
Oct–Nov 1643

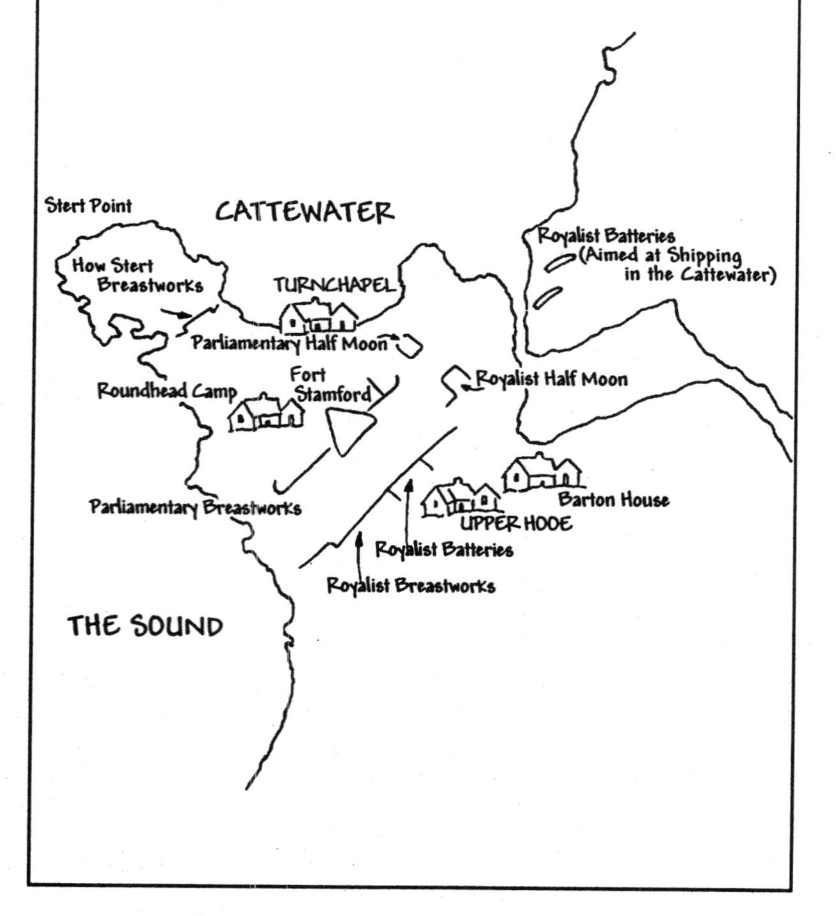
Stert Point
CATTEWATER
How Stert
Breastworks
TURNCHAPEL
Royalist Batteries
(Aimed at Shipping
in the Cattewater)
Parliamentary Half Moon
Fort
Stamford
Royalist Half Moon
Roundhead Camp
Barton House
Parliamentary Breastworks
UPPER HOOE
Royalist Batteries
Royalist Breastworks
THE SOUND

Contents

Chapter 1

The Nation Divides

While Charles Stuart, the distraught King of England recently forced out of his capital by anti-royalist riots, stared up at the royal banner flapping furiously in the breeze atop Castle Hill in Nottingham, people living and working in the port of Plymouth, two hundred and fifty miles away, pondered on what the future held. The year was 1642, civil war had once again come to England and all its depredations and suffering would spread over the land like a plague for the next four years. Plymouth's rise from the medieval period to the accession of the Stuart dynasty reveals ample evidence of the town's maturing importance. The port's strategic coastal position would see control of the town a necessity for both sides throughout the forthcoming struggle.

As a prelude to the outbreak of war it is essential to briefly describe Plymouth and her near neighbours at this time. It is also necessary to outline a number of prominent historical episodes, which are relevant as to why the town turned away from its king and allied itself to parliament. Since the days of King Edward I the Plymouth-Plympton area had been involved in the nation's military strategy during England's wars with Scotland, France and Spain. Plymouth, like other ports along the south coast, found itself utilized as a depot for the gathering of ships and supplies, and as a rendezvous for the soldiers that were to be transported across the Channel for attacks against France or Spain. With the Elizabethan era of Drake, Hawkins, Grenville and Raleigh came a period of savage warfare, which led ultimately to the destruction of Spanish naval power in

1588. It was this age of high seas adventure that put Plymouth firmly on the map, from now on the town's growth and prominence were assured.

The town's ancient defences developed with time, so as to protect Plymouth from attacks, such as the destructive raid, which occurred in August 1403. On this infamous date a French army of 1,200 men sailed into the Cattewater, attacked the town and burned 600 houses. To prevent a repetition a large chain boom was constructed which could be hauled across the harbour in times of danger. Should a hostile fleet approach the port the chain could be drawn up, thus barring access into the harbour. Unable to proceed further the ship-borne enemy would then come under cannon fire from the castle up on Lambhay Hill, whose guns dominated the harbourage. This small, four-towered bastion, built to guard Sutton Pool, had been constructed during the reign of King Henry IV and was under the authority of the mayor and corporation. In the event of an attack each of the town councillors would be assigned his own post in the castle, later the responsibility for defending Plymouth would be transferred to the town's military governor.

As Plymouth grew and warfare evolved so did the need to modernise and extend existing defences. By the end of the sixteenth century a new limestone fort had been constructed on Lambhay Point, southeast of the old castle and directly overlooking the harbour, the Cattewater and Plymouth Sound. This new, much larger and more strategically placed citadel, armed with large cannon, covered all the seaward approaches into Plymouth and made the old castle obsolete. Occasionally used as a storehouse or jail the decaying, almost abandoned structure on Lambhay Hill slowly disappeared until, barely anything remains as a reminder that a castle ever existed there at all.

To guard Plymouth against an amphibious force moving up one of the inland creeks between Sutton Pool and the River Tamar, a number of fortified blockhouses had been constructed. These narrow, claustrophobic artillery towers were dotted along the cliffs at essential points. Two of these mini fortlets protected the approach into Millbay, one on the east bank, one on the west bank. Another on Firestone Bay defended the area between Millbay and Stonehouse Creek, while two more, one at Devil's Point, the other over on the Cornish side at Mount Edgcumbe guarded the entrance into the Tamar. Several of these stone towers were later connected by walls and armed with cannon. The fortified town of Stonehouse, a short walk to the west of Plymouth, with its impressive manor house and high walls was a further deterrent to an invading force considering an attack on Plymouth from the direction of Stonehouse Creek.

The keystone to Plymouth's seaward defence during this period was St Nicholas Island, known today as Drake's Island. This imposing rock lay directly south of Millbay and could only be reached by boat. Enemy shipping moving toward the Tamar or Sutton Pool would pass close to this natural fortress which seemed to rise up out of the sea. To prevent attack the island's medieval chapel was pulled down and a wall constructed around the perimeter as close to the shore as possible. More than a dozen heavy cannon had been ferried over and placed strategically to cover all possible approaches. Towards the end of the sixteenth century Sir Francis Drake, constantly concerned over Plymouth's safety, urged Queen Elizabeth to order a survey with the object of strengthening not only the island but also the town's other defences. As a consequence Robert Adams arrived from London in 1592 and examined the area, making notes of existing defences and planning sites for new forts. Upon completion of his work Adams proposed a strong wall be built to encircle the town and St Nicholas Island be turned into one huge fortress. Due to expense the wall was never built but the island was reinforced. More walls were constructed, tunnels dug and extra cannon transferred over, all under Adams' supervision. In 1602, during the kingship of James I and the governorship of Ferdinando Gorges, further work continued out on the island; barracks for three hundred men went up and the walls and parapet were reinforced. Minor repairs to the citadel would continue until the eve of war and beyond.

The slow build up to the raising of the royal standard in Nottingham and the long, bloody road to civil war grew out of a confused melting pot. Endless political debate, unnecessary executions, imprisonment of the innocent, fear of a return to Catholicism and wars with France, Spain, Scotland and Ireland all combined to foment sedition. Most of England's woes at this time seemed to stem from the rise of the Stuart kings and would not end until the succession of the Hanovarians. As a favourite of Queen Elizabeth, Plymouth, home to many prosperous buccaneers, became an object of envy at court and many courtiers never forgot the queen's high regard for the little port.

A constant thorn in the side of Plymouth's vital maritime trade throughout her history were pirates, who for centuries haunted many a coastal town and spread fear far into the countryside. Raiders would often sweep down on an isolated ship or village, plunder everything of value and kidnap men, women and children, many of whom were sold as slaves, never to return home. King James I made a pathetic attempt to clear the Channel of these scavengers, but in order to do so he demanded £1,000 from Plymouth. The money was not paid and the small naval squadron lying in the Sound remained at anchor, while the corsairs continued plundering and sinking unarmed vessels almost within sight of royal navy lookouts.

Such lack of majestic concern for one of England's most loyal and supportive towns forced many of Plymouth's merchants and fishermen to despise the king's methods. This smouldering resentment against James Stuart rose to a new height in 1618, when one of the town's favourites, Sir Walter Raleigh, was executed on trumped up charges of treason. Since the days of Good Queen Bess, when Plymouth gave more than her share to the wars with Catholic Spain, emotions against that most hated of religions ran high and Puritanism began to take a firm hold of people's ideologies. Unfortunately Elizabeth was long gone and with a Scot on the throne, anti-Catholicism increased in England.

Having failed to work out a marriage between his son Charles and the King of Spain's daughter, James Stuart had been persuaded to declare war on England's old antagonist by Charles and his close friend James Villiers, the conniving Duke of Buckingham. Once again Plymouth was selected as a base of operations and a fleet and army were gathered in the Sound, preparatory to an attack against Cadiz. On March 27th 1625 King James died and his son took the throne. Drunk with power, the new monarch was easily persuaded by Buckingham to continue the war with Spain and the fleet duly set sail. The expedition failed dismally, due mainly to poor leadership and the task force eventually limped back into Plymouth Sound. During the return trip disease had broken out on many of the ships, placing those on board in wretched conditions. By the time the fleet dropped anchor hundreds were dead and many more were dying. When thousands of sick, dejected warriors poured ashore into the narrow streets of Plymouth, before being organised into camps on the Hoe, they inadvertently contaminated the townsfolk. Those who fled into the surrounding countryside to escape spread the plague.

Disease was not the only legacy given indirectly to the community by its new king. Starving, mutinous servicemen soon began a spree of looting. Homes were smashed and shops raided; worse was to follow. Several people were found lying in narrow lanes, robbed or murdered; sometimes a soldier or sailor after a drunken brawl, but occasionally, a blameless civilian. When the camps were eventually broken up and the soldiers disappeared from Plymouth late in 1626, the population had been temporarily stunted. To add to the town's woes King Charles now declared war against his brother-in-law, King Louis XIII of France.

A second flotilla was assembled for an invasion in support of the Protestant cause, which at that moment was fighting for its very existence in Catholic France. The object of this second expedition was the island fortress of Rhe near the town of La Rochelle. Once again, organisation and cooperation failed and the half-hearted attack was repulsed with appalling losses of more than 3,000 Englishmen. The fleet sailed back into Plymouth where death and destruction once more called on the populace. Plague claimed new victims, two lord mayors, Thomas Sherwell and Robert Trelawny numbered amongst the dead, leaving Abraham Colmer to be appointed the third mayor in twelve months. Totalled together the two wasted expeditions caused the deaths of over 1,000 local people, reducing the town's population by more than twenty per cent and all for nothing. Besides the chaos and mortality brought about by military occupation, Plymouth's overseas trade slumped dramatically. King Charles, like his father before him had alienated himself from some of his most loyal subjects, more so by his association with the underhanded James Villiers.

With the fighting over and England's involvement in the Thirty Years' War limited to voluntary enlistment in the various armies serving on the continent, political dissention began to rear its head in parliament. On March 2nd 1629 Charles Stuart found parliament greatly opposed to his numerous money-raising schemes. Frustrated the king used his belief in divine right and ordered the speaker to adjourn the House of Commons. Sir John Eliot refused to be intimidated and violence almost broke out. In retaliation the king ordered the doors to the Commons forced open, but the members prudently fled before the royal command could be carried out. His temper up, King Charles ordered parliament dissolved. Next morning

John Eliot, William Strode, Denzil Holles, William Coryton, Benjamin Valentine and four other members were brought before the Privy Council in the Star Chamber and committed to prison in the Tower of London. Over the years Eliot and Strode not only angered the king and his supporters but they also violently opposed any proposals put forward by Sir James Bagge. The 'Bottomless Bagge' as he came to be known by his opponents was MP for Plympton, owner of Saltram House near Plymouth and a close friend of James Villiers.

Bagge was a blaggard who surreptitiously assisted Buckingham in embezzling money which should have given the English troops of the Spanish and French expeditions comfortable quarters and ample supplies. Being a true royal patriot Bagge had been rewarded for his loyalty in 1624 by a knighthood and an appointment as Vice Admiral of Cornwall. But James Bagge created many enemies during his climb up the ladder. At the top of the list of those who opposed Bagge were John Pym MP for Tavistock, Bevill Grenville MP for Launceston and John Glanville MP for Plymouth. These and others who voiced their opinion were quickly silenced at court, to the anger and dismay of many. James Bagge's twisted fidelity to the crown was further sanctified in 1629 when he was commissioned Governor of Plymouth. The Duke of Buckingham and Sir James Bagge were doing England's new monarch no favours, on the contrary their despicable deceitful dealings caused great hardship to thousands of innocent people. All the time money meant for the treasury kept rolling into the wrong coffers and the shift of public opinion against the king grew ever stronger.

War, disease, loss of trade and politics had already strained the loyalty of the Plymouth people toward their king, now religious discord emerged. The opening round between King Charles and the church-going Puritan population of Plymouth germinated in 1631. Since the year 1572 the town council, by the authority of Queen Elizabeth, had been permitted to select and appoint its own vicar for St Andrew's Church. This amiable agreement continued for almost fifty years and all was well within the mother church. Henry Wallis, a Puritan, held the office of vicar and a Brixton incumbent, Thomas Forde, had been elected lecturer. Shortly before Forde arrived in Plymouth, theological authorities in London mysteriously rejected his appointment. The reason for the rejection was that Forde had opposed Archbishop William Laud's teachings thereby alienating himself from the king and his church leaders.

Three years later Wallis died and the capable but puritanically minded Alexander Grosse was picked as his replacement. From Christow in Devon, Grosse had come to Plympton St Mary's in 1623 and served until 1639, when he moved to a church near Exeter. Sadly Grosse's name was also on Archbishop Laud's blacklist and his nomination as Vicar of St Andrew's was cast aside by the Bishop of Exeter. The town corporation again put forward Thomas Forde's name, but he was refused. Peeved by what he believed to be continual aggravation from Plymouth, King Charles finally took away the town's right to designate its own vicar. St Andrew's however still needed a minister; so the king sent one of his own supporters, Doctor Aaron Wilson, down to fill the post.

A second royalist, Thomas Bedford, was given the position of lecturer over Alexander Grosse, whom the corporation preferred. Wilson and Bedford were met with instant hostility and friction between them and the townsfolk broke out immediately. The new vicar caused trouble for himself by objecting to the orphan's aid and poor hospital, located almost next door to St Andrew's. He also complained about the neighbouring market stalls to the east and he refused to allow town councillors their own pews in the church. Dr Wilson's views also conflicted greatly with the Puritan way of life, but he must have been of durable character as he remained in Plymouth, refusing to be bullied out.

Differences in politics and petty disagreements forced the parishioners to eventually draw up a petition for a new church. With ample support from local parliamentary members including, rather surprisingly two staunch royalists Sir James Bagge, whose dealings with Buckingham were at last under scrutiny and Mayor Robert Trelawny and many local landowners; a petition was drafted and sent to London. King Charles received the application, certifying that the population of Plymouth was too great for one church and requesting the creation of a second church to take the overspill. After six years of delay the king finally agreed, despite the knowledge that a new church would, like St Andrew's, become a rendezvous for Puritanism.

By 1641, due mainly to the efforts of the old mayor Robert Trelawny, work on the new church, to be christened Charles in the king's honour began, however the edifice had to be built on land outside St Andrew's parish boundary. The site eventually selected lay northeast of the old church near Green Street, on a plot of land given over to the council by a local vintner. The right to appoint a vicar for Charles' Church was, rather surprisingly, bestowed upon the people of Plymouth. This act of royal generosity failed to soften the feelings of many toward the king. Shortly after building began on Charles' Church war had broken out, bringing an early halt to construction.

On the eve of civil war Plymouth was a flourishing township of between seven and eight thousand people it was also extremely dirty. Personal waste and other refuse was tossed into the streets and left to rot. Buildings and roads were also in a poor state of repair, particularly around the harbour, where overcrowding predominated. The Barbican, centre of Plymouth's fishing industry, hummed to the perpetual stink of thousands of fish being unloaded daily at Fisherman's Steps, ready for salting and storage or immediate sale at quayside stalls. Despite the employment of scavengers (road sweepers) conditions in the town deteriorated. In fact, so bad had the situation become that in 1634 the corporation received a royal writ, demanding the town be cleaned up immediately. It would take the council almost forty years to comply.

To obtain a picture of the Plymouth area on the eve of civil war, it is necessary to describe as briefly as possible the position of her near neighbours and the various important main roads radiating out to connect them with the port. Over the years Plymouth had grown rapidly outwards, with the exception of those periods when plague ripped through the town. Houses went up in the direction of Stonehouse to the west, the Cattewater to the east and the Maudlyn Ridge to the north. Out in the countryside the villages, which are now suburbs of the city of Plymouth, Plympton, Plymstock, Compton, Stoke, St Budeaux, Tamerton and Knackersknowle (Crownhill) were also expanding. In the 1640s these communities still retained their individualism and were separated from Plymouth by dense wooded ridges, deep valleys and sluggish rivers. Connecting Plymouth with these outlying villages and a half-dozen country manors were a number of well-worn badly-maintained dirt roads. Two thoroughfares linked the town with her nearest neighbour Stonehouse, the direct route via Frankfort Gate (near Princess Street) or by way of New Street and the old mills at Millbay.

The village of East Stonehouse, as it was known in pre-civil war years, had grown up on the east bank of Stonehouse Creek under the tenureship of several prominent families. The Edgcumbes, who inherited the land from the Durnfords by marriage, spent vast sums of money in developing this area, especially the waterfront, bringing in work and helping the village to expand. Dominating the river frontage was the impressive fortified manor house of the Edgcumbe family, while further up the creek stood the towers of an ancient abbey much in decline. To rival its larger neighbours Saltash and Plymouth, East Stonehouse established itself as a borough, but its life as such, was destined to be short-lived. Edgcumbe money also paid for a bridge to be built over Stonehouse Creek that became known in later years as Millbridge. Here a number of corn mills were erected to grind grain for local consumption or export. Passing over the Mill Bridge, from the direction of Stonehouse, a rough road passed through corn fields before swinging off to the left and up towards Stoke Damerell, a cluster of houses near a church on the north bank of Stonehouse Creek.

Running to the north of the Plymouth-Stonehouse-Stoke Damerell Road was the principal route from Plymouth to Cornwall. This highway left the port by Old Town Gate (the northern end of modern Old Town Street) and wound its way out to North Cross. From here the road led down to cross the eastern end of Stonehouse Creek, traversing the stream at a point known today as Pennycomequick. From the creek bottom the road sliced up Alma Road towards Milehouse, from where it ran on through Swilly, passing the recently-built home of Robert Trelawny at Ham. Continuing down toward Weston Mill Lake the route crossed a bridge before threading its way through Kings Tamerton. Today Peters Park Lane has supplanted the old road that eventually terminated on the east bank of the River Tamar opposite Saltash.

The third major road out of Plymouth led to Tavistock and went by way of Old Town Gate directly northwards. This highway lies buried close to modern day Tavistock Road that now follows the older route much like a number of modern motorways follow the ancient Roman roads of Britain. In the seventeenth century North Hill was much steeper and higher than it is today, but despite a difficult climb the road went straight up and over the top of North Hill, then down across the Maudlyn Ridge (Mutley Plain) towards Townsend Hill at the far end. Beyond Maudlyn the road divided; a lesser branch carved a route towards the River Plym, allowing access to the sparsely populated communities of Compton and Eggbuckland.

The main road meanwhile continued ever northwards, swinging left towards Thornhill then back to Venn House before going on to Tavistock. On its way over the moors, a number of side roads branched away from the main track, leading to the manors and villages of Manadon, Widey, Knackersknowle, Trennimans Jump (Roborough) and Elfordstown (Yelverton).

From Gasking or North Gate ran the primary route between Plymouth and the old town of Plympton. This narrow byway curved its way up around the southern end of North Hill, and then ran partially along Lipson Road, before cutting down and across Lipson Creek. The road passed close by Efford Hall and cut its way through thick woodland before reaching the River Plym. Here, at low tide a ford could be utilised and the river crossed. When the long bridge over Marsh Mills was built, this ford was eventually abandoned and almost forgotten except in the old name Ebb Ford or Efford. The new structure was not a bridge in the sense of the word but a long, wide causeway that offered local people and traders easier access to Plymouth from the outlying villages of Boringdon, Newnham, Saltram and Plympton. This practical route spanned the marshland from Crabtree across to the eastern side of the Plym.

Travelling out of Plymouth's East Gate lay the road to Cattedowne, which ultimately came to an end at the Cattewater. Here a ferry allowed people a short cut across the water at Horstone (Oreston) Passage. Once on the east bank, narrow country lanes snaked away towards Hooe, Radford, Plymstock and on into the South Hams. The big name in this area during the civil war period was John Harris, MP for Liskeard and master of Radford House, a fifty-room mansion built near the headwaters of Radford Lake. Radford House had been renown in the old days as a rendezvous for Drake, Hawkins and Howard, and Sir Christopher Harris entertained them all lavishly. It was to Radford House that Sir Walter Raleigh had been confined after his heartbreaking failure up the Orinocco River, before being sent to London for trial and execution.

Many other manorial houses and hamlets were dotted around Plymouth, most remembered today in name only. Back in the seventeenth century these little communities could be reached by travelling along deep, muddy, unkempt lanes. Widey the principal estate north of the town was situated in a valley not far from Eggbuckland Church then a separate parish governed by its own vestry and the county magistrates. Widey House would gain fame during the siege by its intermittent use as a royalist headquarters, but like many grand houses around Plymouth, the estate would eventually disappear at the hands of fatuous councillors. Yeoman Hele, who owned the Widey Estate, also owned Manadon House located to the west of Widey, in the grounds of which was once Manadon College.

Whitleigh Hall, another piece of lost heritage, lying west of Knackersknowle and north of Manadon was the home of John Fownes, the fourth son of Thomas Fownes who had been Mayor of Plymouth during the *Mayflower* episode. Fownes married Catherine Champernowne at Exeter on September 20th 1639, but by the second year of the war he would be a widower. Nevertheless John Fownes would serve the town faithfully during the civil war as a captain. Beyond Whitleigh lay Tamerton Foliot, a separate parish in the rural district of Plympton St Marys. Further out on the banks of the River Tavy stood Warleigh House. Both these outlying hamlets would be used as barracks by royalist soldiers throughout the war. Coming back towards Plymouth, southwest of Tamerton, the proud little village of St Budeaux slumbered peacefully around its historic church. Because of its close proximity to Saltash, St Budeaux would be visited on and off many times during the war by soldiers from both armies.

Moving back even closer to Plymouth to the north of modern day North Road East and roughly where Houndiscombe Road runs, could be found the Houndiscombe Estate, shrouded by a densely-wooded valley. Nothing exists of the estate today, but in the 1640s it was home to the Sherwell family. The most notable members being Thomas Sherwell, MP for Plymouth between 1614-1628 and three times mayor, and his brother Nicholas, who also held the same mayoral office on three occasions. Keame (Keyham), Sir Thomas Wyse's home and Kinterbury (Barne Barton), which belonged to Sir Ferdinando Gorges, were also manors of importance during this period, but over the years these historic buildings have sadly vanished. Besides Keame the Wyse family also owned Mount Wise House, which had been strategically constructed on high ground overlooking Richmond Walk, giving an excellent view of Cornwall and the River Tamar.

Across the Hamoaze, opposite Mount Wyse (Wise) House stood Mount Edgcumbe, the most imposing manor on the Tamar estuary. When the Edgcumbe family took over the Durnfords' property in the later part of the fifteenth century, the family fortune increased dramatically and the name Edgcumbe grew in prominence. In 1638 Piers Edgcumbe, MP for Newport and Camelford, master of languages and a devoted royalist, inherited the estate upon the demise of his father Sir Richard; like many of his Cornish compatriots Piers would remain loyal to the king throughout the war.

To supply Plymouth's ever increasing population with a sufficient amount of drinking water, the corporation was forced to pay for several surveys to discover a new source. The results of these studies revealed that water from the River Meavy high up on Dartmoor could provide the perfect reservoir. If a channel could be excavated across the moor all the way to Plymouth, the town's fresh water problems would be over. In 1585 an act, supported by Sir Francis Drake and Sir Christopher Harris, was passed, authorising the construction of a channel, or leat to divert the Meavy and bring water into Plymouth.

Work on the new waterway began five years later and Sir Francis Drake, sea captain, ex-Mayor of Plymouth, MP for Bossiny and scourge of the Spanish Main was paid £200 to supervise and plan the leat's manufacture. Five months later the construction gang had finished its twenty-mile long meandering trench and on April 24th a great celebration took place in Plymouth as the first water gushed through the leat and down into the town. Mayor William Peperell and the townsfolk eagerly greeted Sir Francis as he rode in, no more would the people of Plymouth have to rely on well water, or so they believed. Little did they realise that royalist troops moving on Plymouth from the direction of Dartmoor, could and often would cut off the supply of water simply by damming the leat at any point along its route.

In 1638 England became involved in yet another senseless war, this time with Scotland. The conflict came about when King Charles undertook to force a new prayer book upon the Scots. The king also contemptuously ordered the Scottish bishops to observe the same saints as their English counterparts, with the exception of a few who were linked to royalty. Riots followed the king's odious command, beginning in a Scottish church and rapidly spreading through towns and countryside. In response the Scots drew up a covenant, declaring that the people of the lowlands were united and would defend their religion against Archbishop Laud's new prayer book. The king, unprepared for war, sent the Marquis of Hamilton north in an effort to relieve the tension simmering in Scotland. Hamilton failed dismally in his mission and by the close of the year preparations for armed conflict were well under way. Unfortunately for Charles Stuart the unity and support of his knights at this critical time was almost non-existent; many made excuses, while others didn't even bother to muster their supporters. Already the English people were making a stand against the king's authority, but even at this late stage King Charles failed to see the writing on the wall.

Money, clothing, equipment, horses and arms were scarce but nevertheless on April 29th an army of sorts set out for the border town of Berwick. Endless exhaustive marching by untrained troops soon made the English war-weary and careless. With no sign of the enemy, a dangerous gap opened between the cavalry and foot. As this opening expanded the Scots saw their opportunity, moving swiftly they frightened the English horse, which panicked and galloped back into their own foot. Terrified by the retreat of the vanguard, the infantry almost broke before turning to meet the foe. The victorious Scotsmen under the able leadership of Alexander Leslie endeavoured to follow, but there was to be no battle. Both armies faced each other and the level-headed Leslie decided to bargain for a victory. Commissioners were now sent into the English camp seeking to negotiate. Had Charles disregarded Leslie's offer, the better trained and better equipped Scots would undoubtedly have given the English a severe thrashing. On June 18th 1639 a treaty was agreed and signed, and the two armies separated and went home bringing an end to what became known as the Bishops' War.

Not long after the border went quiet, King Charles, humiliated at being forced into a treaty by the Scots, broke the pact and a fresh English army was raised. The king called parliament together for the first time in eleven years; by doing so he hoped its members would vote him money for a second expedition. Parliament met in April 1640 in uncertain mood; spotting his chance John Pym took the reins of leadership and a new era in English politics began. With Pym at the helm, the king's desire for immediate money and support went out of the window. Four days after the assembly opened Pym, recalling his despicable internment in the Tower of London, organised a committee. This council was to go over past cases of persecution by the crown against parliamentary members. Pym also passed a list of complaints that should be made good before any money to finance a war would even be considered.

With John Pym determined to thwart his every desire, King Charles used his right to absolute power and dissolved parliament three weeks after its opening. Despite Westminster's refusal to grant him money for war, the king called on his lord lieutenants, commanding them to raise a large army for a campaign in Scotland. The troops were to muster at Newcastle by the middle of September, but while the English were organising themselves, the Scots marched swiftly across the border and invaded northern England. The two armies eventually met on opposite sides of the River Tyne where they remained, observing each other suspiciously for several days. Then an accidental discharge from an English musket killed a Scottish officer and battle began. Fearing revenge the untried English volunteers broke almost immediately, pursued by Scottish cavalry, which had forded the Tyne further upstream in an effort to outflank their opponents. A number of trained officers hastily organised a rearguard and with a nucleus of veteran soldiers they managed to fight off the Scottish attacks, buying time for the rest of the army to retreat on Durham.

Beaten and demoralised, the English soldiery trudged down the road from the Tyne and the victorious Scots moved on to seize Newcastle. The poor quality of his army and lack of morale forced the king to sign the Treaty of Ripon in October 1640, thereby bringing an end to the Second Bishops' War. Humiliated and defeated, the people of England voiced their anger loudly and called on Charles Stuart to assemble parliament. Locked inside his own world of banquets and balls, the king was quite unaware of just how much he had alienated himself from his subjects. Eventually even the walls of the royal palaces couldn't keep the rumours of unrest at bay and in September 1640, against his better judgement, the king called forth parliament.

The following month elections were held throughout the realm to fill the next parliament. In Plymouth Robert Trelawny, a royalist, but a fair man was chosen. Another with similar leaning, Edward Hyde, was picked to be MP for Saltash, while Nicholas Slanning a third royalist, was elected for Plympton. John Pym, the rhetoric parliamentary leader of the Commons again took his seat for Tavistock. Once elected the members met at Westminster in what was to become known as the Long Parliament, which opened on November 3rd 1640 and continued until 1663. Both houses fairly buzzed with conversation, but almost immediately the old animosities flared. Pym a man almost fanatical in his English Protestantism continually opposed the king and his supporters, especially on questions relating to the church, the powers of the bishops and control of the militia. Poor confused Charles Stuart habitually gave in to Pym and feelings toward the monarchy swayed to and fro. People were angry with the king one moment but when they saw him almost bowing to parliament's demands, many grew sympathetic. John Pym now put into action a plan to rid the king of his closest friends whom he believed corrupted his majesty's court.

One of the most prominent of the king's favourites was William Laud, Archbishop of Canterbury an irritable fellow who despised the growing trend of Puritanism, and who showed more than a little sympathy toward the Catholic religion. It had been Laud's revised prayer book that sparked the First Bishops' War. Consequently Laud's name was at the top of Pym's hit list and on March 1st 1641 the archbishop was arrested by order of parliament and escorted to the Tower of London. With popular opinion running against him at the moment, Charles dare not intercede on his friend's behalf. Pym began to believe in the power of parliament and he openly defied the king a second time by arresting another of his staunch supporters, Thomas Wentworth, the Earl of Strafford and Lord Lieutenant of Ireland. Wentworth, a one-time supporter of Pym and Sir John Eliot, owed his high position to a change of allegiance, which made him a close ally to the king. While on a brief visit to his home county of Yorkshire, Strafford was suddenly called to London by his sovereign. Despite warnings from his friends not to leave the security of the north, Wentworth chose to obey the royal command.

Shortly after his arrival in the capital, the Earl of Strafford found himself arrested and imprisoned by order of parliament, or rather John Pym. Wentworth's subsequent trial proved difficult for the prosecution, who had him up on trumped up charges of treason and the verdict hung in the balance. Aware that the day might not go in his favour, Pym proposed an adjournment. Before the trial could resume John Pym played his ace and called for Strafford's attainder. When the king was informed he refused to pass the bill, but on the advice of his timid bishops he passed the responsibility on to a committee. By taking this course of action Charles Stuart believed he could absolve himself of any blame for Strafford's fate and at the same time please his opponents. Once again Pym had achieved his purpose and on May 12th Thomas Wentworth was cruelly beheaded for treason on Tower Hill before a huge cheering crowd.

John Pym's most significant gain during this turbulent period was the king's consent never to dissolve parliament. The ruling monarch always had the option to end any Westminster assembly simply by an order, it would never happen again. The political situation now deteriorated more rapidly as Pym's vengeful reign of terror matched that previously carried out by the king's supporters, though with much less refinement. People who refused information to parliament found themselves arrested and imprisoned without trial, where they lingered for days or even years. Law and order began to disintegrate and England tottered on the brink of anarchy.

With John Pym and his followers in the ascendancy and the split between king and parliament widening daily, many royalist MPs decided to leave London for the safety of their own homes. Amongst those who sought to preserve their freedom in a city so against the king were two westcountrymen, Sir Nicholas Slanning and Sir Bevill Grenville. Slanning born at Bickleigh on September 1st 1606 had become heir to his family estate seven years later, upon the death of his father. Nicholas studied at Exeter and Oxford before travelling to the Netherlands where he learnt the art of war. In 1632 he was knighted by King Charles and afterwards served on the Commission of Piracy for Devon and Cornwall. Later Slanning was made vice admiral for the southern shores of both counties. In September 1625 he married Gertrude Bagge, daughter of the notorious Sir James Bagge, their wedding took place at St Andrew's Church in Plymouth.

Ten years later Slanning was appointed Governor of Pendennis Castle, an important fortification guarding the entrance into Falmouth harbour in Cornwall. During the 'Short' and early part of the 'Long Parliaments' Sir Nicholas represented Plympton in Westminster. Like his friends John Trevannion, Sidney Godolphin and Richard Arundell, Slanning voted against Strafford's attainder. When he left the capital a disenchanted Nicholas Slanning knew what was coming. As in all civil wars family loyalties divide, the Slannings were no exception. Sir Nicholas' cousin John had died in 1633, but his widow Jane, a resident of Plympton, would give her full support to parliament. During the conflict Jane Slanning continually donated cash gifts for the defence of Plymouth, much to her cousin's exasperation.

Slanning's good friend Sir Bevill Grenville, grandson of the famous

Elizabethan sea dog Sir Richard Grenville of the *Revenge* fame lived at Stow in north Cornwall. Although not present at Westminster during Strafford's trial, Bevill Grenville would undoubtedly have voted the same way as Slanning. Matriculating at Oxford in 1611, at the age of sixteen, Grenville represented Cornwall in 1621 and 1624. A close friend of Sir John Eliot, Bevill later stood for Launceston during the first three parliaments of Charles I, before again representing Cornwall in the Long Parliament. By June 1642 there were over forty parliamentary members absent without leave, most like Slanning and Grenville, opposed to Pym's reforms, were either home or on the way. In their absence the House ordered that those missing members should not be allowed into the Commons until their excuses had been heard. If no justification could be found for their absenteeism, a fine would be imposed. John Pym already knew the missing royalists would never return and steps were quickly taken to replace them.

Representing Plymouth in the Long Parliament was the town's old mayor, Robert Trelawny, whose family had shifted from Cornwall to Plymouth back in the late 1550s. Baptized on the 1st of April 1598 in St Andrew's Church, Trelawny had been brought up with the knowledge that one day he would inherit his father's vast wealth. On January 6th 1623 Trelawny married Anne Crooke of Mevagissey and set up home in Plymouth. Ten years later he was elected mayor, following in his father's footsteps. When not tied up with the family possessions in America, or petitioning parliament on behalf of Plymouth's latest church, Bob Trelawny supervised the building of his new residence at Ham, a task that was finally completed in 1639.

Whilst strolling with a friend in London, Trelawny was overheard to declare that the House of Commons could not appoint a guard for itself without the king's consent, under pain of high treason. This was a preposterous statement considering the suspicious nature of those living in the capital at such a tempestuous time. Anti-royalists jumped on Trelawny's comment, his associate was questioned and although he tried to protect his friend, he failed. The fact that Trelawny had spoken of intended guards for Westminster before any had been appointed made matters worse. Robert Trelawny was quickly arrested and questioned. Loyal to his monarch, Trelawny confessed to making the statement and was incarcerated in Winchester prison. Later he was released and permitted to return home to Plymouth, but in March 1642 he was expelled from the House of Commons, his seat being passed over to John Yonge. Trelawny's freedom was to be short lived, for giving open support to the king he would be rearrested again in November.

By the time news reached Plymouth of events in London they had already passed into history, the political situation was changing daily. The same story was being played out all over the kingdom, people were bewildered, who was right, king or parliament? And what news would the next coach or ship bring in, war or peace? The gentry were as divided and unsure as the rest of the population. The looming crisis was not going to become a conflict between rich and poor, but rather between those who believed in the king and those whose faith lay with a people's parliament. The leaders were the wealthy aristocracy and whichever side they elected to fight for, the majority of their tenants would follow.

Meanwhile in London men were continually being questioned and persecuted for their royalist leanings; Robert Trelawny, Sir Ralph Hopton of Somerset, Sir Edward Dering MP for Kent, the eminent writer Dr William Chillingworth and Geoffrey Palmer MP were a few of the more prominent. The Church fuelled animosity against the royalists by fervently calling for the preservation of the Protestant religion and urging violence against Catholicism. As the year 1641 wore on the people of England were beginning to come forward to make their choice.

Finding the capital growing more and more inhospitable, and in a vain hope of receiving support for his cause from Scotland, Charles Stuart travelled north of the border seeking to impress and purchase favours. In October, whilst still in Scotland, ominous waves from the Irish Sea began breaking along the west coast of England, sending ripples inland, upon which rode even more bad news. The Catholics in Ireland had risen against their Protestant neighbours and massacred hundreds of English and Scottish families in Ulster. A horrified King Charles seemed powerless to prevent the slaughter, after all the Irish revolutionaries claimed they were fighting for him. Charles' heart went out to the rebels, but they were murdering Protestants, and England, despite the queen, was fervently anti-Catholic.

With the king absent and no standing army, parliament passed an ordinance in November 1641 giving Robert Sydney, the Earl of Leicester and Lord Lieutenant of Ireland, authority to raise volunteers and money for the purpose of crushing the rebellion in Ireland. Eventually almost 4,000 men were assembled and the money to arm, equip and transfer this force across the Irish Sea was paid out by parliament. Relieved, King Charles quietly gave his consent to the expedition, he could do no less. Command of the horse went to Bevill Grenville's unruly brother, Richard Grenville, while the cavalry was to be under his nephew George Monck of Potherbridge, Devon. Early in 1642 the task force left Chester for Ireland, where the blood bath continued unabated. The war that followed would go on and on for many years, but once again the king had allowed Pym to triumph. Parliament had raised, organised and supplied its own army, though it would fight under the royal banner.

In early December Charles Stuart bravely returned to London taking up residence in Whitehall, in less than a week Pym was again on the attack. A Bill had been introduced in parliament for the militia of England to be placed under Westminster's control, led by a lord general appointed by the Commons. The House voted against the proposal, but John Pym refused to yield, he desired parliamentary domination of the trained bands and was determined to get it. Christmas failed to halt the pressure on the king and London found itself being pulled in all directions. Pym's supporters controlled almost the entire city with the exception of Whitehall and the Tower of London. The latter, one of England's major arsenals, was held by Colonel Thomas Lunsford, a loyal king's man, but Pym was already undermining his position and calling for Lunsford's replacement. Eventually he had his own way and Colonel Lunsford was forced to hand over command of the Tower to Sir John Byron.

Archbishop John Williams of York greatly aided the king's isolation in his own capital by handing a petition in to the House of Lords. In the document Williams complained of the recent forcible eviction of the bishops from the House and stated that, due to an incomplete assembly all Acts and Bills were illegal because of the absence of the said bishops. When Pym learned of the archbishop's protest, he stirred up the Commons and called for the impeachment of all who put their signatures to the document. Both Houses voted in favour and many bishops found themselves arrested and imprisoned. Charles Stuart meanwhile continued to please his opponents, he pronounced the rebellious Irish traitors, despite their misguided beliefs, and he offered Pym the luxurious post of Chancellor of the Exchequer; Pym, as expected, refused the position. With public opinion rising ever higher against him in the Commons, Charles knew he must act soon or lose the game completely.

On January 2nd 1642 Edward Montague the Earl of Manchester and Lord Mandeville, Pym's two strongest supporters in the House of Lords, were accused of treason by Sir Edward Herbert, the king's new Attorney General. Herbert followed up his accusations by pointing the finger at John Pym, John Hampden, Denzil Holles, William Strode and Arthur Haselrig in the Commons. Uproar followed, but none of the five were handed over, the Attorney General's feeble attempt at silencing Pym failed dismally, the king however was not ready to give up just yet. During the evening of January 3-4th, John Pym, expecting his own imminent arrest, decided to stand his ground. Early on the morning of the 4th parliament sat as usual, shortly before noon word arrived that the king's men were on their way with the intention of arresting the infamous five. By mid-afternoon Charles Stuart himself was reputed to be with them. Experiencing a sudden change of heart, Pym, hoping to avoid arrest, decided to leave immediately. Strode however, opposed running and remained stubbornly in his seat.

William Strode was a character of great strength and determination, a survivor who stood by his convictions even if all others weakened. Strode resided at Newnham, near Plymouth but had been baptized at his mother's home town of Bovey Tracey on November 6th 1599. Young Strode, the second son of Sir William Strode, graduated from Oxford in 1619 before going on to represent Bere Alston in parliament. At the age of thirty-five, whilst fervently supporting Sir John Eliot's views, Strode was arrested for disorderly conduct in the Commons and he spent the next eleven years in prison. Unlike the unfortunate Eliot, William Strode survived his ordeal and remained relatively well, considering the length of time he was incarcerated.

Finally released in January 1640, Strode was active in the Commons during the Long Parliament, where once again he represented Bere Alston. Compensated for his unjust imprisonment, but still angered by the eleven lost years of his life, William Strode became one of the king's most rancorous opponents. When he was impeached along with the other four on January 4th 1642, Strode remained seated, refusing to leave the floor. For long fretful minutes, with the footsteps of Pym and the others echoing in the distance, Strode lingered, until his close friend Sir Walter Erle dragged him out barely minutes before the king's arrival. When Charles entered the chamber and found his quarry gone, he tarried only a short time before departing, seething at losing what he believed would have been his moment of triumph.

In London a general voicing of support in favour of parliament followed the king's belated show of royal bravado. Apprentices, militia, sailors and citizens marched through the streets loudly expressing their support for Westminster. With such prevailing pressure in the capital, the king was aware that his own safety was in danger. During the night of January 10th with his family and a small escort Charles Stuart fled from Whitehall, making his way to Hampton Court, then on to Windsor. The notorious five later returned to the House of Commons, applauded by their fellow members and the population of the city. London was now lost to the king and England spiralled more rapidly towards civil war.

Many people in Devonshire, whose own interests lay in a peaceful co-existence between king and parliament, believed their sovereign should take a backwards step and allow parliament to govern the nation accordingly. The assembly of the Long Parliament had recently given the county permission to hand in a petition, which in short complained of the ever-falling economic situation within Devon. Pirates continued to plague the coast, ship money, the threat to Protestantism and bad management in a number of the stannary towns were grievances laid out in the document. Local politicians expressed the concerns of their constituents, but nothing could be done immediately to alleviate their suffering, too much was happening around London for Westminster to worry about affairs in far away Devon.

Despite a rising population, Plymouth's fishing trade was rapidly declining, to add to the town's misery those clergymen, pro-royalist in their beliefs, continually harassed the local parishioners in all matters pertaining to the Church. This was particularly true of Dr Aaron Wilson, who stood out as the leading proponent for King Charles in the community. To burden the county even further, a large number of refugee Protestant and Catholic families, having fled from their homes in war-torn Ireland, had arrived seeking sanctuary within Devon's borders. Fortunately late in January 1642, the House of Commons ordered all non-Protestant Irish rounded up and shipped home. To many in Plymouth it seemed as though parliament was making an effort to stabilize the nation and prevent war.

Throughout the rest of the county, Exeter, despite efforts by the royalist Earl of Bath, gave most of its support to parliament. Of the more rural areas north Devon was against the king's party, while the central portion of the county sympathized with him. The people of south and east Devon were divided and during the coming conflict many would change sides more than once, depending on which faction held the advantage at the time. The influence of the Devonshire gentry also had an effect on the allegiance of many local people, who usually showed little interest in national politics. Of the more affluent Devonian's, Sir Richard Strode, William his brother, Sir George Chudleigh of Ashton and his son James, Christopher Martyn, owner of Chaddlewood, Sir Nicholas Martyn, Sir Shilston Calmady, Sir John Northcote, Sir John Bampfield, Sir John Pole, Sir Samuel Rolle, one of the wealthiest men in the country and two of Sir Francis Drake's descendants, Sir Francis and Thomas Drake, all sided with parliament. Sir William Pole, John Harris of Radford, Sir Henry Cary of Cockington, Sir Edward Carey, Sir Ames Ameridith, Sir Henry Carew, Sir Edward Seymour of Berry Pomeroy, Sir Ralph Sydenham, Richard Culme of Canonsleigh the lord high sheriff of the county, Sir Thomas Hele of Flete, the Champernownes of Modbury and Sir Hugh Pollard all came out for the king.

Although Devon, Somerset and Dorset gave their allegiance to parliament, Plymouth's neighbour across the Tamar remained entirely loyal to King Charles. Cornwall was destined to become a permanent base for recruitment and a perfect avenue for supplies coming across from the continent. Almost the entire Cornish nobility were for the king with the exception of Sir Richard Buller of Shillingham, Sir Alexander Carew of Anthony and Lord John Robartes of Lanhydrock. The hierarchy of town and county began making speeches and nailing up posters urging support for king or parliament, the people like sheep, listened, raised their fists and followed their masters. The very same thing was happening all over England, counties, towns, villages and families were dividing up and preparing for war.

Chapter 2

War

By early 1642 England was breaking up, but not into an organised pattern. Parliament's support came from the southeast, southwest and parts of the Midlands, the king drew his followers from Cornwall, Wales, the west Midlands and the north. Minor skirmishing flared up soon after King Charles fled from his capital. One of the earliest encounters taking place when Colonel Sir Thomas Lunsford and Lord George Digby skirmished with Sir Richard Onslow at Kingston-upon-Thames, twenty-five miles from London. In February the king sent his wife to Holland with high hopes of obtaining assistance from the continent, while he marched north with a small escort.

Approaching Hull, a town stacked with cannon, muskets and powder, the king sent his son Charles ahead to pave the way for a royal visit. Sir John Hotham, a middle-of-the-road parliamentarian and governor of the town, welcomed the prince and lavished generous hospitality upon his royal person. Next morning, April 23rd, Hotham was informed of the king's imminent arrival at the head of an oversized escort. Alerted to the real reason behind such an unexpected visit, Hotham closed the town gates and denied the royal party permission to enter. Receiving no support from the few royalists within Hull, King Charles eventually left and rode on to his most loyal city of York. Once established in the old Viking capital, the king began recruiting for his cause.

In the meantime Westminster sent a party north to discover just what the king was up to in Yorkshire. Charles high-handedly refused to meet with the parliamentary commissioners and they were forced to return to London none the wiser. During the month of May

Charles Stuart ordered the law courts transferred to York; strong protests from parliament were to no avail and the Lord Keeper, Sir Edward Littleton, managed to smuggle the great seal out of the capital thus giving the royalists the law of the land.

On June 1st parliament drew up a draft of nineteen proposals which were sent to the king for his endorsement, but with war fever hotting up and tempers smouldering, it was doubtful he would even consider signing. The document called for such highly-unacceptable concessions as, all officials appointed to high office be made with parliamentary consent and the militia to come under Westminster's control, as would all forts and military posts. Also support for the protestant cause in Europe should be forthcoming as well as reformation of the Church. Charles and his advisors read the petition and, as expected, rejected its asinine proposals. Four weeks later the king issued a general Commissions of Array, which simply meant the lord lieutenants of each county were to muster their respective trained bands in the name of his majesty. Parliament countered by publishing a Militia Bill, calling out those same trained bands on its own behalf.

For almost a month royalists and parliamentarians rallied their supporters; a number of counties were wholly for one side or the other. Yorkshire, Leicestershire and many more were divided. Of the ports, Chatham, Bristol, London, Portsmouth and Plymouth sided with parliament, while Chester, Falmouth and Newcastle retained their allegiance for the king. More parliamentary members left Westminster and returned home to their constituencies in an effort to rally support. The fighting, which so far had been confined to street brawling, now began to take on a more serious aspect. In Manchester casualties were counted when opposing groups battled each other in what, by later standards, would be considered merely an affray. Treachery also showed itself in these early, unpredictable days, when in July Colonel George Goring, parliamentary Governor of Portsmouth, changed sides by boldly claiming the port to be under the royal banner. This habit of switching loyalties would become a common occurrence and an irritation throughout the war.

Plymouth, with its small population, could field very few troops, unlike London, whose trained bands alone numbered 8,000, more than Devon's entire militia quota. However there were a considerable number of capable leaders available to command the defences. These devoted commanders would emerge and rise to prominence at various stages throughout the war, only to fade away later. In order to collect money and fortify, parliament set up a committee in each county to assist the towns and cities, Plymouth's early contribution was to be £500. To oversee the organisation and training of the Devon men and raise even more money or its substitute, usually silver plate, the House of Commons sent Sir George Chudleigh, Sir John Bampfield, Sir John Northcote and Sir Peter Prideaux, all Devonshire men of high esteem, into the Westcountry.

In response to the actions of parliament, King Charles hurriedly dispatched Henry Bouchier, the Earl of Bath, westwards on the 19th of July. Bouchier, a resident of north Devon, tried hard to raise men under the Commissions of Array, despite hostility from many of the locals, which on occasion almost led to riots. What little support Bouchier managed to gain came mostly from country villages, unlike parliament, which was able to draw greatly from the towns. Unaware of Pym's activities in London prior to the outbreak of hostilities, many in Devon saw the king as the man who had initiated yet another unwanted war, and it was this that pushed many in the shire toward parliament.

Local people soon began to organise themselves, Plymouth declared for parliament, as did Exeter and Dartmouth and Sir Francis Drake set about raising a cavalry regiment, which he christened the Plymouth Horse. Although containing many Devon men, this was not purely a Plymouth unit as its name implied; many who joined Sir Francis were from Dartmouth and a score of other locations. Not yet twenty-four Drake had learned the art of fighting during an extended visit to Europe, then in the throes of being torn asunder by over twenty years of slaughter. Upon his return to England in 1640 Francis Drake spent considerable time in conversation with his father-in-law John Pym as well as John Hampden, a close friend of the family and his neighbour, the subject undoubtedly being the declining political situation and the king's refusal to comply.

Thomas Drake and John, both brothers to Sir Francis, joined him in the same regiment, as did his brothers-in-law Elizeus Crymes and Alexander Pym. Barely the size of a troop, the Plymouth horse grew as the war progressed, but Francis Drake only commanded in the early stages, most of his time would be spent at Westminster. Other Devonians followed Drake's lead; John Wear, a gentleman from Halberton raised a regiment of foot within the county, as did Sir Samuel Rolle, Sir John Northcote, Sir Shilston Calmady and many others. On the royalist side, Sir Thomas Hele, Allan Apsley, John Acland and Sir Henry Cary were actively conscripting regiments for the king. How this early system of raising an army worked was simple, individuals with, or in many cases without, leadership abilities would assemble a company in a town or from isolated villages. Once gathered these small groups of men would march to a local muster point, where they joined other newly-raised companies. Eventually these independent units were amalgamated into regiments of a thousand or more and assigned a suitable leader, usually one with a title.

In mid-August Bampfield, Rolle and Northcote received the thanks of a grateful county for their services to parliament. These knights not only managed to raise troops for the cause, but also much-needed capital to finance the war effort. Amidst the upheaval of raising and equipping the various armies being formed all over England, a solicitation was drawn up in Devon and sent to Westminster. This naive petition pleaded for reconciliation between king and parliament. The document was read and discarded, the time for talking was over and Devon's plea for peace fell upon deaf ears.

Across the Tamar the people of Cornwall would side almost totally with their king, but during these early disconcerting months the Cornish people lacked competent leadership. Most of the county's gentry were absent, either on their way home or with the king trying to obtain a command. As a consequence the people were fearful, confused and unorganised. Only Sir Nicholas Slanning was available and he held Pendennis Castle, giving Charles Stuart a safe harbour in the far southwest, if nothing else. Unfortunately Falmouth was too far away to make an effective rallying point for the Cornish royalists.

In July Sir Alexander Carew, MP for Cornwall, Sir Richard Buller, MP for Fowey, Thomas Arundell, MP for West Looe, Francis Godolphin, MP for St Ives and a number of lesser Cornish notables who supported parliament, were sent into their home county to raise the militia against the king. Disorganised and without a suitable royalist figurehead around which to gather, the county seemed ripe for a quick annexation by parliament, providing the move was made sooner rather than later. Unfortunately those selected for the coup were unequal to the challenge. To give credence to their importance, four of the men were honoured by parliament with the title Deputy

Lieutenant of Cornwall, under instructions to maintain the peace. Buller, Carew and their supporters enthusiastically set up headquarters in Launceston, where they began recruiting. Meanwhile the county's most ardent royalists, still awaiting their leaders, kept a low profile.

Due to delays the king's Commissions of Array was not published in Cornwall until August 5th when Sir Bevill Grenville, Sir Nicholas Slanning, John Grylls the county sheriff and others met and posted the proclamation in Launceston, despite verbal opposition from Sir Richard Buller and his parliamentarians. When Westminster learned two of its members had defied parliamentary authority, orders were issued for those involved to come at once to the capital and answer for their behaviour. The insubordinate cavaliers refused and in a bold counter measure Sheriff Grylls called out his rough, untried farmhands on the 17th. The turnout was, as expected poor to say the least, less than two hundred men appeared at the rendezvous site near Bodmin. Fortunately neither side had any passion for a fight, not just yet. The following day a makeshift treaty was drawn up and signed by both parties, an act that would keep Cornwall at peace for a month.

Unfortunately events elsewhere were to have a dramatic effect on Cornwall in the very near future. William Seymour, the aging Marquis of Hertford and the king's Lord Lieutenant for Somerset, arrived in the county of Somerset late in July and posted the king's Commissions of Array. With strong parliamentary backing in the county, Seymour and his small party of prominent royalist concentrated in and around Wells. On August 1st a minor tussle occurred in the streets of Shepton Mallet involving a body of parliamentarians and the royalists under Sir Ralph Hopton and Sir Ferdinando Gorges, one-time Governor of Plymouth Fort. No blood was spilt, and the day ended with Hopton prudently withdrawing.

As the warm summer days wore on parliamentary support grew stronger in the county and the marquis found very few volunteers rushing in to fight for the king. After several weeks of manoeuvring, the royalists found themselves forced out of the shire and into Sherborne Castle, across the border in Dorset. Here doddering old Seymour allowed himself to become bottled up by a mixed force of over 5,000 roundheads from Devon, Dorset and Somerset under William Russell, the Earl of Bedford. Luckily for Seymour the parliamentary army was nothing more than a poorly led, undisciplined rabble. A pitiful excuse for a siege began on September 2nd, and within a few days over fifty per cent of the assembled roundheads had deserted with more going daily. When the better led royalists learned what was happening in the roundhead camps, they boldly came out from behind their walls and fought several engagements with Russell's militia, beating them every time. The situation for the besiegers soon became critical and Bedford was forced to abandon his siege on the 6th.

Although the immediate area around Sherborne Castle was now cleared of parliamentarians, there were still considerable detachments roving around the countryside in search of trouble. Towards the end of the third week of September morale inside the fortified house fell to its lowest. When news came in that Portsmouth had been taken by parliament on September 7th, Seymour decided to quit his position. Two days later the marquis marched out of Sherborne Castle and was allowed to escape by his enemies, whose half-hearted pursuit was unbelievably tardy. By the 22nd the royalists had reached the north coast of Somerset from where they hoped to escape across the Bristol Channel into south Wales. Disappointed at finding only a few boats available, Hertford was forced into a change of plan. Dividing his troops, Seymour with infantry and artillery would use the boats and cross the channel, while Sir Ralph Hopton with the cavalry were to ride through north Somerset, Devon and on into Cornwall.

Hopton arrived at Stowe, north Cornwall, on September 25th having avoided roving parliamentarian patrols. The advent of this small, though eminent company which included the popular Cornish poet Sidney Godolphin and Sir John Berkeley, Hopton's Lieutenant General and Commissary General, had a dramatic affect on support for the king in the shire. When Hopton's little band moved out of Stowe two days later heading for Pendennis Castle and a rendezvous with Slanning, Sir Bevill Grenville and many of his retainers accompanied him. As the column marched down to the south coast, preceded by rumours, it grew in strength as more and more men flocked to the king's standard. When this buoyant Cornish force approached Bodmin, its leaders decided to bypass the town, for a very good reason.

As soon as Sir Richard Buller received word of Hopton's arrival in Cornwall, he issued a proclamation from his headquarters in Saltash, declaring that numerous cavaliers had entered the county in a threatening manner. Immediately the torpid militia were recalled and ordered to converge at Bodmin on the 28th day of September. In the meantime King Charles had drawn up indictments against Buller, Carew and the rest of the parliamentary committee in Cornwall. As Hopton's party rode through the Cornish countryside they were joined by so many volunteers that Sir Ralph changed his mind and decided to move against Bodmin, then occupied by part of Buller's militia. At the same time Sir Alexander Carew and Mr Humphrey Nicholl, a cousin to Bevill Grenville, were riding westwards to meet the royalists and arrange a fresh truce. Naively the two sides met and agreed to talk the following day. As a consequence Hopton withdrew to Mitchell, southeast of Bodmin and the Carew-Nicholl party rode back to Launceston. Hopton and Buller knew their men were undisciplined and many had no stomach for fighting; both sides were thankful for the delay.

At the arranged meeting next morning, negotiations between the two factions terminated promptly with nothing achieved. Hopton now took his army down to Truro while Buller remained around Launceston. In a long distance war of words both sides began accusing the other of unlawful assembly. The question of who was right eventually went to court in Truro, where Hopton spoke up in his own defence. A Somersetshire gentleman in his early forties, Ralph Hopton was a long-term veteran of the endless European war raging across the continent. It was here that he learnt the lessons of modern warfare, fighting at the Battle of Prague, after which he helped escort the Queen of Bohemia and her family into exile. In 1628 Hopton was made Knight of the Bath and later represented Bath as MP. During the Short Parliament he was the member for Somerset and served for Wells in the Long Parliament.

Sir Ralph's wife was Elizabeth Lewyn, widow of Sir Justinian and the daughter of Sir Arthur Capel; the couple married in 1623. Hopton had always been a staunch supporter of the king, though he voted for Strafford's attainder. Due to his exasperating opposition to John Pym, Sir Ralph eventually found himself briefly imprisoned in the Tower of London. In July 1642 Hopton accompanied the Marquis of Hertford into the Westcountry, with the rank of lieutenant general of horse. In August Hopton was expelled from the House of Commons and was ordered to appear before the House as a delinquent.

Unconcerned by Pym's activities in far away London, Sir Ralph presented the Truro court with his commission as lieutenant general of the king's horse in the west, given him by the Marquis of Hertford. The pro-royalist jury gladly acquitted Hopton of the charge of bringing armed men into Cornwall and declared that the law was behind him. The court also expressed its gratitude to Sir Ralph for coming to the county's support. Buller had done nothing to warrant such a verdict, except to try and keep the peace. Sheriff John Grylls now appealed for a posse with which to push the parliamentarians out of Launceston and back across the Tamar, Richard Vyvyan, MP for Tregony, seconded Grylls in his request. With passions running high the motion was quickly passed and Sheriff Grylls ordered the militia to muster on Moilesbarrow Down near Lostwithiel on October 4th.

On the designated day Ralph Hopton was surprised to find almost 3,000 men assembled, all in a variety of costume, some with arms but many without. After a hasty inspection the posse was divided into temporary regiments, lined up and set in motion towards Launceston. The royalist leaders believed that despite a lack of arms and training, the sheer size of this force on the march would force Buller to evacuate Launceston and withdraw without a fight. Unlike his opposite number, Sir Richard Buller was a man of no military experience his only attributes for being in such a position of responsibility were his title and a reputed influence over the people of southeast Cornwall. Unfortunately Buller was not an aggressive commander, neither was Carew or any of the Cornish parliamentary leaders. Possibly their loyalties were still divided, as were those of Sir Richard's good friend Sir William Courteney of Landulph, who resided in Saltash, but claimed himself a neutral.

In his late fifties, Richard Buller had been MP for Saltash in the 1620s, Sheriff of Cornwall in 1637 and MP for Fowey from 1640. The family home was Shillingham, close to the mouth of the St Germans river. With Cornwall dominated by royalists for most of the war, Sir Richard's family was compelled to abandon Shillingham early and move into Plymouth. Fortunately the Bullers owned property in the town and Lady Alice, accompanied by her sister-in-law Sibella, wife of Sir Richard's brother Francis, were able to live there during the war. Sadly Richard Buller was destined to die a sad and disappointed man before the year was out.

While Hopton marched his adventurous army up the narrow roads from the direction of Lostwithiel, Buller waited in Launceston with barely 700 unenthusiastic Cornishmen. The majority of Sir Richard's force came from the eastern part of the county, many unsure why they were there at all. These men resembled Grylls' posse in clothing and poor equipment, but the charisma of the royalist leaders was clearly lacking in the parliamentary camps. Relying on reinforcements, reputedly en route from Devon, Buller did nothing to fortify Launceston and little to organise or train his men. Concerned for his poor position he requested aid from the Earl of Bedford and Sir Samuel Rolle of the Devon Committee. When the reply came back that the Devonshire-trained bandsmen would not leave their home county, a trait familiar with many of the militia units during this period, Sir Richard's despondency intensified, nevertheless he stood his ground, but did nothing more.

By October 6th the inhabitants of Launceston, aware of the royalist advance, were living in fear that should Buller fight and lose, Hopton's men would pillage and destroy their homes. The only way out of such a dilemma would be the immediate departure of the roundheads. The leading citizens of the town held a meeting with Sir Richard, pleaded their case and begged him to leave. Sympathising with their fears, Buller knew his inadequate, lacklustre army could not stop Hopton. With no sign of the reinforcements from Devon, Sir Richard decided to pull out of Launceston. The evacuation began that same afternoon, but his men moved tardily and many supplies were needlessly abandoned.

When Hopton's vanguard eventually reached Launceston, after its unhurried advance from Lostwithiel, his suddenly revitalised troops went on the rampage, looting houses and stores of the wealthier citizens. Sir Ralph himself arrived on the 8th and the pillaging ceased. A proclamation was immediately nailed up calling for the arrest of all those who had taken up arms with Buller. In the meantime a body of mounted parliamentarians arrived in Tavistock due east of Launceston, on the Devonshire side of the Tamar, under the command of Sir George Chudleigh. Buller retreated across Polson Bridge and was joined at Lifton, three miles from Launceston, by Chudleigh. Here the orphaned parliamentary committee of Cornwall set up temporary headquarters. When Sir George learned the size of Hopton's army, he pulled back from the Tamar and withdrew over the moors to Plymouth.

With Buller and Carew now east of the river, the only parliamentary troops still on the Cornish side, was the small garrison in Saltash, a town built on a steep hill sloping down to the Tamar.

The roundhead force in Saltash consisted of a few hundred Cornish parliamentarians under Sir Alexander Carew, whose home at nearby Anthony House he would rarely see again. Carew had been rowed across the Tamar to take command shortly after he and Buller arrived back in Plymouth. About this time two hundred Scottish mercenaries, part of a much larger force on its way from Ireland to serve the King of France, had been driven into Plymouth by a severe storm. Lacking trained soldiers the Scots were persuaded to remain in the town as reinforcements for the meagre garrison.

The Scotsmen agreed to stay, induced by promises of booty and the appearance of two other Scots, Colonel William Ruthven and Lieutenant Colonel James Stephenson, who recently arrived in Plymouth from London. Ruthven, a forceful character took his new-found allies across the Tamar and reinforced the Saltash garrison. Once on the west bank William Ruthven helped Carew organise his small command and threw up a rough fortification above the town to cover the main road. The local people did not want to suffer as their friends in Launceston had, and they refused to help the roundhead soldiers. When Hopton's army was found to be closing in, Carew and Ruthven suddenly had a change of heart. Quickly evacuating Saltash, the parliamentarians hurried down to the waterfront, piled into boats and returned to Plymouth, leaving Cornwall completely royalist.

Forced out of their home county, the parliamentary Deputy Lieutenants of Cornwall, headed by Sir Alexander Carew, transferred first to Plymouth, then later, when that town was threatened, on to Exeter. From the county town the committee made its plans for defeating Hopton and retaking Cornwall. By late October a meeting was under way between the Deputy Lieutenants of Devon and Cornwall with the object of raising money for troops and supplies. On the 29th they wrote to the House of Lords asking that Colonel William Bampfield's veteran regiment be sent to Exeter as a reinforcement to the garrison.

Buoyant after his bloodless victories had cleared Cornwall of the enemy, Sir Ralph Hopton now planned to invade Devon, but as with Rolle's parliamentarian trained bands, the Cornish posse was dead against crossing the Tamar. Unable to cope with such small-mindedness, Hopton revised his plans. For the moment a foray into Devon was out of the question, but he had gained time to raise and train a new army made up entirely of volunteers, an army with which he could march anywhere, unhindered by territorial borders. Throughout what remained of October, Hopton's lieutenants, Nicholas Slanning, Bevill Grenville, John Trevannion and William Godolphin, brought together as many friends and employees as they could gather. These men were taught how to be soldiers and organised in and around Bodmin. By the end of the month some 1,500 volunteers had been assembled, with more arriving every day.

To arm his new command, Hopton scrounged a variety of weapons from county arsenals and disbanded militia. Another vital source of supply was France. Ships from French ports were able to run through the weak parliamentary blockade of Falmouth and anchor safely under the guns of Pendennis Castle. From here the arms and ammunition were transferred ashore, loaded onto wagons and hauled along poor country roads to Bodmin. In the meantime, Warwick Lord Mohun, a Cornish nobleman from Boconnoc House near Lostwithiel, had travelled from the Westcountry to the king's capital at Oxford. Once there Mohun received commissions from his royal highness for himself, Sir John Berkeley, Colonel William Ashburnham and Ralph Hopton, whose earlier commission was from the Marquis of Hertford. This royal directive authorised any two of the four mentioned to take command of the king's forces in the six western counties during Hertford's absence.

With the enemy almost at the door and hundreds of parliamentary refugees arriving from Cornwall seeking sanctuary, Plymouth took belated steps to fortify. The new mayor, Philip Francis, who replaced Thomas Ceely on St Lambert's day, September 17th, would prove to be one of the great cornerstones of parliamentary support in Plymouth. Born April 1600 and baptized in St Andrew's Church, Philip Francis was the son of Philip Francis senior, a local woollen draper. Before the war Francis had been a merchant and the Receiver of Plymouth for the year 1639-40, he had also been a close friend to Jacob Astley, one of the king's most capable officers. Although a dedicated parliamentarian, Philip Francis detested extremism. On several occasions during his mayoralty Philip Francis would refuse to comply with those assigned by Westminster to collect money for parliament, many of whom he knew to be embezzlers. To aid the mayor in fortifying Plymouth the corporation voted to organise a defence committee.

In September 1642, during this vague, unpredictable period of the war, Jacob Astley, royalist governor of Plymouth's military installations, received orders from the king to leave his post and join him as major general in the new royal army. Astley had been governor for almost four years and during that time he had gained the respect of his troops by rectifying the poor pay system suffered by the garrison for years. In his sixties and white haired, Astley, despite his advanced years was a man of sound military experience. In his early life Jacob Astley served in the Netherlands, seeing action at Newport in 1599. He was also present during the siege of Ostend and fought in the European war. Fervently anti-Puritan, Governor Astley never missed an opportunity to barge in on their secret meetings in Plymouth and break them up. Later Astley would be present at many of the larger battles of the civil war and become one of the last to surrender. The transfer of Astley from Plymouth at such a critical time was a tragic error for the royalist cause. With Jacob Astley in command of Plymouth Fort and St Nicholas Island those undercover royalists within the town might have rallied and the war in the southwest may have turned out differently.

With Governor Astley's departure, Mayor Francis and Sir Alexander Carew took charge of the town's fortifications and the island in the name of parliament. All arms and munitions found in Plymouth were gathered in and distributed to the local trained bandsmen and those independent companies hastily being raised. With no set uniform available the soldiers were armed with a variety of muskets, pikes, swords, helmets of various age and design and an assortment of rusting body armour. Private arms were also handed over to the military, while new supplies came in by sea.

It was quite frustrating that all Plymouth's defences faced the sea, the traditional approach of attack, leaving the back door wide open. The council would now have to fork out considerable sums of money to pay for cannon and fortifications with which to protect the town from an enemy capable of attacking the port on its exposed landward side. The near isolation of Plymouth, separated by Dartmoor from the rest of England and the tremendous expense of a large town wall were two reasons why no such defensive line had ever been completed prior to the civil war. But with Hopton just across the Tamar, the port was extremely vulnerable.

Located at the end of a peninsula below several wide ridges running almost east to west, Plymouth lay in an ideal position. These high sharply rising promontories were perfect for the construction of fortifications without exposing the town itself. The furthest of these densely wooded ridges was found to be too extensive to fortify and would have required a considerable army to man. The town leaders, both civic and military, who chose the ultimate site for Plymouth's outer line must have possessed uncanny hindsight for defensive strategy. The threat of attack however was imminent and lacking the resources, the committee ordered a type of council tax levied immediately on all inhabitants. This money would be used for the construction of a rough earthen wall close around the town's immediate precinct.

With lookouts watching for Hopton, townsmen, soldiers and a few hundred borrowed sailors from the navy, helped throw up an earth embankment and dig a shallow ditch out of the hard rock, which, when complete would encompass the town from East Gate around to Hoe Gate. Eventually this rough line would link all the town gates, but its position was vulnerable to an enemy who was audacious enough to move quickly and occupy the high ground above Plymouth, which is today the ridge fanning out east and west of North Hill. Limited by time, money and manpower the defence committee could not authorise work to begin on a more extensive outer line yet. Many knew the inner line to be totally inadequate to withstand a siege. The northern part of the wall ran along what is today the lower part of Beaumont Park and Ebrington Street, before cutting south towards Hoe Gate. Had Hopton been in command of a confident, professional army he could have marched upon Plymouth, planted artillery along North Hill and blasted the town. With insufficient cannon and too few troops the defenders would have been hard pressed to resist for long, fortunately uncertainty and a lack of enterprise on the part of Hopton, saved Plymouth.

While Sir Ralph Hopton was building up his army preparatory to an invasion of Devon, and Plymouthians of all ages and both sexes were feverishly shovelling earth into the shape of a wall, monumental events were taking place in the Midlands, which greatly overshadowed what was happening in the southwest. Having raised the royal standard at Nottingham, the king gathered a small army and marched to Shrewsbury, where Welsh levies were waiting to join him. The royalist army soon swelled to 13,000 well-armed men, amply supplied with artillery. Of equal strength and moving to take on the king was the army of Robert Devereux, the Earl of Essex. This parliamentary force had orders to prevent the royalists from attacking London and, if possible, to protect the Midlands.

By the third week of October both sides were manoeuvring for position and by the 22nd Essex found himself in Kineton, exhausted from marching and countermarching after the elusive king. Suddenly his scouts informed him that the royalist army had slipped in behind him and only the garrison at Banbury now barred the road to London. Prince Rupert, the king's nephew advised attacking Essex rather than leave his army intact to ravage the border country. Agreeing with his nephew Charles Stuart moved forward and lined the royalist army up on Edgehill and here he waited for Essex to attack him. Down below the roundheads also formed and waited, neither side was eager to start the battle.

Frustrated by Devereux's lack of motivation, the king's army eventually moved off its perch and the first full-scale battle of the civil war was on. Shortly after the opening shots Major Faithful Fortescue, commanding a troop of horse under Colonel William Waller in the parliamentary army, suddenly led his entire command over to the enemy and joined Prince Rupert. Born at Buckland Filleigh in Devon in the early 1580s, Fortescue, who failed to live up to his Christian name, would prove an unreliable commander. During the battle of Edgehill Fortescue's troop suffered for their treachery, almost a score were shot or hacked down by their new allies. The reason, the orange parliamentary identification scarves which Sir Faithful forgot to remove prior to his desertion. Fortescue's treachery would subsequently be rewarded when he was given a position in Lord Kilmurry's foot regiment as lieutenant colonel.

For three hours on this warm October day a vicious, stubborn battle echoed across the English countryside, with both sides taking and giving ground and casualties running high. Eventually the fighting died down and the two armies rested for the night, the battle had ended in stalemate. During the dark hours Essex, his troops badly mauled and disheartened, ordered a retreat towards Warwick. The battle was over and, with Essex gone, claimed as a royalist victory which counted total losses in killed, wounded and captured at 4,000; Philip Francis' old friend Jacob Astley being numbered amongst the injured. William Strode the extremist Devonshire parliamentarian had been a witness to the battle of Edgehill. Leaving a glum, reflective Essex, Strode rode to London and announced the sad tidings to a sombre parliament.

Chapter 3

Hopton's Invasion of Devon

With only the River Tamar as an obstacle between parliamentary Devon and royalist Cornwall, skirmishing was bound to occur somewhere along this line, especially in the sparsely-populated countryside to the northwest of Plymouth. Patrols from both armies often collided in small, long-forgotten encounters, which usually came about accidentally. One side out foraging would be ambushed by the other, on a similar errand. The resulting engagement ended with light gains and minimal casualties. These insignificant sideshows would take place around Plymouth throughout the war, but had little significance on the overall picture.

One piece of real estate that saw action early in the war was Mount Edgcumbe House. Its master, Piers Edgcumbe had fortified his home and the shoreline blockhouse with cannon and raised a very small regiment of musketeers from his family, friends and retainers. With himself as colonel, William Scawen lieutenant colonel and his son Richard Edgcumbe as major, Edgcumbe believed he could rely on this little force to protect the immediate area around his home. To use Mount Edgcumbe and its seafront to partially blockade Plymouth, Sir Ralph Hopton sent half of Lord Mohun's newly-raised regiment under Major Walter Slingesby and Captain Edward Coseworth's dragoons over as reinforcements for Edgcumbe. As Major Slingesby approached Millbrook, the nearest village to the house, a grateful Colonel Edgcumbe rode over to meet him. The colonel expressed his fears to the major for the safety of his home, which was still in the process of being fortified. Major Slingesby immediately dispatched a guard to watch over the house, while he and Edgcumbe remained in Millbrook to consider the most advantageous way of protecting the area.

Watching royalist activity in and around Mount Edgcumbe were roundhead detachments on St Nicholas Island and in several coastal blockhouses along the east bank of the Tamar. One of the most advantageous lookout points was Mount Wise House, which was slowly being turned into a mini fortress by Captain Lewis Dick and his company. One dark night, Sir Alexander Carew, now a refugee in Plymouth and in command of St Nicholas Island gathered together a detachment of musketeers from the Stonehouse area. These enthusiastic troops were loaded aboard a number of small boats at the waters edge and rowed across the Tamar. Landing undetected on the stony beach between Millbrook and Mount Edgcumbe, Carew's musketeers moved stealthily forward. Unaware of the raid, a royalist lieutenant and most of the dragoons left as a guard were easily captured, but the few who escaped rode hastily to warn Major Slingesby. Concerned over the size and objective of the roundhead force, Slingesby quickly withdrew the rest of his troops as far as Crafthole, where they were reinforced by several companies of foot under William Arundell and Captain Jonathon Trelawny. Encouraged by these fresh troops Major Slingesby boldly marched back to Millbrook and reoccupied the village. During his absence Alexander Carew, satisfied with the reconnaissance and not wishing to fight an enemy of unknown size, particularly with the Tamar at his back, had already withdrawn back across the river.

Rather than divide his army up to protect the numerous bridges and fords across the Tamar from the Devon side, Hopton used the 500 militiamen under Sheriff John Grylls, which had joined him on the march from Bodmin, to guard these avenues. The rest of the army was pulled back from the border and concentrated, ready to strike out whenever the enemy attempted to invade. Millbrook village, Mount Edgcumbe House and the open area in between was well secured, Slingesby again being left in command. With the frontier safe, Sir Ralph continued to train his embryonic army in camps around Bodmin. Almost certain the roundheads would not attempt another raid against Mount Edgcumbe so soon, the royalists stationed there grew complacent. Then one dark night a second expedition of thirty-six small boats, filled with musketeers, left Plymouth and cut quietly across the Hamoaze toward the Cornish shore. Despite having surprise on their side, the parliamentarians ran into unexpected resistance and were forced to withdraw with a few light casualties, one of which was a Major Fortescue, who had been left behind in the darkness and was captured.

Unhappy with parliament's neglect of their home county and suspicious of Plymouth's loyalty, due to the substantial number of royalists within the town, the Cornish Parliamentary Committee penned the following letter to John Pym on November 11th: *'We wonder much that our county of Cornwall should be so much neglected by you. Since our last Colonel Ruthven with some of ours were invited by the insolency of our Cornish adversaries and their invasion of Devon to try their mettle by falling out upon them as they lay at Millbrook once upon our appearing they immediately fled, leaving to our mercy five of their company, one of which was a lieutenant with their horse and furniture. The sheriff of Cornwall not only continues his malignancy but gives it new accession. The posse comitatus is now raising a second time. This town (Plymouth) is doubted their strength is great 5-6,000 well armed and plentifully provided with money by their taking up the subsidy contribution for Ireland and the county stock. Ours is small which again provokes our petition for a speedy supply, especially of money and arms, pistols, carbines and saddles in the first place. Devon pretends little and will act less. Each procrastination is dangerous to us. We dare not give up our reason. Papers are not safe. We again implore your speedy succour'*. Alexander Carew, Francis Buller, John St Aubyn, John Trefusis, Francis Godolphin, John Carter, Richard Erisey and Thomas Arundell signed the document.[1]

With Cornwall secure and the assembled volunteers armed and partially trained, Hopton believed himself strong enough to march into Devon. The reason for his decision to venture across the Tamar came in the shape of two men, the prominent Plymouth merchant Robert Trelawny, who had suffered imprisonment at the hands of parliament and would do so again very soon, and Sir Henry Cary of Cockington, brother-in-law to Sir Nicholas Slanning. The Royalist Committee of Devon, led by Richard Culme, the county's high sheriff and Sir Edward Seymour of Berry Pomeroy, had chosen Trelawny and Cary to visit Hopton because of their influence with local cavaliers. Trelawny and his associate were in Cornwall to propose a rendezvous between the king's supporters in Devon and those in Cornwall.

At the conference Sir Ralph promised to shift his army towards Launceston and link up with the Devonshire royalists who were to assemble at Tavistock. From here the combined army would march against Plymouth, Exeter and all other parliamentary strongholds within the county. If this joint enterprise proved successful, the far southwestern part of England could be secured for the king. Satisfied with the outcome of the discussion Trelawny and Cary left Bodmin and reported back to the Committee of Devon. Taking a leaf out of Hopton's book, the Devonshire royalists attempted to organise and train their own force, ready for a merger with the Cornish.

For several weeks prior to the invasion, Sir Ralph Hopton planned his route into Devon and secured the crossing points of the Tamar. For once parliament acted swiftly, Lieutenant Colonel Robert Savery and 1,000 men of the county trained bands moved in suddenly and occupied Tavistock, placing a solid block between the royalists in Devon and those in Cornwall. When Hopton finally nosed his way across the Tamar and advanced cautiously towards Tavistock with his 3,000 men and eight cannon, Savery lost his nerve. Considering his men unfit for a major encounter, Colonel Savery evacuated Tavistock and withdrew rapidly over the moors to Plymouth, leaving the enemy with a toehold on the Devonshire side of the Tamar.

Instead of moving briskly in pursuit, Ralph Hopton waited patiently in Tavistock for Culme's posse, which at that time was supposed to be congregating somewhere between Plympton and Kingsbridge. Eventually a few scattered volunteers arrived in Tavistock and informed Hopton that their supporters in the South Hams were still disorganised and therefore unable to join their Cornish allies. With the Plymouth garrison so vigilant, any movement by the untrained Devonshire royalists across Dartmoor would invite attack and possible annihilation.

By late November, Hopton, discouraged at wasting so much time waiting for Culme's non-existent army, decided to march against Plymouth alone. Colonel William Ruthven, judged to be the most capable roundhead officer in the area, had in the meantime, been appointed Commander in Chief of Hampshire, Wiltshire, Dorset, Devon and Cornwall. Taking his role seriously, Ruthven took charge in Plymouth and sent out detachments of mounted men along all roads leading into the town, with orders to watch for Hopton's approach. Ruthven also urged the council to speed up construction of the inner fortifications. Soon the enemy vanguard was observed marching cautiously across Dartmoor in a southeasterly direction, to place themselves between Plymouth and Totnes. Ruthven countered on the 29th by sending 270 men over the Longbridge (often referred to as Newbridge) and out towards Plympton, in an effort to gauge Hopton's strength and plan. This force consisted of two hundred foot and seventy dragoons, the horse was commanded by two energetic young captains, George Thompson and Alexander Pym, the latter one of John Pym's sons.

Next morning, at the tardy approach of Hopton's vanguard, Ruthven's outnumbered observation unit at Plympton, fearing isolation, reported their position as indefensible. Rather than risk being cut off the commanding officer decided to withdraw. On Thursday December 1st, with no sign of the enemy, Ruthven rode cautiously out to Plympton with a small escort to see for himself if he could make a stand or not. Nearing the old town Ruthven detached scouts northwards to watch for Hopton, while he surveyed the area. A short time later, the lookouts dashed into Plympton and reported the strength of the royal army advancing down upon them. Colonel Ruthven immediately abandoned his position and fell back to Plymouth.

Having walked into Plympton unopposed, Sir Ralph set up his headquarters and camps, opened his rough maps and tried to work out how best to tackle Ruthven. With Hopton's sizeable army settling in at Plympton, those royalists in the South Hams gained the confidence to muster and organise themselves under Edmund Fortescue, the new Sheriff of Devon. Hopton appreciated that he would need more foot soldiers if he planned to assault Plymouth with any hope of success and he relied heavily on Fortescue and other prominent Devonshire cavaliers to raise large numbers of recruits from the county. While Hopton waited, royalist sympathisers at Plympton brought food and drink for the Cornishmen and informed on those in the community with parliamentary leanings. Suddenly and without warning, Colonel Ruthven, dynamic and headstrong, launched a surprise attack across Longbridge. This swift hit-and-run raid was designed to see if the royalists would fight and to learn their strength and dispositions.

With a mixed mounted force numbering barely two hundred, Ruthven crossed the Plym and moved on toward the distant foe. When Hopton's outpost spotted the roundhead column, the alarm was drummed out and word passed back to headquarters. Royalist musketeers were immediately lined up and met the attack with a scattered, poorly aimed volley. Ruthven returned the fire and a brief exchange ensued, ending with the outnumbered parliamentarian horse being chased back across Longbridge. Once back on the west bank, Ruthven's men stood to for almost three hours, daring the Cornishmen to cross. A few of the more foolhardy did rush forward in a half-hearted, badly coordinated charge, but were easily beaten off. Fearing an ambush in the thickly wooded countryside, the royalists remained on their own side of the river and Ruthven's men eventually withdrew, leaving a small detachment to watch the crossing. William Ruthven, now called General by his men, returned to Plymouth with renewed confidence and continued improving the town's defences.

Uncertain of Ruthven's numbers or the strength of Plymouth's fortifications, Hopton refused to even consider an attack at this stage. His limited view of the town's expanding earthworks from Saltram and Mount Edgcumbe and reports from spies helped Sir Ralph reach his decision. Another factor was his untried troops, Hopton was not prepared to risk them in what could prove a costly assault, at least not until the Devonshire royalists put in an appearance. For the time being Ralph Hopton was content to throw up his own defences and wait along the east bank of the Plym.

The Cornish army, camped around Plympton, consisted mainly of foot soldiers, with a few hundred horse and a small artillery train. Four regiments of infantry made up Hopton's new army under the leadership of Warwick Lord Mohun, Colonel William Godolphin, Colonel John Trevannion and Sir Nicholas Slanning, the latter no stranger to Plympton. Another regiment under Sir Bevill Grenville had been dispatched to Totnes. This detachment was ordered to watch for parliamentary reinforcements, reportedly marching into the area to prevent the Devon cavaliers from mustering in the South Hams. Grenville was also to collect money and gather supplies and send them on to Hopton's main army. Both Plympton and Totnes subscribed money willingly to the king's cause during this period.

When word of Hopton's presence near Plymouth reached Westminster, efforts to raise more troops in the southwest intensified, three new regiments were to be organised within the county. With Grenville at Totnes, orders were sent from London to fortify the important port of Dartmouth. The House of Commons also raised money to pay for arms and ammunition and a new man was chosen to replace the useless Earl of Pembroke, who since October had been in command of all parliamentary troops in the southwest counties and had achieved nothing. Lord John Robartes of Lanhydrock was selected to supersede Pembroke.

With help so far away Plymouth could only wait and watch, but the town continued to bustle with activity. Soldiers and civilians strengthened the inner fortifications and sites for the outer line of forts were selected and laid out. Cannon were taken from ships and the seaward defences, hauled up through the town and placed in strategic positions, some being located in gardens of outlying houses or on high ground. Meanwhile the Cornish army around Plympton remained passive, small mounted detachments were sent into the countryside to gather forage and loot the homes of known parliamentarians.

In an effort to restrict the garrison from collecting supplies from the area north of the town, Sir Ralph sent part of his army across Longbridge to occupy Widey House, Knackersknowle village and Ham House. Here the cavaliers threw up crude earthworks so as to watch and block any parliamentary excursions. The largest of these works was at Widey where to the west of the house a large redoubt known as Hopton's Work was constructed. A small garrison was stationed at Widey to give protection to its owner Yeoman Hele, a sympathiser to the royalist cause. As a further annoyance to the garrison and civilians of Plymouth, the royalists had cut the town's water supply from Dartmoor on December 5th. Although for the time of year water was in abundance and a supply of fresh drinking water could be brought into the port by ship, the severing of the leat proved a blow to morale and an inconvenience to the townsfolk.

The enemy, lying in wait outside the town, was not the only threat to Plymouth at this time, there were also those who endeavoured to destroy parliamentary support from within. With Hopton's army in close proximity a bad case of pro-royalism suddenly broke out. One of its leading partisans, Dr Aaron Wilson, Vicar of St Andrew's, had already been arrested, placed aboard ship and sent as a prisoner to Portsmouth. A second, more prominent enemy was Robert Trelawny, whose home at Ham would bear the scars of his loyalty to the king, when it was pillaged by a roving detachment of roundheads. Wilson and Trelawny had consistently warned people against contributing money to parliament and of fortifying Plymouth in defiance of the king.

According to Mayor Francis, Trelawny's influence had swayed a considerable number in Plymouth, as a consequence many refused to subscribe to the cause. Robert Trelawny was also accused of trying to persuade the previous mayor, Thomas Ceely, to publish the king's Commission of Arrays in the town. Francis complained that Trelawny refused to lend money to parliament, but gave freely to the king and openly voiced support for his sovereign. Fortunately Philip Francis and William Ruthven countered any seditious royalism by quick arrests and strict imprisonment of all agitators.

In early December Mayor Francis and ex-mayor John Waddon wrote to Sir John Yonge the new MP for Plymouth at Westminster, complaining of Robert Trelawny's treasonable actions. Concerned by Trelawny's transgressions, the House of Commons had already ordered his arrest on November 23rd. When the news finally reached Plymouth several weeks later, Trelawny was immediately picked up and sent to London. Once in the capital, Robert Trelawny was committed to Winchester House, a newly-opened prison for royalists. Here he would remain at the pleasure of the House. Despite several petitions for Trelawny's release on bail during early 1643 the House of Commons refused and he remained incarcerated until his death in 1644. With the arrest and removal of Aaron Wilson and Robert Trelawny the remaining royalists in Plymouth went quiet and the council was able to concentrate all its energy on the enemy outside.

With Hopton's Cornishmen between Plymouth and themselves the Devonshire cavaliers felt secure enough to organise a major muster in the South Hams. Edmund Fortescue of Fallapit, the thirty-two-year-old new royalist sheriff was neither a professional soldier nor a confident commander but he would have to do. Naming Tuesday December 6th as the date for the proposed rendezvous and Modbury, twelve miles east of Plymouth, as the meeting point, Fortescue planned to lead his assembled force over to Plympton and help Sir Ralph Hopton tighten his grip on Plymouth.

On the appointed day several thousand people came from all over Devon and flocked into the little market town of Modbury. To Fortescue's horror very few interpreted the true reason for the muster: men and boys of all ages and professions were present, as were many women and children. Most had no inkling of why they had come and the light-hearted atmosphere was more like that of a carnival. A few of the more level-headed did bring their arms with them. Unaware of the state of the Modbury gathering, Sir Ralph sent Nicholas Slanning riding across country to inform the leaders of his plans for their troops. Reluctant to use a force he had no knowledge of himself, Hopton quickly briefed his subordinate officers at Plympton and with a small mounted escort, rode after Slanning.

When he arrived at Modbury the royalist commander was horrified by the condition of the so-called posse. Despite a large number of the nobility, who assumed their presence would encourage the locals, barely two dozen out of the several thousand assembled were in any fit state to march, let alone fight. In an effort to sort out the mess, Hopton disarmed those whom he suspected would not fight and gave their weapons to those who would fight. Next he selected a score of men, armed and hastily mounted them on whatever horses were available and sent them out to guard the approaches into Modbury. The main route coming in from the east was of special interest to the concerned Hopton because of the roundhead garrison at Dartmouth. However with his own army watching Plymouth from the east bank of the Plym, Sir Ralph believed no threat would materialise from that direction, but a number of pickets were pushed out to watch the roads to the west as a precaution. Hopton impressed upon the sentinels the need for extreme vigilance; his warning would fall upon deaf ears. During the gathering at Modbury, many believed the assembly to be an excuse for heavy drinking and the royalist leaders must have shook their heads in frustration; Fortescue's posse was out of control and good for nothing.

At this point two men rode into Modbury from Dartmouth, greeted Hopton and proposed that he might consider a move in their direction; Sir Ralph believed the idea held some merit. With Plymouth so stubborn and the Devonshire royalists more than useless, a successful advance against this secondary port, only a dozen or so miles east of Modbury, would give the royalists a safe anchorage for shipping and another gateway for supplies from abroad. Sir Nicholas Slanning was again chosen for a ride, this time he was to return to Plympton and inform Sir John Berkeley and Colonel William Ashburnham, left in command there during Hopton's absence, of the new plan. Berkeley was to abandon the partial blockade of Plymouth and strike out for Dartmouth.

Hopton, contemplating his second siege in less than a month, also sent a courier to Totnes, where Sir Bevill Grenville's regiment was stationed. Sir Ralph wanted half of Grenville's command to make haste and come to Modbury for the purpose of protecting the posse.

The presence of Grenville's troops in Totnes had encouraged a number of royalist recruits to join the colours and the town council now decided to come out in favour of the king. Money and plate were eagerly handed over to Grenville's officers in order to help raise and supply a troop of horse for the royalist army. Totnes Corporation also paid out £300 to purchase shovels, picks and ammunition, which was sent to Hopton for his use in besieging Plymouth. With the new plan churning over in his ever-active mind, Ralph Hopton decided to remain in Modbury overnight, consulting with the county leaders.

Late in the night of December 6th the Plymouth high command met to discuss what could be done about the enemy converging on Modbury. Unaware of the poor condition of the posse, the town leaders were gravely concerned. Should such a large force move on Plymouth and unite with the Cornish royalists, the town would find itself in a perilous position. Unfinished forts and the few defenders available could not contend with such an overpowering enemy. Present during the emergency meeting, besides the energetic Ruthven, were a number of the following, Sir Alexander Carew, Sir Richard Buller's brother, Colonel Francis Buller, Sir Shilston Calmady and undoubtedly the aggressive Mayor Philip Francis. At the midnight council Ruthven proposed to lead a mounted force on a roundabout ride, which would by-pass the royalists at Plympton and strike Modbury from the north. This daring plan was eventually approved and at 3 a.m. on the morning of December 7th four troops of horse under captains William Gould, Alexander Pym, George Thompson and Thomas Drake were assembled, along with 100 dragoons, possibly Captain Roland Whiddon's company. Several junior officers asked Ruthven to be allowed to go along just for the chance of some action; he consented.

The colonel inspected his 300 or so troopers, then led them out of Plymouth in the pitch-black night on the road to Tavistock. The column moved cautiously but quickly along narrow country roads, avoiding royalist patrols and the garrison at Hoptons Work. Ruthven then continued northwards as far as the village of Trennimans Jump (Roborough) and from here the raiders swung eastwards over the moors, ultimately coming into Ivybridge. Clattering through the village William Ruthven was rapidly closing in on his objective, now only a few miles to the south.

In the 1640s Modbury was a prosperous marketing community,

lying at the convergence of three roads, one coming in from Plymouth off to the west, another stretching eastwards towards Dartmouth and a third running down to Kingsbridge. Modbury was also the home of one of the county's leading royalists, Henry Champernowne. Hailing originally from Oxfordshire, Henry Champernowne married in 1611 at the age of twenty-one and moved to Devon where the young couple lived with his uncle Sir Richard at Modbury. Henry Champernowne's only military connection prior to the civil war was when he commanded a company of militia during assemblies, but he had never seen action.

While half of Grenville's regiment was making its way slowly along the poor road from Totnes and the posse was coming to after a cold night in the open fields outside Modbury, Colonel Ruthven's column suddenly appeared out of the early morning mist. Drawing swords and pistols the roundheads lined up on the ridge above the village and at a word from Ruthven they advanced. The parliamentarian horse trotted down from the high ground, still wet from the morning dew and with trumpets blaring, they broke into a charge and hit the surprised royalists with such force that the posse scattered almost immediately. Despite outnumbering the horsemen more than four to one the royalists failed to heed their officers and disappeared.

The unfortunate farm boys possessed very few weapons, no organisation and even less inclination to fight, especially after a night of over-indulgent revelry. Captains Alexander Pym and his brother-in-law Tom Drake led their troopers competently and helped the royalists disperse quickly into the countryside. The leaders of the posse, some twenty officers, were at the time of the attack, attending an early morning council in the Champernowne home, a fortified mansion built on high ground on the western fringe of Modbury. Here, as the last of the posse vanished, they made feverish preparations to defend themselves. Colonel Ruthven dismounted his roundhead horse and dragoons and led them on foot against the manor. Once in range, those with musket or pistol opened up a brisk fire on the cavaliers inside. The defenders fought back desperately, hoping reinforcements would arrive. As his men slowly closed in Ruthven, rather than risk lives unnecessarily, ordered the outbuilding set on fire. With a wind fanning the flames toward the main house, the royalists inside began to fear for their safety. To avoid certain death they threw down their weapons and surrendered.

When the royalist officers emerged from the house flying a makeshift white flag, the fighting came to an end. Sir Nicholas Slanning, who returned to Modbury during the night, sought out Hopton and both men endeavoured to rally the posse but found it impossible. Mounting up, the two knights and a small escort rode away, leaving the Devon leaders to face the music. The Champernowne home was totally ransacked as were a number of wagons belonging to the vanished posse. Ruthven's Puritan troopers also pillaged St George's Church, defacing several effigies including that of Sir John Champernowne. Later a large amount of money would be spent on repairing the vandalism; seats, icons, locks and bells all had to be mended or replaced, giving an idea how much damage had been done.

Having secured their prisoners, the parliamentarians found they had bagged possibly the largest cache of prominent royalists ever to be taken in such a small engagement. Edmund Fortescue the High Sheriff of Devon, his brother Peter, Sir Edward Seymour and his young son Edward of Berry Pomeroy Castle, Arthur Bassett, a notable malignant, Captain Henry Champernowne who owned the mansion and Edmund Tremayne. A considerable number of junior officers were also captured, Captain Thomas Wood, Lieutenant William Penrose of Hopton's dragoons, Captain Henry Bidlake of Slanning's foot regiment and Lieutenant William Barnes, who was later to be found under Sir Edward Seymour's command. Two men who would serve Edmund Fortescue upon their exchange, William Hooper and Robert Warren were also taken.

Before Hopton could obtain help from Plympton and Grenville's men arrived from Totnes, Ruthven, with captains Pym, Thompson, Anthony Rouse and Lewis Dick, had ridden off in the direction of Dartmouth with their distinguished prisoners. The larger part of the column made its way back to Plymouth over the same route that had brought them into Modbury. Colonel Ruthven hoped that by dividing his command the enemy would be deceived into believing the entire force was heading for Dartmouth. His strategy paid off handsomely, when the Cornish reinforcements arrived barely half an hour after the roundheads had left, they set off immediately in pursuit of Ruthven's column. During the spirited ride across country, Colonel Ruthven managed to evade several large roving royalist patrols from Totnes with relative ease, before leading his men into Dartmouth, much to the relief of the townsfolk. With the cavaliers so close, William Ruthven decided to remain in the port as a temporary reinforcement for the garrison.

Once rested, Ruthven sent a dispatch to London, praising his troops and detailing his movements. During their brief stopover at Dartmouth the royalist prisoners were well treated before being placed aboard the twelve-gun frigate *Crescent*, which had recently arrived in Dartmouth from Ireland. Thomas Plunkett, the ship's captain, soon set sail, going first to Plymouth, where news of the daring Modbury raid was still being talked about. From Plymouth Plunkett sailed up to Gravesend and arrived there late in December. When word reached Westminster of the *Crescent*'s docking, the commander of the London militia was ordered to send forty musketeers and several barges down to Gravesend. The escort and prisoners were then taken up the Thames to the city, where the captives were landed and divided up to prevent intrigue.

Sir Edward Seymour, Edward his son, Edmund Fortescue, John Fortescue and Arthur Bassett went to Winchester House. Henry Champernowne, Edward Tremayne, Captain Thomas Wood, Peter Fortescue, Henry Bidlake and Robert Warren were taken to the King's Bench. Thomas Shapcote, Thomas Short, Hugh Pomeroy and Thomas Lee or (Leigh) went to the Compter in Southwark. Thomas Lee had been captured by Ruthven on the way to Modbury, and was taken along because of his reputed connivance with Hopton in an effort to avoid losing his own property. Believing Lee a man who would do anything to save himself or his home, Ruthven maintained that he should not be allowed to remain at liberty. The rest of the group, Lieutenant William Barnes, William Hooper, George Bayly or (Baily) and Lieutenant William Penrose, were sent to the Fleet prison. All were committed for high treason in levying war against king and parliament. On December 30th twenty-two year old Captain Thomas Drake, who had joined the *Crescent* when she called in at Plymouth, was ordered to transport the captives to their various prisons.

Shortly after his incarceration in Winchester House Sir Edmund Fortescue was suddenly transferred to Windsor Castle. On the wall of a chamber near the Norman Gate, graffiti was found in the 1800s which reveals the exact room Fortescue was imprisoned in, it read: *'Sir Edmund Fortescue, prisoner in this chamber the 12th day of Annarie 1642, Pour Le Roy C'*. The year 1642 means 1643 in the modern calendar, the new year started on March

25th until the year 1745.

Meanwhile, in the northern part of Devon, strong cavalier forces were gathering, particularly around the homes of two prominent knights, Sir Hugh Pollard of King's Nympton and Henry Bouchier, the Earl of Bath at Tawstock. As in the south, where Plymouth, Exeter and Dartmouth stood firmly for parliament and the South Hams gave fair support for the king, the situation here was similar. Barnstaple, Bideford and Great Torrington were under parliamentary control, while parts of the countryside rallied, if reluctantly, behind their royalist gentry. Colonel John Acland an ardent cavalier from Columb John near Exeter, gathered so many armed men that he was able to gain control of Great Torrington simply by marching in, a move which enabled him to hold the town throughout December. The loss of Torrington put the fear of God into the garrisons of Barnstaple and Bideford, but fortunately Sir Samuel Rolle and Colonel James Chudleigh, son of Sir George, held the former towns in considerable strength. So strong was local confidence in Rolle and Chudleigh that when Hopton laid siege to Exeter, a relief column would be organised in Barnstaple and sent across Dartmoor.

Having failed to intercept Ruthven or unite with the scattered Devonshire posse, whose leaders had become guests of parliament, Hopton knew that with his own army so small and divided he had little chance of capturing Plymouth. Shortly after the fiasco at Modbury and with the Dartmouth plan shelved, Sir Ralph consulted with his lieutenants at Plympton and discussed the possibility of a march against Exeter. Those Devon royalists who escaped capture at Modbury, urged Hopton to move quickly against the county town. They insisted that Exeter was ill prepared to withstand an assault; a ridiculous statement considering it was well known that the city housed 8,000 troops with cannon aplenty. The ceaseless pleading of the Devon royalists eventually had its affect. Hoping to raise more foot and obtain supplies along the way Hopton broke off his weak, partial blockade of Plymouth and marched on Exeter. To watch Plymouth from a distance and protect Cornwall from counterinvasion, Sir Ralph left strong detachments at Mount Edgcumbe, Millbrook and Saltash. Sir Bevill Grenville, who had returned to Totnes, was ordered to join the main army as it advanced eastwards.

Reaching Exeter's outposts at Ide, Alphington and Powderham, the Cornishmen moved swiftly and captured them all with little resistance. Hopton's army edged closer to the fortified city and began throwing up crude earthworks. To blockade the River Exe and cut off supplies for the city from the sea, the regiments of William Godolphin and Grenville, were ferried across to Topsham, three miles below Exeter, thereby almost completely encircling the city. Unfortunately for the royalists the ship used by Grenville to ferry his troops across the Exe was captured, a catastrophic loss that split Hopton's army into two halves and severed direct communication between the two parts. Hopton remained in front of Exeter hoping for at least one success before the year came to a close. With insufficient troops and very few cannon, the Cornishmen could not be expected to conduct a lengthy siege unless the county royalists turned up in considerable numbers and quickly; it would not happen.

To make matters worse, one night, late in December, Colonel William Ruthven, Sir Ralph Hopton's nemesis, left Dartmouth with a picked column of horse, including several of the units which had overrun the Modbury gathering. After an easy ride Ruthven's mounted detachment easily slipped past Hopton's guards and boldly rode into Exeter. Ruthven's arrival rallied the garrison and on December 28th, a parliamentary force left the city and hit Topsham, forcing the royalists to abandon their positions along the east bank of the Exe and join Hopton on the west bank. With December drawing to a close, it became apparent that Hopton had no chance of capturing Exeter, his troops were spread too thin and the artillery woefully inadequate.

In an effort to bluff his way to victory, Hopton asked the city to surrender. His request was refused on the grounds that a large supply of powder and food was stored within the walls and reinforcements were on their way. By now the royalist army had grown agitated and restless, the men had been away from home for over a month and none of Hopton's objectives achieved. Support from local royalists failed to materialise once again and Sir Ralph's despondency dropped to a new low. Open talk of marching back to Cornwall began to spread, and to fuel the misery of the Cornishmen, part of the Exeter garrison struck out on the 31st and hit that section of Hopton's line north of the city. After a brief engagement the royalists were pushed back; for Sir Ralph it was the end.

Hopton called off the siege, abandoning his entrenchments he pulled in his outposts and put his army on the road to Cornwall. The cavaliers took the route back across the inhospitable moors via Crediton, Okehampton and Tavistock. Along the way they were joined by Colonel Acland's small regiment, which had been forced out of Torrington by a reported roundhead column advancing from the direction of Barnstaple.

On December 27th Sir John Northcote received orders from parliament to return to Devon and aid his home county in its hour of need. Northcote left London immediately with a few officers and money to pay recruits and arrived in Exeter early in January, not long after the siege had been raised. Other troops were also being organised, trained and sent either to Exeter or on to Plymouth; a number of these being veteran units from the Earl of Essex's Edgehill army.

With the royalists gone from Plymouth and the much-admired Ruthven, hero of the moment absent, Mayor Philip Francis and the corporation continued to fortify. More cannon were borrowed from ships in the harbour and hauled by bullock to the new gun platforms going up around the town, while money and troops trickled in from London. The old abandoned royalist fortifications north of the town were flattened and mounted outposts re-established.

Occasional skirmishes still took place outside Plymouth. In late December a detachment of royalist horse from Tavistock rode into the village of Crapstone and pillaged the homes of known roundhead supporters, ransacking houses and destroying furniture. Elizeus Crymes, a relative of the Drakes, must have been at home at this time for he was captured, escorted as a prisoner to Totnes and held by the royalists until exchanged. Crymes' imprisonment was only of short duration for by January 1643 he was in Plymouth serving as a captain of the garrison.

In retaliation royalists around Plymouth suffered a similar fate, one Thomas Hake, a schoolmaster from Plymstock and his wife were visited by parliamentary cavalry out on patrol. During such visitations Hake, a known king's man, was often robbed, even the schoolbooks were confiscated. At one stage Hake was arrested, brought into Plymouth and thrown into prison. Here he was starved and had to face the wrath of Colonel Ruthven on one occasion. Eventually Thomas Hake was released, but he was forced to live on charity almost until the Restoration.

For Plymouth the latter months of 1642 had been an eventful period, numerous forts were either in the planning stages or under construction. Hopton's half-hearted siege in early December had proved a complete waste, but it did force the defenders to press on vigorously with their fortifications. Detachments from the garrison under Ruthven easily broke up the royalist posse at Modbury, capturing many of the county's top royalist leaders and raising morale tremendously. Indirectly Ruthven's strike led to Hopton abandoning plans for an attack on Dartmouth and forced him into an unpopular move against Exeter. Ultimately it was Ruthven again who went to the relief of Exeter, forcing Hopton to break the siege and retreat back into Cornwall.

Casualties for the year gave no indication of the horror that was to come, burials were normal, no high rise in deaths from military action and the encounters at Mount Edgcumbe and Modbury saw very little loss, thereby putting many under a false sense of security. On November 30th Sir Richard Buller, the unhappy Cornish parliamentarian, passed away. Sir William Courteney, Buller's kinsman, made every effort to have his friend's body brought home to Saltash for burial in St Stephen's Church, but he failed. The royalist commander in the town, Sir James Colebrand refused Buller an internment on home soil and he was laid to rest in St Andrew's Churchyard Plymouth on December 1st, much to the distress of his family.

After their victory at Edgehill the royalists moved sluggishly towards London, but despite Essex's retreat, the king's commanders were divided on what should be done next. Rupert was all for charging straight into the capital, others believed it would be wiser to wait and hope public opinion might swing their way. It was to be Charles Stuart's greatest error when he cast his vote against his nephew. By the time he realised his mistake it was too late, London had organised itself and the trained bands barred the king's path. Exasperated by his uncle's advisors, Prince Rupert led his cavalry away and spent the time running around the countryside attacking isolated parliamentary strongholds, while King Charles moved on to Oxford. The Earl of Essex meantime detoured around the royal army and entered London on November 7th.

The king had missed his greatest opportunity to capture the city of London and possibly end the war in its infancy. By the second week of November, Rupert was belatedly ordered to march against the capital; by the 12th he was ready to assault Brentford, barely twenty miles from Westminster. Four days later Essex marched back out of the city accompanied by Philip Skippon's militia. The royalists countered by attacking Brentford. Before Essex could reinforce the outpost, garrisoned by only two regiments of foot, Prince Rupert had attacked, broken the defences and captured the town. Rather than risk another full-scale battle so soon, Robert Devereux entrenched his troops at Turnham Green. When the king gingerly edged forward and found Essex outnumbered his own army, he decided against an assault and withdrew to Reading.

Over the rest of the country the two sides were coming off almost equally. Marlborough was captured on December 5th by a royalist force and on the 13th parliamentary dragoons, under Hopton's old friend Sir William Waller took Winchester.

Notes

(1) Page 49: House of Commons Journal.

Chapter 4

Royalist Revival

The year 1643 began with royalist dreams for an early conquest of Devon shattered and Hopton's Cornish army falling back toward the Tamar. During their retreat across Dartmoor, these dejected cavaliers grew more and more despondent. Sir Ralph Hopton had marched them here, there and back again, now mutinous whinging surfaced and it was only the sheer magnetic personality of its leaders that kept the army together. Ruthven compounded Hopton's problems by riding out of Exeter in pursuit and catching up with his quarry at Okehampton. In a brief clash of arms the parliamentarians were eventually driven back, giving the Cornishmen a breathing space, which allowed them to continue their withdrawal unhindered. On January 3rd with Sir Ralph's army on its way out of Devon, a party of roundheads from Barnstaple marched down and regained control of Great Torrington, which had previously been occupied by a small royalist garrison under Colonel John Acland.

Finally arriving in Launceston, Hopton received more bad news, during his absence Saltash had been periodically bombarded by three parliamentary warships and a battery of guns hastily erected on the Devonshire side of the Tamar. The royalist commandant, Sir James Colebrand, did what he could with the limited resources available to him, but lacking sufficient heavy artillery, the defenders could only wait and suffer the shelling. For almost a week the parliamentary guns blasted away at Saltash and fears grew of an imminent full-scale assault. Sir William Courteney of Lanulph, still in Saltash and still claiming to be a neutral, became greatly concerned at the destruction of the town and he wrote to Hopton appealing for help.

Sir Ralph received Courteney's urgent epistle and without further delay he led Colonel John Trevannion's regiment and several companies under Captain William Arundell out of Launceston and down to the river port. When he arrived in town Hopton set to work bolstering existing defences and planning new ones, all the while parliamentary cannonballs crashed down upon Saltash or splashed harmlessly into the river. Due to the strong military presence in the town, roundhead infantry could not now cross the Tamar. Each time a boatload put out from the Devon shore, Hopton's cannon and musketeers would open up and force them back. Eventually William Ruthven, back in Plymouth once again, abandoned the idea of a seaborne assault against Saltash, but the long-range artillery bombardment would continue. Meanwhile parliamentary reinforcements were marching into Devon from Dorset and Somerset, led by Henry Grey the Earl of Stamford, who replaced the useless Earl of Pembroke and the two men who had followed him briefly, Lord John Robartes and Denzil Holles. All three were quickly forgotten and high hopes placed upon this new reputedly, aggressive commander.

Henry Grey, a long-time martyr to gout, was a man of considerable wealth and importance, but little military knowledge. Born around 1599, Grey had been created Earl of Stamford in 1628 and eleven years afterward he accompanied the king northwards during the First Bishops' War. Three years down the line Stamford received the title Lord Lieutenant of Leicestershire and in 1642 he secured the town of Leicester for parliament, thus defying the king who pronounced him traitor. In late July Stamford withdrew from the town and joined the Earl of Essex in Warwickshire. Essex later sent Henry Grey to Hereford, where for more than a month he fought and beat off every royalist attempt to capture that town. Due to increasing pressure, the earl was eventually forced to evacuate Hereford on December 14th and fall back to Gloucester.

Shortly after his arrival in Gloucester, Henry Grey was given command of all parliamentary troops in Salop, Gloucester, Herefordshire and Worcester. No sooner had he taken up his new command than he was, after some hesitation by those concerned, ordered into the southwest. Leaving his own regiment of bluecoats under Edward Massey, Stamford rode through Wiltshire and Somerset and on towards Exeter with only two troops of horse. By January 6th the Earl of Stamford arrived in the county town where he dallied for a time, gathering information on his own forces and those of the enemy.

During the interim period between commanders, William Ruthven, rather than wait for the slow-moving Earl of Stamford whom he despised, possibly out of resentment for his recent high-ranking appointment, devised a plan of his own. First he dispatched a strong body of troops northwards as a decoy, this force was to march on Tavistock, then down to Horsebridge near Gunnislake, ten miles above Saltash on the Devonshire side of the Tamar. Command of this red herring went to three colonels, Francis Buller, son of the late Sir Richard, John Pyne a veteran of fighting at Marshalls Elm and Sherborne, and William Strode. William Strode is not to be confused with the radical Strode from Plympton. This William Strode was a wealthy gentleman from Barrington near Ilchester Somerset. Born around 1589 he had opposed the king's Commission of Array in Somerset and served as a deputy lieutenant for the county before being appointed colonel. The troops these officers led had been sent on down to Plymouth by Stamford as reinforcements for the garrison. Once the crossing of the Tamar was secured by this detachment, Ruthven expected Hopton to withdraw from Saltash to meet the threat to his rear. The evacuation of Saltash would allow Ruthven to cross over the Tamar at this point with his main force, the two separate parliamentary forces would march into Cornwall and converge at a point between Tavistock and Liskeard.

Initially Ruthven's strategy worked, arriving at Horsebridge on January 13th the roundheads found the enemy had smashed part of the structure and thrown up hasty defences along the west bank. After a brief reconnaissance Colonel Strode moved rapidly, his musketeers opened a steady fire from the eastern end of the ruined bridge while he sent his horse and dragoons to cross the river at a narrow, unguarded ford further upstream. Once the mounted detachment was across and in position on the Cornish side, the musketeers charged across the shallow water. When the roundhead horse came pounding in on their exposed flank and rear, the royalist defenders, mostly dismounted dragoons and a few foot fled, leaving behind two men dead and forty-one prisoners with their horses; amongst the captives was a Lieutenant Greenway.

Satisfied with his initial triumph, Colonel Strode secured the crossing by leaving behind a detachment of foot, the rest of the command he took back to Tavistock. That night Buller, Strode and

Colonel John Pyne wrote to Stamford at Exeter announcing their victory and explaining Ruthven's proposed strategy of crossing the Tamar at Saltash next morning, and moving after Hopton. Meanwhile William Ruthven was impatiently waiting with his half of the army along the high ground on the east bank of the Tamar, waiting to cross. Confident that once Strode was across the river the Cornishmen would abandon the river town he waited, rather than risk losing men in a pointless assault.

Ruthven's premonition proved correct, when Hopton learned of the attack across Newbridge he believed his troops in Saltash would be cut off. Consequently he ordered Colonel Walter Slingesby to march from Millbrook with part of his force and take up position to cover the road into Saltash from the north. Later that same evening Sir Ralph received a communication from Launceston describing the rout at Gunnislake and requesting he evacuate Saltash and fall back, as the enemy at Tavistock were too numerous to hold in check. Fearing the loss of valuable troops, should a siege occur at Saltash, Hopton ordered a general retreat towards Bodmin. At first small detachments were left behind to hold Millbrook and Mount Edgcumbe, but later these too were withdrawn.

With Hopton gone, Ruthven sent a dispatch to Strode at Tavistock ordering him to resume his advance. He then crossed the Tamar, reoccupied Saltash, sent detachments to take possession of Mount Edgcumbe and Millbrook and marched north to join Strode's force, which would soon be moving into Cornwall from Tavistock. To guard the Tamar at Newbridge and secure a line for supplies, reinforcements, or a possible route for retreat, Colonel Strode left behind a small guard under Major Simon Worth. The rest of his troops edged cautiously towards a rendezvous with Ruthven somewhere on the road to Liskeard.

Threatened in their home county for a second time, the Cornish soldiers assembled on Molisborough Down near Bodmin, while their leaders met for an emergency council at Boconnoc Park, the home of Warwick Lord Mohun east of Lostwithiel. Here on January 18th the council agreed unanimously to strike Ruthven quickly before Stamford could join him with more troops. As an unexpected bonus for the royalists, three parliamentary ships, laden with weapons of war, had recently been driven into Falmouth harbour by bad weather. The garrison at Pendennis Castle seized the vessels, took off arms, ammunition and money, and distributed the spoils to Hopton's army congregated around Bodmin.

Leaving Bodmin, the well-armed Cornishmen marched towards Boconnoc, skirmishing lightly with advanced elements of roundhead horse. While still in council Sir Ralph Hopton was informed that Ruthven was closing in on Braddock Down, six miles west of Liskeard, he was also told the size of his opponent's army and how many cannon the parliamentarians were dragging along. Lacking sufficient artillery himself, Hopton knew that time was of the essence, consequently he issued immediate orders for his colonels to move early the next morning. To watch Ruthven's movements, mounted scouts were sent out into the dark, bitterly cold night.

Shortly before dawn on Saturday January 21st the royalists, under Hopton's command, began the march towards Braddock Down. Although only a short distance from Boconnoc, the cavalier advance was painfully slow due to a combination of darkness, narrow overgrown roads and several small streams. No matter, the king's men, eager to clear the invader from their county, were in high spirits. Lord Mohun managed to bring along two small iron minion drakes, while Bevill Grenville's regiment marched with fifteen-foot pikes proudly swinging from the shoulder.

Meanwhile William Ruthven's parliamentary army trudged westwards through the same narrow, restricting, muddy lanes as Hopton. Ruthven believed the Cornishmen were falling back towards Falmouth and he pressed on rapidly to a point three miles from Lostwithiel. When his mounted scouts reported a large body of the enemy moving in their direction, William Ruthven was both surprised and mystified. If Hopton was marching against the parliamentarian army he must be confident in his own ability and strong in numbers. This unexpected news threw General Ruthven completely, and with his artillery bogged down in the mud somewhere to the rear, he felt his position vulnerable. Deep inside enemy country, with a hostile force of unknown strength out in front, the parliamentary commander now lost his nerve and the initiative. Changing his plans, Ruthven switched from offence to defence.

Having selected a place to fight, the untried roundhead army formed up on a low hill in open countryside west of Braddock Church. The fields here sloped up from Boconnoc towards Braddock Down and consisted of two heaths, divided by a hedge-lined lane and flanked on one side by a dangerous bog. The roundhead musketeers were posted behind hedges covering the single, narrow road leading back to Liskeard, while Ruthven kept the rest of his foot in line on the cold, open, high ground. The parliamentarians were outnumbered in foot and their artillery was stuck in the mud somewhere between Liskeard and Braddock Church. However Ruthven did possess a great superiority in mounted troops, but for some unaccountable reason, he failed to use his veteran cavalry to break up the alignment of the advancing royalists. The horse, which included the companies of Alexander Pym, George Thompson, William Gould and Thomas Drake, were divided and arranged to cover both flanks.

Preliminary fighting broke out when a detachment of parliamentary cavalry pressed back a party of overeager enemy dragoons, before being forced away themselves by royalist reinforcements. The bulk of the Cornish army soon arrived behind its advance element and drew up on a ridge to the west of Ruthven's position. Drums were enthusiastically beaten and heavy, oversized banners flapped wildly in the wintry breeze, then both sides prayed for victory. The distance between the opposing armies was reputedly so slight that a well-aimed musket ball would most certainly hit a body. Royalist horsemen now trotted around to the flanks of Hopton's foot, facing Ruthven's horse and covered their wings. Pikemen held the centre and musketeers took partial cover behind a small hedge. The two cannon brought along by Mohun and a small detachment of horse remained in position on a low ridge behind the main force as a reserve. In the roundhead line-up were a number of distinguished personalities, Colonel William Strode, Colonel John Pyne, Sir Shilston Calmady, Lieutenant Colonel Robert Savery and Colonel Francis Buller. Colonel William Bampfield, a veteran of Edgehill, with his east Devon regiment was also on hand to lend its battle experience to a somewhat inexperienced army. All now waited and watched in nervous anticipation as the Cornishmen made their final preparations to advance.

The fighting was initiated by a short-range musketry exchange, which, due to poor marksmanship and damp powder achieved nothing and caused little damage to either army. This weak, ineffective duel was kept up for several hours before Hopton, eager to come to grips with the invader, decided to attack. Ordering his two cannon brought into play, Hopton commanded Grenville to lead his pikemen down into the shallow dip between the two armies and up the other side. Slanning, Trevannion and the other royalist regiments, followed Sir Bevill's lead. Ruthven's troops, greatly dispirited by a lack of artillery and Hopton's superior infantry, resisted impotently. All the while Mohun's two cannon added to the misery of the parliamentarians by firing round after round into their lines. Unable to silence the guns, those roundheads in the front rank discharged only a few scattered volleys before the advancing cavaliers reached them. As the Cornishmen hit Ruthven's position his first line snapped completely and fled.

Hopton's horse now moved up the hill in support of the foot and a second parliamentary line collapsed. Hundreds of terrified, undisciplined soldiers, unable to understand their officers, bolted in panic through the narrow lane leading back to Liskeard. On the way they met up with the artillery and supply wagons still stuck fast in the mud. Fearful of Cornish retribution, the gunners and teamsters deserted their charges and joined the rout. Back on the battlefield a number of resolute parliamentary musketeers, held as a last resort, failed to stop the victorious Cornishmen as they overran the remnants of Ruthven's army.

Aware that there was no organised resistance before them, the cavaliers pressed on from Braddock, capturing hundreds of dejected prisoners en route. Ruthven's cavalry turned and dashed from the field so swiftly that they ran down many of their own struggling foot. On the outskirts of Liskeard, pursuit was momentarily halted by a single shot fired from behind hastily-erected barricades, the ball wounding a royalist horse. The shambolic scraps of William Ruthven's army could not stand at Liskeard and the survivors were soon fleeing toward the Tamar. Although not a great battle considering numbers involved and casualties sustained, Braddock Down was undeniably a significant royal victory and for Ruthven his first taste of defeat, a defeat he would never recover from. For Hopton this unexpected triumph was vengeance for the humiliation he had suffered over the past three months.

What had gone so terribly wrong for William Ruthven? His greatest mistake was in not waiting for Stamford, by racing into Cornwall alone, the parliamentarian commander forgot this was not to be a mere raid as had happened at Modbury. Unfortunately Ruthven's poorly-disciplined, substandard army had never fought together before and this showed when the artillery and wagons were left stuck in the muddy lane far behind the infantry. When Hopton suddenly appeared in his front, Ruthven seemed to lose his confidence. As the royalists moved forward and threw artillery shells into the roundhead lines, their military innocence caused many to break. General Ruthven and many of his subordinates failed to inject enthusiasm into their panicky troops and the rot soon spread. The parliamentarian cavalry, which greatly outnumbered Hopton's horse, was also wasted by not being ordered to counterattack, in the end they simply turned and rode away having accomplished nothing. Ruthven had no one to blame for the fiasco at Braddock Down but himself.

As General Ruthven rode toward Saltash, followed by the disheartened remnant of his army, he left behind 1,250 prisoners, five cannon and most of his ammunition and baggage. Killed and wounded were minimal, but cannot be precisely ascertained, at least a hundred can only be a fair estimate. The only Plymouth man recorded as being definitely present at the Braddock fight was William Chapman. A member of the Plymouth horse, Chapman was wounded during the encounter but survived to fight another day. Among those captured was Sir Shilston Calmady, who would be exchanged later. Calmady of Wembury, not far from Plymouth, would become one of the more familiar faces serving parliament in the Plymouth area during the civil war. His small locally-raised foot regiment would spend most of its service as part of the garrison and become one of the town's most faithful and trusted units.

Born in the mid-1580s, Shilston Calmady took over the family estates upon the death of his father in 1611. Seven years later he was knighted at Theobalds by King James I and in 1621 his son Shilston was born, the boy would serve as a captain in his father's regiment throughout the war. Shilston Calmady owned considerable property in Devon, as did his two brothers Edward of Plymouth and Ranleigh, and Vincent, who was lieutenant colonel of Sir John Merrick's foot regiment. Towards the end of 1642 Calmady and his son were active in raising troops in Cornwall for the roundhead cause. Calmady senior was also Deputy Lieutenant of Devon and would later assume the title, Commissioner of Sequestration.

During the retreat from Liskeard, Ruthven's army had scattered in a desperate attempt to escape from Cornwall anyway it could. Rather than allow his own troops to become separated in pursuit, Sir Ralph Hopton gathered in his considerable spoils, occupied Liskeard and rested. Those parliamentary survivors still with Ruthven eventually arrived in Saltash and quickly set about strengthening the town's inadequate fortifications. A disconsolate William Ruthven now pondered on his error of not awaiting the arrival of Stamford's army, reputedly on its way to Plymouth. The mixed force Ruthven had led into Cornwall had been a composition of untried, disorganised foot and veteran, but unruly, horse. This undisciplined roundhead army had fought a determined Cornish force fighting to protect its home territory and been soundly thrashed.

On the other hand Hopton and his lieutenants were greatly respected by their troops and despite earlier setbacks at Plymouth, Modbury and Exeter, the Cornish cavaliers believed themselves ready to pay back. Their chance came at Braddock Down, Ruthven's advance was stopped and his army thoroughly whipped and forced to flee, suffering tremendous losses in prisoners and equipment. The lack of killed and wounded on both sides is ample evidence that any actual fighting was minimal and it was the cross-country chase that stitched the emblem of victory onto Hopton's banners.

The day after the battle Sir Thomas Wrothe, who was in Plymouth at this time, wrote to John Pym at Westminster outlining the fight and consequent loss of artillery. Wrothe also blamed Ruthven for going against Stamford's wishes: *'Besides this attempt was not only without but against the orders of my Lord General. Last of all and not the least but the greatest of all, I doubt we have not been thankful enough for the late and former deliverances, and therefore God did in this action withdraw himself from our assistance. I doubt that one man of note is either slain or taken prisoner, for we yet miss him. His name is Sir Shilston Calmady. Postscript: Your son (Alexander Pym) is now here and very well, and so I hope is my brother. We are not so dejected, but we are preparing to pursue our enemies with as much courage and power, both by sea and land, as ever'.*[2]

Born in London in 1584, Thomas Wrothe had attended Gloucester Hall Oxford in 1660 but left without a degree, though soon after he entered the Inner Temple with his brother Peter. Thomas was knighted in 1613 and upon the death of his father he inherited enough money to purchase the Somerset estates of his cousin Sir Robert Wrothe. He was an avid writer and translated a number of ancient books for his own pleasure. Thomas was also involved with the Virginia Company and in 1620 was on the Council for New England. As busy as ever Wrothe was elected MP for Bridgewater, 1627-8, and Sheriff of Somerset, 1639-40. He felt saddened at the declining state of the English Church and opposed the king in most matters ecclesiastical.

While Ruthven was marching towards disaster at Braddock, Stamford, with eight hundred foot and thirteen troops of horse, arrived in Plymouth to a cheering crowd and the bells of St Andrew's ringing out in welcome. Angry at his subordinate's premature departure, the earl refused to hurry to Ruthven's assistance. Instead he spent several days in Sir Thomas Wrothe's company inspecting the town's defences and being wined and dined by Mayor Francis and the council. Saltash, Millbrook and Mount Edgcumbe were visited and their roundhead garrisons checked. Lieutenant Colonel James Stephenson and 150 men held Millbrook, and Mount Edgcumbe, considered to be a strategically important outpost, was reinforced to forty men under two Scottish lieutenants, Davidson and Livingstone. Sir Alexander Carew, commanding St Nicholas Island, was highly praised by Stamford for his untiring effort, as were the engineers who worked tirelessly on the fortifications.

Satisfied Plymouth was relatively safe and in capable hands, Stamford finally put his small army on the road and headed for Launceston by way of Tavistock. Unaware of the disaster that had overtaken Ruthven's army and believing the Cornish to be in retreat, the earl reached Launceston in good spirits. Now came the bad news, brought in by a number of Ruthven's shattered survivors who limped into town and blurted out their tales of woe. Despite having a considerable force, Stamford, unsure of Hopton's strength or whereabouts, quickly retraced his steps and withdrew across the Tamar. Back in Tavistock, Henry Grey sent riders galloping to Exeter demanding reinforcements.

Rested after his spectacular victory, Sir Ralph Hopton divided his army, now swelled by the county's well-armed militia, and made plans to finish off any enemy troops still in Cornwall. Bevill Grenville, John Berkeley, William Ashburnham, John Trevannion and Nicholas Slanning were sent to Launceston to push back the Earl of Stamford's army, supposedly marching in from Tavistock. Hopton, meanwhile with Colonel William Godolphin and Lord Warwick Mohun advanced on Saltash, still occupied by Ruthven and an inadequate roundhead garrison. When Sunday January 22nd dawned General Ruthven expected the worst. With only 500 demoralised men available, he watched anxiously for Hopton's approach, placing his soldiers in a small, but well-chosen four-gun earthwork above the town gates. To assist Ruthven a sixteen-gun warship from Newcastle, the

Fredrick and William, hired, or rather commandeered by Stamford before he left Plymouth, lay at anchor in the river near Saltash.

Late the previous night Ruthven had received a communication from Captain Alexander Glen commanding the Millbrook garrison. In his letter Glen explained that in the absence of Lieutenant Colonel James Stephenson, who was in Plymouth raising more troops, he had been left in charge and would hold his position to the utmost of his ability.[3] Glen's message must have boosted Ruthven slightly, at least he wasn't alone on the Cornish side of the Tamar, and in addition Stephenson was seeking reinforcements.

The crunch came for Ruthven at 4 p.m. on the 22nd when Hopton arrived before the town and deployed his two infantry regiments in preparation for an attack. When the assault eventually went in the cavaliers expected as easy a victory as they had achieved at Braddock Down. With the river at their backs, the roundheads resisted gallantly for three hours, quite the reverse of their performance the day before, and every Cornish attack was vigorously thrown back. By seven in the evening, the situation was beginning to change, darkness now covered the country and ammunition inside the parliamentary fort was running out. At an emergency council of war it was decided by the majority to abandon the town and take to the boats. Mindful of the vindictive Cornishmen and eager not to be taken, many disregarded Ruthven's plans for an orderly withdrawal down to the river.

Organisation broke down almost immediately and the evacuation turned into a nightmare run for sanctuary. For some unaccountable reason no rearguard was arranged, which would have allowed for an orderly retreat. Instead the roundheads discarded weapons and armour and ran pell-mell down the hill for the boats. At the waters edge only a few vessels were found and the men began to panic, as a consequence many of the boats were swamped and lost. With so many trying to escape there were bound to be casualties and 100 of Ruthven's troops drowned in the frenzy to evade capture.

Eventually General Ruthven and 260 bedraggled and terrified survivors reached the safety of Plymouth, but another 140 had been captured along with all four cannon, muskets, ammunition and stores. The *Fredrick and William* was also taken, along with her crew, sixteen guns and arms for eight hundred men. The master of the ship, one Alderman Allen Ruddock, was later accused of treason by parliament. Ruddock failed to support Ruthven and surrendered his vessel to the enemy rather than escape. It was said the alderman abandoned his ship and fled allowing the enemy to completely pillage the *Fredrick and William*. Hopton later reported a loss of only one man during the battle, a figure too ridiculous to believe. The buoyant cavaliers entered Saltash and ran down to the river bank gathering up prisoners and weapons. The Cornish leaders planned to use the captured ship as a deterrent against any parliamentary attack from the river. Later when Saltash was recaptured by parliament, the vessel was seized and her guns confiscated and used in Plymouth's fortifications.

When the weary and dejected William Ruthven arrived back in Plymouth, fear of a general assault on the town by Hopton's elated army escalated. Nervous eyes peered out from behind the far-from-complete earthworks north of the town, searching for the first sign of royalists' banners coming up over the horizon. Extreme vigilance was the order of the day and all able-bodied men were called upon to defend Plymouth. Despite the heavy losses in Cornwall, those soldiers manning the town's defences were as determined as ever to stop Hopton. Full of fight the parliamentarian soldiery was greatly encouraged by their leaders. At this time Millbrook and Mount Edgcumbe were still held; but rather than leave the small garrisons to face annihilation both were withdrawn shortly after Saltash fell.

To meet the growing emergency, Mayor Philip Francis ordered money paid out of the town coffers to strengthen fortifications. With the outer works still in the preliminary stages, attention focused on the inner line. Extra workmen were hired to strengthen the sod rampart and the perimeter wall of the old Whitefriars' Monastery was reconstructed. More guns were taken from the seaward defences or borrowed from ships, hauled up through the town and positioned at strategically-selected locations. With nothing to prevent the enemy moving through Plymstock to How Stert and placing his artillery on high ground in order to bombard Sutton Pool, work was started on a new earth fort. When complete this isolated fortification would permit parliamentary lookouts to observe royalist activity in the Plymstock area and warn the town of enemy movements. The fort and its encampment were named in honour of the Earl of Stamford. With a second siege expected in as many months, food supplies were hastily collected and stored. Two new hand mills were also constructed at the old castle for grinding corn, and weights were brought in for weighing bread ready for rationing.

Active in raising troops for the relief of Plymouth during the winter months were a number of prominent parliamentarians, Sir John Northcote, Sir Samuel Rolle, Sir John Bampfield, Major General James Chudleigh and his father Sir George. Devonshire militia or trained bands at this time totalled 6,579 men, 4,006 musketeers, the rest pikemen, but these were spread out from the Tamar to the Somerset border and many had joined the royalist armies. Northcote however managed to collect 500 men from Bideford and Barnstaple and these would soon be on their way down towards Totnes, where they would join a new army being raised by James Chudleigh.

Meanwhile the Earl of Stamford, who had tentatively pushed his vanguard as far as Launceston, suddenly found himself threatened by Grenville and almost half the Cornish army. With Ruthven's defeat threatening the morale of his troops and Hopton endangering the route to Plymouth, Stamford pulled back to Tavistock. Here he tarried only long enough to evacuate his supplies before retreating all the way to Exeter, where he set up his headquarters fifty miles from the front. Before leaving Cornwall, Sir Ralph Hopton's cavaliers swore to capture Plymouth, but those eager to utter such promises did not include their own trained bandsmen. After their defeat of Ruthven at Braddock and Saltash, these very same men now disbanded and returned to their homes, reducing Sir Ralph's chances for a successful attack against Plymouth. Nevertheless the royalists under Grenville edged tentatively across the border in the wake of Stamford's retreat and occupied Tavistock.

Late in January, Hopton felt himself ready to move and he issued orders to his regiments at Tavistock to march south and reopen siege warfare against the port of Plymouth. In addition to his own army a few Devonshire royalists joined Hopton, as did a number of trained bandsmen, but only on condition that they were paid. Once Grenville was well on his way, Sir Ralph, Lord Mohun and Colonel Godolphin crossed the Tamar at Saltash with their part of the army and camped north of Plymouth around the St Budeaux area. The troops under Grenville and Berkeley meanwhile came down and set up headquarters at Plympton, cutting the road into Plymouth from the east. Although widely detached the Cornish forces were around the town and in much stronger positions than before.

By the end of the month Stamford, hoping to delay a royalist assault against Plymouth until reinforcements could be assembled and sent to her assistance, proposed a truce, the cavaliers took the bait and agreed. After preliminary talks over locations for the meeting, Kinterbury House, not far from St Budeaux, was chosen, but for some unexplained reason the venue was later changed to Ham House, the home of Robert Trelawny. Sir Ralph Hopton, Warwick Mohun and William Godolphin represented the Cornish army, while Sir George Chudleigh and Francis Buller, went on behalf of the Earl of Stamford.

The conference, scheduled for the afternoon of Sunday January 29th, soon got under way; the main item on the agenda being whether or not Devon and Cornwall could be transformed into a neutral zone. If such an idea was agreed upon, any individual who wished to fight for King Charles could do so, provided he enlisted outside of the two counties. The royalists proposed that all new fortifications thrown up in and around Plymouth since the outbreak of hostilities, should be dismantled and old pre-existing forts turned over to his majesty's authority. Also no money or troops were to be collected for either of the warring factions. After ninety minutes of hot seesawing debate, Chudleigh and Buller refused to agree on the fortification question and the meeting broke up with no settlement. Both sides now withdrew and the brief truce came to an end. Satisfied with the location of Ham House, Hopton shifted his part of the royalist army there and waited for Berkeley, who was not quite in his assigned position.

The next day Hopton edged still closer to Plymouth by camping at Swilly, but before all his troops could arrive, part of the garrison marched out and skirmished with his advance. Godolphin's regiment bore the brunt of the contest alone until reinforcements arrived under Lord Mohun. For three hours the fighting continued before the parliamentarians were forced to withdraw. Sir Ralph Hopton was now able to extend and strengthen his positions, which ran from Stoke village on the right across to Venn House near Mannamead on the left. The royalists held a line running close to where Milehouse, Beacon Park and Pennycross are now, but it was not one continuous line. The cavaliers occupied a number of small loosely unconnected fortifications.

Meanwhile the Earl of Stamford, having recovered from his initial panic after Ruthven's defeat at Braddock Down, poked his head over Exeter's fortifications. Satisfied Hopton was not moving his way he took passage on a ship bound for Plymouth. Once he arrived in the port, Stamford conversed with the military leaders and surveyed the enemy positions. On February 1st he wrote to Westminster declaring the royalists were too strong for him to move against and that Plymouth was in desperate need of money and arms. The jittery earl also informed parliament of the peace conference and its outcome.

While the Cornish army closed the net around Plymouth, Hopton sent mounted detachments out over the moors in different directions, with orders to visit isolated villages. During these forays many parliamentarians were forced to flee from their homes and hide. One such person was John Syms, curate of St Leonard's the church in Sheepstor village, at that time a chapelry under Bickleigh. Syms was a Somerset man who had matriculated from Exeter College Oxford on December 15th 1615 aged sixteen and been ordained priest on September 21st 1623. At the outbreak of war, Syms, his wife Elizabeth and their three children resided in the quiet village of Sheepstor. If not for a daybook, which Syms kept to record, his unique, if biased account of the war years, John Syms would have passed quietly into history and many valuable anecdotes lost forever.

During the first week of February, Sir John Berkeley, having at last reached his assigned location at Plympton, received orders from Hopton to take a mixed detachment of horse and foot and proceed to Kingsbridge, eighteen miles east of Plymouth. Berkeley was to position his force so as to blunt a possible roundhead threat reported to be gathering in and around Dartmouth. The rumour was in fact true, James Chudleigh was in Kingsbridge busy recruiting and training a parliamentary army with which he hoped to take on Hopton. At Berkeley's unexpected approach the alarm was sounded and Chudleigh, not yet ready for a confrontation, was forced to flee along with his poorly-disciplined army, leaving behind a number of confused prisoners and valuable stores.

Satisfied with this successful excursion, John Berkeley had little time to gloat over his triumph. In his absence Hopton had received reports of parliamentary troops gathering at Tavistock. Mounting 500 horse and dragoons, Sir John with Bevill Grenville, William Ashburnham and Sir Francis Hawley, the latter commanding a small regiment of cavalry from Somerset, moved out of Kingsbridge and rode northwards. Finding Tavistock bereft of enemy troops, Berkeley swung his column out of town and continued northeastwards towards Okehampton. Again Berkeley failed to find the enemy, but locals informed him of a roundhead force moving across the moors in the direction of Totnes. Berkeley and his co-commanders decided to follow, but the dragoons were to remain at Okehampton under Grenville.

During the early hours of February 9th, with snow covering the moor and a cold wind biting both man and beast, Berkeley's advance stumbled into Chagford hoping for a warm billet. Fully expecting the reported roundheads to be well on their way towards Totnes, the royalists were off their guard and completely unaware of the presence in town of Sir John Northcote and his 500 men from Barnstaple. These troops had marched into Chagford only hours before, en route to join Chudleigh at Totnes and were resting for the night when the noisy approach of the royalist vanguard was noted and reported. Quickly and quietly the roundheads were roused, armed and positioned.

As the Cornish horsemen rode wearily into the village, shots rang out from the darkness. The leading cavaliers fell from their saddles, the rest reined up and began firing back. Uncertain of Northcote's strength or whereabouts, Berkeley fearing a well set ambush, charged right through Chagford. The running fight which followed was confusing, flashes in the dark indicated musketeers firing, a clash of swords meant hand to hand fighting, an agonising shout told that someone had become a casualty and the thud of horse hooves announced others were making their escape. Eventually the Cornish column extricated itself, galloped clear of Chagford and rode around to rejoin Grenville back in Okehampton. Behind them the royalists left Northcote victorious and a number of killed, wounded and captured. Amongst the dead was the poet Sidney Godolphin, son of Colonel William Godolphin, his premature death would be greatly mourned by the Cornish gentry. Sir Francis Hawley was also shot during the encounter, but his wound was minor and he would recover. Having reclaimed Godolphin's body the royalists buried him in Okehampton and rode back to Plympton, where they rejoined the rest of the army.

The victorious Northcote continued his advance towards Totnes and from there to Kingsbridge. Here, meanwhile, Major General James Chudleigh had returned and was once again gathering an army together. Chudleigh hoped to collect a sizeable force for the expedition against Hopton and his own popular personality helped bring many men together from the southwest. Soldiers from all over Devon, Somerset and Dorset could be found encamped around

Kingsbridge and many more were on their way, all eager to fight.

The Plymouth garrison at this time must have numbered around 3,000 men, inclusive of regulars, trained bandsmen, sailors and the survivors from Braddock. The recently-arrived London greycoat regiment of Colonel Sir John Merrick, under Lieutenant Colonel Vincent Calmady, was also a welcome addition to the town. One of the most active local parliamentarians at this time was Mayor Philip Francis. On February 7th the Earl of Stamford, greatly impressed by the man, wrote to the speaker of the House of Lords declaring: *"The mayor of Plymouth is as brave a man as ever breathed"*.[4]

A letter, which appeared in a tract dated February 20th 1643, described an event that was more propaganda than fact, but reputedly involved the popular mayor. In the pamphlet Sir Nicholas Slanning was supposed to have written a letter to the chief gunner of one of the outer forts. This unnamed person, an old pre-war acquaintance of Slanning's, was to load his cannon with gunpowder and paper in place of cannonballs. When the royalists launched an arranged attack the paper defence would allow them to overrun the fort. The gunner's reward for his treachery was to be £100.

Slanning's supposed letter was intercepted and handed over to Mayor Francis, the gunner was consequently arrested and Philip Francis wrote back to Slanning, appertaining to be the said gunner and agreeing to the offer. As the royalist attack went in the fort's guns opened up and blew the assault to pieces. Sir Ralph Hopton and 800 of his men were reported killed. This kind of propaganda permeated the English civil war from the beginning; the fact that Hopton was not injured and no such battle recorded condemns the incident as pure fabrication. On the other hand treachery did occur many times in and around Plymouth during the war, and although the battle and greatly exaggerated losses are to be ignored, the offer from Slanning, who knew many in the town, could have held some credibility.

During this period Philip Francis' strong personality made up for Stamford's weak indecisiveness and Ruthven's despondency after his recent defeat, and the mayor remained the foundation for Plymouth's continued resistance. Almost equal in numbers to the royal army, which was separated into two distinct parts by the River Plym, the garrison believed itself ill-prepared to dislodge the entrenched Cornishmen. The unfortunate setback at Braddock contributed greatly to the town's defensive policy at this time. No one was willing to risk another defeat and with the enemy settled behind their fortifications the roundheads were satisfied to watch and await developments.

When a large parliamentary force was rumoured to be gathering in South Devon for the relief of Plymouth, the Earl of Stamford had a sudden surge of renewed confidence. He quickly made preparations to join the fight at the earliest opportunity. The target for the new roundhead strike was the village of Modbury, where Hopton had recently quartered two of his foot regiments, those of Sir Nicholas Slanning and Colonel John Trevannion, under the overall command of Sir John Berkeley. Although only a short march from the rest of the royal army, the Modbury detachment blocked the roads into Plymouth from the east and cut the town off from the South Hams. By occupying Modbury, Hopton was also preventing Chudleigh from making a surprise attack against the rest of his army around Plymouth. Also supplies could be collected and transported westwards for use by the Cornish troops and recruits enlisted. The appearance at Modbury of armed royalists gave added protection to local supporters of the king, two of the more prominent being John Harris at Plymstock and Sir Thomas Hele of Flete, a huge mansion lying several miles west of Modbury.

Harris, like Piers Edgcumbe, Sir Thomas Hele, Sir Henry Cary, Sir Edward Seymour and many other leading Devonshire royalists was descended from noble stock and the Harris family had resided at Radford since the reign of King Edward IV. When Sir Christopher Harris died in 1623, the family estate, built at the head of Hooe Lake, was left to his sister Joane, who married a John Harris of Lanrest in the parish of Liskeard, thereby keeping her surname. Their first child, Christopher, married Bevill Grenville's sister, but died childless, leaving his brother John to inherit the family estate. On July 16th 1637 John Harris married Elizabeth Champernowne in Plymstock Church and he served as MP for Liskeard until January 1643, when along with his friend Sir Edward Seymour, he was dismissed for deserting the House and joining the king's parliament at Oxford.

Nearing fifty at the outbreak of war, Harris found life at the king's new capital unsuitable and he returned home to better protect his estate. John Harris fortified Radford House to the best of his ability, but with insufficient troops and weapons, he was forced to ask Hopton for help. Later Harris was said to have commanded a foot regiment, but in all probability his only authority was over those few troops who helped garrison his home. Sir Thomas Hele, whose residence was less than ten miles from Radford House, was a cousin to Sir Alexander Carew and many of the Rolle family. On May 28th 1627 Hele had been created baronet, nine years later he was Sheriff of Devon and in 1640 MP for Okehampton. Sir Thomas served the king during the war by commanding a small cavalry regiment, raised mainly from Devonshire royalists.

In the event of trouble at Modbury two additional royalist foot regiments, stationed at Plympton, were less than three hours away, while the rest of Hopton's army was encamped around Stoke and Mannamead. If an attack against Modbury materialised it was doubtful any of these units could reach Berkeley in time to be of help. To aid his royalist confederates, John Harris passed on valuable information concerning roundhead defences and troop movements in Plymouth, but with a strong enemy garrison holding newly-erected Fort Stamford on the high ground which commanded the Plymstock area, there was little more he could do.

The threat to Sir Ralph Hopton's widely-dispersed army appeared towards the end of the third week in February. The parliamentary high command had been busy planning a concerted two-pronged attack against Modbury for weeks and had assembled plenty of troops for the offensive. The principal force would march from Kingsbridge in the east, while a secondary, much smaller column was to strike from Plymouth in the west. Since Braddock Down parliament had been feverishly drawing every spare unit in the county together. From north Devon Sir John Northcote and his 500 men marched into Totnes, elated after their minor victory at Chagford. Major General James Chudleigh and his father Sir George assembled the Devonshire trained bands around Totnes, Colonel John Wear came down from Exeter with a small detachment and Captain Nicholas Roope, merchant and true patriot with almost eighty horsemen, all equipped at his own expense, rode in from Dartmouth. Also heading for Kingsbridge were colonels John Pyne and Edward Popham with part of the Somerset trained bands and a detachment of Dorset horse. To make up the numbers a body of badly-armed locals, intent only on plunder, also converged on the village.

Nevertheless by February 20th Chudleigh's command was reputed to number some 9,000. This rather high figure is a gross exaggeration, a fair estimate would be around 7,000, of which three quarters were fighting men. With his force assembled and a large train of supplies, Chudleigh marched to Kingsbridge, fourteen miles southwest of Totnes, a route which would allow the roundheads to approach Modbury from below. General Chudleigh and his subordinates were hoping for total surprise. Arriving in Kingsbridge later in the day, James Chudleigh set up a supply depot, dispatched foragers and sent scouts up the road toward his objective eleven miles away. Early on the morning of the 22nd General Chudleigh's massive army, marched along the narrow, twisting country road towards Modbury.

While the roundheads converged on Kingsbridge, a meeting took place in Plymouth, where the Earl of Stamford, recently arrived from Exeter and full of fight, announced to Lieutenant Colonel Vincent Calmady, that several companies of his London greycoat regiment were needed. The detached companies were to form a mixed column along with several companies of the town trained bands under Captain Christopher Martyn and a number of dragoons and cavalry. This force was to move out of Plymouth during the night, filter past the royalist camps and attack Modbury from the west in conjunction with Chudleigh's assault from the east. Of the troops from Plymouth, the militia should never have been sent, as the men were untrained for such an important mission.

To defend the village of Modbury, Slanning and Trevannion had perhaps 1,500 foot, many of them veterans of recent engagements, a few local cavalry and five cannon. Upon word of the roundhead advance from the direction of Kingsbridge, part of the royalist force moved out of Modbury and lined a number of hedges and makeshift breastworks thrown up east of the town, overlooking a narrow sluggish stream. Crossing Huttons Bridge at Aveton Gifford, the parliamentarians closed in on Modbury from the southeast. Meanwhile the Plymouth detachment, having discreetly been ferried across the Cattewater, advanced very slowly, avoiding enemy lookouts at Radford. Their arrival at Modbury was delayed when the troops stopped off at Flete House in order to pillage the residence of Sir Thomas Hele. During the raid, one of Captain Martyn's militiamen, James Cowre of Ugborough was slightly wounded, becoming possibly the only casualty suffered by either side. By the time the Plymouth column was back on the road, encumbered by prisoners, twenty horses and much plunder, fighting had already broken out off to the east.

The second battle at Modbury began at noon on Tuesday February 22nd, when half a mile from the town, Chudleigh's vanguard, under Sir John Northcote, ran into enemy musketeers lined up on a hill covering the approach into the village. Partially protected by thick hedges, the royalists began shooting down onto the advancing roundheads who were toiling forward through the wet mud. Fortunately for the north Devon foot, the enemy matchlocks were inaccurate and slow to reload. Despite a good defensive position, supported by cannon, casualties amongst the parliamentarians were relatively light. Although Chudleigh outnumbered the enemy by more than four to one, only half his army was on hand. This and the tenacity of the Cornishmen, made the fighting at Modbury hard going.

Finally through a shortage of ammunition and sheer weight of numbers pressing uphill, the cavaliers were ousted from their commanding position and forced to leave their cannon and a number of prisoners behind. The withdrawal of the Slanning-Trevannion regiments, which fell back in good order from hedge to hedge, may have been due to the arrival on their right flank and rear of the Plymouth detachment, which had finally joined the battle. The royalists, although in retreat, refused to be pressed and they fought hard as they fell back through Modbury, inflicting casualties on the enemy with every volley. Darkness descended but the fighting continued, silhouetted by torchlight and burning buildings.

Chudleigh's men followed on the heels of the retreating Cornishmen, picking up prisoners as they went, a number of the more disreputable soldiers broke off to loot and set fire to houses. Weary and discouraged, many of the cavaliers finally broke and fled northwards over Sheepstor Bridge or down a lane leading towards Ayleston Brook that is still known today as Runaway Lane. One small group of diehards occupied the old Champernowne House. This building had been well fortified and the last of the royalists held out here until the early hours of the 23rd. With the situation growing more desperate, the survivors voted to break out. Aided by darkness the majority managed to slip away, leaving sixty dragoons behind as a rearguard. These men remained until daybreak when they took to their horses and galloped away after their comrades, easily evading the roundheads who were too busy looting Modbury. The Plymouth horse and other cavalry detachments eventually picked up a small number of the rearguard detachment and herded them back to

Modbury. Had the column from Plymouth moved more swiftly and positioned itself to cover the western exits of Modbury, and Chudleigh's men been better organised and disciplined, the royalists would not have escaped so lightly.

At the battle of Modbury, Hopton's army suffered approximately 100 killed, 200 wounded and 100 captured. Sir Nicholas Slanning was rumoured to be amongst the slain, but this story, like so many, turned out to be false when he reappeared later at Plympton. Five cannon a thousand muskets, or so it was claimed and many other materials of war were taken by the parliamentarians, who reported their own casualties at only eleven killed, a few wounded and no more than a dozen captured. These numbers are obviously miscalculated in killed and wounded, Chudleigh's losses must come closer to the royalist total. This disparity in casualties between two sides is so typical of the time. The victor always minimised their losses, while maximising their opponent's. Captain Roope, the Dartmouth merchant who fought in Chudleigh's army, paid money out of his own pocket for the care of his wounded men.

The figure for the royalist dead is probably nearer the roundhead number and the prisoners more than likely include many of the wounded. Roundhead losses are much too low, the veteran Cornish infantry must have inflicted at least the same number of killed and wounded as they received, if not more. Three of the recorded parliamentary wounded were Thomas Searle, Edward Millard and George Gibbs, the later from Holsworthy. One of the immediate results of the battle, besides forcing the cavaliers from the field, was that Henry Bagley, the zealous royalist Rector of St George's Church in Modbury, took his very large family out of the village and fled into Cornwall.

Coinciding with the two-pronged attack on Modbury was a pre-arranged sortie by part of the Plymouth garrison, under Stamford's personal direction and aimed at Hopton's siege works. This was planned as a diversionary attack, to prevent the royalist from reinforcing their troops at Modbury. Although Hopton managed to force the assailants back, the ferocity of the assault, coupled with news of the disaster in the South Hams, persuaded Sir Ralph to raise the siege of Plymouth and retreat to Tavistock. When the Slanning-Trevannion detachment finally marched back into Plympton early next morning, they found their comrades breaking camp. Hopton's artillery, which was too bulky to haul over wretched country roads, was transported to the Tamar and shipped straight across to Saltash. Five of the heavier pieces had to be abandoned, due to lack of animals and time. The horse and foot rendezvoused on Roborough Down and from here the royal army marched on to Tavistock, followed at a respectable distance by part of Chudleigh's force. Unfortunately, with the fighting over, many of the roundhead militia saw no reason to stay with the colours and large numbers began to desert.

The second siege of Plymouth was now over and once again engineers from the garrison moved out in Hopton's wake and demolished the abandoned enemy earthworks. Even though his three sieges to date had ended in failure, Sir Ralph Hopton still managed to retain the respect and confidence of his subordinates, unlike the Earl of Stamford. While Hopton fell back across Dartmoor, those roundhead troops following in his tracks, were halted and assembled on Roborough Down. Alarmed by the high proportion of desertions, Stamford disbanded the majority of Chudleigh's trained bandsmen and allowed the men to return to their farms in preparation for spring planting. The earl accompanied by the deputy lieutenants of Devon, then returned to Plymouth, where they were entertained before leaving for Exeter.

With Hopton gone, the Earl of Stamford, at the head of a 1,000-man escort left Plymouth and marched to Modbury for a consultation with James Chudleigh, to work out a plan for pursuing the enemy. Unfortunately before a decision could be reached, a call for a truce rang out from Cornwall. Despite the parliamentary success at Modbury and the breaking of the siege, Stamford agreed to the proposal and a date was set for negotiations to begin, though Westminster had not been informed. The conference was to take place at Mount Edgcumbe House during the week of February 28th-March 6th.

The idea for the cease-fire came from the royalists and was no more than an excuse for Hopton's army to lick its wounds, resupply, rearm and recruit. Not all parliamentarians were taken in, some believed they should play the same game, others like Thomas Gewen resented such arrangements and he spoke openly of his indignation.

On March 3rd Sir George Chudleigh wrote to London in an effort to explain Stamford's agreement to the peace talks: *'The great blessing of God upon our late endeavours, hath rendered the undisciplined forces of this county manageable to defend it against a small invasion. But consisting chiefly of trained bands altogether incapable to follow our victory into Cornwall for many unanswerable reasons, as the case stands yet, therefore we have thought fit to accept our enemy's importunity for a treaty, hoping to increase our volunteers, and to get supplies for our trained soldiers, whose affections to their families and husbandry carry them from us daily in very great numbers with their arms. We ask for arms and power to use Martial Law'.*[5]

During the negotiations, dignitaries from both sides met as arranged and suggested a lasting peace. The Cornish representatives proposed that no troops should move out of either county, this would mean parliamentarians in Devon could not aid their supporters in Somerset. The roundhead commissioners felt uneasy at such strict terms, but they eventually agreed. To prove their good intentions, those present took communion together and proposed a second meeting, to take place in Exeter.

Almost forgetting the trouncing at Braddock Down, many parliamentarians believed the Cornish royalists could be defeated and suspected the motivation behind this truce. It becomes more curious therefore, why the local roundhead leaders agreed to a continuation for a further twenty days. Only Sir George Chudleigh and a few pessimists believed the army was not yet ready to fight Hopton, thus a continuance was believed beneficial to both sides. During the truce, a meeting took place in Exeter, attended by many prominent citizens from numerous Devonshire parishes, including John Syms, curate of the church at Sheepstor. The reason for this council was to organise a tri-county association, to consist of Devon, Somerset and Dorset, its aim, to confine the war to Cornwall, a dream that would soon be shattered.

During the prolonged, vacillating truce, Henry Grey, the unpredictable Earl of Stamford travelled regularly between Plymouth and Exeter, disbanding his large army and allowing many of the troops to return home. It was hoped by a few of the more easily-led that the four westernmost counties of England, could negotiate some kind of permanent neutrality, with the protection of said shires of prime concern. Fortunately the House of Commons considered any treaty without the authority of parliament illegal. King Charles at Oxford also denied knowledge of any such truce and refused to condone such action. Concerned by these events, Westminster sent Edmund Prideaux and Anthony Nicholl, the later MP for Bodmin and a relative to both Bevill Grenville and John Pym, into the Westcountry. These prominent gentlemen were to assess the situation in Devon and report back as quickly as possible.

Upon their arrival Prideaux and Nicholl immediately began to bombard the House of Commons with the latest intelligence concerning the putative truce. Fearing a possible royalist coup, Westminster sent orders to the mayor of Exeter and the deputy lieutenants of Devon, commanding them not to allow Sir Ralph Hopton or any of his followers into the city, the proposed rendezvous for the next meeting of the peace commission. Mayor Christopher Clark obeyed his strict mandate from parliament and those royalists who arrived at the city gates for the second conference were surprised when they were denied entry. The delegation was informed of Westminster's decision and told to wait at the West Indies Inn, a hostelry in St Thomas, then an outlying village, where they would be met by a group of parliamentarian representatives. The royalists were mainly from Cornwall, the roundheads from Devon and Dorset. Sir William Waller, commanding parliamentary forces in Somerset was dead against any local treaty and he used his cavalry to prevent those appointees from Somerset from attending the conference.

At the rendezvous on Tuesday March 14th the royal commissioners proposed that all forts in Devon and Cornwall, erected since the outbreak of war, should be flattened and the troops disarmed. Trade between the two aforementioned counties should be unimpeded and any force, either for king or parliament, moving into these two westernmost counties was to be stopped. All prisoners, military and ministerial, were to be released and Hopton with his army, be permitted to join the king freely and without hindrance. The parliamentary representatives, having learned that Cornish soldiers were fortifying Saltash, disagreed with almost all of Hopton's proposals. Consequently the meeting ended with distrust on both sides, but with a third rendezvous proposed and a further ten days added to the truce period. With no word from Westminster on whether to prohibit the talks which were destined to begin again in Plymouth, Edmund Prideaux and Anthony Nicholl gave Mayor Francis permission to allow the conference to go ahead.

The third parley proved as pointless as the previous two, once more a great deal of talking ended in indecision and by now both sides realised it was only a matter of time before hostilities would break out anew. Prideaux and Nicholl, aided by such hot-blooded parliamentarians as Christopher Clark, Philip Francis, Thomas Gewen and a host of others, effectively undermined all attempts at forming a separate neutrality. The date set for the expiration of the truce was April 22nd but neither side wished to be the one to reinstate armed conflict. The fruitless talks had not prevented Hopton and Stamford from building up their forces, on the contrary the time was not wasted and had been greatly utilized to train and recruit both armies.

Continually suffering from gout, Henry Grey ordered three fresh regiments of foot raised in Devon, calling up those very men he had disbanded only a month before. Colonel John Wear went back to work and assembled his unit in Crediton. This regiment, raised at Wear's own expense, had fought well at Exeter and Modbury and was one of the better commands in the county. Captain Robert Bennett, whose cousin Sir Humphrey Bennett commanded a regiment in the king's army, mustered his company at Torrington, ready to rejoin Sir Samuel Rolle's north Devon regiment. Meanwhile Sir George Chudleigh, now Governor of Plymouth Fort, Philip Francis and many others in the town proclaimed their continued support for parliament.

With winter's dreary weather lingering, fighting over most of the country was minimal. Heavy rains turned bad roads into bottomless mud, making movement of artillery and horses almost impossible. Skirmishing continued throughout the winter months, but no serious campaigns were attempted. When combat did occur both sides had varying success and failure. In Lancashire the royalist Earl of Derby, James Stanley, had moderate luck against the parliamentarians, but he dealt savagely with towns and people alike. In neighbouring Yorkshire, George Goring, the man who as a roundhead fled from Portsmouth and joined the king, was about to besiege Leeds, only to be talked out of the project by wiser heads. The Midlands saw parliament gain the upper hand when Lord Brooke captured Lichfield. On February 22nd Queen Henrietta, having travelled to Holland for the purpose of securing foreign support for her husband, slipped through a weak ineffectual roundhead blockade and landed at Bridlington with arms and ammunition.

(2) Page 73: Letter from Sir Thomas Wrothe to John Pym, January 20th 1643. Oxford Bodleian Library, MS Nalson 2 fols 288-9; by kind permission of the Oxford Bodleian Library.
(3) Page 75: Buller Papers, pages 89-90, Edited by R. N. Worth, Plymouth City Library.
(4) Page 81: House of Commons Journal.
(5) Page 88: Letter from Sir George Chudleigh and four others to the Committee of Lords and Commons for the safety of the kingdom, March 3rd 1643. Oxford Boleian Library. MS Nalson 2 fols 326-7; by kind permission of the Oxford Bodleian Library.

Chapter 5

Disaster for Parliament

The month of March saw the end of an era in Plymouth, unable to cope with defeat Colonel William Ruthven, the town's early hero, left for London. Poor Ruthven blamed himself for the army's dismal failure at Braddock Down. All too eager to claim the laurels of victory he had refused to wait for Stamford and ultimately led his command to disaster. Almost immediately after his departure, royalist newssheets attacked Ruthven. Enemy propaganda declared that General Ruthven made plenty of money out of the war, and with the prospect of peace in the southwest plunder would be in short supply. In January John Pym wrote to William Ruthven from the House of Commons asking for an account of the money he had received from the customs. Ruthven must have sent Pym a satisfactory reply as no further action was taken. The cavalier version of Ruthven's departure from the war also claimed his wife, residing in Exeter at this time, had left to join her husband without paying a number of bills. Base statements of this calibre were made in an effort to discredit the reputation of the most successful parliamentarian leader of the Westcountry's early struggle against royalist aggression.

Behind the peace facade, roundhead and royalist continued reorganising and reinforcing their armies. In Plymouth, with Philip Francis' help, the little garrison was brought up to 3,500 foot, a number of sailors borrowed from the navy made up a sizable proportion of this force. Also included were 400 trained bandsmen and 500 cavalry. A further 1,200 foot, under Sir John Northcote, were camped on Roborough Down, a short march from Plymouth.

The navy helped considerably during this period, by conveying supplies into the port from London and other places and allocating well-trained gunners to man the heavy cannon dotted around the forts. Since the arrival in the Westcountry of Sir Ralph Hopton, both armies had stripped the countryside around Plymouth of forage and the town's limited stock of food was beginning to run dangerously low.

Although supply ships regularly sailed into Millbay and Sutton harbour their cargoes were proving insufficient, especially with so many refugees arriving. With the prospect of famine looming, Mayor Francis detained a number of grain ships en route to Spain and purchased their cargo by force, paying the masters a fair rate in return. When parliament learned of the mayor's action an ordinance was passed to indemnify Philip Francis for any monies paid out. Francis also received permission to continue this practice as long as he believed it necessary.

By early March the defenders of Plymouth felt so confident of holding the town that the forty-gun frigate *Lion*, resting at anchor in the Hamoaze under Captain Ludovic Dick, was ordered to sail and join the Earl of Warwick's fleet. This two-year-old vessel, having spent a brief period refitting in Sutton Pool under the diligent eye of Mayor Francis, was now deemed ready to join Warwick's flotilla. Hopton's departure and the truce helped terminate the need to keep the *Lion* in port.

The Cornish army was also being supplied by sea, mainly from the continent via Falmouth harbour. A second, but more important source of supply for the royalists at this time was Plymouth itself. Early in March three ships belonging to Robert Trelawny, the *Richmond*, *Little Richmond* and *Tiger*, sailed from Plymouth. Using royalist agents and captains, the ships were landed in Falmouth and seized by Sir Nicholas Slanning, no doubt by pre-arrangement. Silver plate, gold, gunpowder, muskets, swords, match, salt, wheat, pork and sugar were found on board and confiscated. This blatant show of treachery probably swayed the House of Commons from acceding to another bail petition from Trelawny, still a prisoner in Winchester House; in fact the House refused outright. With such a build-up of arms and supplies by both sides, fighting was bound to break out and soon.

Despite the truce, skirmishing on the outskirts of Plymouth continued, when royalist scouts rode too close and were attacked by parliamentarians out on patrol. On occasions the cavaliers were rowed across the Tamar on cattle rustling raids. During one such foray a Captain William Pomeroy, from Plymouth and Mr Nevil Bligh, a Cornishman, were captured by a detachment of the Plymouth horse under Captain Nicholas Boscowan. Both men were escorted back to Plymouth ready to be transferred by ship to London. Originally from Bodmin, Nevil Bligh lived at Carnedon near Launceston and was married to a Plymouth girl; he had been aboard the *Fredrick and William* when the vessel was captured at Saltash.

Later the royalists offered to exchange Sir Shilston Calmady for Bligh, but the offer was refused, the reason being that Bligh had been one of the principal signatories of a petition sent from Cornwall to King Charles back in 1642. This document informed his majesty that all those who signed the document would lay down their lives to defend his royal person and pressed the king not to listen to parliament. Bligh, possibly with the connivance of a royalist sympathizer or through bribery, managed to escape from Plymouth by cutting his hair off and disguising himself as a roundhead. Later he was to be found serving as a captain in William Coryton's royal regiment of foot.

Plymouth at this time was being used extensively as a prison for captured royalists, due mainly to its position, hemmed in by water. On March 13th the House of Commons ordered Captain Creface Riley, then being detained at Newgate prison, Captain Edward Darcy, Captain George Darcy prisoners in the Gatehouse, ensigns Richard and Thomas Shelley and Cufs, Captain Ogelby, cornets George Wyshart and George Gordon, prisoners in Lord Peters House, be transferred to Plymouth. Due to numerous escape attempts, not by the aforementioned officers, but by other royalists, parliament sent these captives west for better security. Mayor Francis, as if he hadn't enough on his plate, was to be in charge of their safety, however, if he considered it unsafe to detain them in Plymouth, he was authorised to transfer them to either Barnstaple or Lydford.

In early March parliament ordered commissioners to assess each county and collect taxes from all persons according to the value of their estate. Responsibility for collecting the money on parliament's behalf was assigned to a number of trusted officials, notably Sir George Chudleigh, Sir Francis Drake, Sir John Northcote, Sir Samuel Rolle, Sir Nicholas Martyn, Robert Savery and Sir Shilston Calmady. At first Devon was assessed at £3,000 per week, but after a huge outcry, this figure was reduced to £1,800, still the highest in the country. Cornwall had only to pay £625 and Exeter £50/10s. Later, on May 7th a further demand for more taxes was ordered those possessing estates were to pay one fifth of their yearly income in duty. Any bishop opposed to parliament was to have his property sequestered, as were those MPs serving the king. To seize estates and money from delinquents on parliament's behest, the following commissioners were named, William Gould, Thomas Boone, Charles Vaughan, Thomas Gewen, John Champneys and George Peard esquires. Christopher Ceely, Richard Evonds, Moses Goodyear merchants and Richard Evans and Christopher Clarke the younger of Exeter. Amongst those marked to have their property confiscated were Robert Trelawny, Sir Edward Seymour, Sir Hugh Pollard and Sir Thomas Hele. Trelawny, Seymour and Pollard were being held prisoner by parliament at this time and Hele was with the king. An interesting story abounds that Sir Edward, shortly after his confinement to Winchester House, managed to file through the bars of a window and jump out. Unfortunately he landed on the back of a startled guard who was so winded and shocked at the prisoner's audacity he was unable to cry out or prevent Seymour's escape. This incident is all the more plausible when the treatment Seymour suffered at the hands of parliament, after the war, is taken into consideration. He was imprisoned and kept in confinement long after many other, more prominent royalists, were released.

For a moment disaster to the parliamentary cause loomed, not from the enemy across the water, but from far off Westminster. On March 30th with the truce still in effect and no sign of its termination, parliament proposed to reduce the forces defending Plymouth, Portsmouth and the Isle of Wight to their original garrison strength before the outbreak of war. Fortunately this proposal was quickly and quietly shelved.

Unimpressed by the efforts of the Devon committee to unlawfully seek out a separate truce with Hopton, Westminster sent numerous messages to cease all such activity. In response Sir George Chudleigh and his fellow commissioners wrote to London on April 17th apologising to the Committee of Safety for even contemplating such a process. Chudleigh explained in his letter that the only reason such talks were ever initiated was to prevent the spilling of blood. As the deadline for the end of the truce approached, part of Stamford's army was making its way slowly towards Lifton, four miles from Launceston. Fortunately the earl was still in Exeter suffering from gout and the burden of command passed to Major General James Chudleigh. This capable young officer had managed to concentrate 1,700 foot and five troops of horse at Okehampton before beginning his march westwards.

Chudleigh's hastily-raised vanguard consisted of troops from Colonel William Bampfield's regiment, part of Sir Samuel Rolle's north Devon trained band regiment and possibly part of Sir John Bampfield's northeast Devon regiment. Several hundred volunteers from the navy were also present as well as captains Thomas Drake, William Gould and Alexander Pym, who commanded three of the five mounted companies available. The energetic Chudleigh could not hope to achieve great results with the small force on hand. Why Stamford had not given his subordinate all available troops is a mystery. It was probably Henry Grey's lack of confidence which forced him to retain 1,800 foot and three troops of horse in Exeter. Whatever the reason James Chudleigh would soon find himself in a dangerous position with his closest support being all the way back at Plymouth.

At midnight on April 22nd it was all over, the so-called truce came to an end. Learning there were barely 1,200 cavaliers in Launceston awaiting a general rendezvous of all Cornish regiments, Chudleigh marched toward the Devon-Cornwall border by way of Polson Bridge. Expecting reinforcements from Plymouth at any moment, James Chudleigh saw no reason to delay. Only a few hours before the roundheads crossed the border, royalist scouts noted the activity east of the bridge and reported the news to Sir Ralph Hopton. Being a Sunday and despite the imminent danger, Hopton ordered his troops to attend prayers in the town church. As the service concluded, frantic reports came in from anxious pickets, announcing the enemy had crossed the Tamar at Polson Bridge and were assembling in fields ready to ascend Beacon Hill less than a mile from Launceston. Chudleigh had moved rapidly, his small cavalry detachment under Thomas Drake easily brushing aside a company of royal dragoons, which shamefully abandoned their post at the bridge and fled. The only opposition now was Sir Bevill Grenville's regiment, but help was near. Hopton kept half his foot in Launceston and led the rest up Beacon Hill to support Grenville. Other Cornish units were converging on Launceston Slanning, Trevannion, Godolphin and Mohun were pushing their foot hard, while Sir John Berkeley with the horse and dragoons, rode as fast as their mounts would allow.

For now, though Hopton, Grenville and Thomas Bassett, who had recently replaced William Ashburnham, were alone with 1,200 musketeers and pikemen. Hopton's early strategy was dominated by his lack of numbers and he chose to remain on the defensive until reinforcements arrived. The key to Launceston from the direction of Polson Bridge was the commanding elevation known as Beacon Hill, to the southeast of the town, and it was here that the Cornishmen threw up their defences; boxes, barrels, sacks, anything found was utilized. Most of the royalist foot were positioned on the summit except for a detachment of musketeers. These were the forlorn hope and they were sent down the slope to take their place behind a hedge near the eastern base of the hill. Shortly before the first parliamentary attack, Colonel William Godolphin and most of his regiment arrived; grateful for their timely arrival Hopton placed these fresh troops beside Grenville. Godolphin brought royalist numbers up to well over 2,000, almost equal to Chudleigh's little army, which had now lost its advantage.

Shortly before 10 a.m., James Chudleigh lined up his foot, sergeants badgering privates into some sort of alignment, while banners were held aloft, their dazzling colours and designs fluttering in the light breeze. When ready, Chudleigh sent his infantry forward cutting their way through the undergrowth towards the base of Beacon Hill, less than a mile away. When the roundheads came within range, Grenville's forlorn hope put match to powder and let fly a scattered volley. Once they had discharged their weapons, it was a feverish few minutes while the royalist musketeers attempted the difficult task of reloading.

First a fresh ball was pulled from its pouch, a powder charge from one of the bandoliers kept on a belt over the shoulder, was tipped down the barrel, the ball dropped down and a wad rammed in after the ball. The musket was then primed, aimed with the aid of a rest and fired using a lighted chord. However, despite these elaborate instructions many shots were wasted, as most of the volley missed its target and the roundheads were in amongst the musketeers before they could reload. Chudleigh's fifteen-foot pikes were thrust through the hedge and the cavalier skirmishers fell back up the slope. To add weight to the parliamentary assault, several brass cannon were placed on a rise, where Major Sam Price, of Colonel William Bampfield's regiment, urged his gunners to throw round after round upon Hopton's defenders. After initial roundhead success, Chudleigh's foot suddenly ran into more solid opposition; the reason for such an increase in Cornish resistance was the arrival of Major Walter Slingesby and the horse under Sir John Berkeley. These troopers were dismounted and placed in the line and the battle degenerated into a kind of seesaw fight up and down Beacon Hill, with Chudleigh's outnumbered foot unable to get any further than the lower slopes.

Finally, after more than six hours of long-range musketry and brief short charges, the roundheads were exhausted. Hopton now saw the opportunity for a counterattack. Quickly pulling one of his regiments out from behind the barricades and three troops of Berkeley's horse, Sir Ralph sent them around on a flanking march behind the hill and woods to his right, out of Chudleigh's view. This detachment was to sweep in against the roundhead left and rear, seize Polson Bridge and cut off the escape route of the parliamentarian army, trapping it on the west bank of the Tamar.

Fortune this day was on the side of Chudleigh, who by now was losing a number of men to desertion. Many had never seen action before and these simply left the line and strolled back to the bridge, where they could rest and quench their thirst. At around 5 p.m., while Hopton's unobserved flanking force was moving into its position, Sir John Merrick's London greycoat regiment arrived at Polson Bridge. These seven hundred men led by Lieutenant Colonel Vincent Calmady had force marched all the way from Plymouth to join Chudleigh. Sergeant Major Thomas Fitch and 100 soldiers of Sir John Northcote's regiment also joined Chudleigh at Polson Bridge at this time.

During the eight-mile march from Tavistock, Fitch's detachment had strayed and ended up somewhere downriver from the main fighting. Fortunately they spotted a troop of royalist horse trotting up the west bank and after a brief exchange across the water both sides pulled back. Observing the direction in which the enemy rode away, Fitch took a similar route and soon found himself on the right track. Eventually Tom Fitch arrived at the bridge, just in the nick of time as it happened. But for these late arrivals, Chudleigh's entire command would have been scattered or captured and Hopton would undoubtedly have taken Polson Bridge. Calmady's greycoats and Fitch's trained bandsmen formed up and beat off the royalist flanking force, pressing the Cornish foot back towards Beacon Hill and thereby saving a way out of Cornwall for their comrades. With the flank attack blocked, Fitch positioned his men to protect the approaches to the bridge, while Calmady advanced to reinforce Chudleigh's battered lines on the lower slopes of Beacon Hill. Having merged the various roundhead forces, General Chudleigh was able to stabilise his lines at a critical moment when all seemed lost.

At 7 p.m., with the sun finally setting, the fighting died down. Hopton's army was by now almost complete; Slanning and Trevannion having recently arrived and Sir Ralph now outnumbered Chudleigh by more than two to one.

The parliamentary commander realised he had no hope of taking Launceston, the royalists were in a commanding position and his own army was beginning to fall apart, with the exception of Calmady's Londoners. Had Hopton made one final effort he could have overrun and captured the greater part of the parliamentarian army. Fearing just such a manoeuvre, James Chudleigh made immediate plans to save his command and get safely back into Devon. Before he was able to disengage his army, Hopton sent in one last probing attack. Despite their fatigue, the roundheads stood fast and beat off this final assault.

Finally at 9 p.m., after almost twelve hours of constant battle, the parliamentarians withdrew across Polson Bridge, leaving behind their dead and a small supply of powder. Major Sam Price, in command of the small artillery battery, wanted to abandon one of the guns, but Chudleigh himself organised its rescue and saved the piece. A half-hearted royalist pursuit ended when the abandoned roundhead gunpowder stored in a small barn exploded, causing a number of royalist casualties. Losses for the day must have numbered at least a hundred on either side, possibly more, but no record has been found to give a true account. Two royalist officers were buried in St Mary's Launceston shortly after, Captain James Bassett on April 24th and Ensign John Arundell the following day.

Chudleigh's skill helped him extricate his little army from the field and take it back to Lifton with a loss of only forty men during the retreat. Once in Devon the army was split up and the troops returned to their pre-battle posts. Captain Robert Bennett, with his company and the sailors, marched up to the Barnstaple-Bideford-Torrington area with orders to fortify those towns for parliament. The London greycoat regiment turned south and headed back to Plymouth. Unable to hold Tavistock, Chudleigh saw no point in leaving a force there, so he sent Sergeant Major Fitch's company to Plymouth. With the remaining 1,200 foot and four troops of cavalry James Chudleigh withdrew over the moors towards Exeter. The royalist horse did not press the roundhead rearguard far, well aware of Chudleigh's uncanny prowess, they secured their prisoners and returned to Launceston.

While burying the dead and caring for his wounded, Sir Ralph Hopton learned from scouts that the parliamentary army had divided and that Chudleigh's' men were camped in a state of uneasiness at Okehampton. Hopton saw an opportunity to destroy this part of Chudleigh's army before it could reach Exeter. At a council of war Sir Ralph outlined a plan of pursuit to his subordinates and issued orders for the army to march next morning, April 25th. By the evening of the next day the sluggish royalist advance only managed to reach Lifton. The following morning Hopton's badly-strung-out column, consisting off 3,000 foot, 600 horse and dragoons and four cannon trudged on to Bridestow, six miles from Okehampton. A small body of mounted Devonshire cavaliers, led by the county's new sheriff, Sir Henry Cary joined Hopton at this point.

An ardent royalist and brother-in-law to Sir Nicholas Slanning, Cary had alienated his home village of Cockington near Torquay, by siding with the king. Despite pressure from friends, Cary refused to alter his allegiance and he would serve King Charles throughout the war to the best of his ability. After the capture of Edmund Fortescue in December 1642, Cary had been appointed royalist Sheriff of Devon, he would later be responsible for raising a regiment of foot and a small regiment of horse for King Charles.

Whilst the cavaliers rested at Bridestow, a brief skirmish broke out between Hopton's vanguard and Chudleigh's pickets, resulting in the latter withdrawing. At this point Sir Ralph received confirmation that the parliamentarians were thoroughly disheartened and only waiting for wagons to shift powder and supplies, before continuing their retreat to Exeter. This news came from a reliable royalist spy and it spurred Hopton into ordering a night march and a dawn attack against Okehampton.

Chudleigh's scouts were also out this night, peering into the darkness for any movement. At 9 p.m. they rode into Okehampton and reported that Hopton's army was closing in. The roundhead commander, true to form, refused to panic, despite problems securing enough animals to haul out his supply wagons. Instead of abandoning his camp and beating a hasty retreat, Chudleigh planned to utilise the darkness and the terrain. With the artillery already en route to Exeter, General Chudleigh placed 600 of his infantry in line on the western edge of Okehampton, to cover the retreat of his horse, which he was going to use in a large-scale ambush. Leading his mounted arm, reduced to only 108 troopers after the recent desertion of most of Captain Pym's company, Chudleigh rode up to Sourton Down, a high windswept, inhospitable ridge, cut by the rough road from Bridestow.

At Sourton, Chudleigh found an ideal depression in the moor and quickly divided his 108 into six eighteen-man sections. Three of these groups were commanded by captains William Gould, Alexander Pym and Thomas Drake, while captains William Fenton, Downing and John Lutterell from Rolle's foot regiment took charge of the others. The 108 were assigned positions along the south side of the track and ordered to keep out of sight, hidden by the darkness and the depression. The six junior officers were under strict orders not to fire until the enemy scouts had passed and the main body was well up; Chudleigh was counting upon complete surprise.

When Hopton's van rode past the ambush site, somewhere around eleven that night, whispering cautiously and scanning the little countryside visible to straining eyes, Captain Drake held back as commanded until the main body of royalist horse sauntered up. Suddenly Drake stood in his stirrups and led the eighteen men under him forward in a reckless charge, firing pistols and yelling orders to add credence to the bluff. Despite an accidental discharge only seconds before, the surprise was total. Drake in the style of his legendary ancestor, dashed in amongst the bewildered cavaliers firing, slashing and calling out "Charge on, they run!"

In company with one of the detachments, James Chudleigh joined in the melee and from four different directions the rest of his men rose up out of the ground adding to the enemy's dismay.

So rapid and ferocious was the ambush that it smashed right through Hopton's mounted van, numbering 300 men, and hit the stunned foot soldiers behind. Had the parliamentarians not stopped to plunder the royalist dead and captives, the charge might have achieved more than was intended. Those few under Gould, Drake and Pym, who maintained the momentum of the assault, managed to fight their way almost to Hopton's cannon, which were by now cluttered with fleeing foot and galloping horse. Around these very guns Bevill Grenville and Warwick Mohun arranged part of their infantry. This action undoubtedly saved the royal army from what could have been an embarrassing disaster. Grenville's staunch line of pikemen and musketeers were soon joined by Sir Nicholas Slanning, who arrived with part of his own regiment and ordered a row of sharp stakes placed in front of the royalist cannon, in an effort to deter the headstrong roundhead horse.

Meeting with this unexpected wall of steel and wood, Chudleigh sensed one more charge might bring victory and he endeavoured to rally his cavalry for a final effort. Orders were also despatched for the roundhead foot to come up and join the battle, but already his outnumbered horse was beginning to waver. The infantry, unaware of events and lacking artillery support had marched back to Okehampton and could not be brought forward. With no fresh troops available General Chudleigh decided to withdraw. To mislead the enemy he sent orders for his musketeers to leave their match chords alight and set them on the down. In order to keep up the bluff Chudleigh led his mounted men forward once more, this time they were aided by thunder and lightning, which crashed down over the moor, sending rain falling in torrents. Once again rapiers sliced into unprotected flesh and those pistols with dry powder sent their loads into bewildered and confused faces. Satisfied the royalists would not march against Okehampton this night, James Chudleigh recalled his buoyant horsemen, gathered his wounded and withdrew. A detachment of twenty-two men was left in the area to watch the enemy and report on any movement.

Sir Ralph Hopton had had enough, hundreds of his troops had scattered during the disconcerted fight, many others stood confounded and terrified, fearful of this up-and-coming young parliamentarian general. The most immediate consequence of the night fight was Hopton's retreat back to Bridestow, and when dawn broke next morning Chudleigh found himself the victor of the field. As far as the eye could see the road was strewn with the debris of a defeated foe. One thousand muskets and pikes were eventually collected, five barrels of gunpowder, many horses, twelve drums, three flags and a large quantity of other military flotsam. Sir Henry Cary, the Sheriff of Devon, who was with the royalist dragoons during the engagement, managed to elude capture by disguising himself as a woman, or so it was said, and slipping away in the darkness. Cary would rejoin Hopton a week later.

The most important single item picked up on the Sourton battlefield was a set of papers written by King Charles and addressed to Hopton. The contents of these letters revealed the king's instructions for Sir Ralph to march into Somerset and included a list of prominent royalist supporters in Devon. Besides the loss of his private correspondence and vital military equipment, Hopton suffered sixty killed and wounded and twenty prisoners. At dawn on the 28th the defeated Cornishmen limped back into Bridestowe, soaked and dejected by the sudden disaster. Once the storm abated Hopton led his command back into Cornwall.

According to one of the captured royal letters, which were eventually sent on to the Earl of Stamford, still tormented by gout, Chudleigh had spoilt an obvious attempt by the Cornish army to join Prince Maurice, who was waiting for Hopton in Somerset. When Stamford read these dispatches he jumped from his sickbed and began issuing orders for an immediate concentration in west Devon. Hopton would definitely make a second attempt to move into Somerset and Stamford was determined to smash him before he could link up with Maurice.

Back in Launceston Sir Ralph Hopton rested his army for several weeks, gathering supplies and recruiting. Whilst in camp, soldiers were still not safe, accidents were a way of life in the military, on April the 30th, Lieutenant Henry Maynard of Lord Mohun's regiment and three other men were scalded. Though not fatal, the men were most certainly incapacitated for a short time. Soon his confidence returned and he marched back to Okehampton, where memories of Sourton Down still haunted him. The royalist commander was making his second attempt at joining Prince Maurice. Mounted patrols were dispatched across the moors to check the route, but these detachments soon returned with ominous news that a large parliamentarian army was moving on Okehampton from the direction of Exeter. This intelligence forced Hopton to cancel his planned march across north Devon and retreat back into Cornwall, where he divided his army in order to cover all the crossing points of the Tamar.

What Hopton's scouts had spotted was the vanguard of Stamford army, which left Exeter on May 11th. The earl was moving so as to hit the royalists in north Cornwall, thus negating the Tamar river line and making it indefensible to Hopton. If he moved quickly Stamford could force his opponent down into Cornwall and gain the advantage.

To tackle Hopton, Stamford and James Chudleigh had gathered a substantial army numbering 5,400 foot, 1,400 horse and dragoons, thirteen cannon, one mortar, a full wagon train bursting with supplies and munitions of war and a considerable chest of money to pay the soldiers.

The troops that made up this army were a mixed batch; Sir John Merrick's Londoners under Lieutenant Colonel Vincent Calmady, Colonel John Wear's Devonians and Sir John Northcote's regiment, the survivors of Colonel William Bampfield's command, minus their commander who had recently defected. The trained bandsmen under Sir William Russell and Sir Samuel Rolle made up the foot. The mounted force was under Sir George Chudleigh and consisted of numerous individual companies.

The royal army, in comparison, was almost all Cornish, well led, but at this time badly scattered along the west bank of the Tamar. Slanning with 1,000 men was in Saltash, Mohun with another 900 rested around Liskeard. 700 men under John Trevannion garrisoned Launceston, while Bevill Grenville and his 1,200 lay at Stratton barring the easiest route into Cornwall. Other foot under Thomas Bassett, William Godolphin and the horse under John Berkeley were dotted about the countryside gathering forage. Sheriff Grylls, meanwhile, made every effort to organise and train the county bands in and around Bodmin.

By the 13th the roundheads were concentrating in Torrington, less than two days' march from Bude, the major town of northeast Cornwall, whose population was largely sympathetic to parliament. The following day, as a fast was held in Exeter for the success of Stamford's command, the earl boldly led his army forward. Two days later the roundheads crossed the border and were on Cornish soil east of Stratton. Henry Grey now foolishly detached 1,200 of his horse, almost all his veteran cavalry under Sir George Chudleigh, with orders to cross the Tamar at Newbridge far to the south. The irrational reasoning behind Stamford's detachment of his mounted troops was to attack Bodmin and break up the sheriff's posse. The loss of Sir George's' expert cavalry would have tragic consequences on the forthcoming battle and add to the growing evidence of the earl's inadequate leadership.

After an easy march and increased skirmishing with parliamentary cavalry around Efford Mill south of Stratton, Hopton arrived on the scene with reinforcements for Grenville. Sir Bevill had been observing the roundhead advance, outnumbered he could do little else. The concerned royalist leaders watched helplessly as Stamford's foot clambered up the key position in the area, a steep-sided ridge named Stratton Hill north of the village. Once established on this grassy north-to-south running promontory, less than two miles from Bude, Stamford sent out his remaining horse, numbering less than 200 men, to reconnoitre and select a suitable spot for camp.

Stamford meanwhile lined up all fourteen pieces of his artillery on the very top of the hill in a rough semi-circle, facing west, northwest and southwest. The eastern side of the ridge cut sharply downhill to a thick wooded valley, an almost impossible venue for attack, thereby allowing the roundheads to concentrate all their available firepower against one front. To protect the artillery Stamford's foot regiments erected crude breastworks on top of an old iron-age fort. Most of the infantry were then lined up father out around the crest of Stratton Hill, while a forlorn hope marched down the slope and took cover behind thick hedges. By going over to the defensive Henry Grey had lost the initiative and he handed Hopton the advantage of how the battle was to be fought.

Shortly after 4 a.m. on Tuesday May 16th Hopton's skirmishers moved forward and began exchanging musket fire with the roundhead forlorn hope.

An hour later the main royalist body formed and advanced up the western slope, which unlike the eastern ridge, fell away gently, making it easily accessible for infantry. Despite being outnumbered Sir Ralph had gone on the offensive as he had at Braddock Down four months before, hoping to panic the opposition. The royalist commander divided his 2,400 men into four brigades, each supported by two cannon. Slanning and Trevannion would move in directly from the west, Berkeley and Grenville from the southwest, Mohun from the south, and from the northwest Godolphin and Bassett. To guard against a possible flanking attack by roundhead cavalry and to act as a reserve, Colonel John Digby with 500 horse and dragoons positioned himself off to the west and waited.

At a signal from Hopton the four-pronged royalist attack began, only to be thrown back by heavy musket fire. Realigning for a second attempt the cavaliers moved off, but again they were repulsed. Two more charges ended in similar fashion, men on both sides were fighting hard. Northcote's regiment, Rolle's, Wear's, Calmady's units and Colonel William Bampfield's survivors under Lieutenant

Colonel Sir Robert Wingfield held the ridge, and many believed they could beat Hopton, if only the commander-in-chief was as confidence. These veterans easily beat off every assault and were ably supported by Sir William Russell's troops and a unit of marines from Plymouth. As the morning wore on the fighting went on unabated and continued in this way into early afternoon.

After ten hours of battle, Hopton began to grow increasingly anxious, Stamford still dominated Stratton Hill while his own army had made no headway. As an added concern, royalist musketeers and artillery were down to their last four barrels of gunpowder. To cope with the emergency, Sir Ralph ordered the shortage kept from the men and commanded all his regiments to reform and advance upon Stratton Hill simultaneously, using pikes and reserving the musket until the crest had been gained. Possibly due to weariness, hunger or lack of confidence in the Earl of Stamford, who remained back with his horse and left the fighting to his capable, though frustrated, number two James Chudleigh, the parliamentarians suddenly found themselves being hemmed in from three directions by the long, deadly royalist pikes. Why Stamford never launched a counterattack is difficult to understand considering the size of his army and the heavy ordnance available to him.

Unable to stem this final wave of Cornish determination sweeping up the hill at them, the roundhead foot suddenly fell apart and withdrew back from the crest, abandoning their cannon. Now the enemy swarmed up over Stratton Hill, meeting around these silent guns from three different directions. Why the remaining cavalry was never ordered to charge at this crucial point in the battle, in order to break up what would have been the final royalist attack can only be speculated upon. Losing heart completely, Henry Grey now deserted his army and rode away with the reserve cavalry.

Sensing disaster, Chudleigh hastily gathered a body of pikemen and thrust his way forward, counterattacking the Grenville-Berkeley brigade. The initial shock at first pressed back the cavalier pike block, knocking Bevill Grenville to the ground in the process. However Berkeley rearranged his musketeers and these men now opened fire, sending the roundhead pikemen reeling backwards. Within minutes Chudleigh's brave band had vanished, killed, wounded or scattered, their gallant commander, a prisoner, stood fuming at Stamford's cowardice.

Somewhere around 3 p.m., the successful four-pronged royalist assault ended and Hopton's jubilant army held the crest of Stratton Hill. The captured artillery was now swung around and made ready to support one final charge against Stamford's camp. Disheartened by the unexpected royalist victory, the loss of Chudleigh and Sir Robert Wingfield, both captured, the death of Lieutenant Colonel Vincent Calmady and the desertion of Stamford with his cavalry, the remaining parliamentarian foot broke and fled. Many threw away their weapons and sat dejectedly awaiting capture, others disappeared into the brush. Colonel John Wear left with Stamford, thereby avoiding the fate of Chudleigh and many others.

The parliamentary camp was taken with little effort and roundhead losses would have been far greater but for a staunch rearguard action by Vincent Calmady's London greycoats and the marines from Plymouth. Their heroic last stand allowed those companies still with the colours to escape from the field. Eventually the fighting died out and Stamford's survivors withdrew towards Okehampton or Barnstaple. Henry Grey himself rode across Dartmoor and on to Exeter, almost without stopping. Only a fraction of the royalist horse went in pursuit of the retreating foe, Hopton wanted to use the majority of his cavalry to go after Sir George Chudleigh's raiders. Losses for the battle of Stratton numbered 300 roundheads killed and 1,700 wounded and captured. Also taken were all fourteen guns, 2,000 muskets, pikes, seventy barrels of gunpowder, provisions for a large army and a chest of money amounting to £5,000. Many of the officers taken were escorted to Launceston and held there until exchanged the following July. Hopton's reported casualties were eighty killed and many hundreds wounded, some of whom died later.

What of Sir George Chudleigh and the 1,200 roundhead cavalry detached by Stamford to break up the trained bands around Bodmin? Having crossed into Cornwall the parliamentary column, which included the Plymouth horse under Thomas Drake, rode straight for Bodmin, well behind enemy lines. Chudleigh's brigade soon reached the outskirts of the town and the raiders fanned out to hit the ill-prepared militia from several directions at once. Initially the badly-equipped cavaliers fought back with any weapon available, but eventually the better-led veteran troops under Chudleigh prevailed. The roundhead horse finally succeeded in capturing the town with a loss of only ten men and the Cornishmen rapidly melted into the countryside. Sir George Chudleigh released a number of roundhead prisoners held in the town, threw out guards and settled down to await the arrival of the Earl of Stamford. Later when news filtered into Bodmin of the disaster at Stratton, Chudleigh feared Hopton would concentrate his entire force against him and cut off his escape route out of Cornwall, so he quickly made plans to leave.

Leaving his prisoners and plunder in the hands of Sir Bevill Grenville, Hopton offered up prayers in gratitude for his unexpected victory, then made preparations to follow his cavalry and cut off Sir George Chudleigh's column. With the exception of Grenville's regiment, the royal army marched down toward Launceston, only to learn that their quarry had evacuated Bodmin and was already back across the Tamar. The humiliating defeat of a well-supplied roundhead army in north Cornwall by a force half its size was a devastating blow to parliamentary hopes in the southwest and caused great anxiety in Plymouth.

John Syms the puritan minister wrote of the disaster in his daybook: *'Our army was routed at Stratton, where the enemy took from us near 700 prisoners, our arms all our great guns, powder, ammunition, carriages. And our horse being gone that day for Bodmin under the command of Baronet Chudleigh, who hearing of the rout at Stratton wheeled about for Plymouth, but with such delay as if he intended to have had them all cut off, as his son had betrayed the fate at Stratton for they come for Plymouth but staying there not above three or four days, went for Exeter'.*[6]

Ten days after Stratton, James Chudleigh, now a dispirited prisoner, found his gaolers extremely chivalrous and comfortable to converse with. Fascinated by Hopton's magnetic personality, his ability and the loyalty of the Cornish soldiery, Chudleigh pondered upon the cowardly way Stamford had handled his own army. Born in 1618, Chudleigh's early military service was in 1640 when he served as a captain under the Earl of Northumberland during the First Bishops' War. At the time of Strafford's trial young James was the courier ordered to carry several messages between the army camped in the north of England and the king. This incident became known as the army plot, which called for the northern army to march south, take over parliament for the king and await developments. When the conspiracy was discovered and discussed in parliament, Chudleigh gave evidence to the commission against King Charles. Chudleigh's evidence brought an angry reaction from Charles Stuart's supporters, they would remember this youthful upstart in the future.

James Chudleigh went on to serve in Ireland until 1642, when he returned to England and offered his sword to the king at Oxford. The days of the army plot now surfaced, and many recalled Chudleigh's so-called evidence. Receiving the cold shoulder, James took his service to Westminster and was made Sergeant Major General of Parliamentarian Forces in Devon. After six months of excellent leadership at Modbury, Polson Bridge, Sourton Down and Stratton, Chudleigh did the unthinkable, he joined the royalists. Believing he had been forced into changing sides, James Chudleigh lost much of his previous enthusiasm. Given the rank of colonel, Chudleigh would command a regiment in Prince Maurice's army and die in action before the year was out.

Chudleigh's father, Sir George, and his cousin, Captain Thomas Drake, were greatly distressed by James' treason, indeed the incident almost shattered poor Sir George. Back in Exeter, the Earl of Stamford seized the chance of taking the pressure off himself by speaking out loudly against Chudleigh's treason. He also insisted that Sir George had something to do with his son's change of coat. Depressed and disgusted, George Chudleigh resigned his commission as General of Horse and Governor of Plymouth Fort rather than face the disgrace that was bound to follow Stamford's uncalled for declaration. Several weeks later Sir George Chudleigh asked the king for a pardon, agreeing to remain loyal to his majesty, but refusing to fight against parliament.

George Chudleigh's career had been varied, born at Ashton in Devon in 1582, George married Mary Strode, daughter of Sir William, with whom he had six sons, two of whom would change loyalties during the war. In 1622 Chudleigh was made baronet and two years later served as MP for Tiverton, in the 1625 parliament he held the seat for Lostwithiel. July 1642 found him selected by parliament to be one of their commissioners responsible for collecting money and plate for the war effort. In early 1643 Chudleigh was one of the representatives involved in peace negotiations with the Cornish royalists and was on the Devon committee to assess and levy a national tax on all persons. Sir George also held the important post of Governor of Plymouth Fort, Mount Wise and other fortifications within the town. When the Chudleighs ended their service with parliament, Devon lost two of its most eminent leaders to the regret of many.

With Stamford's army scattered, sheltering behind fortifications at Plymouth, Dartmouth, Barnstaple and Exeter, Hopton's route into Somerset and unification with the Marquis of Hertford and Prince Maurice lay wide open. The latter with a force of 1,500 horse, 1,000 foot and eleven guns had marched from Oxford in the middle of May to meet the victorious Cornishmen, but their advance had been painfully slow. Meanwhile Sir Ralph Hopton planned his second attempt to capture Exeter, at this time held by approximately 5,000 troops. With the county town out of the way, the royalists could march out of Devon without fear of attack, but what of Plymouth and the other parliamentary towns? Hopton had a simple answer, he would forget about them, relying on local royalists to rally and prevent the roundheads from harassing his flanks and rear. Strong garrisons would also be left at Millbrook and Saltash, supported by plenty of artillery and the Cornish trained bands.

Satisfied with his arrangements, Sir Ralph Hopton shifted his main army of 3,800 men quickly from Launceston to Okehampton, where a small body of roundhead horse withdrew at his approach. From here Hopton sent Dr William Cox, clergyman and spy, to boldly ask for Exeter's surrender. When Cox rode into the city his true intentions were immediately suspect, consequently he and his accompanying trumpeter were arrested. When the cleric was searched a letter from Major General James Chudleigh, addressed to his father, was discovered. The communiqué inferred that Sir George, recently arrived in Exeter, should leave the service of parliament and come into the royal camp. Cox was tortured and incarcerated on board a ship anchored near Topsham by order of the Earl of Stamford. Later the vessel set sail for London where Dr Cox was imprisoned.

With the capture of Cox, Hopton forgot about Exeter, but placed small detachments to the north and east of the city, with orders to harass Stamford and prevent him from raising a fresh army. Local royalists were also ordered to draft in as many men as they could and send them to reinforce the nucleus of this new force. Sir John Berkeley was detached by Hopton and sent to command the mixed bag of royalist units around Exeter and forge them into an army. Eventually Berkeley would bring order out of chaos and begin the second royalist siege of Exeter. In the meantime Sir Ralph concentrated on moving his little army safely through Devon. On May 24th the Cornish regiments left Okehampton and marched forward in the direction of Crediton.

Despite strong parliamentary garrisons on his flanks, at Barnstaple and Exeter, and his rear, at Plymouth, Hopton felt confident the victory at Stratton had so unnerved his enemies they would remain quietly behind their fortifications, his assumption would prove correct.

Fortunately for Hopton, the roundheads, fearing another defeat, did not molest the Cornish advance across the moors. By May 28th Hopton had reached Tiverton where he expected to meet opposition. Surprised to find the town bereft of defenders, Sir Ralph rested several days before marching into Somerset. Finally on June 4th the two royal armies met at Chard north of Honiton. To oppose this sizable force came an old friend of Hopton's, Sir William Waller, with orders to stop the Cornishmen. Unfortunately Waller's advance was too leisurely and before he knew it Hopton and Prince Maurice had merged.

Shortly after the battle of Stratton, Plymouth received a demand for surrender from the Cornish side of the Tamar; it was of course refused. Hopton believed his victory over Stamford had totally demoralised the defenders and the town was ripe for submission, on the contrary the garrison remained as defiant as ever. Once Hopton's army crossed into Somerset, Plymouth relaxed and for the next three months the defence committee contented itself with perfecting fortifications and skirmishing with enemy patrols. Occasionally the garrison felt brave enough to move further afield.

Late in May a substantial task force, exaggeratedly reported to number 800 foot and 150 horse, left Plymouth and moved eastwards, their target Flete House. With most royalist troops absent under Hopton or gathering around Exeter, only a small body of dismounted cavalry occupied the house. All demands for surrender were refused and minor skirmishing broke out between the two sides. Eventually a detachment of parliamentary sailors arrived hauling a large cannon. The sight of this artillery piece rumbling up the road unnerved the outnumbered defenders and they quickly agreed to surrender. Thirty cavaliers marched out of the house behind their lieutenant and his ensign, along with many valuable horses. Despite the absence of Hopton and the success of this raid, the roundheads of Devon did not feel confident enough to take on the royalists in another pitched battle.

During Hopton's absence the people of Plymouth switched their attention to the royalist Sheriff of Devon, Sir Henry Cary and his growing band of supporters. Emboldened by the victory at Stratton and Berkeley's strengthening blockade of Exeter, Cary ordered his men to hit the homes of any parliamentary sympathisers. These incursions grew in frequency and boldness to such an extent that at one time road communication between Plymouth and Exeter was temporarily cut.

As a consequence Mayor Francis wrote to John Yonge the town's MP on June 15th complaining of a situation made worse by numerous desertions from Plymouth: *'We are here in a deplorable condition, our whole country being harrowed by Sir Ralph Hopton. Lately in their going forth and the forces left behind them joining with those of the sheriff raised by his power, plunder as well in our parts in the south as those in the east about Exon'.*[7]

Low morale and a lack of regular pay was the main cause of Plymouth's siphoning manpower. By the end of June the situation had deteriorated further despite continued contributions from those loyal to the cause. Mrs Jane Slanning donated £50 for the town's defences on June 19th, her example was followed by her nephew Peter Treby, Lady Alice Buller and many others. Unfortunately royal privateers continually wreaked havoc amongst Plymouth's maritime trade and with little money coming in from outside, the corporation found great difficulty paying its assessment taxes. Despite these upsets the loyalty of the population on the whole remained firm.

Outwardly Plymouth looked strong, work on the exterior line of earthworks was progressing slowly and although not extensive, the line was beginning to look formidable. The four main forts under construction at key points along the high ground above Lipson Creek and Stonehouse Creek, gave lookouts a perfect view of the northern approaches. When completed these forts would not be large bastions, brimming with cannon and full of troops, on the contrary, each would be garrisoned by a number of gunners and one or two companies of foot. Eventually a trench system would connect the main forts, while a number of intermediate fortlets would be thrown up at strategic positions between the primary works. The town's defence committee assumed that any attacking force would be hard put to surprise the town, as an assaulting column would have to cross water and scale steep cliffs to reach its objective. Therefore many soldiers were camped behind the main forts, from where they could move rapidly and deploy at any threatened point. The only real avenue of attack was via the Maudlyn Ridge and here the defences were stronger. Roadblocks were thrown across the roads into the town during the hours of darkness as an added precaution.

Captain Cooper commanded the bastion known as Lipson Fort, at the western end of Mount Gould Road overlooking Lipson Creek. Holywell Work, a smaller fort to the left of Lipson commanded both the higher part of Lipson Creek and a portion of the Maudlyn Ridge; Captain Adrian Anthony commanded here. Maudlyn Fort, further along, covered the main road into Plymouth from the north and was located where the Blind Institute once stood. This important fortress, known as the 'Great Work' was the keystone of the outer line, as it stood almost in the centre. Away to the left rose Pennycomequick Work, built upon rocky ground to cover the Saltash Road and the upper reaches of Stonehouse Creek. This earthwork was positioned between what is now North Road Station and Caprera Terrace. Captain Richard Clarke commanded Pennycomequick. Most of the cannon emplaced in these new forts were borrowed from ships in the harbour and many of the gunners were displaced seamen.

Besides these major works new forts were already in the planning stages, with sites at Eldad Hill and Cattedown being surveyed. Other points under examination were Laira Point, at the confluence of Lipson Creek and the Plym and the woodland above Houndiscombe Farm, between Maudlyn Fort and Pennycomequick Work. The sea front was as strong as ever, in fact to supplement the outer forts many of the cannon from the coastal defences had been transferred inland. Sir Alexander Carew competently commanded St Nicholas Island since his appointment to the post by Colonel Ruthven on January 20th. The island's small but efficient garrison was well drilled and regularly visited by clergymen who, since the resignation of Sir George Chudleigh, preferred to make sure of their loyalty. The imposing Plymouth Fort dominated the harbour approach and was commanded by Captain Thomas Arundell, while smaller guard detachments occupied Mount Wise House and the numerous blockhouses along the Hoe foreshore.

To watch for enemy movements in the Plymstock area and protect the sea approach into Sutton Pool, the defence committee had already begun constructing Fort Stamford on How Stert. Stamford's early garrison was to be a combined force of sailors and soldiers under a Captain Cuskett. This isolated earthwork would later be extended to enclose a tented camp for the garrison and a storehouse, but it would always lack cavalry and thereafter suffer by an inability to scout the countryside efficiently. The troops in Plymouth during the summer months numbered several thousand, many of whom were veterans of Braddock Down, Modbury, Polson Bridge and Stratton; seamen and militia made up the number. Despite the inadequate size of the defending force, Hopton's absence gave the defence committee time to find reinforcements. A bonus to Plymouth came in the month of May with the return of Sir Shilston Calmady, recently exchanged by the royalists and soon back on duty with his troops.

However, behind Plymouth's brave facade, the town was suffering from internal corruption. Money sent by Westminster to pay the garrison went missing, was mislaid, lost or stolen. Two men, Master Charles Vaughan and Thomas Gewen, were charged with handling this money. Vaughan, supposedly a gentleman from Exeter, was on January 17th 1643 appointed treasurer for sequestrations in the county of Devon, with deputies in Dartmouth, Barnstaple and Plymouth. Vaughan already held a number of important posts with parliamentary authority. On January 13th the House of Commons appointed Vaughan to be in charge of the records for the county of Devon, he was also to take over the office of clerk of the peace. The previous clerk, a royalist, had been captured by Ruthven at Modbury in December 1642.

Thomas Gewen of Boyton in Cornwall, besides being Vaughan's brother-in-law (he married Anne Vaughan at Werrington Church on March 4th 1608) was also his deputy in Plymouth. At one time Gewen had been the Cornwall auditor, and in the late twenties he was one of those who fuelled the militia chaos in Cornwall, when he refused to provide arms for the trained bandsmen and ordered his own officers not to attend the musters. In 1639, Gewen, along with Sir Richard Buller and many others ignored the call to march north during the war against the Scots. Gewen loudly supported John Pym's policies and in mid-1642 King Charles replaced Thomas Gewen, Buller and eight other Cornish peace commissioners. Later Thomas Gewen left his home county and joined the parliamentarians in Devon.

Lacking wages to pay its troops, the Plymouth Corporation found itself forced into levying a tax on the townsfolk. Not yet aware of Vaughan and Gewen's fraudulent activities, the pair were given authority to organise the collection of all taxes. As official sequestrators these men had legal sanction to scour the countryside around Plymouth, Dartmouth and Barnstaple, literally robbing the homes of royalists and their supporters. Those who had nothing, or refused to pay were arrested and imprisoned. Others such as Abraham Biggs of Plymouth lost his home in Vauxhall Street, when in his absence the previous owner died. Mayor Francis sequestered the house and used it to store military equipment. Vaughan and his deputies carried out their instructions with ruthless efficiency. People from all walks of life were accused of non-payment and thrown into the dirtiest and dampest dungeons, until a ransom had been secured. Fortunately Vaughan and his brother-in-law would come to grief when they made the mistake of crossing Philip Francis.

Since landing at Bridlington, Queen Henrietta, along with soldiers, arms, munitions, powder and artillery, joined the Earl of Newcastle at York. Later she would move south and join her husband at Oxford on the 13th of July. Another of the king's relatives, Prince Rupert, achieved limited success capturing Cirencester in February and Birmingham and Lichfield in April. While the king's nephew and his most aggressive commanders were winning in the Midlands, the Earl of Essex and his parliamentary army marched cautiously out of London and bombarded Reading on April 16th. Despite a frantic effort by Rupert and the king Reading fell. Meanwhile Rupert's brother, Prince Maurice, commanding a small army, met Sir William Waller, a parliamentary officer of limited capabilities, at Ripple Field near the Severn on April 13th. Although Maurice beat off Waller, parliament retained control of the Severn valley. The prince then moved to join his uncle in the failed attempt to relieve Reading. Subsequently he returned west as lieutenant general under Hertford.

Notes

(6) Page 109: John Syms, A daybook of some special passages and mercies, British Library, Add 35297; by kind permission of the British Library, London.
(7) Page 113: Letter from Philip Francis to Sir John Yonge, June 15th 1643. Oxford Bodleian Library, MS Nalson 11 fols 194; by kind permission of the Oxford Bodleian Library.

Chapter 6

Desperate Times

In July bad news filtered into Plymouth after the Hopton-Maurice-Hertford army fought a hard battle with Waller's parliamentarians at Lansdown north of Bath. As at Edgehill, nightfall brought an end to the fighting and in the darkness Waller withdrew his battered army. The Devon horse brigade, under recently-promoted Colonel William Gould, which had ridden away from Exeter to avoid the siege, fought in Waller's army, and the companies of captains Thomas Drake, George Thompson and Nicholas Boscowan maintained their fiery reputation. On the royalist side, Sir Bevill Grenville had been mortally wounded during the fighting and the following day, July 6th an ammunition cart exploded, badly injuring Sir Ralph Hopton. After several weeks of incompetence on both sides, culminating in Waller's defeat near Devizes, the road to Bristol, England's second largest port, lay wide open for the king.

With Waller's army dispersed, the royalists arrived before Bristol on July 23rd where they were joined by another small army under Maurice's brother Rupert. Old Ferdinando Gorges, one-time commander of Plymouth Fort, sent Prince Rupert a detailed plan of the city's defences. Having examined Gorges' map the prince sent in a demand for surrender on the 24th. Governor Nathaniel Fiennes refused and the next morning royalist cannon opened up. Two days later the infantry launched its attack, but parliamentary cannons and musketeers caused great destruction amongst Hopton's veterans. The murderous fire from the city walls cut down Sir Nicholas Slanning, John Trevannion and Colonel Walter Slingesby, but the assault continued. A breach was eventually made in one of the walls and the cavaliers, who greatly outnumbered the defenders, poured in. Unable to stem the tide Fiennes capitulated.

Securing Bristol, Prince Rupert moved north towards Gloucester, while Maurice marched his army down into Dorset, where he made a feeble attempt to capture Lyme Regis. Failing to obtain the port's submission, Maurice crossed the border into Devon and joined Sir John Berkeley, then in the process of tightening the noose around Exeter. Sir Ralph Hopton meanwhile, had been appointed Governor of Bristol and the shattered remnant of his once proud Cornish army made its way home. With most of its original leaders dead and Hopton upgraded to the post of governor, the men had no desire to remain so far from their families. Despite the disintegration of the Cornish troops, Berkeley, who commanded all royalist forces in Devon during Hopton's absence, still possessed a substantial force. Royal reinforcements had recently arrived in the Westcountry to boost Berkeley's strength and the Devonshire royalists trickled in to join the colours.

Throughout the summer Westminster's anxiety for the southwest increased, what spare troops the House of Commons could gather were hurriedly dispatched by ship for Plymouth. Nothing it seemed could stop the king's armies from capturing the entire southwestern peninsula. Dorchester, Weymouth and Portland, all in Dorset, had been lost, but hopes were high that Stamford could hold Exeter. Despite warnings that if Exeter fell, Plymouth would be the next target, the port's defence committee managed to scrape together a column of reinforcements, which was duly dispatched to Exeter. By the middle of July the situation had turned critical. Henry Grey steadfastly refused to allow his subordinates to make any attempt at breaking the enemy siege lines, thus allowing Berkeley to pull the noose even tighter. Sir Alexander Carew on his way up from Plymouth with the reinforcements, headed first for Dartmouth, where he picked up as many men as that garrison could spare, then on to Torbay. Here he met up with the navy under the Earl of Warwick, and it was decided that with its heavy naval guns the fleet should sail up the Exe and break the siege from below. Carew's relieving force boarded the vessels and the flotilla sailed up the coast towards Exmouth. Arriving at their destination, part of the infantry, reinforced by a number of sailors, disembarked, stormed into Exmouth and overran its inadequate defences, capturing guns and prisoners.

Crossing the Exe, the roundheads captured a four-gun battery known as Exmouth Fort, but as they advanced towards Exeter they met heavy resistance and were forced back. In the meantime the Earl of Warwick moved on up the river with six ships filled with infantry, only to meet strong resistance at Topsham, where the Exe divided. Berkeley had previously sunk several boats near Topsham to block this avenue, now as Warwick's ships came in range of the obstructions, hidden cannon blasted him back downriver. Warwick made several attempts to put more troops ashore, only to find his vessels being riddled with shot. A receding tide finally forced Warwick to abandon three of his ships, picking up Carew's detachment he finally withdrew.

With Warwick's reduced fleet disappearing over the horizon, Sir John Berkeley turned his attention to a new threat, a fresh parliamentary army gathering in north Devon. Without weakening his siege lines, Berkeley detached 300 horse and dragoons under Colonel John Digby, and sent them northwards to deal with this danger. Digby established a camp at Torrington, where 700 Cornish recruits joined him. Lacking infantry, Colonel Digby decided to train his new men to fight on foot. By the end of the third week of August the Barnstaple parliamentarians, led by newly-promoted Colonel Robert Bennett, joined with those of Bideford, bringing the total available to around 800. On the 19th this force, led by colonels Bennett and Robert Pawlett, marched on Torrington.

Of the two commanders Robert Bennett had achieved the early fame. Born at Hexworthy, Bennett, in his late thirties, had taken over William Gould's foot company in December. A month later this unit was attached to Sir Samuel Rolle's regiment and in February it saw action at Modbury. During the stagnant truce period Bennett's company disbanded. Ordered to reform again, the Devon men went to Exeter with the Earl of Stamford. Bennett rejoined his command at Torrington in April and marched with his regiment to disaster at Stratton. During the retreat, Bennett, having lost his personal trunk, made his way to Barnstaple where he helped Colonel Pawlett strengthen the defences and raise new troops.

News of the roundhead advance from Barnstaple soon reached Colonel Digby, whose own command now totalled over a thousand men. Unsure of the size of the enemy column snaking its way toward him, Digby decided to wait behind Torrington's crude earthworks. When the parliamentarians failed to appear on schedule, Digby believed the entire advance was nothing but local propaganda; as a consequence he disbanded his Cornish recruits. No sooner had the men scattered than a messenger arrived at Digby's headquarters with a report that the enemy were closing in. With little time and so few men available, Colonel Digby reacted quickly. Planning an ambush at Norwood Stream, Digby placed his 200 horsemen in concealed positions along the river.

Being mostly untried militiamen, the Barnstaple-Bideford column was ill-prepared for combat. When Digby's cavalry pounced out of the greenery the dumfounded roundhead vanguard broke and fled with barely a shot fired. As they ran the royalist main body sprang up and fired their muskets at the confused mass, spreading such panic that the column disintegrated. The survivors later rendezvoused in Bideford, less 400 men killed and wounded, but mostly missing. John Digby followed up his unexpected victory with a swift march on Bideford, which he laid siege to. In the weeks that followed, Digby's jubilant little army captured Appledore, stormed into Bideford and moved on to Barnstaple, which surrendered on September 2nd. The fall of the north Devon towns meant no relief could now come to Exeter from that direction. Coupled with the repulse of Warwick's fleet, the city looked doomed.

The incompetent Earl of Stamford surprisingly retained command of Exeter's defences. On July 27th he found time to write to his friend, the royalist Sir Edward Seymour, proposing to exchange a number of prisoners held by him for a similar number in royal prisons. What Stamford was actually seeking was the return of his servant Mr Thomas Davies, captured at Topsham and held in Taunton. The earl emphasised that: *'If there be a general exchange it would be an act of charity'*.[8]

As an example of his continuing misconduct, Stamford wrote a letter to King Charles in early August, urging the king to rid himself of his advisors. Anticipating Exeter's fall, Henry Grey also proclaimed his own faithfulness in an effort to ingratiate himself with his sovereign. As August wore on, hot and sticky, supplies and money began to run low.

On September 4th a bombshell fell that seriously damaged the parliamentary war effort in Devon. Exeter, the county town capitulated to Sir John Berkeley and Prince Maurice. After four months of constant royalist activity, which cut off every avenue of escape and slowly strangled the city, Exeter had finally submitted. With ammunition and powder almost gone and no relief in sight the

Earl of Stamford agreed to surrender. Henry Grey had never been a capable military commander, he preferred to wait behind Exeter's walls rather than be at the head of an army taking on the enemy in the field. On the only occasion he did take command, he planned badly and left the fighting to his subordinates; as a consequence he was soundly thrashed. With the defection of James Chudleigh, who was with Hopton outside Exeter, and the resignation of Sir George Chudleigh, Stamford's own loyalty began to waver. What finally forced Stamford's hand may have been the recent treachery of Sir William Russell, the Earl of Bedford and parliamentary Lord Lieutenant of Devon and a turncoat.

The defenders of Exeter marched out on the 7th, Prince Maurice granting similar terms to those offered Bristol by his brother. The officers and men were to leave their arms stacked and march away from the city. Units included in the surrender were Colonel Sir William Russell's foot, Sir John Northcote's regiment, Colonel Richard Saunders' command, Colonel John Wear's Devon foot regiment now reduced to 150 men. Several companies of Colonel William Bampfield's old regiment and the survivors of Merrick's London greycoat regiment were also in the garrison at this time. A number of those who left Exeter went to Plymouth, they included Stamford, Sir Francis Drake, Sir Nicholas Martyn, Sir John Bampfield and Sir Samuel Rolle, others dispersed, but many returned to their homes never to fight again. A few were persuaded to join the royal army, while poor Sir John Northcote was kept a prisoner until exchanged in 1645, by which time his old regiment had been disbanded in London.

John Northcote, of Hayne in the parish of Newton St Cyr, was a wealthy Devonshire baronet in his mid-forties. Educated at Exeter College Oxford, Northcote entered the Middle Temple in 1618 and was Sheriff of Devon, 1626-7. In 1640, during the war with Scotland, he found himself with the king in York, later he sat in the Long Parliament as MP for Ashburton and in July 1641 was created baronet. At the outbreak of war, Northcote greatly aided parliament's cause with his influence and wealth, so much so in fact, that he was exempted from the king's pardon in November 1642. During the autumn of the same year Sir John's regiment of Devonshire trained bandsmen saw action at Sherborne Castle, and in late December he was ordered by the Commons to return to Devon to help prepare his home county for defence. Northcote raised a new, much larger regiment, said to number almost a thousand men.

Northcote's regiment fought at Chagford and Modbury in February and at Polson Bridge in April. Shortly after the last battle, Sir John received reinforcements, which took his total to well over a thousand. These men were from Lord Brookes' regiment which had suffered heavily at Edgehill and later at Lichfield, where Brookes' himself had been killed. Badly under strength, Brookes' command was broken up and several of its companies sent into the Westcountry. Northcote's amalgamated regiment fought well at Stratton and many of the men escaped capture and retreated towards Exeter. Trapped inside the city by Berkeley, Northcote and his men remained until surrendered. Sir John's capture and eventual release ended his military career. On May 7th 1645 he would resume his seat in parliament and two weeks later Sir John Northcote took the solemn league and covenant.

Granted a royal pardon, Sir Henry Grey rode to London where he arrived on the 16th. Standing before the House of Commons, Grey tried to explain his reasons for surrendering the city of Exeter. Offended by his personal pardon, which had been written into the articles of capitulation, the Commons ordered an enquiry. Almost immediately the earl's poor leadership surfaced but Stamford countered by laying the blame for his misfortunes upon his subordinates. Parliament would have none of this and it was decided he should never again command an army. One reason for Stamford's downward spiral may have been the plight of his widowed mother, Dame Elizabeth Grey, who on September 6th had been forced to petition parliament for relief, not only for herself, but also for her daughter-in-law. Elizabeth had lost all her estates in Ireland and her son Captain Richard Bingley, Stamford's brother, had been killed. Grey would continually pester Westminster for what he called justice, but he had lost the confidence of his superiors and his soldiers.

Prince Maurice made Berkeley Governor of Exeter and dallied in that city until September 19th then, instead of marching directly on Plymouth, he advanced towards Dartmouth with an army of 7,000 men. En route the prince detached 500 dragoons with orders to occupy Totnes and prevent supplies being sent downriver to Dartmouth. Upon news of Exeter's surrender, Plymouth's defenders feared the royalists would sweep down and overrun the undermanned port, but when Maurice moved against Dartmouth, their fears turned to relief. Once the prince captured Dartmouth, as he undoubtedly would, Plymouth would be his next objective, but for now the defence committee had a little longer to prepare. However the town had not been left entirely at peace, Colonel John Digby, the man who had so easily subdued north Devon, was already on his way with 3,600 well-equipped soldiers, hoping to add more victories to his tally.

Securing Barnstaple, Bideford and Appledore, Digby began his advance across Dartmoor on September 13th. Arriving in the Plymouth area, Colonel Digby prudently examined Plymouth's northern defences and found them too formidable for his small army to assault. Leaving detachments of observation at Widey, he skirted the great forts north of the town and moved his army through Plympton to Plymstock, setting up headquarters at Radford. From here Digby felt more secure and he detached cavalry up towards How Stert to observe Fort Stamford. Wagon convoys were sent out into the countryside to bring in provisions from the surrounding area. Colonel Digby's manoeuvres cut Plymouth off from the rich food crops in the South Hams. Eventually the royalists would dig siege lines and plant heavy artillery at Oreston Hill and Hooe, allowing them to edge closer and closer to Fort Stamford. Such tactics would ultimately allow the cavaliers to isolate Fort Stamford and Digby's gunners would be able to fire at ships sailing into Sutton harbour. Prince Maurice's lack of foresight and Digby's failure to strike while the iron was hot lost the royalists one of their best opportunities to capture Plymouth.

The loss of Exeter and Digby's arrival at Plymstock followed a deep morale shattering episode, which could easily have lost Plymouth to the enemy without a shot being fired. Within the town there was a considerable number of royal sympathisers, many of whom were prominent figures. As parliament suffered defeat after defeat in the county, many of these closet cavaliers, encouraged by the success of the king's forces, came out and voiced their opinions. A minority however, were still sceptical and remained silently anonymous. Sir Alexander Carew, commander of St Nicholas Island, keystone to Plymouth's seaward defences, was rumoured to be one of the latter.

The only surviving son of Richard Carew of Anthony in Cornwall and his first wife Bridget, Alexander was born on August 30th 1609 and grew up a close friend of Bevill Grenville. He was also a cousin to Sir Thomas Hele of Flete. In 1631 Alexander married the daughter of Robert Rolle and he later represented Cornwall as a knight of the shire. During the Long Parliament Carew and his friend Grenville sat as MPs for Cornwall, but the following year Alexander was back in his home county raising money and troops for parliament. Eventually forced to leave Anthony House and flee into Plymouth, along with many other Cornish parliamentarians, Carew found himself in command of St Nicholas Island.

As the months wore on and royalist victory's in the southwest mounted, Carew's loyalty was rumoured to be swerving in a dangerous direction. Fearing for his family and property, Carew corresponded secretly with Piers Edgcumbe across the water and Sir John Berkeley who was busy besieging Exeter. In the exchange of letters, Alexander reputedly discussed the possibility of surrendering St Nicholas Island to the royalists. By this act Carew hoped to ingratiate himself with his king. At first Sir Alexander's fidelity to the cause appeared unbreakable, but with so many defeats and defections, rumours, begun by one of his own servants, started to circulate. Whispers spread, first around the island, then into the town, that Sir Alexander Carew was furtively meeting with Piers Edgcumbe on his estate late at night. It was reported that the two conspirators were planning for a body of cavaliers to be shipped over from the Cornish shore. Once on the island these men would quickly round up the garrison and secure the island and its cannon for the royalists.

Since July, Philip Francis, grieving for his wife Margaret who had died recently, grew more and more suspicious of Carew's allegiance. He also believed Captain Thomas Arundell, Governor of Plymouth Fort, was another whose loyalty ebbed and flowed. One day the mayor met privately with Captain Richard Evans, a local merchant and a friend he could trust. Francis relayed his doubts to Evans, who in turn informed Sergeant John Hancock and gunner Benjamin Fuge, two of the island's most dependable soldiers. Hancock told Evans that he would watch Carew carefully, but then Francis added that if treason were discovered, all concerned in its revelations and any subsequent arrests would be well rewarded.

Philip Francis communicated his suspicions and fears to London and on August 1st Westminster ordered Sir Alexander Carew and Thomas Arundell to come up to the capital for questioning. At first the evidence Francis needed was hard to ascertain, but eventually Carew's nocturnal visits to Mount Edgcumbe were noted. Upon receipt of parliament's directive, Sir Alexander agreed to come ashore and put his accounts in order. Later he changed his mind and was again observed slipping across to Mount Edgcumbe. Finally on August 19th the House of Commons ordered Sir Alexander to give his oath that he would attend parliament. If he came at once to London, Carew would be free to lodge at Lord Sheffield's home, if he refused he would be arrested and confined under the sergeant-at-arms. In the meantime Francis sent Timothy Alsop, a local merchant, over to the island to inform Carew of pay due to him. Alsop asked Carew to come ashore for his money and he agreed, but he never left the island. Frustrated, the mayor conscripted Francis Godolphin and John St Aubyn and sent them to St Nicholas Island, with orders to entice Carew off the rock, they too returned alone.

On August 26th Philip Francis changed his tactics and dispatched masters Randall and John Wills to the island. Both men preached regularly to the island's garrison and Francis hoped they could succeed where others had failed. The two ministers also carried written orders from the mayor for Sergeant Hancock to arrest Sir Alexander Carew, but by the time they arrived at the wharf, he was already under guard and waiting to be shipped across to the mainland. Unaware of Sir Alexander's arrest, the mayor, anxious to close the episode once and for all, filled a number of boats with soldiers and pulled away for the island. At the wharf Francis was told the news, relieved by the loyalty of the rest of the garrison, he thanked them all. Sergeant Hancock was promoted immediately to ensign and given temporary charge of the island and the rest of the men were promised their overdue wages. Philip Francis then escorted the dejected, former commander down to the boats.

Carew's mistake was in waiting for his pardon from the king to be stamped with the official seal of England; the delay proved his undoing. After being taken across to Plymouth, where a clamouring crowd yelled for a hanging, Alexander Carew was sent to London for trial and ultimately the executioner's block. Had Carew's treachery succeeded and the enemy captured St Nicholas Island, Plymouth's sea front defences would have been ruptured irreparably and her supply route with the outside world cut. The speaker for the House of Commons, William Lenthall, thanked the mayor for his zeal and courage in maintaining Plymouth's continuing stand against tyranny.

Unfortunately Carew's treachery was not an isolated case, Captain William Brooks of the frigate *Providence*, serving under the Earl of Warwick and anchored at Plymouth, was also discovered in an act of sedition. Brooks attempted to turn over his ship to the enemy, but he was caught before completing the dastardly deed. Evidently Captain Brooks had received a letter from his latest wife, inciting him to change sides and take the *Providence* to Bristol, now under the king's banner. Not sure what to do, Brooks handed his wife's letter to the Earl of Warwick and avowed his loyalty. Despite his protestations, William Brooks secretly corresponded with Sir John Pennington, the royalist naval commander. In his communication Brooks announced his intention to sail the *Providence* to Bristol. As with Carew, Brooks was betrayed by his own men. On September 13th they intercepted his letter to Sir John, arrested and locked him up and sent the communiqué to Warwick. Brooks was later sent to London for trial.

On September 14th, the day after Brooks' treachery was uncovered, Mayor Francis, Sir Shilston Calmady, Lieutenant Colonel Robert Savery, John Hawes, Thomas Arundell (back in Plymouth after convincing Westminster of his faithfulness), Francis Godolphin and Richard Erisey, sent a joint letter to Westminster. These devoted parliamentarians announced that every attempt at treachery had been thwarted and the letter explained in detail their fortunate conclusions. Treason and uncertainty was rife during the summer of 1643, not only in Devon but also in the capital, where distrust and suspicion permeated every governmental building. Prison escapes were on the increase in London, and to prevent bribery, prisoners were transferred from one gaol to another, unfortunately even these stringent measures failed to halt the corruption.

In March, Sir Hugh Pollard, a Devonshire royalist from King's Nympton, who had been captured at Sherborne in September 1642 and held captive in London, was permitted to move to his own house in Holbourne. Pollard declared he had not served against parliament and never would. On June 12th Pollard was ordered confined to close imprisonment due to a rumoured plot against parliament. Fearing for the security of its high-ranking royal captives, Westminster tightened security. By September Hugh Pollard, now in the Tower of London, was awaiting confirmation of an exchange for Sir John Saville, a prisoner of the king. Henry Champernowne, taken by Ruthven at Modbury back in December 1642, was held first at the King's bench, then transferred to Lord Peter's House and finally in August to the Compter in Southwark. A month later the House of Commons agreed to his exchange along with Mr Thomas Lee, Mr George Bailey and Lieutenant William Penrose for Captain Butler, Lieutenant Garrett, Richard Penwarne and Ensign Henry Keckwich, being held by Sir John Berkeley and all taken during the recent fighting in the southwest.

With Exeter and north Devon completely dominated by the king's forces and the town's plunging morale, brought about by the treachery of Sir Alexander Carew and William Brooks, Plymouth looked ripe for plucking. Once in position, Colonel John Digby's cannon would add to the town's misery by firing across the Cattewater. The ever-active defence committee ignored it all and continued to burrow, fortify and reinforce the incomplete earthworks that protected Plymouth. A redoubt named New Work was nearing completion at the junction of what is today North Road and Eldad Hill. This fort overlooked Stonehouse Creek and Millbridge and covered the approach from Stoke Damerel. On the opposite end of the outer line, a small three-gun fort, known as the Laira Point Work was almost finished. This important earthwork enabled lookouts to observe enemy movements north of Lipson Creek and around Saltram House and protect the right flank of Lipson Fort.

During the summer months, the town council and the defence committee, concerned over the unfinished outer line, decided to splash out more money and reinforce the inner line with a layer of stone. All existing forts on the interior line were subsequently strengthened by a covering of masonry or demolished and completely rebuilt; the trench was also deepened and gates repaired. Inappropriately-named Fort Stamford was also heavily bolstered at this time. Cannon, borrowed from the warship *Providence,* were taken ashore and hauled up the cliff to give the earthwork added firepower, and a large padlock secured the magazine. No matter how hard the defenders worked though Stamford's isolated position made it a tempting target for the enemy; it was only a matter of time before they would move against it.

As one Devonshire town after another fell to the enemy, Plymouth became a magnate for the many small companies that escaped the royalist net. These individual units were directed to rally at the town as a last hope. One such unit was Captain Wadding's company from Totnes, this forty-six-man detachment received twelve days' pay from Totnes Council in August. Each man received 18d per day for his service; not a great deal considering. With reinforcements difficult to obtain, parliament gave a number of royalist prisoners the option to join her armies or remain incarcerated; a practice well established by both sides. On August 17th royalist prisoners held in London were offered the chance to join the garrison at Plymouth. The few who agreed to go swore an oath never to fight against parliament, they were then discharged from gaol and sent by ship to Plymouth. Once ashore these reformed cavaliers were distributed amongst the regiments defending the town, but many were distrusted and branded as reformados.

September saw the popular Philip Francis step down from the mayoral chair, to be replaced by John Cawse, a man who, unlike his predecessor, could not work well with others in authority. A merchant and local magistrate, Cawse now in his second term as mayor, resided in Whimple Street with Elizabeth, his wife of over twenty years. This new mayor was stubborn, resentful and short-sighted where military matters were concerned. The biggest difference between Francis and Cawse was that Cawse was ill-prepared for the traumatic year ahead. Most fortunately for the new mayor, the onus of responsibility for the defence of Plymouth would soon fall upon the shoulders of several hard-hitting officers who were already on their way from London. Upon completion of his term, John Cawse would serve on the defence committee for Plymouth until his death in March 1645. Philip Francis in the meantime, continued to support the town as captain of a local trained band company.

Another well-known, albeit less popular personality also slipped out of the picture this summer, but his departure was more permanent. Although generally despised by Plymouthians for his extreme royalism, Dr Aaron Wilson the unrestrained Vicar of St Andrew's Church, having been imprisoned the previous year, suffered irreparable damage to his heath during his confinement. After great difficulty, Wilson's friends managed to obtain his release, but it was too late. Dr Wilson died in Exeter on July 7th, having been free only a short time. Some of the less-radical felt remorse at his passing and George Hughes allowed Dr Wilson to be recorded in the burial register of St Andrew's on July 8th.

Since the loss of Bristol, parliament considered Plymouth the most important port in the southwest, and with Exeter gone the House of Commons decided to reinforce the garrison immediately. Six hundred soldiers were assembled in Portsmouth, mostly from Colonel William

Gould's hastily-raised foot regiment. Gould would be returning to an area familiar to himself, where as a cavalry officer he had fought many times under Colonel Ruthven. Besides Gould's 600 troops, parliament also managed to accumulate a supply of arms, ammunition, 200 barrels of gunpowder and a large sum of money. A further £4,000 taken out of a loan to Westminster from the city of London would also be available for Plymouth. To command the expedition, parliament selected a Scot, Colonel James Wardlaw. Wardlaw fought at the battle of Edgehill, where he commanded a regiment of dragoons and later served on the Earl of Essex's council of war.

Gould, Wardlaw's second-in-command, of Hayes and Dunscombe had been baptised on September 14th 1615 at St Thomas' Exeter. At twenty-two he was married, by twenty-seven he was a widower with two children. In 1642 William Gould commanded a foot company in Sir John Bampfield's regiment at St Thomas near Exbridge, with the rank of captain. Later in the year he transferred to the cavalry and saw action at Braddock Down, Polson Bridge and Sourton Down. During the Stratton campaign Gould rode with Sir George Chudleigh and missed the fiasco in north Cornwall. After the retreat, Gould was promoted and given command of all the parliamentary horse in Devon.

In 1643, as Hopton advanced through Devonshire on his way to join Prince Maurice, the Devon horse brigade retired from his front and eventually joined Sir William Waller. With Gould at its head, the brigade fought at the battles of Roundway Down and Lansdown, before retiring with Waller all the way to London. The Devon horse was later shipped back to its home county a portion at a time and Gould, without a command was given charge of a newly-raised foot regiment, made up of *'Poor boys from the southeast'*.

From the moment of his arrival in Plymouth, William Gould, a man as Puritan as Cromwell, served the town with all his heart. Gould would take an interest in every aspect pertaining to the defence of Plymouth, from the layout of the siege lines protecting the port, to Church and civic matters. Colonel Gould resented blasphemers and drunks and would punish those responsible. Later Gould took over the reins of command from Wardlaw and showed such strength and determination that he was made Governor of Plymouth and Sheriff of Devon; both positions he retained until his sudden and untimely death.

Sailing from Portsmouth on September 17th, the ship conveying the reinforcements for Plymouth, stopped off at the Isle of Wight, where the men stepped ashore in order to preserve their health. The next stop was Torbay, then Dartmouth, which by this time was closely besieged by Prince Maurice. Wardlaw left 100 men there as a token reinforcement to the outnumbered garrison, but his orders were for him to press on for Plymouth and he promptly obeyed. The Wardlaw-Gould contingent finally sailed into Sutton Pool to a large cheering crowd on September 30th. Unfortunately jealousy marred their arrival. The new mayor, John Cawse, immediately resented Wardlaw's appointment as military governor, because his own responsibility for the town's defence came to an end. This simmering hostility between civil and military authority would cause continual friction between the two during the critical months ahead.

The newly-arrived detachment from Portsmouth, though weak in numbers, raised the garrison's hopes considerably. Their spirits rose even higher when Wardlaw announced there was to be no question of surrendering Plymouth to the enemy. While the new governor brought his troops ashore and replenished the town's powder supply, neighbouring Dartmouth was fighting for survival. Prince Maurice's aggressive approach was at first gallantly thwarted by the defenders, who managed to hold the royalists back for almost a month. Their heroic resistance and eventual sacrifice gave Wardlaw and Gould ample time to beef up Plymouth's defences.

Having marched from Exeter via Totnes, the king's nephew arrived in front of Dartmouth on September 19th. Here he merged his army with a detachment of Devonshire royalists under the popular Sir Edward Seymour. Upon his incredible escape from prison, Sir Edward returned to Devon and on April 16th 1643 he was commissioned by the Marquis of Hertford to recruit a force of 1,500 foot. Unable to raise the quota needed, Sir Edward saw minor action in Cornwall but spent most of his time skirmishing with parliamentary soldiers from the Dartmouth garrison prior to the port's close siege. Refusing to surrender, Dartmouth, ill-prepared for siege warfare, could only watch while the enemy dug earthworks out of the wet soil and hauled up heavy cannon. To stop provisions from entering the River Dart the royal navy seized all available boats. To prevent reinforcements coming up from Plymouth, strong detachments were posted at Totnes and Salcombe.

Finally, in early October, after weeks of petty skirmishing, the royalist artillery was in position and on the 4th it opened up. From their advantageous positions Maurice's gunners were able to pour a devastating blanket of iron and stone down against the centre of the town's defence. Subsequently when the prince sent his infantry in, they easily drove a deep wedge through the heart of Dartmouth, cutting the castle off from the town and dividing the defenders. Victory for the royalists was now only a matter of time, but it came quicker than many expected. On September 6th Dartmouth surrendered, giving up a large band of prisoners, supplies and fifty cannon. Trapped in the harbour were forty-four ships of various sizes and thirty-two barques, many loaded with assorted cargoes.

Many believed Dartmouth had been betrayed from the inside, John Syms wrote in his daybook, October 6th: *'Dartmouth by machinery is yielded to the enemy upon quarter. Our men were to depart by sea many of our soldiers there took up arms'.*[9]

One of the tragic casualties of the fighting at Dartmouth was James Chudleigh, killed at the head of his foot regiment. Dartmouth was quickly secured, prisoners exchanged and Sir Edward Seymour made governor on October 4th. Maurice now set his sights on Plymouth, which had ignored an appeal to surrender, sent in by Digby the day before Wardlaw's arrival. Colonel Digby had addressed his communication to the: *'Seduced mariners and soldiers in Plymouth'* and promised them freedom to return to their homes if they would quit the rebellious town. Digby also offered those parliamentarians who would join the royal army six shillings a week as payment; no one took his offer seriously. Unfortunately for the royalists, the prince and many of his soldiers had been struck down by sickness while in Dartmouth. This unexpected setback caused considerable delay to the planned offensive against Plymouth and left Digby pacing his headquarters in frustration.

Throughout the late autumn and early winter months, diseases, such as typhus and influenza, which struck down many of Prince Maurice's soldiers soon raged in Plymouth. Wretched weather and overcrowding meant the town was rife for an outbreak and when it came it put many a poor soul in his or her grave and the plague did not discriminate. Prisoners suffered worse, due to cramped conditions, rats and poor amenities. The situation eventually grew so bad that Mayor Francis proposed the transfer of all prisoners to a much cleaner environment. Despite the changes prisoners continued to die; during August and September, ninety people were buried in St Andrew's Churchyard alone, five a day during some periods; it would get much worse.

When Dartmouth initially came under siege, a number of political prisoners held there were transported to Plymouth. With typhus spreading Philip Francis thought it wise to keep these new arrivals in the Marshalsea. To prevent the prisoners from dying and lose parliament such valuable assets, the war council in Plymouth compromised with the captives. Four of the more prominent, Messrs Kelland, Hoddy, Yeard and Giles Loman offered £800 for liberty, their proposal was accepted and the quartet released. Those who were fortunate enough to purchase freedom and escape the plague that stalked the narrow streets and fortifications of Plymouth were few and far between. For the less advantageous there was no escape.

Thanks to Maurice's enforced stay in Dartmouth, Plymouth gained an entire month, giving Wardlaw not only the time to strengthen fortifications, but also the opportunity to launch several counter thrusts against Digby. The first of these jabs took place in the early hours of October 8th when Wardlaw selected 300 soldiers, placed them in small boats and sent them across the Cattewater. The objective of this amphibious force was the enemy outpost at Hooe, a small village nestled at the bottom of a valley between Radford and How Stert. When the boats beached near Turnchapel, the soldiers disembarked and waited until dawn.

When the first streaks of daylight appeared on the horizon the raiders re-embarked and rowed around to Hooe. Minutes later the roundheads leapt from the boats and rushed through the shallow water. They struck so swiftly the cavaliers were caught completely off guard. Several scattered shots were fired and two of the parliamentarians were hit, but the enemy guard was dispersed. A royalist captain, an ensign and fifty-two other soldiers were captured, as were a number of small arms, two colours and three barrels of gunpowder. Before the survivors could raise the alarm and reinforcements rush to the area, the roundheads secured their captives and spoils and withdrew. The following day, October 9th, a soldier named Daniel Douglas was executed in Plymouth. It is likely that Douglas was one of the prisoners taken at Hooe, recognised as a deserter from the garrison and summarily put to death for treason.

A week later, on October 15th, Colonel Wardlaw, spurred on by the success at Hooe, organised a second foray, this time the raid was aimed in the opposite direction. At the appointed hour two hundred musketeers and a body of horse headed north, along the road to Knackersknowle via the Maudlyn Ridge. At a point near the village, less than two miles from Plymouth, several troops of enemy horse were observed camped on outpost duty. Once again the parliamentarians struck rapidly and easily overran the encampment, capturing some thirty prisoners with their horses and arms. The survivors jumped into the saddle and fled in the direction of Trennimans Jump (Roborough).

Leaving the infantry to collect the trophies and return to Plymouth, part of the elated horse charged up the road in reckless pursuit. When the van of the retreating cavaliers met up with a second royalist detachment near Trennimans Jump, the two forces combined and counterattacked their pursuers. Surprised by this sudden turn of events, the roundheads numbering less than a score, found themselves surrounded and being called upon to surrender. Fortunately one of the parliamentarians had his wits about him, Michael Searle, a dragoon officer from Somerset, who would rise in rank and prominence during his time at Plymouth, yanked on his reins, put spurs to flanks and broke through the enemy cordon. Lieutenant John Chaffin, second in command of Captain Thomas Halsey's troop and several others followed Searle's daring example. Eventually the royalists managed to escort away only three or four prisoners from the field. Wardlaw's second raid had proved as successful as his first, but it would be his last, Prince Maurice was fast approaching with a large army and many guns.

Throughout October Colonel John Digby had been slowly, but steadily reinforced and as more and more royalist troops arrived, he was able to extend his lines. The strongest build-up of cavaliers was around Plymstock, but as the month wore on Digby was able to strengthen and extend the detachments north of Plymouth. An isolated outpost was also established at Tamerton, where forage and recruits could be gathered. As a bonus Digby managed to commandeer thirteen small boats, which his men had hauled overland from the River Yealm to Pomphlett Mill. With these he planned to launch a night assault against one of the forts at Prince Rock, but for some reason the plan never went into operation.

Guiding the town's spiritual resistance during these crucial months, was as important as its military leaders strategic planning. With Dr Wilson long gone, Thomas Bedford, lecturer, had taken over the pulpit of St Andrew's, but being as ardent a royalist as Wilson, his days were numbered. Despite warnings Bedford persisted in reading anti-parliamentary sermons, as a consequence he was arrested and thrown into gaol. On September 4th Bedford was ordered by the House of Commons to be sent by ship to London to answer for his delinquency. Either on the voyage, or in the capital, Thomas Bedford died.

On the 21st of October, George Hughes, a man recommended for the post by Westminster since July, was at last appointed Vicar of St Andrew's, to the satisfaction of all. Hughes was indeed a fortuitous man, being born in Southwark in 1603 when his mother was fifty-two years of age. Always a non-conformist, Hughes was, at one time commanded by Archbishop Laud to stay silent in his zealous beliefs. With the outbreak of war, George Hughes was found preaching in Tavistock; when Hopton occupied the town Hughes and his family refugeed to Exeter. With that city's ultimate capture in September, the Puritan minister and his family were permitted to leave, possibly due to the recent death of his wife. After a brief period in Coventry, Hughes accepted the offer of St Andrew's and he left the Midlands for the Westcountry. George Hughes would remain in Plymouth throughout the war, serving his parishioners to the best of his ability for the next eighteen years.

On the same day George Hughes was appointed to St Andrew's, October 21st, the royalists launched their first assault against the town's most isolated outpost. Thus began the hardest-fought battle of the civil war around Plymouth. The combined royal army camped on the outskirts of the port numbered almost 10,000 men; made up of nine regiments of foot and five of horse, supported by a large compliment of artillery. The largest concentration of troops was with the prince, moving steadily through Plympton to positions north of the town. Digby remained in charge at Radford with three regiments of foot, five companies of cavalry and a number of batteries. Due to Colonel Digby's increasing activity around Plymstock, Wardlaw expected an early attack to come from this direction, but he believed it would be an amphibious assault against one of the forts along the river at Prince Rock. Consequently he failed to adequately reinforce Fort Stamford or evacuate its garrison. Wardlaw's reason for leaving the 300-man garrison out on a limb may have been to use the very isolation of the garrison as a beacon, to attract the enemy and draw in royalist men and materials. By focusing upon Stamford, Maurice would ultimately weaken his forces north of the town. Wardlaw knew Prince Maurice would need to snip off this redoubt before concentrating entirely on Plymouth. So by sacrificing Stamford, was Colonel Wardlaw buying more time for the town?

With the king's nephew barely an hour's march away, Colonel Digby finally felt confident enough to attack the large bastion on top of How Stert. His choice was ideal, remote and awkward to reinforce; Stamford could be plucked off the roundhead map with relative ease, or so he believed. The fort had been constructed on a low ridge, but it was small, badly positioned and its left flank could be turned. Once this happened the garrison, with their backs to the sea, would have little chance of escape. Built of earth, wood and loose stone, Fort Stamford faced south and overlooked Plymouth Sound, the Cattewater, part of St Nicholas Island and Plymstock. To protect the exposed left flank and prevent an enemy moving upon its rear by way of Turnchapel, a small fortlet had been raised east of Stamford looking down upon Oreston and Hooe. Breastworks also protected the garrison's encampment located behind the main fort. Stamford's few cannon were manned by a number of naval artillerists, while the defending infantry consisted of men from Colonel William Herbert's regiment, a few survivors of Calmady's London greycoats and part of Colonel William Gould's new regiment, but there was no cavalry available.

During the night of October 21st a detachment of royalists moved silently up towards Stamford from their camps around Hooe and Radford. Covered by the darkness Digby's engineers quickly and quietly threw up a rough earth wall, well within small arms range of the main fort and in such a position to be able to cut off the Stamford garrison from their flank work. At first light the garrison was shocked to find the enemy so close and feverishly fortifying their new advanced line. To give himself a breathing space and reopen the garrison's escape route, Stamford's commandant launched an early attack against the audacious enemy. Captain Richard Corbett, one of Gould's company commanders, was to lead the charge.

Digby's musketeers took up their weapons, lined the crude breastwork and blasted the attack back, then his horse charged in and cut the roundheads to pieces; lacking cavalry, Corbett withdrew. Undeterred by this setback, the parliamentarians made further attacks against the enemy line, and one of their half-moon works (small demi-forts, hastily thrown up to protect the flanks of a central position). After three hours of fierce fighting and heavy casualties, the stubborn roundheads gallantly overran the line and its supporting half-moon, capturing fifty-one prisoners including a Captain White.

That night thirty men, under an ensign, were left in the captured fortlet as a guard. Either by fear, treachery or cowardice the enemy recaptured the half-moon work without a shot being fired to warn the Stamford lookouts. As a consequence the worn-out parliamentarians were forced to do it all again. A second major assault was therefore launched against the enemy position on the 23rd. Once more the royalist position was overrun after bitter, bloody combat, but the roundheads suffered further heavy losses and not enough reinforcements were coming in to replace the casualties. Four top commanders, including the gallant Captain Corbett, shot in the head and killed, had fallen so far, making total losses for the garrison at twenty killed and 100 wounded.

Another intrepid company officer who died during the early fighting at Stamford was Captain Richard Sandall. Sandall had been a dragoon officer who fought at Lansdown and Roundway. After Waller retreated to London, Sandall made his way into the Westcountry and found himself commanding a foot company in Fort Stamford. Having fought courageously, Sandall was killed and his body ferried across to Plymouth, where he was interred in St Andrew's. Corbett's body was not brought back until the 28th, possibly due to the boat owner's reluctance to run the risk of losing his vessel by making the hazardous trip. On the 25th of October, one Edward Oliver was executed in Plymouth, he may have been the soldier who betrayed his comrades three days before, or another captured deserter.

The roundheads tore down as much of the enemy fortlets and breastwork as they were able, hoping to deter the cavaliers. To strengthen their own position the parliamentary commander organised his tired soldiers into working parties. These men threw up new walls to the right and left of Stamford, thus extending their own position and taking in the flattened royalist works and most of the ridge. Half-moons were also constructed on either flank, but the garrison could not effectively man the entire fortification.

The exhausted roundheads continually looked over their shoulders for reinforcements, but only a few boatloads ever arrived. Wardlaw, for some reason known only to himself, kept men and valuable supplies from being thrown across the Cattewater. He knew the isolated fort was of no practical use to Plymouth's main defence and more than likely relied upon its delayed capture to buy him time. On the other hand Stamford's loss would enable the enemy to completely secure the east bank of the River Plym and release more troops for Prince Maurice's offensive against the redoubts north of Plymouth. Stamford's forfeiture would also allow the enemy to establish artillery on the cliffs from where they could bombard the lower part of the town and those forts along the west bank of the Plym.

Digby's engineers continued to throw up breastworks parallel with the defender's line and push their cannon closer and closer to Fort Stamford. To protect the guns the royalists also constructed two strong emplacements, which they filled with soldiers. The more cumbersome pieces of artillery were left on Oreston Hill, well within range of Stamford. By November 3rd the cavaliers had, according to highly-exaggerated accounts, two hundred cannon of various size and calibre and were close enough to bombard Stamford. The closest battery faced Stamford's south wall, another was on high ground just behind, while more guns were at Oreston, in a position to hit the vulnerable left flank and its detached fortlet.

On the same day, the House of Lords moved that the town of Plymouth, being under siege and of such great importance, should not be lost. Accordingly a committee of lords and commons was ordered to meet and consider what should be done for preserving and relieving Plymouth. Those selected for the committee were the earls of Northumberland, Pembroke, Lord Viscount Saye and Sele and Lord Wharton, later, in a twist of irony, the Earl of Stamford's name would be added to the list.

Two days later on the 5th Digby's gunners opened up, tossing iron balls and great stones ranging from six to twenty-four pounders into Fort Stamford. To heighten the effect and scare the town, a number of those guns on Oreston Hill turned their attention to the ships lying at anchor in Sutton Pool. Unable to protect themselves, these vessels sailed around and took refuge between St Nicholas Island and Millbay, where they were safe from the royal gunners. The Fort Stamford garrison was not so fortunate, it had nowhere to go; soon the ramparts were systematically ripped apart, deal boards were splintered, wool sacks scattered and earth sprouted into the air. The defenders shovelled the mud back into place, but against such a storm they were unable to keep ahead. Also the powder magazine was in constant danger of being hit. Men and cannon were disabled and covered in debris, while soldiers in the forts along the Plym watched in awe, powerless to help as their friends wilted under the tremendous fire. The fort's commander raised a signal to the town that he was in distress, but no help came.

Outnumbered and totally outgunned, the parliamentarians could do nothing and the bombardment continued into the next day. Frustrated by the heroic defence, Colonel Digby at last readied his command for what he believed would be the ultimate strike. The target for the attack was the main fort itself and its neighbouring half-moon. Suddenly a ship full of troops was observed sailing towards Plymouth and Digby feared a counterattack from the Cattewater. Consequently he stood his entire command ready, in front of Radford House. Three regiments of foot and five troops of horse waited, but the ship ran into Plymouth and Digby turned his full attention back to Fort Stamford. Several companies of horse, one from his own cavalry regiment, under Major Jonathon Trelawny, another from Sir Francis Hawley's and a third from Lieutenant Colonel Thomas Monk's regiment under Captain Thomas Stuckley, were sent on up the hill. The remaining horse and foot followed a short time later. About this time two mounted companies of Devonshire horse appeared at Radford, sent to Digby's aid by Sir Henry Cary.

The royalist artillery meanwhile continued blasting away at Stamford from the south, east and southeast, until two of Stamford's portholes and their cannon were knocked down and a huge breach made in the wall. As a sign of recognition Digby's men placed a bay leaf in their headgear, while the word for the day was 'Victory'. The royalist foot soon arrived at the half-moon work, directly south of Stamford's left flank breastwork. Here they waited for Digby to order up all those troops remaining at Radford. Once assembled, the foot with a loud shout charged toward the roundhead half-moon. As trumpets and drums blared and rattled the cavaliers stormed the little work, forcing its defenders to flee, first to Stamford, then down towards Stert Point (Mount Batten). Forty dazed prisoners were captured in the work and escorted away.

Using movable breastworks as cover and hauling up a number of ladders, the royalists were able to close rapidly on Stamford from three sides. The heavy bombardment forced the parliamentarians to keep their heads down and allowed Digby's men to manoeuvre into a position from where they could assault the breastworks east of Stamford. To fill up the trench surrounding the fort, faggots were pushed up and thrown in, giving the assailants a makeshift drawbridge. With only seven artillerists remaining out of thirty-six and less than fifty soldiers fit, Stamford's commandant looked to his supplies. Barely two barrels of powder were left and not much ammunition, despair turned to panic and it was decided to capitulate before Digby stormed the redoubt. The defenders agreed to surrender at 4 p.m. on condition that they be allowed to march out with colours flying, arms in hand, a cannon in tow and prisoners exchanged. Colonel Digby honoured the bravery of the survivors by agreeing to these conditions.

Those roundheads who managed to avoid capture retreated back toward Stert Point, where a small breastwork had been thrown up across the narrow isthmus. Demoralised and aware of the numbers Digby could throw against them, these men stood defiant only as long as was necessary. Soon they received orders to abandon their position and were evacuated by boat to Plymouth. Condemnation for the loss of Fort Stamford was placed upon the shoulders of Mayor Cawse, because he would not, or could not save the garrison. However both Wardlaw and Gould must also share the blame, as both stood by while the little garrison was annihilated.

Sadly, of all who took part in the gallant fighting around Stamford most have been lost to history, only a few names remain. Two of the parliamentary captains Richard Corbett and Richard Sandall were brought back to Plymouth and buried in St Andrew's, as were a number of others who succumbed to their wounds. The majority of the dead were interred in pits near Fort Stamford, where they remain to this day, unmarked and forgotten. One survivor of the garrison, William Chapman, who as a cavalryman had been wounded at Braddock Down and recovered in time to fight at Fort Stamford, was so severely wounded he had to be carried down to a boat and ferried across to Plymouth; he would never walk again. Another unfortunate was John Kittoe, wounded in the hand and captured by the royalists, possibly during the assault against Stamford's flank work. As he was marched to the rear Kittoe was hit on the back of the head by the butt of a musket. Later he was exchanged, but his wound never healed and John Kittoe eventually went deaf.

Stamford's loss was a morale blow to Plymouth, as the enemy were able to place cannon upon How Stert and fire directly into Sutton Pool. Royalist lookouts could also see part of the outer line and observe roundhead movements within the town. Fortunately parliamentary shipping was able to use Millbay, where supplies were landed and transported the short distance to the town by wagon. The only damage ever recorded by royalist artillery firing from How Stert was when a solid shot fell upon the Hoe, knocking off a piece of the windmill. It is hard to believe that no other loss was ever suffered; no doubt occasional shot fell onto the town, especially in the Barbican area. Wreckage of a vessel sunk in the harbour has been dated to the civil war, the ship had reportedly been sunk by enemy artillery. Exchange of fire must have been frequent during this period, due to the close proximity of the two sides, but it has gone unrecorded.

While the fighting raged around Fort Stamford, a secondary engagement broke out near the Lipson Work, when a royalist attack was sent in. This assault was to draw attention away from Fort Stamford and keep the parliamentarians from detaching troops for its relief. Lacking motivation, the royalists were easily repulsed, without serious loss to either side. A few days later Colonel Wardlaw, irritated by Mayor Cawse's perpetual contention toward his authority, took over full control of the town's defences. Despite Cawse's anger over Wardlaw's attitude, the mayor could do nothing. All royalist sympathisers within the town were ordered to be arrested; Johnathon Sparkes, Edmond Fowell and two other deputy lieutenants were among those caught in Wardlaw's net. Later Sparkes and Fowell would be sent to London, to be arraigned before the House of Commons. The troops, seamen and townsfolk of Plymouth were then bluntly informed by Wardlaw that he would set the town on fire before surrendering. Colonel Wardlaw's radical actions were approved by parliament.

On November 4th the council of war, urged on by Wardlaw, issued a vow and protestation, which was to be published in the assemblies by the ministers of Plymouth. All soldiers and civilians of the towns of Plymouth and Stonehouse were to take the vow; those who refused would be noted and a special watch kept on them. The following day, Wardlaw and Mayor Cawse led the garrison and townspeople in swearing the vow and protestation of loyalty to parliament, which had been nailed up at various points throughout the town and in the siege works. On November 11th Colonel Wardlaw wrote to parliament explaining the loss of Fort Stamford and describing the good condition of the rest of the town's defences. He also sent a copy of the oath sworn by the inhabitants for Westminster's approval. The House of Commons praised Wardlaw's actions and ordered a letter of thanks to be sent to Colonel James Wardlaw.

As in many of the parliamentary garrisons dotted around the country, Plymouth was critically short of men and supplies. Colonel Gould complained to London that half the original 500 men brought into Plymouth back in September were dead, wounded or sick. Gould also protested the mayor's attitude, especially towards Colonel Wardlaw, over who commanded the local trained bands. The mayor demanded that the town captains retain traditional charge of their companies, while Wardlaw kept command of all other troops.

William Gould added that he blamed Stamford's loss on the hostility between Wardlaw and Cawse: *'We have met with many difficulties, chiefly in the settling of the authority of the said colonel to the command of the militia here, which hath been mainly opposed by some of the town, who strive to uphold the mayor in the managing of the military affairs, which he is not capable of, and the soldiery will not submit unto. This occasioned the loss of Mount Stamford'.*[10]

Such a situation could not work, two individual commands fighting independently against a common foe, behind the same walls, was a recipe for disaster.

Both Wardlaw and Gould were appalled by the recent condition of St Nicholas Island; short of ammunition and badly provisioned, no wonder Gould would be given a special commission from London to take the reins of power and place the island under his own charge. Captain Thomas Arundell and his successor, a Mr O'Rourke, both proved ineffective in governing the island.

Wardlaw would later resent Gould's popularity and bad blood between the two senior officers would add to the town's mounting problems. With arms, munitions and supplies so short, it seemed as if courage alone was sustaining the defenders of Plymouth; courage and a little luck.

(8) Page 120: Letter from The Earl of Stamford to Sir Edward Seymour, July 27th 1643, Seymour Letters, 1392M/1643/12; Devon Record Office, Exeter; by kind permission of Muncaster Castle.
(9) Page 131: John Syms, A daybook of some special passages and mercies; British Library. Add 35297; by kind permission of the British Library.
(10) Page 141: Letter from Colonel William Gould to William Lenthall, November 15th 1643. Oxford Bodleian Library, MS. Nalson 3 fols 153-4; by kind permission of the Oxford Bodleian Library.

Chapter 7

Fighting for Survival

On November 11th Colonel Wardlaw wrote to William Lenthall, the speaker for the House of Commons. In his letter Wardlaw described the loss of Fort Stamford and explained the advantage of its dispossession, in allowing him to better defend the town. The colonel also expressed the dissatisfaction he sensed within the town since the royalist army arrived in the area and told of his plans to combat sedition: *'I believe the neutralists do desire that the town might be delivered up: Whereupon, for fear that either through treachery of the townsmen, or for want of experienced men, I seized the fort and island, the castle and magazine, that in case the town should be forced and overpowered with strength by the enemy, and knowing this place of such great concernment, that through God's assistance I would keep them until supplies and relief come'.*[11]

The desperate situation in Plymouth did not prevent Wardlaw from gathering in as much forage as he could before the enemy completely cut off access to the region north of the town. On the same day he penned his communiqué to Lenthall, Colonel Wardlaw selected several troops of horse and a body of musketeers. This detachment was ordered to escort a number of wagons out to Thornhill, load them with hay and wood and return. In command of the escort was Major Elizeus Leighton, another survivor of Waller's Lansdown-Roundway campaign. In compliance with orders Leighton led his command up North Hill, along the Maudlyn Ridge and on to Thornhill. Suddenly a party of royalist horse appeared and Leighton's enthusiasm replaced his caution. Preferring not to fight, the cavaliers reined up and rode away, but Major Leighton gave chase, pursuing the enemy as far as the village of Knackersknowle. Here they caught up with the royalists, killing a captain and several troopers.

As was usually the case with cavalry during the civil war, Leighton's men had gone too far. While they were enjoying their minor victory, the roundheads failed to notice a much larger party of royalists bearing down. Major Leighton saw them at the last minute and tried to reorganise his troops for a fighting withdrawal, but it was too late. Leighton fought heroically, but he was struck five times during the clash and loss of blood forced him to surrender. A number of his men were also taken and the survivors rode back to Thornhill. Here they picked up the wagons and musketeers and escorted them back to town. The foolhardy, but gallant major would later be exchanged and promoted.

Seven days after the Thornhill fiasco, Colonel John Digby at Fort Stamford, offered the Plymouth garrison terms for its capitulation. In this, his second such offer, Digby promised pardon for all and guaranteed protection of personal property: *'To the Mayor and Governor of the town of Plymouth. That you may see our hearty desires of a just peace, we do summon you in his majesty's name, to surrender the town, fort and island of Plymouth, with the warlike provisions thereunto belonging, into our hands for his majesty's use. And we do hereby assure you, by the power derived to us, from his majesty upon the performance here of, of a general pardon for what is passed. And engage ourselves in our honour, to secure your persons and estates, from all violence and plunder, we have now quitted ourselves on our parts, and let the blood that shall be spilled in the obtaining of these just demands (if denied by you) be your guilt. Given under our hands at Mount Stamford the 18th day of November 1643'.*[12] John Digby, Thomas Bassett, Peter Killigrew, John Wagstaffe, Jonathon Trelawny, Richard Prideaux, John Arundell, Thomas Monck, William Arundell, John Downing and Thomas Stuckley signed the proposal.

Wardlaw flatly refused Digby's offer, but already the enemy were beginning to close in on Plymouth from the north. Having crossed the Plym in mid-November, Prince Maurice sent his engineers up to Compton and Mannamead to find suitable positions for artillery. Soon batteries and redoubts sprang up along the high ground north of Lipson Creek, opposite the town's outer line. Eventually the royalists would occupy positions extending from Townsend Hill down to where Lipson Creek joined the Plym, with minor outposts covering points further to the west. On November 17th as a prelude to the close siege, the royalists organised a piece of showmanship for the benefit of their own commander and the Plymouth garrison. The remnant of Hopton's original Cornish army mustered at Saltram, close to Longbridge, where Prince Maurice reviewed them, the rest of the royal infantry rendezvoused at Fort Stamford. Pleased with his veterans, the prince met with his subordinates and formulated plans for the capture of Plymouth.

Initially a number of proclamations were issued from the royalist headquarters at Plympton. One of which was aimed at the communities dotted around Plymouth. The royal decree was to be read out in every church; those clergymen who refused would face persecution and imprisonment. Supplies from these outlying villages were to be commandeered for the use of the army and if the villagers refused, their property would be confiscated. Meanwhile the royalist infantry followed their cavalry around to the north of Plymouth and were soon observed setting up camps on the high ground overlooking Lipson Creek.

Wardlaw countered Maurice's movements by rebuilding the high hedges that connected the outer forts. Alone these isolated bastions were a deterrent against attack, but in a siege situation the individual earthworks were nothing but boulders upon a beach, and the tide could sweep in around them without hindrance. To impede such action, old hedges, previously torn down, were replaced thereby connecting the forts and preventing an enemy force from slipping in between. Maudlyn Fort, considered the most important of the outer works, was strengthened and an extra gun platform added near the main road. To fill in a huge gap in the outer line between Lipson Fort and the Plym, Wardlaw ordered a recently-constructed fort, sited halfway along the line, to be strengthened and the Laira Point Work, on the extreme right of the line, to be reinforced.

Meanwhile Westminster continued to receive letters urging the parliamentary leaders to relieve Plymouth, not only from Wardlaw, Gould and Mayor Cawse, but also from the Earl of Warwick, who in a very short time would be promoted Lord High Admiral of England. On November 11th Warwick wrote to William Lenthall, declaring Plymouth's great importance and stating that it was parliament's only western port and its fall would prove fatal to the cause. Warwick was trying his utmost to raise a fleet with which he could force his way into Plymouth Sound through the small royalist blockading squadron under Sir John Pennington. Another who showed concern at this time was Colonel Ralph Weldon, an officer who one day would assume the governorship of Plymouth. Late in November, Weldon, then at Blackfriars, wrote to the House of Commons. Either from information received, or a brief visit at some time, Weldon declared that the Plymouth garrison had not seen full wages for many months and the troops there were in great need of relief.

Westminster responded as best it could, the recruiting of Colonel Sir Edward Harley's regiment, which was earmarked as reinforcements for Plymouth, was hurried along. With only half the number of men needed under arms, Sir William Waller was asked if he could spare 500 foot. Despite assurances that his troops would only be on loan to Plymouth, Waller refused, declaring he had no men to spare. Consequently on December 4th Harley's incomplete regiment was ordered on to Plymouth. The Earl of Warwick was to transport the reinforcements down to the Devon port and provide 200 barrels of powder. Much-needed money for the beleaguered garrison was also found at this time from the sequestered estate of the royalist Sir George Sandys. Further cash, available from imports and exports coming through customs was set aside for the use of Plymouth, Poole and Lyme Regis.

Those trapped behind Plymouth's walls were not the only people to suffer physical and mental hardship during the winter of 1643. Farmers in the South Hams found they were unable to send food into the garrison due to threats from Digby's troopers. These very same cavaliers would often swoop down on farms and commander horses, cattle and grain for their own army. Roving bands of royalists also alienated many people in south and west Devon by sudden acts of terrorism, not only against parliamentarians but also against neutrals. On November 18th Tavistock received one such visit, homes were pillaged and a number of innocents arrested and sent to the notorious Lydford gaol. As a consequence of these activities, Colonel Wardlaw and the people of Plymouth had to rely on limited supplies, stored in warehouses, and fish to sustain them.

During this time, John Syms, the ardent Puritan curate of Sheepstor, was forced to flee from his home. Crossing Dartmoor,

Syms hid in Brixton, not far from Plymouth; while on the run his home was ransacked and royalist patrols combed the South Hams seeking him out. With Brixton becoming too hot, Syms was forced to move on and he walked back across the moors and stayed with the Elford family at Longstone, across the valley from Sheepstor. John Syms had been a witness to Prince Maurice's hideous proclamation to round up all parliamentarians and requisition supplies. Now his own parishioners were forced to gather food and send it without payment to the royalist army besieging Plymouth.

Maurice the king's nephew, had been born on December 25th 1620 and was the third son of Fredrick V, elector palatine of the Rhine. Fleeing from their home in Prague in 1629 the family settled in Holland. At the age of seventeen Maurice and his brother Rupert joined the army of the Prince of Orange and learned the art of war. In 1637 Maurice went to study at a French university, where he stayed for two years before returning to Holland and the army. With war clouds descending over England, Maurice accompanied his brother Rupert across the Channel to fight for their uncle.

At the initial cavalry encounter at Powick Bridge on September 23rd 1642, the two royal princes fought together and gave a good account of themselves, though Maurice received a head wound during the fighting. In the following February, the pair again achieved success when they stormed Cirencester. A month later the brothers were split up and Maurice received orders to protect Gloucestershire and stop Waller from running amok. After achieving victory over his opponent at Ripple Field, Maurice was promoted lieutenant general, to serve under the incompetent Hertford. At Chewton Mendip, Maurice and Sir Ralph Hopton thrashed a parliamentary force on June 10th but Maurice suffered a second head wound.

At twenty-two Prince Maurice, much less gifted than his older brother Rupert, was both headstrong and cruel and many of the king's military advisors disliked his heartless persona. Maurice had picked up his brutal methods on the continent, where the ways of the soldier had etched themselves upon his young, receptive mind. During his campaigns as commander of the Western army, Maurice often betrayed those to whom he promised mercy, looting, rape and destruction were usually the order of the day, after offering mercy and protection of property for the surrender of a town or garrison. Such open infidelity hardened Plymouth's stance against the prince's often-believable overtures.

Maurice's odious proclamation was directed in part to the trained bandsmen and other so-called rebels within the town, and it commanded these very men to withdraw or *'Be called traitors and be persecuted with fire and sword'*. His dramatic words made no difference, the majority of ministers in southwest Devon refused to read the proclamation. Many were subsequently arrested, or like John Syms forced to flee from their homes. Despite royalist threats of retribution and the commandeering of all supplies, a small number of farmers still managed to smuggle supplies through the enemy lines to the hungry population. The weak royal naval blockade also failed to prevent parliamentary ships carrying provisions, money and occasionally reinforcements, from slipping through to Millbay.

Well aware that his efforts to starve Plymouth into submission were failing, Prince Maurice formulated plans for an attack against one of the key forts north of the town. Preceding the planned assault, Ellis Carkeet, a mariner serving as an artillerist in the Maudlyn Fort, was arrested for attempting to convert Roger Kneebone, the chief gunner of that work. Carkeet had spoken on several occasions to Kneebone and finally believed the time was ripe to make his move. Assuming from their intimate conversations that Kneebone was sympathetic to the king, Carkeet tried to convince him to blow up the powder magazine. Chief gunner Kneebone, a local man, whose family lived in the town, was a staunch parliamentarian and he immediately informed his superiors of the discussions between himself and Carkeet. Kneebone's action led to the seaman's immediate arrest and interrogation.

Like Kneebone, Ellis Carkeet was a local man, whose family also resided in Plymouth. Thirty-eight years old in 1643, Carkeet and his wife were expecting another child. What reason could have persuaded a man to turn his coat at such a time, the possibilities are too numerous; the recent fall of Fort Stamford, the poor conditions, dwindling rations, persuasion from royalists within the town, bribery or the strict Puritan code then in practice. Whatever the reason, Carkeet's endeavour to subvert such a man as Roger Kneebone failed miserably. The fact that as chief gunner of the Maudlyn Fort, the most important bastion on the outer line, Kneebone would have to be one of the most trusted of men, makes Carkeet's choice a bad one. He might have been more successful with a gunner from one of the other forts; fortunately for the town Carkeet made a bad judgment.

With Carkeet's seizure and imprisonment, two of his fellow conspirators, Moses Collins, attorney, and Henry Pike, vintner, fearing arrest, fled to the enemy. Once safe the two men passed over vital information on the layout of the town's defences to Prince Maurice. Pike, like Carkeet, was a Plymouth man, whose wife Susan had recently given birth to a son. It is difficult to comprehend why two local men should abandon their families at such a time and join those who might cause them harm. Prince Maurice quickly utilised the valuable intelligence given by Pike and Collins on Plymouth's outer defence system for his planned assault.

Dividing up their cannon into batteries, royalist engineers had positioned them in forts along the high ground above Lipson Creek. The five main royalist earthworks ran in a line almost opposite the town's northeastern works. One rose above Lipson Mill at a place called Crow Down, another known as 'The Mount' was built at Mannamead. The third was on Hill Crest, a fourth stood behind Hyde Park Terrace and the fifth was on Mutley Plain itself, between what is today Belgrave Road and Ford Park lane, directly in front of Maudlyn Fort. Satisfied with the arrangements, Prince Maurice opened the ball on November 28th with a preliminary long-range artillery bombardment, concentrated mainly against the Lipson Fort. For several days gunners on both sides sent roundshot arching over Lipson Creek, but little damage was done to the earthworks, the wet soft soil simply soaked up the huge cannonballs.

The royalists kept up their cannonade for three days, hoping to use it as a screen to push infantry across Lipson Creek and onto the south bank. Fortunately the engineers who built Plymouth's defences had chosen the best ground. The space between Lipson Fort and the creek was precipitous and overgrown and in the winter very wet and slippery. Even now, with modern roads the route up from Lipson Creek (Alexandra Road) is still steep and simply walking up it is tiring. Unable to force a crossing, Prince Maurice decided upon an attack against one of the other forts further to the east, which would divert the defenders' attention away from Lipson Fort. If all went to plan a large royalist force would cross the creek lower down where the ground south of the creek was less precipitous.

The early hours of Sunday December 3rd were extremely raw and a bitterly-cold wind whipped up Lipson Vale. The few roundheads on guard at Laira Point Work, the easternmost fortification on the outer line, stamped their feet to keep warm. As a consequence the pickets were not as alert as they should have been. Across the creek to the north, hidden by the night, the turncoats, Henry Pike and Moses Collins, guided 400 royalist musketeers down from Compton, this was to be Maurice's diversionary column. Silently the cavaliers assembled under their officers at the waters edge before being led across Lipson Creek. Unfortunately for the roundheads the enemy had chosen well, as the tide was right out allowing easy access across the stream at this point. Pike and Collins had no trouble leading the raiders over to the south bank and with the exception of the deeper middle channel, the crossing went as planned. Once on dry land the royalists moved quietly around the shoreline of the Plym below the Laira Point Work so as to come in behind the unwary lookouts.

Laira Point was a small, new earthwork, mounting three cannon and guarded by a detachment of musketeers. Its strategic position allowed the parliamentarians to observe enemy movements on the east bank of the Plym and to the north of Lipson Creek. Unfortunately the night was dark and the sentinels careless, they were totally unprepared for what was about to happen. Suddenly out of the darkness the royalists swept up the rocks and engulfed the little earthwork from almost every side at once. The inadequate, somnolent garrison was quickly overwhelmed and captured along with all three cannon, before any resistance could be organised. One of the parliamentarians did manage to fire a warning shot and while the cavaliers wasted time wondering what to do next, Plymouth hurriedly prepared a task force to retake the lost fort at first light. Three hours after its loss, 450 horse and foot had been assembled for the reconquest of the Laira Point Work. Several parliamentary merchant ships anchored in the Plym close to Laira Point with orders to drop supplies off at the fort, now found themselves in a precarious position. The captains were offered the chance to surrender their vessels or be blown out of the water by cannon fire. The captains agreed to talk over the royalist offer and negotiate.

During the Pike-Collins raid, Prince Maurice held the bulk of his army ready near the village of Compton. When news came in that the Laira Point Work had been secured, the prince ordered a second, much larger force down the slope towards a position close to Lipson Creek. Here an extensive hedge provided ample cover for the royalist officers to muster their units in safety. Perhaps as many as 2,000 men were to take part in the assault; mainly foot with a detachment of horse. Rather than risk a night fight, which could end in disaster, Prince Maurice waited until dawn to give the order to advance.

As the first streaks of daylight broke through the cold December night, one of the royalists' cannon at Fort Stamford fired a warning shot. Lookouts there had spotted a column from Plymouth moving along Tothill Ridge towards Laira Point Work undetected by the cavaliers now occupying that place. The signal was misunderstood, but it also came too late, the main advance across Lipson Creek had began. Royalist banners fluttered briskly in the cold breeze as drummers beat the troop, a call to move forward into action. Shortly after the shot from Fort Stamford and while Maurice's principal force struggled across Lipson Creek, the concealed roundheads on Tothill Ridge loomed up in front of Laira Point Work and counterattacked.

The roundhead commander sent in his horse first, 150 of them under Captain John Wansey, a veteran officer who had fought at Lansdown and Roundway. The fighting was fierce and for a time the issue hung in the balance as both forces were evenly matched, but the determination of the Plymouth men gave them a fighting edge. As luck would have it, the left hook of Maurice's main body, which had crossed the creek, saw their comrades in trouble and sloped off to help. Captain Wansey led a charge right into the cavalier line; waving his sword above his head, this noble officer was shot from his horse and killed. The fighting continued and the reinforced royalists gradually pushed back the gallant roundheads. Unable to recapture the fort and greatly outnumbered, the Plymouth men found themselves counterattacked. Added to the untimely death of Captain Wansey, this proved too much for them and they broke. The cavalry rode away, and the foot dropped their muskets and fled westwards across three fields towards the main Lipson Fort.

This great redoubt rose up on the western end of Mount Gould Road to the east of Freedom Park, where the garrison watched as survivors from Laira Point Work withdrew in their direction. With the parliamentary retreat, a small detachment of royalist horse, inspired by their own success, rode down toward the inner line of defences. Here they came face to face with the stone ramparts of Resolution Fort and here they were blasted back. After a brief exchange with the soldiers manning the walls, the frustrated horsemen disappeared as quickly as they had come.

Meanwhile those roundheads who retreated to the Lipson Work now used this bastion to rally. With the refugees from Laira Point, a new line was formed under the supervision of Colonel William Gould, who had arrived shortly before and remained relatively composed considering the threat. Observing the disaster to his right flank, Gould had previously sent riders off to the forts on his left and down to the town in search of reinforcements. To prevent the garrison from concentrating a substantial force, Prince Maurice threw weak diversionary attacks against the other forts on the line. Royalist artillery also opened fire on Maudlyn and Holywell. Under manned and under pressure themselves, these redoubts could spare very few troops, but when grouped together with the survivors from Laira Point and a detachment sent up from the town Colonel Gould had amassed between 1,000-1,500 men.

By the capture of Laira Point, and their subsequent movement westwards toward the very walls of Lipson Fort, the royalists had effectively punched a large hole through the outer defence line. Now with more troops crossing Lipson Creek and joining those advancing from the east, Prince Maurice held a tremendous advantage. All he needed to do was press the attack, overrun Lipson and roll up the rest of the line; victory was within Maurice's grasp. Unfortunately for the king's army, all that followed was delay and ineptitude. The sight of Gould's new line, running down away from Lipson Fort, the cannon on the ramparts and the incoming tide sweeping back into the creek behind them were crucial factors that may have forced the royal commanders to hesitate. Their vacillation gave the defenders sufficient time to bring up a few more troops and to arrange for a separate detachment to march up from the inner works and come in behind the enemy.

The longer the two sides faced each other, the more advantage the defenders gained, and the more discouraged the royalists became. After several half-hearted attacks by the cavaliers were easily repulsed, a drummer approached Gould's line with a demand for surrender. Colonel Gould and his subordinates scorned the offer and the man was sent away with a cannonball over his head. Now 200 musketeers of the town's trained bands arrived, these were the companies of Philip Francis, Christopher Martyn and Richard Evans. Their timely arrival provided a great boost to the troops already on the line. A small drake was also wheeled up to a crossroads at this time, and when the piece began firing at the enemy its uncanny accuracy caused havoc amongst the royalist horse. Unable to bring their own artillery across the muddy river, the cavaliers could not respond to the drake's fire. With all attention focused on Lipson Fort, the detachment of roundhead musketeers moving up by a circuitous route to come in on the royalist left rear flank continued undetected.

Aware of the flanking manoeuvre, Colonel Gould waited until a suitable passage of time had been allowed for this detachment to get into position, before making his move. Considering the size and composition of his force, William Gould finally ordered a counterattack, which was to be carried out by every available man. As drummers began beating the charge the parliamentary foot bounded toward the astonished cavaliers, yelling 'God is with us!' Roundhead and royalist clashed in the muddy fields east of Lipson Fort; musket, pike and sword were brought down hard, fracturing bone, tearing flesh and splintering weapons. Horses and men fell screaming and dying on the cold, wet grass. In the thickest part of the fight, Colonel Gould was thrown to the ground when his horse was killed. Helped to his feet, an aide brought him a fresh mount, but in a short time this animal was also hit but not killed, allowing Gould to remain mounted.

Minutes after William Gould launched his counterattack, the sixty-man flanking detachment appeared behind the enemy left wing and opened a devastating fire into their backs. This unexpected attack caused immediate panic and a number of royalists broke. Hit simultaneously from two directions and confused by their own leaders' lack of aggression, the cavalier line buckled. First individually, then in groups and soon by the hundred, the disheartened royalists began to break and run for safety. A number of officers called for a general retreat; the signal was given but there was to be no organised withdrawal. Despite a previously-devised plan for just such an emergency, the distressed cavaliers fled pell-mell, slipping and falling down the ridge toward Lipson Creek. Unfortunately while the royalists were dithering about east of Lipson Fort, the tide had turned and Lipson Creek was now full of water.

As the royalist horse and foot slithered down the muddy, bloody slope, Colonel Gould's victorious troops followed in their wake. With no structured rearguard, the roundheads had ample time to set up their muskets and fire down on the enemy milling about in the valley below. The gunners in Lipson Fort compounded their torment by lobbing roundshot over their heads. Many royalists were killed attempting to swim across the creek, others were dragged to the bottom by heavy equipment, or died on the riverbank.

Meanwhile the captains of the parliamentary ships anchored off the Laira Point Work, were locked in prolonged consultation with royalist officers concerning the possible surrender of their vessels. Unaware of the disaster off to the west, the small detachment of cavaliers holding the fort listened with keen interest to the sounds of battle. Suddenly word filtered in of disaster, defeat and retreat, the soldiers in Laira Point fearing capture abandoned the work and made their way down to the creek. All communication between the ships' captains and the royalists now ceased. With the threat of being sandwiched between two fires, one from Fort Stamford and the other from the captured cannon in Laira Point Work, gone, the ships moved closer to the mouth of Lipson Creek. Here they anchored and fired their guns up the valley, adding to the chaos and confusion of the royalist retreat.

On the field a belated mounted rearguard was hurriedly assembled by those royalists still fighting, but it was quickly isolated from the retreating army, forced eastward and pursued down to the deepest part of the creek. Here many of the more heavily-armoured drowned in the muddy waters or surrendered. With the rearguard defeated, the Sabbath day battle, or Sunday fight, came to an end, it had been a close run thing, but ended in final victory for the gallant defenders. With the fighting over both sides gathered up their casualties and glowered at each other across Lipson Valley.

After a promising start, Prince Maurice's subordinates had called a halt and prudence replaced speed; a decision that passed the initiative over to the parliamentarians. Had the royalists moved with more purpose and coordination they could have overwhelmed the outnumbered defenders and ruptured Plymouth's outer line. With Lipson eliminated, the forts to the west would have been outflanked and the town's surrender less than a week away. Colonel Gould on the other hand displayed dazzling leadership ability, considering less than a year before he commanded only a troop of cavalry. William Gould took his place beside his men, refused to panic, organised reinforcements and showed such an aggressive front that the enemy was thrown completely off balance. At the opportune moment Gould counterattacked with such ferocity that the enemy could not stand.

Hit from two sides the cavaliers broke and fled from the field.

Names of roundhead officers who fought at the battle are difficult to find, but on the following brief list some or maybe all took some part in the fight: Sir Shilston Calmady, Philip Francis, Richard Evans, Christopher Martyn, Henry Hatsell, another militia captain. Major Michael Searle, only recently promoted, would rise to lieutenant colonel before the month was over for his intrepid service. Captain Henry Northcote, Captain John Wansey and many others also played their part. Of the hundreds of ordinary soldiers who fought to save the day most are lost to history, however a few names have been found.

All told twelve parliamentarians were reportedly killed on the field, 100 more were wounded, many of whom died later, and forty captured. The majority of those taken were captured at the fighting around the Laira Point Work and included Captain Lieutenant Richard Row, Lieutenant Nicholas Upton and ensigns Crocker and Francis Rolle. The greatest loss was that of Captain John Wansey, who was buried in St Andrew's Churchyard on December 7th. Interred alongside their intrepid captain were six other troopers who perished on the day: William Burgess, Thomas Frank, Richard Green, Oliver Mathews, John Worth and Bernard Warne. The majority of the dead from both armies were laid to rest in pits somewhere behind the outer line. One poor soul who ended up here was a soldier named Michael Bloye, killed on the field, leaving his wife Elizabeth and three children to endure a harsh future.

Of the wounded, one, a trooper named Samuel Caswell, lingered in pain until December 22nd when death finally brought him peace. Another, George Gibbs from Holsworthy, serving in Captain Thomas Halsey's troop, was shot in the shoulder. Gibbs survived primitive surgery and later rejoined his command. Another who lived to tell the tale was Walter Morrell, a Plymouth mariner who was so badly wounded during the fighting that he lost his right arm. Royalist losses were far greater; 300 killed and wounded were reported and thirty-two captured. Colonel Gould's men also picked up hundreds of assorted weapons that lay strewn across the fields, thirteen barrels of powder and two teams of horses to be used for hauling away captured artillery. As a reward for their efforts the town sent barrels of beer out to the brave defenders. Major Searle gave his troops a bonus for their gallant conduct throughout the battle. Mayor Cawse, overcome by the occasion, announced gloriously *'The Lord showed himself wonderfully in our deliverance'.*

Shortly after the Sabbath day fight, Mr Sampson Hele, whose son was in Plymouth fighting for parliament, came to the outworks with a surrender demand from the prince. Arriving without the customary trumpeter or drummer, Hele was verbally abused and threatened to such an extent that he was persuaded to promise to pay a large sum of money towards the clothing of the garrison. Upon receipt of Mr Hele's guarantee he was released.

An interesting sideline, which could be connected to the battle, took place on December 14th and 15th when two entries in St Andrew's register read: *'Walter Pike and Richard Reede, trooper, slain'.*[13]

One or both of these men may have been in league with Moses Collins and Henry Pike, if so were they convicted of treason. Pike more than likely was a relative to Henry Pike, as for Reede he may have been one of the sentinels on duty at Laira Point and turned a blind eye when the enemy attacked. On the other hand both may have been innocent and in the post-battle frenzy, when the fear of treachery rose again, could have been used as scapegoats and executed as examples. Sedition within the town was being treated with a hard hand during December; before the month was out two other men, William Skynner and Thomas Sellar would be taken out and executed.

Despite the harshness of close-contact warfare, the siege of Plymouth was not all death and deprivation, the town did witness the occasional tender moment during those dark days of December 1643. On Sunday December 10th, a week after the Sabbath day fight, a crowd gathered in St Andrew's Church to bear witness approvingly as Captain Thomas Halsey married Joane Harris. Halsey, thus became one of only two officers to wed in St Andrew's during the war, the second was Captain Mathew Cousins, who would lead Elizabeth Doltson into St Andrew's on October 7 1645. Halsey, one of the many unsung heroes to emerge, had previously fought at Lansdowne and Roundway under Waller, before being shipped to Plymouth with his troop back in September 1643. As Thomas Halsey and his bride took their vows, the cannonading from the outer line could be heard in the distance, but its significance failed to spoil their day.

During the early hours of December 13th a mixed bag of royalist foot and horse congregated, the infantry were from Colonel Bullen

Reyme's regiment, the 200 cavalry from Colonel John Digby's horse. Before daybreak this detachment marched down Compton Hill towards Lipson Creek. Crossing over they struck a new demi-fort named Lipson Mill Work, which had been thrown up on the steep ground below Lipson Fort to watch for enemy units crossing the creek and to prevent a surprise attack. The determined assault was greatly aided by darkness, but the defenders were up to the task and they threw back the attack with great conviction. Being so close to Lipson Creek this new fort would be considered more of a hindrance to the roundheads than a help, and it would later be abandoned and flattened. It was probably at this fight that Captain James Anderson, one of Wardlaw's officers, was killed. Anderson had previously served in Sir John Merrick's regiment, fought at Exeter and made his way to Plymouth, where he joined the garrison; his death was a sad loss.

Following the royalist failure to capture Lipson Fort, the Plymouth defence committee ordered the Maudlyn Fort to be strengthened. Colonel Gould expected Prince Maurice to hit this important bastion at some stage during the siege, especially since Ellis Carkeet's discovered treachery and the fact that one of the enemy earthworks had been thrown up less than half a mile from its northern wall. In obedience Maudlyn's earthen walls were thickened and as an added deterrent a demi-culverin, which had been captured on a ship en route to Ireland was earmarked for Maudlyn. This huge cannon had been brought into Plymouth at just the right time. Unloaded, the culverin was hauled up North Hill by oxen and placed on a specially-built platform close to the pivotal fort. A number of volunteers were needed to help draw the cannon up the steep slope and Quartermaster Richard Clapp was forced to pay out 10s 6d for the transportation of the gun.[14]

On the morning of Monday December 18th, royalist gunners suddenly opened up a determined bombardment, concentrating their ordnance mainly against the Maudlyn Fort. The defending artillerists, having the advantage of higher ground, returned the compliment with equal tenacity. This counter battery fire was aimed at the royalist's most forward fortification, which stood on Mutley Plain itself, close to where Ford Park Road joins the ridge, and it proved highly effective. Roundhead gunners lobbed their shot right into the royalist earthwork, causing the cavaliers to abandon their guns and seek shelter. The artillery duel continued until Wednesday evening, when the firing finally died away.

Throughout the siege, the women of Plymouth carried beer and other provisions up to the front line to relieve the defenders. Occasionally they were fired upon and several found bullet holes in their clothing, but they refused to stop their errands of mercy.

During the night of the 29th a detachment of enemy musketeers, numbering around 200, left the safety of their own lines and stealthily made their way across the Maudlyn Ridge, using hedges as cover wherever possible. Silently this cautious column headed down into Houndiscombe Woods and up to an open field less than several hundreds yards from the main roundhead line and so sited that it was almost between the Maudlyn Fort and the Pennycomequick Work off to the west. In a corner of the field the cavaliers quickly set to work, digging the cold, wet soil and throwing up a crude earthwork. These trespassers were aided in their work by heavy rain, darkness and the carelessness of the officer commanding the roundhead guards.

When dawn broke on the morning of December 21st the surprise on the faces of the Maudlyn lookouts must have been exceeded only by their disbelief. This new, intrusive cavalier outpost was so close to the parliamentary line that it threatened communications between two of their major forts. Time was now the most important factor for the defenders. Colonel Gould would have to oust these royalist squatters before they had time to capitalise on their initial gains.

Within minutes sixty soldiers, mostly from the Maudlyn garrison, had been assembled and were sent against the royalist position. A fair amount of self-esteem was at stake here, as the garrison troops wanted very much to redeem themselves. Being totally inadequate for the task at hand the preliminary attack although heroic, was doomed to failure. The assault by the outnumbered Maudlyn detachment was thrown back easily and rather than risk annihilation, it was sensibly decided to await reinforcements.

Several nerve-racking hours came and went, during which time nothing happened. Colonel Gould concluded that Prince Maurice was not going to support his forward detachment. Despite its vulnerable position, the new royalist earthwork was a considerable threat to the garrison. Satisfied that Prince Maurice's inertia had doomed his isolated garrison, Gould collected every soldier that could be spared from less endangered points. By 9 a.m. the roundhead commander had managed to bring together a substantial force of horse and foot and he now lined them up ready to counterattack. The second parliamentarian assault went in shortly after nine, and by sheer weight of numbers the roundheads were able to secure a foothold in the enemy earthwork. Unfortunately the defenders were as determined to hold their piece of property and a counter-assault quickly ejected the parliamentarians.

A third attack ended in similar fashion, with the assailants thrown back by heavy fire and vicious hand-to-hand combat. Colonel Gould however was resolute in his strategy, he did not want the enemy squatting right under his nose, so he prepared a forth column of attack. Using fresh troops, Gould urged the men forward. This time the royalists, weary and short of ammunition, were unable to stem the tide and within minutes they had been overwhelmed. Roundhead soldiers poured over the sodden mud walls and smashed into the exhausted defenders. Hand-to-hand fighting exploded all over the little fort and the butt end of the musket became the favoured weapon as men charged forward and ripped each other apart for half an acre of nothing. Finally, when the smoke cleared and the shouting died away it was all over. The surviving cavaliers abandoned their fort and withdrew into the cover of the woods, from where they made their way back to their own lines.

The victorious roundheads now demolished the outpost in order to prevent the enemy sneaking back and reoccupying the place. In the New Year the defenders would erect a demi-fort on slightly rising ground northwest of the main Maudlyn Fort in order to prevent the cavaliers from repeating their manoeuvre. The fighting had once again been hard, as is attested by the day's casualties. Twenty parliamentarians were dead, amongst them Ensign Ferdinando Grimes, who was buried on the 23rd. The wounded totalled sixty, the majority of whom recovered to fight another day. A second ensign, Samuel Hart, was badly wounded; he lingered until January before dying and was finally laid to rest on the 9th. The royalists had captured half a dozen prisoners, a Lieutenant William Harwar amongst them. Harwar and two of his men were surrounded by the enemy during one of the earlier assaults and captured. Prince Maurice lost 100 men killed, wounded or captured during the badly-executed venture, his own trumpeter being among the prisoners.

After the engagement, parliamentary officers found great difficulty in restraining their elated troops, many were eager to press on along Maudlyn Ridge to attack the enemy artillery. Fortunately they were quickly brought to their senses. For the royalists, the stagnant outer line surrounding Plymouth must have looked unbreakable. Despite a shortage of manpower, ammunition, and food for the defenders, the siege was not progressing well at all. A full major assault had ended in failure and an attempt to cut communications between Maudlyn and Pennycomequick proved equally disastrous, mainly because the initial assaulting party had not been supported properly. The royalist artillery could not batter the earth forts into submission, and even treachery had failed to achieve an advantage for the prince.

The day following the unsuccessful royalist thrust between Maudlyn and Pennycomequick, the roundheads awoke to find the enemy withdrawing artillery from their forts. Three days later, on Christmas Day, the siege was lifted, on the very day Prince Maurice promised his army would be in Plymouth, not a good birthday present for his royal highness. Dejected by the town's defiance, disease which had broken out within his own dirty encampments and most of all by a lack of sufficiently heavy siege guns and ammunition the prince decided to abandon his positions and depart. Several weeks before leaving, Maurice had written to Sir Edward Seymour, Governor of Dartmouth, requesting guns and ammunition. When they failed to materialise the prince sent further communications demanding the guns, and asking Seymour to send them down with all speed. Sir Edward failed to comply and when the guns did not arrive the end of the siege was imminent. The royalist commander pulled his army back towards Tavistock in order to rest and reorganise his command, ready for another attempt against Plymouth in the spring.

Before leaving the area Maurice did two things, first he issued a warrant to the constables of Eggbuckland and St Budeaux, threatening prosecution to any persons sending cattle, provisions or manpower to aid in the rebellion. Secondly he commissioned Sir Edmund Fortescue to rebuild the fortifications at Salcombe and occupy the tiny port for the king. After his exchange Fortescue had returned to Devon and on the 9th of December he received his commission from the prince; Fortescue would perform his duty to the best of his ability. To prevent supplies reaching Plymouth from the South Hams and continue a partial blockade of Sutton Pool, Prince Maurice left Colonel John Digby in the area with a small command. Lacking sufficient men and materials, Digby could not hold the extensive royalists' works north of the town, so he set up headquarters at Plympton and kept most of his troops on the east bank of the Plym between the Longbridge over the marshes, near Plympton and Fort Stamford.

As a parting shot Major General Sir Thomas Bassett, commanding Sir Nicholas Slanning's old regiment, called out to one of the parliamentary officers who was observing the royalists dismantling their forts. Bassett shouted across that God had fought against his cause and if he could be convinced that he was on the wrong side, he would hang himself to save taking up arms again in such a quarrel. The close siege of Plymouth was over for the time, but the army brought down by Prince Maurice had used up a considerable amount of cattle and forage from the area north and east of the town. With a lack of sustenance the townsfolk and garrison were forced to tighten their belts and rely on supplies coming in by ship. Having withdrawn as far as Tavistock the cavaliers settled down and remained there for a considerable time before receiving fresh orders to pack up and march eastward. During his brief tenure at Tavistock Maurice was promoted to command all royalist troops south of the Thames, consequently in the New Year he left a number of sick soldiers in Tavistock and led the rest of his army across the moors towards the Dorset border.

For a while speculation abounded in London that Plymouth had succumbed to the royalist siege, but as with so many rumours throughout history it proved to be no more than hearsay, but it could so easily have been true. The day after the royalist departure, December 26th, parts of two of the main earthworks collapsed due to heavy rain and freezing weather, an incident that may have proved disastrous had it happened during the fighting. With the enemy gone the existing forts were now rebuilt and reinforced, thick hedges between the lines were dug up and the old cavalier earthworks levelled. Extra cannon were transferred from the sea defences to the outer line to replace worn out ones. Troops who had stood guard were rested, their uniforms and weapons repaired and ammunition stores replenished. Skirmishing between opposing units out on patrol flared up again in the area between Plymouth and Buckland, where the royalists had established an outpost.

The biggest killer of the war was not the cannon nor the musket, but disease; the plague that ran riot in Maurice's camps also played havoc with the defenders and took a great toll of both armies. With the leat cut and little fresh water or food coming into the town sickness multiplied and deaths increased. Burials in St Andrew's for December alone totalled 107, almost five times the normal quota. This figure exceeded December 1642 by forty and December 1641 by ninety-two. Amongst the internments for the month were sixteen troopers, not all however were victims of the plague, many had succumbed to primitive surgery. Hundreds of soldiers who died from all causes were buried in pits close to the forts, therefore the true death rate for December 1643 is much higher and will never be known. Counting those killed in the battles around Lipson and Maudlyn, compounded with others who died from disease, the total for the month must be closer to 400.

Plympton and Tavistock also suffered greatly from the effects of typhus at this time. Amongst the burials registered in St Mary's are a number of cavaliers; civilian and military. The royalists who arrived after the surrender of Dartmouth had carried the disease with them. Once settled in camps, bad wintry weather, inadequate clothing and unhealthy sanitation helped knock out hundreds of soldiers. Even Plymstock suffered, forty persons, including soldiers, were laid to rest in the little cemetery during December 1643. Refugees and prisoners arriving from Dartmouth before its surrender helped typhus establish itself in the port, while royalists captured during the siege and interred in the town's overcrowded gaols facilitated the spread of the disease and people died at an alarming rate. Entire families were killed through disease during the war years, small children being the most vulnerable. St Andrew's records many instances where the mother would follow her children to the grave, sometimes on the same day. With prisoner exchanges slow and disorganised many captives perished. Of those who survived, a fair proportion never fully recovered and when released, a high proportion hobbled back to their homes, never to fight again.

One day, so the story goes, a sudden influx of pilchards into Sutton harbour gave Plymouth an ample supply of fresh fish, staved off starvation and saved the town. Whether this is true or just another rumour will never be known. The reality was that the two plague-infested months of November and December saw upwards of over 600 soldiers and civilians from both sides die in and around the town. The war was beginning to take on a more sinister and terrifying aspect for everyone. It was not only siege and disease that were harassing the local population, royalist privateers and the blockade were ruining the town's economy. As for her fishing industry that had almost disappeared completely. Plymouth however survived and unlike many towns its defenders had cracked the enemy ring and forced the besieging forces to retreat, but the war was far from over.

The year 1643 proved a highly active year for Plymouth and her people, several sieges had taken place and many small, vicious battles. Numerous acts of treason had also appeared and been stamped out. Across the rest of Britain the year began with the prospect of peace, but the king's arrogance and parliament's unreasonable demands spoilt any hopes of a settlement. Both sides saw success and failure in Yorkshire, Lancashire and the Midlands. Oliver Cromwell was winning in East Anglia, while George Goring was back as a royalist and beating Sir Thomas Fairfax on Seacroft Moor. Sir Hugh Chomley followed Goring's example and changed loyalties, turning Scarborough over to the king without a fight. During the summer the royalists were beginning to gain the upper hand after the Earl of Newcastle badly mauled Sir Thomas Fairfax at Adwalton Moor on June 30th.

Meanwhile in the south, the Earl of Essex, having captured Reading manoeuvred leisurely towards Oxford, but he was forced to abandon his half-hearted attempt at besieging the king's capital when Prince Rupert struck at Chalgrove Field on June 18th. Due to the success of Sir Ralph Hopton's little army at Lansdowne, Roundway and Devizes, Rupert joined his brother and Hopton and the three combined their talents against Bristol. This vital port surrendered on July 26th. Lincolnshire also felt the wrath of the royalists, and by the middle of August the Earl of Newcastle had taken Gainsborough and Lincoln, as well as many smaller towns.

With such victories under their belts the king's advisors should have voted for a march on London; Rupert wished it so, but his tactical advice was ignored and Charles chose to attack Gloucester instead. Consequently the cavaliers arrived outside the town on August 10th and demanded its surrender, but Gloucester refused and the royalists brought up their heavy ordnance. As the weeks wore on with nothing gained, the king was suddenly shocked to learn of a large relieving force on its way to Gloucester under the Earl of Essex. When the roundheads reached the Severn, not far from Gloucester, the royal army packed up and left. Now the king was handed another perfect opportunity to march on London. Most of the capital's trained bandsmen were with Essex, and if he could move quickly, Charles Stuart would soon be in a position to sweep away the few defenders and enter his capital before Essex could react. To hold back the earl, Prince Rupert's cavalry would use hit-and-run tactics.

Fortunately for parliament nothing went right for the king, at first he managed to keep ahead of the roundheads but took far too long marching across country. Arriving at Newbury on September 19th, the cavaliers, weary after almost two weeks of constant marches, were attacked the next day by Essex. A bitter engagement followed which lasted from seven in the morning until seven at night, seesawing backwards and forwards. The fighting finally ended in a stalemate, but with little gunpowder left in the royal supply, King Charles was forced to step aside and withdraw towards Oxford, leaving Essex to march home. By poor advice and a tardy advance, the king had lost his second opportunity to capture London. As the royalists pondered on what might have been, parliament was forming an alliance that would bring thousands of Scottish soldiers in on their side. These reinforcements would soon be operating against the Earl of Newcastle's army in the north of England; the tide of war was beginning to turn against the king.

Although the year had ended well for the royalists, the future looked far brighter for parliament. Sadly John Pym would not live to see success, for on December 8th the great statesman passed away. He died it was reported of an internal abscess, cancer killed him. Pym's body remained in state at Derby House, where people were permitted to look in and see him, then on the 15th he was interred with great ceremony in Westminster Abbey. Attending the funeral were Pym's two sons, Alexander and Charles, and the members of both Houses, ten of whom acted as pallbearers, one of which was Pym's good friend Mr William Strode.

Notes

(11) Page 143: Excerpt taken from, the copie of a letter sent from the commander in chiefe of the town and port of Plymouth, to the honourable William Lenthall, Esq. Speaker of the House of Commons, concerning the late, great fight at Mount Stanford. Thomason Tracts E.76 (11); by kind permission of the British Library.
(12) Page 144: A true narration of the late siege of Plymouth from the 15th day of September 1643 until the 25th of December, Thomason Tracts E.31 (15); by kind permission of the British Library.
(13) Page 156: St Andrew's Church burials, West Devon Record Office, Plymouth.
(14) Page 157: State Papers 28/128 PT2, National Archives, London; by kind permission of the National Archives London.

Chapter 8

Colonel Gould's Ascendancy

Early in January 1644 Colonel James Wardlaw resigned his position as Governor of Plymouth. Constant bickering between civic and military authorities within the town and recurring illness picked up during the siege, forced Wardlaw to this decision. Colonel Wardlaw's post was quickly taken over by Colonel William Gould, who since January 1st held the title of Parliamentary High Sheriff for the county of Devon. On the 22nd of the month Gould also took on the additional responsibility of St Nicholas Island and Plymouth Fort. Despite his resignation, upon Wardlaw's official replacement by Gould, the former governor complained bitterly to parliament and a progressive bad feeling developed between two men, who had worked so well together.

For Wardlaw it was too late, a letter written by him in February and sent to the lord general was handed over to the committee for Plymouth, Poole and Lyme. In his dispatch Wardlaw explained the differences existing between him and Colonel Gould, nothing changed and James Wardlaw would eventually disappear from the scene. Wardlaw was not the only person to object to Gould's appointment. Others less able to take on such a responsible task, also felt slighted and jealous of Gould's promotion, none of this made any difference, William Gould remained in command.

Governor Gould's first priority upon taking office was to strengthen Plymouth's fortifications. Although Digby's undersized army still manned their cannon along the east bank of the Plym, it was not strong enough to completely invest the town or launch a major assault despite a small reinforcement, which arrived in late

December. Subsequently Colonel Gould was given the breathing space he needed and he used the time to completely flatten the remaining enemy earthworks north of the town. Hedges that could have been used to conceal a royalist force, such as those along Lipson Creek, were pulled down and foragers were sent out to gather sustenance and wood from an area already stripped bare by Prince Maurice.

William Gould, a passionate Puritan, having set his mind to protecting Plymouth now endeavoured to purge the garrison of drunkenness, swearing and licentious behaviour. Sundays were to be given over to the Lord and soldiers were advised, but not ordered, to attend divine services. The numerous clergymen in Plymouth at this time are evidence of the sway Puritanism held over the population. Many church ministers from outlying communities had been compelled to leave their own parishes by royalist depredations; with the rest of Devon under cavalier control Plymouth remained the only haven open for them. Men such as Stephen Midhope, Francis Porter, Christopher Lawrie, John Wills, George Shugge, and Mr Randall found themselves without a church, and took to walking amongst the soldiers in the various forts around the town ministering to their needs. One man, Abraham Cheare, a trained bandsman, was elected Chaplain of Plymouth Fort without his knowledge. Cheare disliked his new position, as it took him away from the military life, consequently he discharged himself and assumed his post in the fort.

To keep Plymouth and her defenders alert and to remind them that war was but a stone's throw away, John Digby's gunners periodically lobbed cannonballs into the town. Those cannoneers manning the guns in Plymouth Fort returned the enemy fire, but little damage was done to either side due to the range and quality of powder. The navy usually suffered the most, with enemy batteries in strong positions at Fort Stamford and Mount Edgcumbe, any shipping sailing into the sound had to run a gauntlet of iron and stone before anchoring safely in Millbay.

In mid-January two ships, the *Swallow* and *Leaper* arrived in Millbay from Deal, with part of Colonel Sir Edward Harley's regiment on board as reinforcements for the garrison. The journey had not gone well for these new troops; near the Isle of Wight bad weather forced the ships to turn back. Eventually the two vessels set sail again and this time completed the trip. One of the company commanders, Captain Francis Hakluyt, wrote to Harley in London complaining of the inadequate conditions aboard and asked his commanding officer to instruct the Plymouth defence committee to supply his troops with clothing and other necessities. Upon disembarking at Plymouth Harley's companies were not immediately assigned to a specific unit, which caused another captain, Thomas Rea, to protest. In his letter Rea, also informed Harley that the Cornish royalists were raising new forces with which to subdue Plymouth.

During this relatively inactive period, Colonel Sir Francis Drake took leave of his regiment, not that he was actively involved with the Plymouth horse much before this time. Recently King Charles, possibly at the instigation of Drake's uncle Sir George Chudleigh, offered Sir Francis a royal pardon, hoping to entice him away from parliament. Drake declined the offer and remained true to the cause. Riding to London, Sir Francis Drake met up with his friend Charles Pym, son of the deceased statesman John Pym. Both men put their signatures to the Solemn League and Covenant, a document proclaiming preservation of parliament and king, as well as Presbyterianism and religious reforms. The covenant also affirmed to maintain the unity of England, Scotland and Ireland. The Solemn League and Covenant was a document to be signed by all parliamentary officers by order of Westminster, no matter what their individual beliefs were.

Fighting for the New Year began in earnest on January 26th when a party of royalist horse from Plympton and Buckland, both substantial royalist outposts, skirmished with detachments of Gould's foragers. Later Captain Thomas Halsey rode out of Plymouth towards Tamerton, six miles away and attacked a small body of enemy horse camped close by the creek. Halsey easily routed the cavaliers, capturing nine troopers with their horses and arms. Captain Halsey's men broke up the encampment and rode back to town. A month later, on February 24th, Captain Lieutenant John Chaffin, a Dorsetshire soldier rode out of Plymouth with part of Captain Halsey's troop and headed north. Reaching Trennimans Jump Chaffin surprised the royalist guard, who broke almost immediately and fled over the moors towards Tavistock. During the brief pursuit the roundheads killed several of the enemy and captured three officers and seven troopers. The chase continued for more than a mile before Chaffin called a halt and withdrew, having suffered only two men wounded.

A second encounter at Trennimans Jump took place on March 15th, in which one of Colonel Gould's men was captured during a reconnaissance near the village. When news of this incident reached Plymouth, newly-promoted Major Halsey once again rode out at the head of his cavalry. Almost simultaneously a body of cavalier horse was on its way from Trennimans towards Knackersknowle. These two opposing forces collided somewhere in-between and Major Halsey, the first to react, ordered a charge. This manoeuvre took the royalists completely by surprise, and after brief resistance they fled back the way they came and took shelter in their guardhouse. Halsey kept up the momentum and attacked the guardhouse, overwhelming the place, killing three men and capturing six others. Having released their own man, Halsey's troop rode back to town with prisoners, horses, nine muskets and two drums.

Late in February the committee for both kingdoms (England and Scotland) ordered Sir John Bampfield and Mr Edmund Prideaux to report to London on the situation in Devon. Cavaliers had plundered Prideaux's home and his wife and children had been forced to flee to London. Bampfield's House at Warleigh had also been looted and was being used by the enemy as an outpost. As a consequence Sir Edmund was compelled to live on money sequestered from royalist estates. Both Prideaux and Bampfield obeyed the summons and appeared before the committee, where they told of Plymouth's continued defiance. They also informed the members of dissatisfaction within the army, caused by a lack of regular pay, which had forced many officers to borrow in order to keep their men from deserting. Unfortunately the committee could do very little to rectify the situation immediately. Money had been earmarked for Plymouth, but the roundhead cause was suffering cash flow problems almost everywhere.

In the middle of March, Sir Richard Grenville, one of the most treacherous and contemptible men to emerge during the war, according to parliament, arrived in the Westcountry. Grenville's advent in the Plymouth area was by order of King Charles, and he held instructions to recruit Cornish volunteers. Forty-two years of age in 1644, Sir Richard, the younger brother of the late Sir Bevill Grenville, had recently returned from Ireland where he had been fighting rebels. With the trouble in Ireland diminishing in importance and the war in England developing, Grenville believed it was time to go home and reap greater glory. Late in 1643 he boarded a ship bound for royalist Chester, unfortunately the vessel docked at the parliamentary port of Liverpool. Suspected as a king's man, Grenville was escorted at once to London, where he found great difficulty persuading parliament of his loyalty. Eventually Grenville's implorations worked and the parliamentary authorities were satisfied. Sir Richard suddenly found himself a lieutenant general of horse, with an appointment to Sir William Waller's army.

For several months Grenville recruited under Waller's supervision and parliament considered promoting him to the governorship of Plymouth. Then in early March, while Waller was planning to attack Basing House, Grenville turned his coat and rode for Oxford where he joined the king. During his brief time with the roundhead army Sir Richard had been elected to the council of war, where he learned Waller's immediate plans, these he handed over to his grateful sovereign. Due to Westminster's misplaced trust and Grenville's treachery, the people of Plymouth grew to hate Sir Richard and he was placed high on parliament's most-wanted list. Grenville was not initially given a command, the king was hopeful that his family name and reputation would enable him to raise a new Cornish army. Thus Grenville's first mission was that of recruiting officer.

Grenville set up headquarters at Fitzford, the home of his wife, near Tavistock and waited for volunteers to begin trickling across the Tamar. To pass the time Sir Richard satisfied a number of personal vendettas by arresting several old acquaintances, one was sent to Oxford and another was hanged without trial. Sir Richard and the commander of the royalist forces around Plymouth, Colonel John Digby paid a number of courtesy calls on each other during the early spring. It was on one of his excursions to Plympton that Grenville's extreme brutality emerged. Whilst returning to Fitzford, after a conference with Digby, Grenville's escort came across a detail of roundhead soldiers out cutting wood somewhere north of Plymouth. Outnumbered and on foot, the terrified parliamentarians were herded towards Sir Richard. Questioning informed him that the men were from the garrison. Callously Grenville ordered one of the men to hang his companions, which he reluctantly did and was then run through with a rapier for his trouble.

Despite Digby's higher authority, Grenville made his initial contact with the Plymouth garrison on March 18th when he arrogantly sent in a communication addressed to Colonel Gould and the officers of Plymouth. In his letter Grenville tried hard to justify the reasons that made him change sides. He also explained he had been offered the governorship of Plymouth by parliament, but believing the port would eventually fall to the king's forces, he declined the offer and went to serve his sovereign. Colonel Gould replied aggressively to the turncoat's communiqué: *'Though your letter meriting our highest contempt and scorn, which once we thought fit by our silence (judging as unworthy of an answer) to have retired. Yet considering that yourself intends to make it public, we offer you these lines that the world may see what esteem we have of the man notorious for apostasy and treachery and that we are ready to dispute the justness and equity of our cause in any lawful way, whereto the enemy shall at any time challenge us, you might well have spared the giving us an account of your dissimulation with parliament'.*[15] Gould went on to declare that he was grateful Sir Richard was against the town rather than for it, and he called the king's advisors mischievous and denounced them all.

Grenville's original letter to Gould was accompanied by a small booklet entitled *'Iniquity of the Covenant'*. Colonel Gould handed the tract over to the council, who ordered it burned in the market place. The town's hangman carried out the command in front of a cheering crowd. A proclamation was then nailed up which stated that any person in possession of such a book should hand it in or be treated as an enemy of the town. William Gould was at the pinnacle of his success and he relished the idea of taking on Grenville, sadly it was not to be.

On March 27th the unthinkable happened, Colonel Gould, Plymouth's most beloved commander died, succumbing to the plague, which was rife at this time; his death was greatly mourned by all. Stephen Midhope, one of the army chaplains wrote a touching sermon for William Gould and dedicated it to Sir John Bampfield, who took over temporary command of the town. The text for the sermon was from Revelations 14. Bampfield of Poltimore and the owner of Warleigh House was no soldier, he had been MP for Tiverton in 1621 and Sheriff of Devon in 1634. Created baronet on July 14th 1641, Sir John was the third son of Sir Amias Bampfield and son-in-law to Sir Thomas Drake. As Deputy Lieutenant of Devon in 1642 Bampfield was ordered by parliament to raise and train the county militia and collect money. Early in 1643 Sir John was active in organising the trained bands in north Devon along with Rolle and Northcote, but this was his only military experience.

Due to his lack of martial knowledge, Sir John did not retain command of Plymouth for long. On April 16th the town's defences were taken over by Mayor John Cawse, Colonel John Crocker and Lieutenant Colonel Robert Martin. Colonel James Wardlaw, still suffering from some unspecified malady, must have been in Plymouth at this time as it was he who transferred the authority of the town to the triumvirate. The mayor and his two officers were to cooperate and govern Plymouth until parliament appointed a new commander. Crocker and Martin were possibly from the same locally-raised regiment, Martin being the most aggressive. A veteran of many engagements around Plymouth and Exeter, Robert Martin was more a fighter than an organiser and both Cawse and Crocker considered him most suited to command. Consequently on May 1st Martin was given full charge of all military operations, while Cawse and Crocker kept control of civic affairs.

Robert Martin assumed his new responsibility with as much vigour and energy as his popular predecessor. Captain Henry Hatsell, considered by some to be one of the garrison's more capable officers, retained command of St Nicholas Island and Captain Samuel Birtch held on to Plymouth Fort. Colonel Gould had assigned both men to their posts and Martin believed them capable of maintaining their charges. Hatsell would eventually rise from militia captain to Vice Admiral of Devon, and whilst in command of St Nicholas Island he improved its defences and cared for his men.

Shortly after the death of Colonel Gould and during one of town's many designated fasting days, a group of local children were playing outside the recently whitewashed St Andrew's Church. Inside Mr Sherwell was busy preaching the word of God, when suddenly the children sounded the alarm by calling out "Arm, arm!" The congregation rushed from the church, a number of officers present drawing their swords, fortunately it was all a misunderstanding, the children were only playing at war, much to the annoyance of the flustered congregation.[16]

John Syms, the adventurous refugee from Sheepstor, now living in Plymouth and without a church, had returned to the port in February. Unable to remain in his own village because of persecution by John Nosworthy and other pro-royalist constables, Syms made his way across Dartmoor. Utilising the leat and avoiding cavalier patrols along the way he eventually arrived safely. With so many clergymen in the town Syms was forced to visit the various forts, gathering groups of soldiers about him. To these warriors he administered the new oath of the Solemn League and Covenant. This verbal bond had been issued by parliament in February and was to be taken by all men over eighteen years old. The oath was intended to bind those who swore by it to parliament's cause.

By early April the royalists were firmly established along the west bank of the Tamar, at Mount Edgcumbe and Saltash and along the east bank of the Plym, centred mainly around How Stert, Fort Stamford, Saltram and Plympton. Other detachments manned outposts at St Budeaux, Warleigh, Trennimans Jump and Widey, but together they numbered no more than 3-4,000. Plymouth on the other hand could muster almost 3,000 regulars and militiamen. With the cavaliers so dispersed the advantage remained with the defenders who were on interior lines, from where they could concentrate and strike out with superior force. The over-extended royalists, unable to closely besiege the port were prone to attack from a dozen different directions. With his army so scattered, Colonel Digby would be hard-pressed to rapidly reinforce any detachment that came under attack.

On the 12th of April a flotilla of fourteen ships, conveying food, water, munitions of war and 200 reinforcements, defied the weak royalist blockade and ran into Millbay harbour. Enemy guns could rarely reach this haven and with insufficient troops to completely invest Plymouth, Digby was greatly frustration each time a vessel sailed in past his cannon. The royalist gunners opened up anyway and threw cannonballs at the target. Most of the shot fell harmlessly into the sea, but occasionally a strike was made. As more a defiant gesture, Captain Birtch's gunners in Plymouth Fort randomly fired back at the enemy in Fort Stamford. On the same day the convoy arrived in Millbay, a lucky shot from the fort hit a group of royalist soldiers gathered about their kettles, killing and wounding several men. Jubilation must have been at frenzy pitch during this exceptional incident, as such hits were extremely rare.

Shortly after taking sole command at Plymouth, Lieutenant Colonel Martin received a report that a body of 500 royalists were quartered in and around St Budeaux Church. In actual fact there were only 160 recruits and thirty veteran musketeers from Saltash under a

Major George Collins of Richard Grenville's budding foot regiment. Martin believed Grenville himself was in the area, but parliamentary intelligence, often poor at best, was once again incorrect. John Grenville, the fourteen-year-old son of the late Sir Bevill Grenville, and nephew to Sir Richard was actually in command of the St Budeaux detachment.

Robert Martin decided to strike quickly before the enemy could consolidate his position and block a valuable route for the garrison foragers. Several hours before dawn on April 16th Colonel Martin led his 600 musketeers and 120 horse out on the road toward St Budeaux via Ham and Kings Tamerton. To prevent royalist reinforcements being dispatched from Plympton, a substantial diversionary force was detached and sent out in the direction of Longbridge. This re-routed column would split into two smaller detachments; the larger force headed on down to Longbridge, the smaller mounted column rode up towards Knackersknowle. During the advance of the main body under Martin, a stupid mistake by a guide caused the parliamentary horse to take the wrong road, thus leaving the foot to march on to St Budeaux alone. Colonel Martin's reduced force now numbered 300 foot and a dozen horsemen, undeterred he pressed on.

Skirmishing broke out somewhere in the countryside between Ham House and St Budeaux. With many of the muskets failing due to damp powder, the outnumbered cavaliers found themselves pressed back by hand-to-hand fighting. When Martin's men arrived in St Budeaux village during the early hours, they quickly formed up and made straight for the church. John Grenville's ill-equipped and badly-trained recruits watched as these veterans lined up, unfurled their standards and advanced. This was enough for many of the novices, the majority discarded their weapons and fled towards Saltash passage. A number of the musketeers and a few fearless volunteers barricaded themselves in the church, while a second group opened fire from the cover of nearby hedges.

Colonel Martin's men pressed forward and returned the cavaliers' scattered fire with more orderly volleys. Slowly but surely the royalist position deteriorated and Grenville's survivors knew that no relief would come. They resisted as long as they were able, but eventually with no way out Major Collins ordered his men to surrender. Only two cavaliers had been killed, but forty-four were captured; amongst them a Lieutenant Andrew Cory, Captain Richard Porter's ensign, twenty horses, 100 muskets and three barrels of powder. Due to a lack of roundhead horse, Major Collins, Captain John Tavinor, the last from Bevill Grenville's old regiment, Captain Porter, a Captain Vacy from Tamerton and many others managed to mount their horses and ride away to safety.

Robert Martin secured his spoils and returned to Plymouth, where many of the prisoners changed their allegiance and joined the garrison, a common trait for the period. Had the roundhead cavalry not gone astray the bag of captives would have been far greater. The detachment heading towards Knackersknowle searched the village, but only managed to pick up a single roving royalist trooper before turning back. Eventually the misguided cavalry rode back to the town, embarrassed by the affair.

Three days after his initial success Colonel Martin struck again, this time he sent 200 musketeers and a detachment of cavalry out in the direction of Hoptons Work, the old cavalier earthwork near Widey House. Enemy cavalry had often been spotted in this area and Martin hoped to capture prisoners for interrogation. As a consequence he ordered the forlorn hope not to attack until the main body arrived. Unfortunately his words were wasted, the advance guard, unable to contain itself rushed toward the surprised royalists. The cavaliers were able to get off a single volley before abandoning their position and fleeing to a nearby hedge for better cover, pursued at a distance by the roundheads.

Such was the momentum of the parliamentary attack that the royalists were forced to leave their second position and retire to anther hedge further back. The retreat continued until the enemy reached a small breastwork, thrown up previously to protect the approaches to Longbridge. Soon parliamentary reinforcements arrived and the royalist defence collapsed. A lack of ammunition curtailed further roundhead success and with royalist reserves moving down from Plympton, they broke off the attack and withdrew. Due to the nature of this engagement casualties were light. Roundhead sources indicate one man slightly wounded and another shot in the back. This unfortunate fellow lingered in great pain for several days before dying. It is quite possible that Thomas Harding, a soldier who was buried in St Andrew's on April 23rd was the poor wretch shot in the back at the Longbridge fight. Had the forlorn hope obeyed Martin's original order not to attack alone, more might have been achieved. Unfortunately strict obedience to orders was a rarity in the civil war.

Robert Martin continued piling pressure against the fragile royalist blockade. On April 27th he gathered together a party of thirty musketeers from the Prince Rock Forts, loaded the men into boats and sent them across the Cattewater. Their objective was a small enemy outpost somewhere up Pomphlett Creek. The roundhead raiders arrived so quickly that the cavalier guard was taken completely by surprise. Those few who escaped left behind six horses, a number of arms, a drum, food and sixteen of their comrades. The unlucky captives were bundled back to the boats, and the roundheads pulled away for the west bank just as a body of royalist horse from Plymstock appeared galloping along the east bank.

Not all the action around Plymouth took place on land; idle seamen loafing around on ships lying at anchor in Millbay would occasionally form themselves into small groups around an officer. This elite unit, sometimes augmented by musketeers from nearby forts, would wait until nightfall, take a small boat or two and furtively row out hugging the South Devon coast. Some of these forays were quite impudent in their procedure. On April 25th a packet boat crammed with roundheads left Plymouth and put out for the Channel. Before long the vessel managed to overhaul a bark laden with cloth, hides and other luxuries and sailed it back into Plymouth.

The following day, a Sunday, a similar incident netted a ship from Falmouth loaded with wine, part of which was destined for Mr William Scawen the royalist Governor of Millbrook. Three acquaintances of Scawen's on board were also captured but later released. A number of the more daring raiders went almost as far as Dartmouth in search of adventure. These would land in some obscure cove; the crews would then disembark and probe the area, rounding up sheep, cattle, horses and whatever else they could find, then return. Larger vessels on their way to Plymouth occasionally captured prizes en route and towed them into the only friendly port left in the far southwest. On May 18th a number of parliamentary ships sailed into Millbay with six captured merchantmen; coal, wheat and flour were amongst the cargoes. Such minor seaborne hit-and-run raids were of little military significance, but they often raised morale considerably.

Trouble for the garrison during this period was not wholly confined to the besieging royalists. Since the death of Colonel Gould and the arrival in the area of the psychopathic Sir Richard Grenville, dissatisfaction surfaced once again, fuelled by royalist sympathisers. Many of the more unobtrusive culprits were women; one, a Mrs Springwell, was exposed, arrested and confined in Plymouth Castle, which served as a prison for malignants and traitors. Mrs Springwell was accused of corresponding with the enemy, and of sending clothing through the lines to the turncoat Moses Collins. She even invited the enemy to assault Plymouth and offered her home to a cavalier major named Harris, once the town had fallen. Valuable information on weapon stores and gunpowder locations was also passed on to the enemy fortunately her treacherous activities were curtailed by arrest and imprisonment.

With the royalists so close, two men, George Henwood and William Shugby, deserted the town after taking the oath and covenant. Despite a general pardon issued to all soldiers who left the garrison and joined the king's forces, Henwood and Shugby failed to return. Both were subsequently captured during a skirmish at Roborough wearing royalist colours. The pair were tried by military court martial and found guilty of desertion. George Henwood and William Shugby were hanged upon the Hoe on April 8th. Their trial and execution was a resolute example to others who contemplated changing sides and gave out the message that Colonel Gould's policies would be continued by his successors.

Many of the encounters between roundhead and cavalier resulted favourably for the former, due mainly to the defenders' interior lines. With the enemy distributed over a huge area, and in many cases almost isolated by rivers, the parliamentarians were able to strike with concentrated force against their outposts and return home before Grenville or Digby knew what was happening. However the garrison did not have it all their own way, in early April a ten-man roundhead raiding party was captured and sent under escort to Dartmouth, where they were imprisoned. To counter what the royalists believed to be the superior numbers of the Plymouth garrison, Colonel John Digby sent several messages to Sir Edward Seymour, Governor of Dartmouth, requesting arms and ammunition.

On April 8th Digby wrote a letter to Seymour asking for thick poles, twenty feet or more in length, shovels, arms and a supply of lead for making bullets. Digby emphasised that he was desperate for ammunition. His request was followed on the 22nd by a further communiqué, this time the colonel desired pikes and 100 matchlocks as soon as they were produced. Money to pay his troops was also needed and Digby urged Seymour to send whatever he could spare. Clearly the royalists around Plymouth were running short of almost everything needed to maintain their tenuous positions. Manpower was also in short supply, as is evident by Sir Thomas Hele's warrant to the constable of Eggbuckland and other parishes. Hele's warrant ordered the presence at Modbury of all able-bodied men with whatever arms they could find. Owing to Grenville's brutality and the failure of previous musters, the turnout was lamentably small and with Digby so short of arms, any recruits raised would have proved more a hindrance than an asset.

The spring of 1644 saw a further blow to royalist ambitions for capturing Plymouth, which had its roots in far away Dorset. Prince Maurice appeared in front of the port of Lyme Regis in early April to besiege this small town on the south coast close to the Devon border. The prince hoped to have more success here than he had at Plymouth. To bolster his small army Maurice sent orders to Exeter and Plymouth, requesting reinforcements from Berkeley, Grenville and Digby. On May 7th Sir Edward Seymour was commanded to bring his own regiment of foot and as many soldiers from the Dartmouth garrison as could be spared. Seymour loathed leaving his comfortable billet and his response was sluggish to say the least, forcing Maurice to send a second order urging Sir Edward to speed up his departure from Dartmouth. Eventually Seymour left Sir Ames Ameridith, his brother-in-law, in command of the port and joined the prince. Maurice must have reconsidered leaving such a valuable port short of troops, for by June Seymour was back in Dartmouth with his regiment.

Although Robert Martin was considered a capable, temporary commander for Plymouth, local parliamentarians organised a petition calling for the appointment of Lord John Robartes to take full charge of the town's affairs, both military and civil. This petition, no slight on Martin's character or ability, was sent to London and presented to the House of Commons on May 10th. Parliament however was already speculating on someone suitable to take the reins of command from Lieutenant Colonel Martin, but the town would have to wait until June for its wishes to be complied with.

Meanwhile the energetic colonel, who had assumed full command of the military on May 1st, continued his pestering forays against the besiegers. On the 2nd of May a detachment of parliamentary horse surprised a royalist guard detail at Efford. The unfortunate cavaliers were gathered around their kettles when the roundheads came upon them. Unable to escape, all seven were captured along with their horses and escorted back to town. Nine days later, on the 11th, 140 foot and 100 cavalry left Plymouth and headed for Trennimans Jump. At first everything went well, the enemy was dispersed and prisoners taken, but during the return journey the situation changed dramatically.

As the column wound its way back to Plymouth, several hit-and-run assaults were launched against the parliamentarians by roving units of royalists. The disciplined rearguard beat off these stinging raids and the column continued its withdrawal. The heaviest attack came from a body of thirty horsemen based at Warleigh House. These riders came up and made an aggressive charge against the rear of the column shortly after it left Trennimans Jump. Fortunately a strong body of roundhead horse was on hand. Counterattacking, the parliamentary horse broke up the assault, inflicting seventeen casualties in the process. Eventually the parliamentarians reached the safety of the outer works. The large bag of prisoners was sent on to the castle where they were incarcerated. One man however, a Richard Grey, one-time member of the garrison was court martialled and executed on the 13th.

Robert Martin followed up his success the next day with a reconnaissance in force, only this time he directed his attention across the Hamoaze, towards Mount Edgcumbe. The parliamentary raiders were transported over the water by boats and landed unopposed on the stony beach. Quickly they bypassed the small, fortified blockhouse and attacked uphill against the main house, reportedly occupied by Colonel Piers Edgcumbe and thirty musketeers. However with numerous cannon dotted around the mansion the parliamentarians may have been wary of launching a full-scale assault against the place. After a minor probing attack was easily repulsed, Colonel Martin was satisfied he had achieved his goal and he withdrew his men back to their boats. The strength of the royalist garrison and their unresponsive efforts at cutting off Martin's retreat gave him just the ammunition he needed. Once back in Plymouth the colonel planned a second, much larger and more aggressive expedition against Mount Edgcumbe.

Early on the 15th of May, Colonel Martin dispatched Captain

Haines with 300 foot to the Cremyll Work, opposite Mount Edgcumbe. Once at the battery Haines and his men were to be ferried across the water to secure a beachhead. When Haines had established himself on the enemy shore, Martin himself would join him with twenty horsemen. Haines, another of the garrison's gallant officers who would give the ultimate sacrifice for parliament, landed his infantry as arranged. For some unaccountable reason the royalist pickets failed to detect Haines and he was able to move swiftly, capturing a small coastal battery and the blockhouse without a shot fired. Those of the enemy who managed to elude capture fled through the woods to the main house and Captain Haines sent the signal for Colonel Martin to join him.

Arriving on the beach, Martin sent a pre-prepared communication under a flag of truce to the commander of Mount Edgcumbe House: *"To prevent the effusion of Christian blood I do hereby require you immediately to deliver Mount Edgcumbe House unto me for ye use of the king and parliament. And ye shall have fair quarter, which if you refuse I have acquitted myself from the guilt of blood which be spilt in obtaining my just desire".*[17]

Martin's offer was refused, and not wishing to waste time and lives storming the heavily-fortified house, he quickly altered his plans. With only the three captured cannon available and no gunners to serve them, Colonel Martin left detachments at the blockhouse and at strategic points around the mansion to keep the cavalier garrison inside. With the rest of his force he trudged up the hill towards Maker Church, a short walk away. At the approach of the roundheads the small royalist guard locked itself inside the church and took up positions to defend themselves. Martin's dynamic leadership had instilled boldness in his troops and as they approached the secular building they fanned out and opened up a steady fire. While the stonework was peppered and the windows shattered, those inside knew their time was up. Soon resistance ceased altogether and the cavaliers threw down their weapons and surrendered.

Due to its location, Maker Church tower gave the observant eye all round vision for miles. Leaving a small guard here to watch and report, Robert Martin sent another detachment down to Cawsand, while he marched with the main body towards another battery located between Maker and Millbrook. The earthwork was found abandoned and the raiders moved on Millbrook, less than two miles from Maker. As he approached, Colonel Martin was informed that 250 royalists held the village; the parliamentarians minus their detached units numbered less than 200. Nevertheless Colonel Martin doubted the size of the enemy force and advanced on Millbrook. The outnumbered enemy put up only weak resistance before running away, leaving the victors to gather up prisoners, arms, artillery and powder. Unable to haul the cannon back up the steep hill, Colonel Martin ordered his men to push the guns into the sea. The earthwork at Inceworth Point was selected as the next target, but before Martin could make his move, the lookouts in Maker Church signalled to him that enemy reinforcements were on the march from the direction of Saltash. This news terminated Martin's foray and he ordered his troops back to their boats. The withdrawal was made at a leisurely pace, with a score or more prisoners in tow, along with cattle, arms, ammunition and powder. En route to the beach the main body was joined by the Cawsand detachment, which had driven away a royalist detail stationed there.

Arriving back at the beach, the spoils were loaded aboard boats and Colonel Martin believed he had time for one more attempt at capturing Mount Edgcumbe House. Enemy cannonfire and heavy musketry easily repulsed the weary roundhead infantry who only half-heartedly assaulted the mansion. Unable to reach the main house, the parliamentarians were able to set fire to the outbuildings and banqueting hall before falling back. Satisfied with his limited success, Martin led his men down to the boats and they made the crossing unhindered, while royalist cavalry rode up to the house only minutes after the roundheads pulled out.

Disembarking near the Cremyll Fort, Colonel Martin marched back to Plymouth with his prisoners, many of whom were later exchanged. Despite having achieved so much the parliamentarians had failed in their chief object, to take Mount Edgcumbe House. On the other side of the coin the raid demonstrated the weakness of the royalist forces in the Millbrook area and greatly raised the morale of the raiders. Casualties for the affair had been light; Martin lost one lieutenant and three privates killed and a few wounded. Amongst the injured was George Gibbs of Holsworthy, a trooper in Major Thomas Halsey's unit. Only recently recovered from a previous wound suffered during the Sabbath day fight, Gibbs was hit in the hand by a musket ball and had to be helped back to Plymouth by his comrades. Several others died of their wounds, one of these was Thomas Greepe a St Budeaux man, whose brother John had died in January 1643. Tom Greepe took his family into Plymouth at the start of the war, but his wife and daughter both died in January 1643. Thomas Greepe's burial is recorded in the registers of both St Budeaux and St Andrew's. Corporal Edward King, another respected veteran, lingered until the 19th before succumbing to his wounds.[18]

Back in Plymouth, Colonel Martin discovered that during his absence Sir Richard Grenville had made a half-hearted assault against part of the town's outer defence line. Grenville's reconnaissance in force had been aimed at the Maudlyn Work, but the attack lacked strength and coordination and was easily repulsed by cannonfire. Parliamentary successes around Plymouth were mainly due to the fact that her leaders were defiant, energetic and able to command respect from their men. The royalists on the other hand endured a less than happy existence, occupying isolated earthworks and under constant threat of a lightning raid from the garrison.

The fighting continued, on May 22nd a detachment of Colonel Martin's troops, which included Captain Arthur Gay's local company, assaulted a party of cavaliers camped around Warleigh. The royalists managed to barricade themselves inside the house and the roundheads attacked, burning the outbuildings in the process. Due to a lack of numbers, the parliamentarians were unable to storm the main house. Next they changed their tactics and tried to blow up the house with grenades and powder; this also failed. With no way inside, the roundheads secured a small number of prisoners and horses and withdrew.

During the return to Plymouth, royalist reinforcements crossed the Tamar from Saltash and joined those at Warleigh. This combined force now went in pursuit of the raiders. Near Hoptons Work the pursuers caught up and a clash of arms occurred. Reinforcements from Plymouth were soon observed galloping to the rescue and the cavaliers broke off and swung away heading for Efford. The fighting around Warleigh House and the subsequent pursuit cost the Plymouth garrison a number of killed and forty wounded. Amongst the latter was Stephen Webb, one of Captain Arthur Gay's company. Painfully wounded in the thigh, Webb survived the ordeal of surgery but would suffer from the wound for the rest of his life. Late in May, Captain Gay crossed the Tamar and made a foray into enemy territory. The complete surprise of the raid allowed Gay to bring away prisoners, livestock and, with the greatest of effort, a solitary cannon.

Several events occurred in Plymouth during the month of May and although of no military significance, they are interesting. On the 10th, Charles' Church, which still remained unfinished and covered with a temporary roof, saw its first wedding. Secondly, on the 31st, Sir Nicholas Martyn's wife and children arrived in Millbay. Lady Martyn managed to secure passage aboard a parliamentary warship lying off Dartmouth and had been brought down the coast to safety. Also on this final day of the month, two royalist troopers rode into the Plymouth lines and surrendered. Having deserted their own army, the men joined the parliamentary cause. This was not unusual and was followed on the 20th of June by a Mr Jeffery from Cornwall, who came into the town with thirty-five men, many of them mounted, they were followed later the same day by another half a dozen, most of whom joined the garrison.

June began as May ended, both sides were still in their respective fortifications, and skirmishing north of the town remained rife. On the 11th a troop of horse rode out of Plymouth heading for the village of Shaugh. When they returned, they had in tow a number of horses, thirteen bullocks and one prisoner. Tamerton and Buckland were also visited, and boat raids became almost daily occurrences; not all of them successful. One of the more ambitious parliamentary boat forays of the month was to Bigbury Bay and it netted several valuable hostages. Mr William Lane, Rector of Aveton Gifford Church was a tenaciously outspoken royalist and a well-known local troublemaker. Although he himself escaped detection by the roundheads, his two sons Richard and John were caught when the parliamentarians, having disembarked at Bigbury, marched up the Avon river towards Aveton Gifford. Also captured were the church curate and a royalist captain. The parliamentarians herded a few rustled sheep back to the boats hidden in a creek almost a mile from the village, while the prisoners, only half-dressed, were forced to carry the booty. The raiders returned to Plymouth on June 13th and the sorry-looking captives were incarcerated in the old castle, where, reputedly, they suffered greatly.

On June 14th the *Hector* sailed into Millbay harbour, on board was Colonel James Kerr, with orders from Westminster to assume the governorship of Plymouth and command of all parliamentary troops in Devon and Cornwall, which effectively amounted to those in the garrison. Kerr's name had been put to the Committee of the West on May 9th by Sir William Waller, who declared that Kerr was a most able and trustworthy officer. Sir John Bampfield and Thomas Drake accompanied the colonel on his journey to Plymouth. Before reaching the port, the *Hector* called in at Lyme Regis, here Kerr and his officers talked briefly with Lord High Admiral Warwick. The earl was, at that moment, supporting the hard-pressed parliamentary defenders of the port in their effort to crack the tight royalist siege works. Warwick explained to Kerr that he had recently received a communication from Plymouth urging him to pressure parliament for money and a new governor. Whether or not the colonel had been supplied with an ample money chest is not known.

The town council wined and dined its new commander, despite a shortage of money for such luxuries, and the townsfolk gave him a rousing welcome. As mentioned before, Kerr's arrival was not a stain on Colonel Martin's honour. Robert Martin's daring raids and courage did great justice to his temporary leadership and Kerr gave him enormous praise for his work over the past month. Nevertheless parliament believed the responsibility for such an important post was more suited to someone of Colonel Kerr's experience. Had Martin the resources available, no doubt he could have achieved much more and risen even higher in the town's esteem.

James Kerr had an interesting career before his transfer to Plymouth. According to several sources he had served in the Swedish army of Gustavus Adolphus during the Thirty Years' War and been wounded on several occasions. Possibly due to his injuries, he later returned to his native Scotland. With the outbreak of civil war Kerr was commissioned lieutenant colonel of dragoons and within a short time found himself Governor of Cirencester. In February 1643 the garrison was attacked and captured by Prince Rupert. Upon his exchange, James Kerr joined Waller's army, was promoted to full colonel and fought at Lansdowne, Roundway and Cheriton. Finally on May 10th, Kerr received orders to take command at Plymouth, but more than a month would pass before he arrived to take up his new post.

Despite lacking money, arms, food and manpower, and notwithstanding the achievements of Colonel Martin, Colonel Kerr and Mayor Cawse refused to cooperate. In fact there were not many people John Cawse could get along with. This sour relationship between military and civic leaders was a constant thorn in the side of the town's defence committee. Four days after his arrival Colonel Kerr, who became the third Scot to command in Plymouth, reorganised his forces. All available regiments were drawn out near Lipson and the troops listened as Kerr's commission was read aloud. New officers were elected to replace older, less able men, and others promoted. Due to a heavy loss of officers over the past few months, Kerr was forced to bring in replacements or promote junior officers. Numbered amongst those who had succumbed to wounds or disease since December the 1st were Captain John Wansey, Captain James Anderson, Captain Adams, Captain Philip Beaumont, Captain Humphrey Burton, Captain Richard Roe and Colonel William Gould.

For his previous good service in the Westcountry, Thomas Drake was advanced to major of all the horse at Plymouth, Colonel Sir Edmond Fowell retained charge of the Tinners trained bandsmen, Elizeus Crymes became his lieutenant colonel, and Mr Sampson Hele's son was promoted to major of the same unit.

Captain Christopher Martyn retained his rank but was reduced to the command of only forty-five volunteers. The competent Lieutenant Colonel Michael Searle lost his position but remained in Plymouth. This was not the first time such a thing had happened to Searle, earlier in the war he was a captain commanding a foot company in the Earl of Stamford's army. Later he was a major in Colonel William Strode's regiment, but was discharged after only a month on the 21st of August 1643. By early September Searle was found in Plymouth serving as a captain.

Major Thomas Drake, recently honoured by parliament for his commendable service so far in the war, had been absent from Plymouth for a considerable time, having travelled to London earlier in the year. While in the capital Drake spent money lavishly, much of it wages destined for his regiment. Grateful to be away from the strict Puritanism of Plymouth young Drake enjoyed London and remained in the city for over four months. During this relatively quiet period, Major Drake, having returned with Colonel Kerr, and bored by the inactivity, rode out of Plymouth one morning. When he returned his cousin and close friend Christopher Chudleigh, the twenty-four-year-old youngest son of Sir George Chudleigh, and brother to the late James Chudleigh accompanied him.

Drake and Chudleigh were soon observed walking and talking together, and many officers and soldiers grew uneasy. The defeat at Stratton and, what many believed was the Chudleigh treachery, were still fresh in the minds of many. When Chudleigh was appointed a cornet in Drake's regiment, the Plymouth horse, bad feelings multiplied and open discontent broke out in Plymouth. Many saw Chudleigh as one who could cause trouble and, given the opportunity, turn weak-minded men against the roundhead cause. Within a week of their arrival, Drake and Chudleigh, aware of the animosity building against them, left Plymouth and went over to the enemy. Having been escorted to Richard Grenville's headquarters, the pair announced they were now for the king. Grenville signed passes for the two men to travel on to Oxford, where they were to proclaim allegiance to King Charles.

Shortly after their desertion, the House of Commons received a letter from Plymouth explaining the incident. Meanwhile Thomas Drake was welcomed at the king's capital by the Governor of Oxford; the king being away campaigning against Waller. Over the next few days Drake bravely denounced parliament, while he waited for a pardon. During this period Drake must have pondered on his rash decision, which may have been forced upon him by his cousin, or the attitude of his fellow officers in Plymouth. On the other hand it may have been his brother's unceasing loyalty that nagged at him. The king had previously offered Sir Francis Drake a pardon to entice him away from parliament, possibly at the request of his uncle Sir George Chudleigh, but Sir Francis had declined the offer. Unexpectedly Tom Drake suddenly changed his coat a second time, hoping for clemency he left Oxford alone and made his way back to Plymouth.

Along the road Major Drake was picked up by a roving patrol of roundhead horse and without suitable papers he was escorted to London. Once in the capital, Drake explained his controversial action away by declaring he had temporarily lost his mind. The entire matter was then placed into the hands of the Committee of the West. Thomas Drake was subsequently held in the custody of the sergeant at arms while his very influential family and friends spoke up in his defence. Drake was indeed fortunate, Lord Robartes, William Strode, his uncle, and the old Mayor of Plymouth, John Cawse, all wrote to Westminster on his behalf. Finally on July 26th Major Drake was released from confinement and discharged. There was however a penalty, Drake was not to leave London without first consulting the committee and receiving a passport. Major Thomas Drake never returned to his regiment or Plymouth during the course of the war.

On the day that Colonel Kerr held his grand review at Lipson, a detachment of roundhead horse rode out towards Efford, where the enemy had established an outpost. Unaware that the royalists had been alerted to their approach, the parliamentarians pressed on along a confined lane. Suddenly they found themselves the target of a well-set ambush. The cavaliers rose up from behind a hedge and opened fire. Reeling their mounts backward the roundheads found the narrow road too tight to manoeuvre in. Two troopers, Samuel Petherbridge and John Webber, were killed in the panic and three others captured. Once clear of the lane, the parliamentarians reformed and charged, forcing the cavaliers to retreat. Later a Plympton woman told an acquaintance in Plymouth that the royalists had lost thirty killed and wounded during the encounter; an obvious exaggeration.

During the fourth week of June a much more significant engagement occurred, that began when several reports reached the town of a band of royalist horse creating havoc in the countryside. This roving detachment, part of Grenville's command, was continually looting homes in and around Plympton. In an effort to end such wilful destruction, a party of roundhead horse moved out of Plymouth during the night of June 24th heading initially for Shaugh. The plan was to bypass enemy outposts without being observed and attack Plympton from an unexpected direction. The surprise was such that the roundheads were able to rustle a number of enemy horses and capture a bewildered lieutenant before heading back to Plymouth via the Longbridge, the most direct route home. Unable to catch the royalist vandals before they were reinforced, retreat became the only option open to the roundheads.

The cavaliers were soon in pursuit, but when the parliamentarians reached a point below Hoptons Work, a detachment of friendly musketeers was found lining a hedge. Something now went terribly wrong; a second body of royalists appeared causing the parliamentary horse to panic and bolt towards their own infantry, running down several men in their effort to escape. Captains Haines and Gabriel Barnes were captured during the fighting and Captain Henry Gosnal was wounded in the leg. The roundhead foot eventually stabilised and delivered a steady fire at the cavaliers. Simultaneously the horse composed itself and returned to the fray.

During the escalating engagement, Colonel John Digby received a rapier cut to the face from Cornet Bushell. Bushell's weapon also caught one of Digby's eyes, causing him such a serious injury that the royalist colonel would suffer from it for the rest of his life. Although Digby survived, reports of his death were soon circulating as far away as Lyme Regis. Another casualty of the fighting was Colonel John Arundell, son of the royalist Governor of Pendennis Castle. During a personal melee with a roundhead captain named William Braddon, a Cornishman, formerly of Colonel Gould's regiment but recently transferred to the cavalry, John Arundell was mortally wounded and captured. During a counter charge by the parliamentary horse, twenty prisoners held by the enemy made a dash for freedom, amongst them captains Haines and Barnes.

Having suffered a reported sixty killed and wounded and forty-four lost as prisoners, the royalists broke off the attack and withdrew. The garrison losses were thirty killed, wounded and captured, four of whom were buried in St Andrew's the following day, another on the 26th and a trooper on the 27th. Colonel Arundell was carefully conveyed back to the town, but he died at the Maudlyn Fort. Later the gallant captain's body was returned to the royalist lines. One of the wounded cavaliers was Henry Browne of Plympton, who served as a gunner under Digby. Browne had received a bad injury to the hand and was captured. Incarcerated in the Marshalsea, he soon fell sick due to the appalling conditions. Upon his release Henry Browne could no longer serve, and he never regained the use of his hand.

On the 29th of the month a party of roundhead foot crossed the Plym via the ford near Efford and made for Saltram Quay. With the tide beginning to turn speed was of the essence. At their approach the royalist guards quickly disappeared and the parliamentarians moved on, only to come upon the main enemy line. The cavaliers had utilised a long breastwork on high ground and here their pickets fell in beside them. When the roundheads advanced uphill, they were met by stiff resistance. Reinforced by a detachment of horse, the royalists pressed the assault back down towards the water. Finding the tide sweeping in behind them the parliamentarians were forced to abandon their attack and flee across the deep ford. As they withdrew the cavaliers lined the shore and peppered them with musket balls.

The raid had proved totally fruitless, barring a few prisoners.

The roundheads suffered six killed, thirty wounded and half a dozen captured. Amongst the burials for St Andrew's for June 29th-30th are six soldiers, John Scritchet, Richard Housewife, John Heath, John Boyes, Daniel Cooper and Fortinatus King. All were killed in action and it is likely they are all from the failed attack described above. The following day the royalists made a retaliatory raid against Stoke. Being outside the main defensive perimeter, the village was not considered a military objective and the raiders managed to round up a number of horses and a small herd of livestock. Also a local man, Mr Yolston, was taken away as a hostage, possibly for objecting to the theft of his animals. Being a Sunday, by the time the alarm had been raised in Plymouth and a force assembled, the enemy had vanished.

Due to the severity of his wound, Colonel Digby felt unable to continue in command of the royalist force blockading Plymouth, so he handed over full authority to his co-commander Sir Richard Grenville. Eager to accept, Grenville was incapable of taking advantage of Plymouth's isolated condition due to his own self-interest. By order of the king all property belonging to those in rebellion against him, was to be seized in order to pay for the royalist war effort. Like many, Sir Richard mutated this royal decree to make himself a rich man. Amongst those who had their property sequestered by Grenville were the Earl of Bedford, Lord John Robartes and Sir Francis Drake. Besides what he skimmed off for his own personal needs, Grenville was allocated £1,000 plus per week, the so-called county contribution for the royalist armies. No doubt part of this payment also ended up in Sir Richard's pockets. To crown his venality, Sir Richard kept his estranged wife Mary and their children from the family home at Fitzford, and continued to use the house as his headquarters.

Royalist officers who did not obey Sir Richard's despotic orders vigorously, and those civilians who objected to his brutal approach, were imprisoned or executed. Others who refused to subscribe found their cattle stolen, their homes plundered and their crops burned. With troops in short supply Grenville began rounding up all men of military age and conscripted them into his army, an army that was fed with food commandeered from local farms and villages. Truly Sir Richard Grenville was living up to his nickname of 'Skellum' Grenville.

If Grenville treated his own men and innocent civilians with such ruthlessness, how did he treat his enemies? With equal contempt and a brutality more intense than many ever witnessed. Sir Richard saw parliamentarians as traitors and as such the punishment should fit the crime. All roundhead dignitaries and officers captured by his troops were sent to the notorious Lydford Castle or Exeter gaol. The prisons of the civil war were notorious for disease and deprivation; Lydford was one of the worst. Located to the north of Tavistock, Lydford had a reputation for barbarity that sent prisoners destined for its gloomy dungeons into a cold sweat.

When Grenville arrived in the southwest, all prisoners that fell into his hands were either killed, or marched over the moors to Lydford. Here they were crammed together into damp vaults beneath the castle. Maltreatment, disease and hunger brought death to many and the numbers were slowly whittled down. When the Earl of Essex invaded the Westcountry in the summer of 1644, the royalist guards at Lydford fled, leaving the prisoners to fend for themselves. One of the survivors was Lieutenant Colonel John Hals of Efford in Cornwall, who served under Colonel Nicholas Boscowan as second in command of the Plymouth horse. Captured in one of the engagements around Plymouth, Hals was thrown into Lydford. Surviving his traumatic ordeal, Lieutenant Colonel Hals gave ample evidence as to the cruelty of the gaolers, who executed parliamentarians without trial and tortured them for their own satisfaction. With Essex's later defeat and the return of the royalists, Lydford would once again resume its role as military prison and a number of fresh, prominent captives would be herded inside its grim dungeons.

The only parliamentarians in the county of Devon in the early summer of 1644 were either behind earth ramparts at Plymouth, locked up in royalist gaols or in hiding. Sir Richard Grenville continued to raise more troops, but these were slow in coming forward. Those who were impressed into service were usually brought in under guard and watched lest they desert at the earliest opportunity. The blockade of Plymouth looked as if it would go on all through the summer, Colonel Kerr was secure behind his ever-expanding fortifications and the royalists remained concentrated in their numerous strongpoints, north, east and west of the town. However, events further afield were about to have a dramatic affect on Plymouth's isolated position.

On January 19th, some 20,000 Scots, under Alexander Leslie, at the invitation of parliament, crossed the border and invaded England. The royalist Earl of Newcastle, outnumbered by more than two to one, fell back before Leslie's advance and sent an urgent appeal to the king for reinforcements. At first the royalists could do nothing, but the Scottish advance was so leisurely that King Charles would later be able to dispatch his nephew Prince Rupert to help Newcastle. By the spring of 1644 though, Newcastle had fallen back to York where Leslie's mighty host, reinforced by several parliamentary armies, had bottled him up.

In Cheshire, Nantwich was the setting for a royalist defeat on the 25th of January, when Sir Thomas Fairfax and Sir William Brereton joined forces and successfully attacked Lord Byron; Fairfax later went on to besiege Lathom House in Lancashire. After a winter of rest and recruitment around Winchester, Sir Ralph Hopton was joined in March by Patrick Ruthven, the Earl of Forth. These two men marched their combined army out to meet Sir William Waller. Roundhead and cavalier collided on March 28th at Cheriton, and after a fierce engagement Hopton and Ruthven withdrew. The victory was celebrated in Plymouth on April 10th with a day of thanksgiving.

King Charles, still at Oxford with a large army, made up his mind to leave part of his command behind and with the rest march on Worcester. Charles hoped that Essex and Waller, whose armies had merged, would split up and he could attack them one at a time. His first attempt failed, and the roundheads advanced rapidly against him, forcing the king back to the safety of Oxford. A second attempt was made on June 3rd and this time Charles was able to reach Worcester three days later. For some strange reason and against Westminster's wishes, the two parliamentarian commanders now made a rather unexpected move. Waller remained to watch King Charles, while the Earl of Essex decided on his own initiative, to march down into Dorset and relieve Lyme Regis.

By the middle of June, Essex was closing in on the Dorset port and Prince Maurice was forced to raise his siege and retreat into Devon. Urged on by Lord John Robartes, the Earl of Essex decided to advance further westwards, hoping to draw support away from the king and build up his own army with recruits. Left behind with only the London trained bands and a few odd regiments, Waller was to prevent the king following Essex. When Charles received intelligence of the earl's misguided trek, he saw the perfect opportunity to destroy two separate parliamentary armies at his leisure. Accordingly on June 29th, after reinforcements joined him from Oxford, the king marched along the Daventry Road, skirmishing with Waller as he went. Battle finally exploded at Cropredy Bridge over the River Cherwell. Waller came off second best in the engagement and fell back, but during the retreat his army disintegrated, leaving a joyful king to re-enter Oxford. Here Charles Stuart, delighted that the first part of his plan had worked so well, resupplied his army and quickly set off in pursuit of Essex.

Notes

(15) Page 170: A continuation of the true narration of the most observable passages in and about Plymouth from January 26, 1643 till the present, Thomason Tracts E 47 (1); by kind permission of the British Library.
(16) Page 171: John Syms, A daybook of special passages and mercies, British Library, Add 35297; by kind permission of the British Library, London.
(17) Page 179: Letter from Colonel Martin, reproduced from Transactions of the Plymouth Institute; by kind permission of the Plymouth Athenaeum.
(18) Page 181: St Andrew's Church burials, St Budeaux Church burials, West Devon Record Office, Plymouth.

Sir John Clobery
(Courtesy of Mr J Hardacre, Winchester Cathedral)

Blockhouse at Mount Edgcumbe which was attacked several times by Parliamentarians. (Author's photo)

Lord John Robartes of Lanhydrock in later years.
(Portrait by Sir Godfrey Kneller, courtesy of the National Trust)

Sir Alexander Carew.
(Courtesy of the National Trust, Sir Richard Carew Pole of Anthony House, Lorna Yabsley, Cameracraft)

Defaced Effigies, Modbury Church. *(Author's photo)*

Civil War Cannon found on Burrows Hill, Plymstock. *(Author's photo)*

The Memorial to Colonel John Birch at Weobley Church.
(Courtesy of the Rev. Bob King, vicar of Weobley Church)

In Hope of a Resurrection to Eternall Life
Here is Deposited the Body of
Coll John Birch
(Descended of a Worthy Family in Lancashire)
As the Dignities He arrived at in the Field; and the
Esteem Universally yielded him in the SENAT-HOUSE
Exceeded the Attainments of most; so they were but the
Moderate and Just Rewards of his Courage, Conduct
Wisdom and Fidelity. None who knew him denyed him ye
Character of asserting & vindicating ye Laws & Liberties of
his Country in War, and of promoting its Welfare and
Prosperity in Peace; He was borne ye 5th of Sept. 1626
And died a Member of ye Honble House of Comons
Being Burgess for Weobley
May ye [illegible]th 169[illegible]

Henry VIII Blockhouse, Firestone Bay, protecting the coast.
(Author's photo)

Ruins of Palace Court, Plymouth. (Author's photo)

St Margaret's Church, Westminster. The final resting place of Colonel Nicholas Boscowan, John Pym and William Strode amongst others. (Author's photo)

Runaway Lane, Modbury, an escape avenue for the royalists after the battle of Modbury. (Author's photo)

Colonel St Aubyn in later years.
(Courtesy of James St Aubyn, St Michael's Mount, Marazion, Cornwall)

Chapter 9

The King Moves West

Having relieved Lyme Regis, the Earl of Essex moved into Somerset. At the same time Prince Maurice, dejected after his continuing failure to capture a south coast port, withdrew his army back towards Exeter, where he joined forces with Sir John Berkeley. Earlier Berkeley had had the foresight to write to his friend Sir Edward Seymour at Dartmouth, warning him to secure his garrison as Essex would more than likely be marching into Devonshire. Later in the month royalist anxiety increased further when a letter from Sir Richard Grenville reached Seymour informing him of a plot by local parliamentarians to seize control of Dartmouth. The rebels were to be assisted in their endeavour by a detachment of troops supposedly on their way from Plymouth, the plot never materialised.

When he reached Chard, Essex dispatched a force under Lieutenant Colonel Robert Blake with orders to capture Taunton, and by July 10th Blake had achieved his goal. For some reason though Essex was in no hurry to press on. The lord general believed he had ample time and rested his army for a week. Meanwhile the king, fearing for the safety of his queen, presumed to be still in Exeter, was already hot on Essex's trail. Fortunately Queen Henrietta had left Exeter on June 30th and took carriage for Falmouth. Two weeks later as her husband was nearing Bath, the queen boarded a ship bound for the continent.

In early July both Houses announced an ordinance appointing commissioners for the five southwestern counties. Those selected were to raise money to pay for more defences and more troops. Of the twenty-eight representatives for Cornwall many had been or soon would be involved in Plymouth. Notably amongst them being Lord Robartes, Francis and George Buller, Thomas Arundell, Francis Godolphin, John St Aubyn, soon to be elected Sheriff of Cornwall, Nicholas Boscowan of Tregothan, an officer in the Plymouth horse, Thomas Gewen, Anthony Rouse and Robert Bennett. Eminent amongst Devon's contingent were Sir John Bampfield, Sir Edmond Fowell, Sir Shilston Calmady, John Crocker, Robert Savery and John Lutterell, soon to be elected Sheriff of Devon, as well as John Cawse and the redoubtable Philip Francis.

Finally on the move once again, Essex advanced through Axminster, Tiverton and Crediton, bypassing Exeter with its substantial garrison under Berkeley and Maurice. The king himself marched down from Bath and entered the county town on July 26th. In Plymouth meantime, Colonel James Kerr received news of Essex's approach, though he was unaware of the king's pursuit. Kerr knew that once Essex was close Grenville would lift his blockade and run for the Tamar. Consequently Wednesday July 10th was observed as another day of thanksgiving for the continual defiance of the garrison. This same day saw a weak royalist cavalry detachment chased out of Hoptons Work and pursued towards Buckland Down. Realising their main body was nearby, the cavaliers halted near the gallows and turned to face the foe. The roundheads drew rein, contemplated momentarily, then withdrew in the direction of Longbridge.

Simultaneously a company of eight sailors rowed over to How Stert, crept up towards old Fort Stamford and surprised the enemy guard. After a brief exchange the seamen were forced back to their boats, losing one man killed and several captured. Their withdrawal was covered by guns in the earthworks along the west bank of the Plym and by those of Plymouth Fort, but they in turn came under counter-battery fire from enemy cannon in Fort Stamford.

The following day, July 11th, the *James* and three other warships sailed into Millbay under the Earl of Warwick, bringing in sixty soldiers and a number of refugees from Dartmouth. Two days later a force of 200 men boarded a ship and slipped out of Plymouth. These could have been the men Grenville wrote to Seymour about earlier. The vessel sailed around the coast and anchored not far from Salcombe, where the soldiers were landed. Once disembarked the infantry marched down toward the village. Undefended, the

Plymouth men had no trouble capturing a ship and seventeen prisoners. One intrepid officer called on the old castle to surrender but the small royalist garrison refused. Unable to remain long the soldiers were taken back on board ship and returned to Plymouth, where they arrived on the 15th.

Two days later, a royalist drummer appeared at one of the outer forts. The man was immediately escorted to Colonel Kerr, where he announced that Sir Richard Grenville wished to call a nine-day truce. Kerr had no doubts that such a proposal was being offered to cover Grenville's true intention, which was to withdraw his army safely before the advancing army under Essex could trap him. Kerr was no fool and he denied Grenville the necessary time he needed to withdraw his army without hindrance. As a consequence Sir Richard was forced to maintain his position in front of Plymouth, despite orders from Prince Maurice to detach most of his foot and send them to Okehampton, where the prince was collecting an army with which he hoped to stop Essex. At the time Grenville's communiqué was being taken to Kerr, Sir Richard sent an urgent dispatch to Seymour at Dartmouth pleading for reinforcements; Sir Edward, as usual, could spare neither men nor materials.

With rumours rife and general uncertainty in the air, military activity around Plymouth decreased significantly, as the king and Essex were both heading towards the Tamar, neither side wished to initiate a major confrontation at this stage. The royalists were content to watch the town from a distance, while their opponents were happy to remain behind their fortifications and await the arrival of Essex. To alleviate the monotony, prisoner exchanges were arranged between the two sides. On the 14th of July nineteen roundheads, held captive at Plympton, were exchanged for an equal number of royalists incarcerated in Plymouth. This was followed three days later by a chivalrous gesture on the part of Thomas Killigrew. A party of elderly women and children, whose husbands and friends were in the service of parliament, had been gathered up by Killigrew and sent across the Tamar to Plymouth. The following day, July 18th, forty-one parliamentarian soldiers were exchanged for forty-one royalists. Some of the roundheads released were from Lieutenant Colonel Vincent Calmady's regiment and had been held in captivity since their capture at Stratton fourteen months before.

With Essex closing in on Tavistock, Grenville was forced to hastily abandon his positions north of Plymouth and concentrate his army on the east bank of the Plym. Alerted by Grenville's recent offer of a truce and well aware that he might slip away, Colonel Kerr maintained a careful watch on the enemy. Conscious that something was in the air, Kerr ordered five companies of foot and a detachment of horse to assemble near the Maudlyn Fort. On Friday July 19th this mixed force headed towards Longbridge by way of Maudlyn Ridge, Townsend Hill and Efford. Grenville, in the meantime, was preparing to abandon his positions along the east bank. Two local women relayed news of the royalist evacuation to the parliamentarians and Colonel Kerr altered his plan. Believing the enemy would cross Longbridge and take the shortest route into Cornwall, he decided to set up an ambush above Efford Hill.

The roundhead infantry took up their concealed positions and the cavalry rode down towards Plympton in order to entice the enemy into attacking. At first all went well, the cavalier horse spotted the roundheads and pursued them back in the direction of their waiting foot. Suddenly, an accidental discharge from a parliamentary matchlock warned the enemy. The royalists drew rein, turned and galloped back towards Plympton before the trap could be sprung, and the roundheads sullenly returned to Maudlyn Fort. Four days later, Grenville put his army on the road and slipped away.

One who accompanied Grenville on his retreat was a cavalryman from Captain John Chaffin's company. This trooper was a hostler and had been acquainted with Henry Pike, the traitor who had conspired with Moses Collins and others to blow up the Maudlyn Fort. With his arms and a good horse, the trooper galloped away from the garrison one night and joined the enemy.

Retreating with his 800 men, Sir Richard marched rapidly northwestwards, hoping to reach Tavistock before Essex, and block the most direct route into Cornwall. Unfortunately Grenville left it too late, Essex had arrived in Tavistock earlier than anticipated and Sir Richard was forced to cross the Tamar above Gunnislake, at Horsebridge. Satisfied the enemy were gone, Colonel Kerr sent detachments out to scour the enemy positions and make sure they had all left. The first men to arrive in the old royalist works found the cavaliers had stolen away so quickly that they left behind most of their heavier equipment. At Plympton eight cannon were found and hauled back to Plymouth and four more were retrieved from Fort Stamford.

With Grenville gone and the town safe, Essex sent Colonel Kerr an order to send him 1,000 reinforcements from the garrison; Kerr had no choice but to obey. With most of her best troops marching across the moors towards Tavistock, Plymouth was left with only a few companies of horse, a detachment of sailors and the local militia. To command the newly-created Plymouth brigade, Essex elected Lord John Robartes, the man chiefly responsible for the army's continued advance westwards. Robartes had recently been appointed Lord Lieutenant of Devon and Cornwall, with responsibility to relieve Plymouth and gain support for the parliamentary cause in Cornwall and he looked forward to his new obligation.

No doubt Robartes' principal concern for an advance into Cornwall was the liberation of his family, then being held as hostages by the royalists and the recovery of his home. Despite an offer of exchange from parliament for the children of Lord Arundell of Wardour earlier in the year, nothing had been accomplished and Robartes' children remained unwilling guests of the king. Lord Robartes constantly assured Essex that if he crossed the Tamar, Cornwall would rise up for parliament and he would be a step closer to ending the war.

Essex and his 10,000-man army had arrived in Tavistock on July 23rd, and the only resistance they met came from a detachment of 150 royalist soldiers, foolishly left behind by Grenville to protect his property at Fitzford. The rest of his troops he kept on the west bank of the Tamar. Noting the size of Essex's army the commander of the royalist garrison knew it would be sheer folly to fight. A huge estate on the edge of Tavistock, Fitzford could not be defended with only 150 men. However, when two roundhead regiments advanced against the house, a number of royalist skirmishers hiding behind a hedge fired a scattered volley. Angered by such defiance the roundheads wheeled up a cannon and aimed it at the hedge.

Wishing to avoid a massacre the royalist commander sent out a flag of truce, requesting a parley to discuss surrender. Next morning, before any arrangements had been made, the parliamentarians rushed the house, still flying its white flag. The cavaliers threw down their weapons and begged for mercy. The roundhead commander declared that if they were all Englishmen they would receive mercy, but any Irish found amongst them would not be so fortunate. The royalists were soon rounded up and the spoils listed, two cannon, muskets, pistols other equipment and money. A number of the prisoners took the covenant and joined the earl's army, the rest were taken away.

To hold up the advance of Essex until Launceston could be fortified, Grenville left several hundred foot and horse in front of Horsebridge, the rest he withdrew and put to work building fortifications around the town. Meanwhile, the troops from Plymouth joined the earl at Tavistock, these men were from the regiments of James Kerr and Anthony Rouse and were commanded by Lieutenant Colonel Robert Moore and Lieutenant Colonel Robert Martin. Having delayed for several days, and pressured all the while by the eager Robartes, Essex finally pushed on towards the Tamar, and on July 26th he attacked Horsebridge, (also referred to as Newbridge).

After several determined attempts to cross the bridge were repulsed by well-placed royalist musketeers, the roundheads pounded forward a third time. In the foremost part of the fighting was part of the Plymouth horse under Major Lahearne. This final attack unnerved the enemy and within minutes the demoralised cavaliers fled, leaving behind a number of casualties strewn over the west bank. Lord Robartes, leading the Plymouth foot regiments, managed to round up 150 prisoners and Essex was delighted. His own casualties numbered 40-50 killed and wounded, but he was now on the Cornish side of the Tamar. The following day the Saltash garrison, fearing encirclement, hastily evacuated the port and marched away to join Grenville. When a detail from Plymouth was rowed across the Tamar to occupy Saltash, they found several more pieces of ordnance abandoned in the fort above the town.

As Grenville, still in Launceston, strived desperately to raise more troops and find arms in a county denuded of both, he received a variety of news. He was informed of the rout at Newbridge but more importantly, he was told that the king was in Exeter with a large army. Abandoning Launceston, Grenville fell back towards Truro.As he retreated a buoyant Lord Essex marched on to Bodmin, but the situation had already changed for parliament. Unaware of Sir Richard's strategic thinking, Essex was being led into a tight corner, while the king with 15,000 troops, was already moving across Dartmoor with the intention of closing the door behind him.

Pleased with the way the campaign was progressing, Charles Stuart reviewed Prince Maurice's troops on Dartmoor and called on the people of Devon to rally and support him. Unfortunately royalist depredations in the county for the past two years had alienated many from their king's cause, and those who did come forward and enlist in the royal army were few in number. Nevertheless the king was satisfied with the condition and size of his force and on July 29th he advanced to Bow, fifteen miles northwest of Exeter. The only sour note to the king's advance was news of a tragic defeat for Prince Rupert's army on July 2nd. Although he didn't know it at the time, the consequences of the battle on Marsten Moor would be the loss of virtually the entire north of England to parliament.

Meanwhile Essex pursued Grenville down towards Lostwithiel and snapped hard at his heels. Sir Richard continued his retreat through Truro and on to Penryn, thirty miles beyond Bodmin and close to Falmouth. A jubilant Essex followed him, though now with more caution, and occupied Bodmin late in July. Here he dallied, waiting for the support Robartes promised him would come once he had crossed the Tamar. Robert Devereux must have been kicking himself, Cornwall was almost totally royalist and fewer recruits came forward here than for the king in Devon. Lord Robartes thought it was time to disappear for a while and he marched the Plymouth brigade down to visit his home at Lanhydrock and occupy the port of Fowey. Suddenly aware of his blunder, Essex continuously informed of the king's progress behind him, decided to halt his pursuit of Grenville. The earl believed his army could still march back out of Cornwall by way of Tavistock or be ferried across the Tamar via Saltash.

Then on August 2nd a bombshell landed, a sweating courier galloped up to Essex's headquarters carrying an urgent dispatch, the king's army was in Launceston. Well and truly caught between two royalist armies, Essex knew he was now cut off from direct contact with Devon. Angry and frustrated the earl rapidly shifted his command to Lostwithiel, a town on the River Fowey south of Bodmin. Occupying Lostwithiel would give the roundhead army a route to the English Channel and keep their communications with the navy open. In a letter to Westminster, dated August 4th, Essex announced his frustration at the way in which a large royalist army had been permitted to march through the Westcountry without molestation. The lord general then went on to explain his reasons for selecting Fowey as a base from which to procure supplies by sea. At about this time Grenville received orders from the king to advance against the parliamentarians with his own army, which had been reinforced by the Cornish militia, bringing his numbers up to almost 2,500. As Essex fell back the king and Grenville pressed forward from two different directions and the roundhead soldiery, with dwindling supplies, contemplated on the failings of their commanders.

Back in Plymouth August the 3rd was an exceptionally windy day. The ketch *Providence*, anchored in Sutton harbour, found herself continually buffeted as her crew endeavoured to fill the vessel with supplies destined for the Earl of Essex's army. One person on board was John Syms and he remembered how the ship sailed out of harbour on the following morning and was almost immediately blown onto the rocks near How Stert. Despite several holes in her hull the *Providence* managed to reach the open sea and headed for Fowey, being repaired en route.

Robert Rich, the 2nd Earl of Warwick and cousin to Robert Devereux, arrived at Plymouth and was appalled at the condition of the town, left almost bereft of first-rate troops. Warwick's main concern was that, if Essex met with defeat in Cornwall, there would only be 1,000 soldiers and seamen available to man four miles of defences. Of this number 200 had been detached and sent across the Tamar to occupy Saltash. As reinforcements, Warwick rounded up 100 of his own sailors and sent them to bolster Colonel Anthony Rouse in Saltash. To supplement Plymouth's ordinance, the ship *Fredrick and William*, lost to the enemy in 1643, was found at Saltash and brought around to Plymouth. Warwick now commanded that her sixteen guns be taken off and transferred up to the forts.

In his late fifties, Robert Rich was an enthusiastic adventurer who had been attracted to the new colonies in the Americas and greatly enjoyed privateering on the high seas. The latter brought him into conflict many times with the East India Company, but it did not stop him. Rich also served as MP for Malden on two occasions, in 1610 and 1614, and in 1625 he was appointed Lord Lieutenant for the county of Essex. None of these domestic titles prevented Warwick from continuing his privateering. Being a member of a strong Puritan family and detesting the extravagance of court life, Robert Rich veered away from the king and his supporters over the years. More and more he sided with those who were against the king's policies and he grew increasingly outspoken. In February 1642 Warwick was appointed Lord Lieutenant for Essex and Norfolk, but parliament realised his maritime skill and on March 10th promoted him admiral of the fleet. A year and a half later, Robert Rich rose even higher when he was elevated to the post of

Lord High Admiral of England in command of all the navies.

Assuming the protection of Plymouth in the absence of Essex, and most of the garrison was his responsibility, Warwick made plans to improve the defences. To stop enemy gunners firing at his ships from Mount Edgcumbe House, the earl decided to attempt its capture.

Rather than risk losing valuable troops, he sent over the following demand for the surrender of Mount Edgcumbe House and its garrison on July 30th: '*Robert Earl of Warwick, Lord High Admiral of England, Ireland, Wales and Captain General of his majesties seas and royal navy. To ye commander in chiefs of Mount Edgcumbe. I do hereby summon you in the name of the king and parliament forthwith to render to me Mount Edgcumbe, now in your keeping, for the use of his majesty and parliament with all things in it. Else you may expect the rigours of war, I being resolved otherwise to enforce your speedy obedience. You are to return me your answer by this bearer, my Lieutenant. Warwick, Aboard his majesties ship* James *in Plymouth Sound, July 30 1644'*.[19]

In the absence of Colonel Piers Edgcumbe, Warwick's flourishingly titled communication was answered simply by Henry Bourne: *'Noble Earl of Warwick, whereas you have summoned me in the name of the king and parliament, to render unto your lord the house Mount Edgcumbe, may it please your honour, I am here entrusted to keep the house for my master Colonel Edgcumbe, till his return, to whom, as I conceive, it doth justly belong. Your humble servant Henry Bourne, Mount Edgcumbe House, July 30th 1644'*.[20]

His bluff having failed, Warwick contented himself with using his fleet to bombard the royalist gun positions along the Cremyll waterfront. Greatly concerned for the plight of Plymouth, the lord high admiral wrote to London on the 18th of August, declaring that should the town fall, the entire west would be in danger. Warwick also explained his difficulty keeping peace between Governor Kerr and Mayor Cawse, the former could be replaced, the latter, unfortunately, could not.

The precarious position of Warwick's cousin Essex soon became evident in Plymouth. Messengers, who slipped through royalist patrols, or returned on ships brought in the news of an ever-worsening situation. To make matters even more disheartening, westerly winds prevented Warwick's ships from supplying the parliamentary army hemmed in around Lostwithiel. Should the king destroy Essex's army, Plymouth would be the next target. Mayor Cawse and Governor Kerr still continued to contradict each other on all matters. Two reasons for such antagonism may have been Kerr's strict discipline and his choice of subordinates. Whatever the justification, with less than a thousand men and the few seamen on loan from Warwick's ships, Kerr and Cawse should have worked together for the good of the town at this critical juncture; it never happened.

With the area around Plymouth momentarily free of enemy troops, supplies ceased to be a problem. The ships arriving in Sutton Pool were bursting at the seams with provisions and ammunition earmarked for Essex. With contrary winds blowing up the Channel, the armada in the two harbours built up and Warwick was able to siphon off supplies for the use of the garrison. Colonel Kerr in the meantime was not idle, he sent out mounted patrols, improved defences, trained the militia and kept in communication with Saltash. Unfortunately Plymouth did not have a say in what happened next, events down in Cornwall would determine the town's destiny.

By the second week of August the two royalist armies of King Charles and Sir Richard Grenville had closed in on Essex, and were only separated by the River Fowey. The royalist capture of Respryn Bridge allowed these two armies to link up. Once united the cavaliers, under the eyes of their king, began to hem in Essex from the north and east. On the 9th the earl was summoned to surrender, he refused, believing he still had several options open to him. Unfortunately Essex's generalship, already poor, deteriorated rapidly. From a good commanding position atop the hills surrounding Lostwithiel and the Fowey river, Essex tragically misused his army, the results were to prove devastating.

Despite being outnumbered by the royalists the odds were not great, and the parliamentarians were nearly all veterans, which evened up the disparity in numbers. Essex continually compounded his mistakes, orders were misunderstood, troops were being sent back and forth between the various fortifications and several of the most strategic sites were either insufficiently manned or not occupied at all. Many of his subordinates believed the earl did not know what to do. Lord Robartes was proving equally inept and he brooded openly over the loss of his home, which had been taken over by Grenville on the 11th.

For the 10,000-man parliamentary army, the situation was becoming more and more irretrievable with each passing day. Unable to stand, Essex found himself pushed from one strong position to another back down the valley towards the sea. On the other hand the king was in high spirits and fought the campaign like an expert. On the 13th the royalists surprised Essex by capturing Polruan Castle, which had been left weakly garrisoned. This triumph gave the cavaliers complete command of the east bank of the Fowey river. To hammer more nails into Robert Devereux's coffin, a mounted relief column, under Sir John Middleton, was defeated near Bridgewater by Sir Francis Doddington. Seven days later, on the 21st of August, the entire royalist army advanced down both sides of the Fowey, swamping Restormal Castle in the process. Once again Essex had failed to use his army properly. Restormal dominated Lostwithiel and was a keystone in the roundhead defences, inadequately garrisoned the castle fell easily.

By now many of Essex's subordinates had grown frustrated and confused by his mishandling of the campaign. Essex though still retained a glimmer of hope that Waller would come to the rescue. Unfortunately at that very moment, Sir William was licking his wounds at Farnham and would never arrive. It seemed as if nature was also against parliament, heavy winds continually prevented Warwick's ships from coming in to land much needed supplies. Nevertheless the roundheads were still able to scour the countryside in the direction of Par, a town half a dozen miles to the west, for forage, but time was rapidly running out. Essex was finally denied this avenue of supply on August 23rd when George Goring with his cavalry and 1,000 foot advanced and occupied Par.

Despite mounting setbacks, Devereux maintained his communications with Warwick's fleet, but the line was unstable at best. John Syms aboard the *Providence* gives a good description of the trauma of one such journey: "*August 27th. The wind blowing E.S.E. because it was we gave ground to ride in, we came off Fowey harbour the winds oft as a whole being very lofty and the sea very tempestuous and boisterous and which was most dangerous we work upon the sea shore. We had fearful gusts for about three hours and more in so much as many in the ship if most men in the ship were afraid what would become of us. We fixed aft our out foretop yard and were much afraid of our main mast, the ship went? With one side near close to the water and the waves dashing into the ship, but at last being thus betwixt fear and hope it began to be somewhat clear and after awhile we espied Rame Head and so, by God's providence, the wind coming southwest, we came into Plymouth harbour the same day about eight of the clock".*[21]

On the night of August 30th, Essex dramatically concluded he could not break the royalist ring and at an emergency council of war he decided to give his cavalry a chance to punch its way out. The infantry would march down to Fowey from where they could be ferried out to the fleet and shipped back to Plymouth. During that night the royalist guards, pre-warned by deserters of the roundhead cavalry's planned breakout, were reinforced and told to be alert. Regardless of all their security measures, Sir William Balfour led 2,000 parliamentary horse safely out of the bottleneck. The Plymouth horse remained behind, having decided to suffer the same fate as the rest of the army. Essex would later speak well of this little band of horsemen from the Westcountry.

As Balfour's cavalry broke out and rode away into the dark, unfamiliar countryside, the Earl of Essex abandoned his defences around Lostwithiel and marched his infantry down muddy trackways to new positions less than two miles from the village of Fowey. With heavy rain lashing the dispirited column, a number of artillery pieces and wagons had to be sacrificed for the sake of speed. The new parliametarian position would be centred on Castle Dore, the last good ground before the coast. When the king found his opponent gone, he sent his army in pursuit, and when he caught up with Essex he wasted no time. Lining up his guns and foot King Charles launched an attack against the parliamentary centre. In the fighting around Castle Dore part of the Plymouth garrison troops held a precarious position along with two other regiments on the right of the line. Here they fought all day and into the early evening, then as darkness closed in, so did disaster. The cavaliers suddenly broke through on the roundhead right, forcing the defenders to retreat away from the river. Those captured were sent back to Tavistock under guard, to be imprisoned in cramped gaols, where many died of ill-treatment and disease.

Finding the enemy advancing down the west bank of the River Fowey, in order to push him away from the village and Warwick's fleet, the Earl of Essex did a despicable thing. Along with Lord Robartes, Sir John Merrick and a number of their close companions, he deserted the army, rode down to one of the coves and took passage for Plymouth on a fishing boat. Essex had abandoned his troops without even informing his senior subordinate, Major General Philip Skippon, who although wounded, was left to console the men and do what he believed best. It would have been better for the army if Essex and his cronies had run off a month earlier; the options open to Skippon now were limited.

After a brief meeting with his brigade commanders, Skippon all for fighting his way out, was voted down. Reluctantly he agreed to surrender the army on September 2nd. The king allowed the parliamentarians to march out without arms, except for the officers, who, as a courtesy, were permitted to retain them. The sick were to be taken aboard Warwick's ships and transported home. All told some 6,000 men and forty-two cannon were captured at Fowey and it was parliament's biggest defeat. An entire army of 10,000 well-armed veterans had marched into Cornwall and been completely devoured. What followed for the survivors would be worse than anything they had yet endured.

Meanwhile Sir William Balfour's cavalry, after several bitter clashes with the pursuing royalists under George Goring, managed to reach Saltash, having lost no more than 100 men during the ride. Balfour rested briefly in the town before crossing the Tamar and riding into Plymouth on September 1st. Balfour's news of the Fowey disaster sent a chill through the defence committee. Either from orders or fear, Balfour's valuable cavalry quickly took its leave of Plymouth and rode away in the direction of Lyme Regis. George Goring continued to chase the roundhead horse, but his pursuit was lackadaisical and the cavaliers never caught up. Due to an injury sustained during the retreat from Fowey, Sir William Balfour was forced to remain in Plymouth until he was sufficiently recovered.

Late in the afternoon of the 2nd, with rain still pouring down, 6,000 disconsolate roundheads marched out of Fowey under guard and made their way up to Lostwithiel. Despite orders from the king, a substantial number of royalist soldiers and locals assembled en route. These people insulted, robbed and beat up many of the exposed parliamentarians. Unable to help their straggling comrades, the main column headed for the border in the direction of Okehampton. Three days later, Philip Skippon led his shabby, demoralised army into the Dartmoor town. During the first phase of its doleful march the column had been greatly reduced, and in fields along the line of retreat many soldiers lay murdered and stripped of their clothing. In Okehampton, Skippon commandeered food and his ravenous men wolfed it down before continuing on towards Tiverton, where the vanguard arrived on the 6th. Eventually 1,000 weary, starving survivors straggled into Poole. This remnant later went on to Portsmouth, while other individual groups trickled into Plymouth or made their way to Southampton.

Shortly after Skippon's surrender, the Earl of Warwick's fleet sailed up the Channel to Portsmouth, dropping many of the wounded off at Plymouth en route. Worried citizens and soldiers clamoured around these new arrivals, pressing them for news, all of which was bad. Warwick expected the port to fall and not wishing to be stranded himself he left behind his vice admiral, William Batten, along with eight ships to support the defenders. Batten was a man who had been associated with the sea for most of his adult life, as a master in the royal navy or involved in commerce. In 1638 he acquired the post of surveyor for the royal navy, and in March 1642 he was appointed to be Warwick's second in command.

Batten saw early action along the east coast of England, and in February 1643 he learned that a ship had sailed from Holland carrying arms and ammunition for the king. Spotting the vessel unloading its cargo at Bridlington, William Batten opened fire, unaware that he was actually firing on the Queen of England. His service later brought him to the south coast. While in Plymouth, Batten did his utmost to raise morale, extra sailors were landed from the fleet and communications between Plymouth and Saltash kept open. When the House of Commons learned of the many wounded from Essex's army being dumped at Plymouth, Sir Gilbert Gerard, Treasurer of War, was ordered to pay Philip Francis fifty shillings for a surgeon's chest, with which the injured could be cared for.

On September 3rd Sir Richard Grenville, under orders to join Goring and press after Balfour, disobeyed his king and decided on a plan of his own. Hoping to gain a personal victory, he cast an eager eye on Saltash. With the help of Sir Edward Waldegrave, the commander of a small horse regiment, the town was easily occupied and all eleven guns captured without a shot being fired. The 400 defenders, under a nervous Colonel Anthony Rouse, having abandoned Saltash, fled across the Tamar shortly before the royalists appeared. Almost simultaneously the Earl of Essex arrived at Plymouth, and as he stepped ashore he was greeted with the news of Saltash's loss. Enraged Essex, rather hypocritically, believed Colonel Rouse had left Saltash too hastily and at first the colonel was refused admittance into the town. By mid-afternoon though, Essex had a change of heart, possibly recalling his own desertion, and Rouse and his anxious command were allowed in.

Many were convinced that Anthony Rouse had behaved cowardly whilst in command at Saltash. Indeed during his occupation of the town it became common knowledge that Rouse openly discouraged his troops, announcing they would get no pay and that they should expect to be stuck on the Cornish side of the Tamar all winter. Rouse did not play a significant part in the siege of Plymouth, but he was present from 1643 onwards. Anthony Rouse, the son of a Cornish gentleman, now in his late twenties, rose from captain of horse in 1643 to colonel of a foot regiment in 1644, having served at both Exeter and Plymouth.

When Essex arrived in Plymouth, such were the feelings against him for deserting his army that he tarried only a short time before leaving. Boarding a ship he sailed for Portsmouth to await the arrival of his foot, which at that moment was struggling across the Devon moors. Like Rouse, Essex must have sensed the hostility aimed at him in Plymouth, especially since the cream of the town's defenders had been sacrificed in Cornwall. Why Robartes was considered any better than Essex is difficult to understand. Despite the disaster and Robartes' improper escape, the mayor and his councillors still wanted him as governor. John Cawse hoped Kerr would be superseded and Robartes was his choice. Consequently when Essex and Merrick sailed away, John Robartes remained to assume the mantle of governor.

Many commended the Plymouth brigade for their gallantry and fighting spirit; the troops of lieutenant colonels Martin and Moore had fought well during the Earl of Essex's fruitless campaign. Sir Shilston Calmady also praised the conduct of the garrison troops from Plymouth in a letter he sent to the House of Commons. Now with the defeat of the army and 15,000 royalists marching on Plymouth, the greatly-outnumbered defenders waited for, what many believed, would be the inevitable onslaught.

(19) Page 209: Letter from the Earl of Warwick to Mt Edgcumbe House, reproduced from Transactions of the Plymouth Institute; by kind permission of the Plymouth Athenaeum.
(20) Page 209: Letter from Henry Bourne to the Earl of Warwick, reproduced from Transactions of the Plymouth Institute; by kind permission of the Plymouth Athenaeum.
(21) Page 211: John Syms, A daybook of special passages and mercies, British Library, Add 35297; by kind permission of the British Library.

Chapter 10

The King Pays His Respects

Securing the captured ordnance, wagons and weapons, and having rested his army sufficiently, King Charles marched towards Tavistock, which he reached on September 5th. Four days later the royalist army strolled across the moors towards Trennimans Jump. From here part of the queen's regiment of horse rode on to reconnoitre Plymouth's outer defences. Colonel John Cansfield commanding the regiment, expected little resistance as he led his horsemen towards the port. Approaching the outer line of forts along Tavistock Road, Cansfield was shocked to suddenly find a body of parliamentary horse bearing down on his column. Unprepared for a fight, the royalists turned and fled, pursued by the roundheads almost to Trennimans. Observing the entire king's army spread out before them, the parliamentarians prudently withdrew.

Aware of Plymouth's renowned fortitude, King Charles sent a solitary mounted trumpeter to the town, requesting the port's surrender. The royal letter carried by the messenger contained the usual promises, no loss of privilege, no royalist garrison and pardon for all, soldier and civilian alike. Picking up the trumpeter a roundhead patrol escorted him into Plymouth, locked him up for a day and released him on condition that the next time he brought such an insulting communication he would be hanged. Later in the day a parliamentary drummer took the defence committee's official response back to the king; it was an emphatic no!

Next morning, Tuesday the 10th, the royalist army marched down through Knackersknowle, Mannamead and Compton, where they deployed and set up their camps and baggage park in the area known today as Vapron Road. The king's headquarters were further back at Widey Court, whose owner Yeoman Hele was an eminent supporter of his majesty. Prince Maurice must have recalled contemptuously the disastrous events of ten months previous, as he selected a point above Lipson Creek for his centre of operations. From here Maurice could stare across at the site of his earlier defeat.

Royalist troops edged their way slowly nearer to the town's outer line, skirmishing lightly with roundhead dragoons and horse in the orchards and fields around Thornhill. Eventually superior numbers began to tell, and the Plymouth men were forced to fall back down Townsend Hill and along the Maudlyn Ridge toward their main positions. The enemy pursued until the guard at the Maudlyn Fort opened up, but they did not fall back. Instead they took up an advanced position behind a high hedge barely 150 yards from the Maudlyn Fort. Losses during the arrival of the king's army were light, with only a few killed and wounded on either side.

Royalist gunners now manhandled twenty-eight heavy cannon up into positions along what is today Seymour Road and placed them in crude batteries running east and west, almost opposite the roundhead forts. The foot regiments raised their standards on high ground near the guns and waited. As the cavaliers moved into position the parliamentary gunners opened up. The enemy replied and gunsmoke soon began to drift down into the valleys. This long-range artillery duel would prove more of an inconvenience than a threat, and the only casualties recorded from Plymouth were a woman whose leg was taken off and a man who lost an arm.

Plymouth's position at the time of the king's approach looked desperate, despite the strength of her outer forts. Manpower was critically short, deaths from sickness, already rife, rose rapidly with the sudden influx of wounded from Essex's defeated army. As a consequence shops in the town closed and all available men were given arms and sent by Colonel Kerr to bolster the outer line. All told there were less than 3,000 troops manning the forts and guns along the outer line. The nucleus of this force were several small regiments; those of Colonel Crocker, Lieutenant Colonel Thomas Fitch's, Sir Shilston Calmady's, the few companies of Kerr's and Rouse's regiments that had remained in the town during Essex's campaign and Sir Edmond Fowell's trained bandsmen. Numerous little companies of horse were also on hand, but totalled together they still numbered less than a third of the force available to the king. Never before had the town been in such a perilous position, nor the enemy so strong.

To increase the number of defenders, Captain William Batten further depleted his squadron by drafting seamen for shore defence. Recently many of his sailors had been working on How Stert, throwing up an earthwork across the lower part of the peninsula. Now with the king before the town, the work ceased and the men were transferred to the outworks. With a good supply of powder, ample food and a population used to fighting under siege, the sight of a formidable, victorious army, led by the King of England, did nothing to intimidate the garrison.

In the capital Plymouth's predicament took temporary precedence over the re-equipping of Essex's army and other important matters. On September 7th the Lords and Commons decided to dispatch a number of regiments and fresh supplies of food, ammunition and clothing to the port. Orders were sent to Colonel William Strode, commanding him to send 5-600 men. Further requests were sent to Colonel Anthony Stapely at Chichester, Colonel Ralph Weldon and Colonel John Owen, the latter commanding the city of London yellow auxiliaries, then at Weymouth. In addition Colonel John Birch's Kentish regiment, also stationed at Weymouth, was ordered to Plymouth. Unfortunately the response was poor, excuses were given by nearly all the commanders not to go, only Birch obeyed, but even he contravened his superiors' wishes. Colonel Birch was to take ship and only disembark at Plymouth if the king's army stood before the town. Had the king withdrawn, Birch was to sail back to Weymouth. By the time the Kent regiment arrived the royalist army had gone, leaving only Grenville before the town, but Colonel Birch disembarked his companies nonetheless.

As an added boost to the town's courageous defenders, Lord John Robartes was appointed governor on the 7th, though he would not take over from Kerr immediately; Robartes' sheer presence greatly inspired the town in its hour of need. The new governor had a point to prove, he needed to regain the confidence he had lost during the fiasco at Fowey. Born 1606 into a family that had made its fortune from the tin and wool trades, John Robartes, a strict Puritan, attended Oxford University in 1625. Upon the death of his father, nine years later, John took over the family estates as Baron Robartes of Truro. In the meantime he had married Lucy Rich, daughter of the Earl of Warwick. In 1640 Robartes became Lord

Lieutenant of Cornwall and upon the outbreak of war he organised a small garrison for his home at Lanhydrock.

Soon Robartes received orders from the Earl of Essex to join him and command one of his newly-raised regiments. John Robartes served with great distinction at the battles of Edgehill, Newbury and Lostwithiel. Many commented on Lord Robartes' courage on the field, but many more remarked on his unfriendly nature and overbearing manner. What Robartes lacked in demeanour he would make up for by an ability to inspire confidence and raise the morale of the Plymouth garrison. Most of the townsfolk knew Robartes' fine house had been given over to Sir Richard Grenville by the king and that the royalists were holding his children captive. On his abandonment of the army at Fowey, they shrugged their shoulders and put it from their minds, he was here now as the redoubtable leader of their defiance.

When Colonel James Kerr was eventually able to transfer full authority over to Robartes, he himself would be ordered by Essex to report to him at Portsmouth. If Kerr ever did get to Portsmouth and meet with Essex he didn't remain there long; considered an asset to Plymouth, he was back in the port by early 1645.

With dissatisfaction fervent amongst the population, Robartes wrote an early letter of concern to London on the 18th, informing Westminster of the situation: *'This town has been assisted by the vice admiral, who still rides here and had the whole fleet done so the king probably would not have attempted this place. The soldiers who remain being so ill-paid, are low in courage, but loud in complaints.*

Many of the inhabitants are cold and indifferent, weary of a two-year siege. The ammunition scant and such as a little time will exhaust, besides want of arms, deadness of spirit, and I doubt not a disaffected party within.

This day upon the return of the trumpet, it is probably that the enemy will storm the works. If they form a siege time will be allowed for an after supply'.[22]

For the time, Robartes, Kerr, Batten and the mayor put aside their separate differences and concentrated mutually on stopping the enemy and raising morale. Skirmishing between the two sides broke out somewhere along the line almost hourly. Numbers of wounded were conveyed back down to the town, those that survived were fortunate, others whose wounds were so bad that they died, were buried in St Andrew's. Many who succumbed on the field were placed in pits behind the lines and their graves might never be found.

On the 11th of September, the day Cornwall's trained bands assembled at Mount Edgcumbe in order to take over the protection of the Tamar river line, the king left Widey and rode out towards his artillery. As Charles Stuart reached the batteries above Lipson Creek, the royal standard was recognised by the Maudlyn Fort gunners. These men, proficient in the service of their cannon, defiantly fired their own salute. Undaunted by the garrison's impertinence, the king chatted leisurely with his officers during the cannonade, recalling his wife's words that he should not linger too long in front of Plymouth. Unfortunately King Charles had already missed his greatest opportunity to capture the port. Had he moved directly after his victory at Fowey and launched an all-out assault, the town might have fallen. By allowing the defenders time to shake off the loss of Essex's army and giving Robartes, Kerr and Batten time to encourage the garrison, he lost the initiative.

Concerned over previous attempts at storming strong defensive positions, the king watched as part of his infantry moved down, what is today the Hyde Park Ford-Park-Hillside area, to attack the large Pennycomequick Fort. The battle which followed was loud and confusing and ammunition was expended as if it were going out of fashion, but it was no more than a slugging match. Despite Captain Richard Clarke and his gunners throwing cannonball after cannonball at the determined cavaliers, the enemy managed to get in close to the defenders by utilising a number of hedges on the slopes below the fort. Reinforcements from the town double-timed up to Pennycomequick, and with troops sent down from Maudlyn, they formed a strong, unbreakable barrier. The royalists could get no closer and eventually the king called off the attack, only to allow it to be resumed during the night. The results were the same; the royal army suffered even more casualties and withdrew. Several half-hearted attacks against Stonehouse, and again at Pennycomequick were also easily repulsed. All the time the monotonous dull cannonade between the two armies continued, with little effect.

Once the losses had been counted, the king shifted to an entirely different mode of warfare, bribery. Lord George Digby, the elder brother of Colonel John Digby and also the king's secretary of state and one of his favourites, sent a woman into the roundhead lines with a sealed letter for Lord Robartes. When his lordship read the communiqué, he must have smiled wryly to himself. Digby promised Robartes great reward and high rank if he would hand over the town of Plymouth. With his children still in royalist custody, his lands sequestered and his plundered home being used by Sir Richard Grenville, Robartes scoffed at the king's offer. He would never betray his trust nor his father-in-law, the Earl of Warwick.

Robartes sent word of Digby's offer to the committee of both kingdoms: '*This morning there came a woman with a sealed letter from the Earl of Digby, the original I send you, and immediately after the summons Grenville summoned the town while the lord general was in it, but being a fugitive he received no answer.*

I hear nothing of our horse but that they are gone eastwards; had they attended the kings movements I do not see how he could have attempted this or any other place. You know well the importance of this place and how much better it is to defend than regain, the sad aspect of which induced me to stay here a few days to see if I could contribute anything to the public advantage'.[23]

The fighting around Plymouth during the five days was surprisingly minimal, considering the size of the royal army and the make-up of the defending force. The king never launched a full-scale assault, and the reason for this might have been the failure of an earlier costly siege. Bristol and the horrendous losses sustained there caused his majesty to shy away from a full-blown frontal offensive. Another reason for Charles' apprehensive strategy in front of Plymouth may have been the fear he felt for the safety of his capital. Since Rupert's defeat and the loss of his army at Marsten Moor back in July, the king believed he needed to get home as soon as possible, before parliament organised itself and attacked Oxford. Whatever the reason, on September 12th King Charles packed up most of his artillery and marched away from Plymouth, never to return.

Upon the departure of the royal army a tremendous cheer went up from the defenders. First they had trounced Hopton, then Prince Maurice, Colonel John Digby, Sir Richard Grenville and now the king himself, a great achievement for a small town. In the hope of capturing prisoners and booty, and in order to observe the enemy, a body of roundhead horse left the lines and wound its way cautiously along the Maudlyn Ridge in the wake of the cavalier rearguard.

Left behind to the mercy of the garrison was a large number of royalist sick and wounded. These men had been so badly injured in the recent fighting they could not be moved. Wagons were now sent out to the royalist camps and the wounded brought into town, where many subsequently died of their terrible injuries. Once the siege had been raised forty enemy prisoners were taken out of the overcrowded town gaols and transferred to London by ship.

Losses suffered by the defenders of Plymouth and her civilians are difficult to estimate for the month of September. Burials in St Andrew's from battle, disease and natural causes numbered eighty-six, other interments, either behind the front lines or in pits, probably trebled this figure. Not a particularly high proportion of losses, but high enough especially when added to the 1,000 soldiers lost in Cornwall. Lord John Robartes and Captain William Batten now reorganised the town's defences. Men voluntarily left their premises closed to help work on the outer forts and to take turns at guard duty until suitable reinforcements arrived. Foraging parties were once again free to roam the area north of the town, which had been stripped almost bare by the king's army. Enemy forts were flattened and the open sections between the main roundhead forts were closed in.

On September 26th Robartes took time to write another letter to the House of Commons appealing for aid: *'Neither money nor ammunition have yet come for the supply of this place. The want of the former makes sundry officers unwilling to stay here and the want of the later will make them unable.*

The inhabitants are so exhausted that they are not able to support a third part of the garrison, which I conceive in the lowest proportion should be 2,500 foot besides the townsmen and 400 horse.

If twelve ton of match, four ton of lead and 1,000 shot each for saker, minion and falcon, with 200 barrels of gunpowder were sent down, these would supply the present until a further magazine were provided, which I leave in your consideration'.[24]

With Vice Admiral Batten riding at anchor and only a small royalist force quartered around Plympton, Lord Robartes felt confident of holding Plymouth for parliament.

On the same day, Major Willis was given money to purchase provisions for the soldiers of Colonel Kerr's regiment at Southampton, where they were awaiting a ship to take them back to Plymouth. Captain Martin had already received a small amount of money from quartermaster Richard Clapp in Plymouth for the relief of Colonel Rouse's regiment, located somewhere between Poole and Weymouth. These men were the survivors of the two regiments sent into Cornwall with Essex.

After the departure of the king, Sir Richard Grenville, general of the king's forces in Devon and Cornwall remained behind to blockade Plymouth to the best of his ability. To contain the parliamentarians, Grenville was left with only 800 men; Sir Richard must have been confident because he promised to capture Plymouth by Christmas, as Prince Maurice had boasted a year before. Once again Grenville set up headquarters miles from his base of operations; this time he utilized Buckland Abbey, the sequestered home of Sir Francis Drake. Until he could raise a much larger army, the Tamar and Plym would form the ideal natural barriers to pen in the garrison. During the next few months Grenville's provost marshals and cavalry harried towns and villages around Plymouth, rounding up reluctant volunteers for his new army.

On September 17th Plymouth accepted its third wartime mayor. Twelve days later out went the antagonistic John Cawse and in came the more accommodating Justinian Peard. Born at Goodleigh near Barnstaple in 1597, Peard grew to become a prominent merchant. On April 27th 1631 Justinian Peard married Elizabeth Taylor in Exeter Cathedral and by 1642 he and his family were living in Plymouth. Peard invested considerably in property at home and abroad, but sadly during the war years Justinian Peard would lose five of his children. Unlike his predecessor, Peard was well received by the town's military authorities and cooperation between the army and civilian authorities gelled well for the next twelve months.

Between Peard's election and appointment, the first reinforcements promised by parliament reached the port and marched ashore. These were Colonel John Birch and his 800 Kentishmen, who arrived from Weymouth on September 20th. Birch was under strict orders from Sir William Waller that should the king raise the siege of Plymouth, he was to bring his regiment back to Weymouth. Birch, for some mystifying reason, failed to carry out his superiors' command and he would remain in Plymouth for nine months, proving an effective ally.

A short time after the king's departure, Joseph Grenville, a sixteen-year-old royalist, made his way voluntarily into the Plymouth lines, where he announced his intention of joining parliament. Hearing of the incident and learning that the boy was a relative of Sir Richard Grenville, Lord Robartes valued the boy's treachery. Believing he had one over on his opponent, Robartes gave young Grenville the rank of captain. For a week Captain Grenville grew in popularity and made many friends in the garrison, until the eighth day. With discontent over pay and conditions spreading through the parliamentary lines, Grenville had taken mental notes and sounded out a number of what he believed were dispirited officers.

When he listened in on a conversation between Lieutenant Colonel Michael Searle, the disgruntled officer who had been replaced by one of James Kerr's officers and several others, Captain Grenville's ears pricked up. Lieutenant Colonel Searle complained bitterly of having no pay for weeks and boasted that he would never again serve parliament. Grenville managed to separate Searle from his companions and spoke to him privately offering £3,000 to Searle if he would turn his coat and betray Plymouth. Appalled by the youngster's perfidious offer, Searle stalled for a while so as not to alarm the boy, then went immediately to Lord Robartes and reported the incident.

Joseph Grenville was arrested at once and interrogated before a council of war. The boy refused to say anything, and with the prisoner unwilling to defend himself, the court had no option but to find him guilty of sedition; consequently he was sentenced to death. When word of the incident reached Sir Richard Grenville, the royalist commander made every effort to have his kinsman pardoned and exchanged, offering any amount of money. Annoyed at being taken in, and bearing in mind the way his own children had been ousted from their home by the royalists, Robartes refused Grenville's overtures. A gallows was set up at Mount Gould and on September 26th, to the rage of Sir Richard, Joseph Grenville was hanged in full view of both sides. It must be said in the boy's defence that although only sixteen years old, Joseph Grenville died with dignity and bravery, still refusing to talk.

Fighting flared up seriously again when Robartes sent 700 foot and horse across the Tamar by boat in the early hours of October 4th. Landing near Saltash, the roundheads easily routed the small garrison left there by Grenville and reoccupied the town. Satisfied with his initial success, Robartes sent a second expedition across the water, this time aimed at Millbrook. The village fell as easily as Saltash had and put Grenville in a very unhealthy position. The cavalier commander feared for his communications with southeastern Cornwall. With Saltash and Millbrook in enemy hands, Grenville's blockade of Plymouth had been greatly reduced.

Robartes believed his troops could maintain their positions along the west bank of the Tamar if he could be substantially reinforced, consequently he hurried off another dispatch to London: *'This morning, with a party of foot we assaulted and took Saltash, which may be kept if your lordships send in time a good supply of men and ammunition. Yesterday there came on shore from the Isle of Wight fifty-two soldiers including corporals under the command of Captain Baskett.*

Of the Plymouth foot which went from hence 1,000, there are come back with Lieutenant Colonel Martin only 200'.[25]

Grenville had to do something and quickly, any delay would enable Robartes to take further offensive action, and the entire royalist position around Plymouth would be in danger of falling apart. Sir Richard rose to the challenge, within hours of Saltash's loss, he planned a counterattack, which was to go in before Robartes could cram in more troops. With extra guns and ammunition sent up by Sir Francis Bassett, royalist High Sheriff of Cornwall, Grenville crossed the Tamar above Plymouth and, reinforced by the Cornish trained bands, he closed in on Saltash. Robartes now reacted as Essex had at Lostwithiel, he sat back and allowed the enemy to deal with Saltash and Millbrook at their leisure.

Once on the west bank, Sir Richard Grenville wasted little time; to prevent the enemy from attacking his back he ordered a detachment around to assault Millbrook. With the rest of his force he was now able to focus entirely on Saltash. Those parliamentarians defending Millbrook were so surprised by the speed of the royalist counter offensive they were unable to organise a suitable defence. Unsupported and with the Tamar at their backs, the roundheads put up only weak resistance before fleeing with a loss of forty men killed and wounded and thirty-three prisoners.

When a courier rode up to Grenville before Saltash and informed him his rear was safe, he set about recapturing the town. The 700-strong garrison, flabbergasted by Grenville's sudden appearance, feverishly fortified its position, but morale was already sinking. The first royalist attack went in on Saturday October 5th, less than twenty-four hours after Robartes' men had first taken possession of Saltash. This assault came in haphazardly and was easily beaten back with heavy loss to the attackers. When reinforcements joined Grenville the next morning, he sent in a second attack. This time part of the town near the river was overrun, despite intense fire from the defenders and the assistance of a parliamentary warship, which had sailed up the Tamar and was firing its guns at the royalists. Suffering heavy casualties, the Cornishmen hung on to their gains and could not be dislodged. Soon they began expanding their foothold, but the roundheads would not give up.

On the 7th brutal hand-to-hand fighting allowed the parliamentarians to evict the cavaliers and consolidate their position. By now the defenders, having refused several offers to surrender, were tired and way past their best. Supplies of food and ammunition were dangerously low and many troops were dead on their feet. During the evening Sir Richard planned a two-pronged assault against the port for the next day. At 1 p.m. on the 8th, two regiments of cavaliers charged the barricades, one from the south the other from the north. What followed was two hours of confused, bitter fighting. The roundheads were slowly but surely pushed back and the battle flowed into the narrow, slippery streets. The defenders were eventually pressed down towards the river, resisting as long as possible. A few managed to find boats and escape, but the majority, between 4-500, were killed, wounded or captured; the final surrender took place at 3 p.m.

Grenville jubilantly claimed between 4-500 roundheads killed during the battle and 100 more captured. No doubt he misread the lists; the figures should have read 100 killed and wounded, 4-500 captured, royalist killed and wounded must at least have equalled parliamentarian losses. Having promised quarter only if the garrison surrendered before he captured the place, Grenville, still volatile after the execution of Joseph Grenville, threatened to put to death all prisoners taken. Fortunately the king heard of his general's insane threat from a letter hurriedly sent to Prince Rupert by Colonel John Ashburnham. Grenville, who probably never meant to go through with his threat, was commanded by King Charles not to even consider such actions against prisoners of war.

Charles Stuart knew that executions on such a scale would only bring retaliation and drive those still neutral into parliament's service. No doubt Grenville did hang a small number of captives as an example. Both sides often meted out this kind of retribution with great wantonness in the days of the civil war. By retaking Saltash and Millbrook, Richard Grenville had restored his direct communications with Cornwall and Lord Robartes had lost a large number of troops he could ill-afford to lose. Why Robartes sent 700 men into hostile territory and then left them to be gobbled up without support is difficult to comprehend. Despite his popularity with the population of Plymouth and his previous record, Robartes was not a competent tactician.

As reported by Robartes on October 4th, sometime late in September or early October, Lieutenant Colonel Robert Martin had arrived back in Plymouth with 200 survivors of the Plymouth brigade, much to his wife's relief. The fighting around Lostwithiel and the calamitous march to Portsmouth took a dreadful toll on the lieutenant colonel, for within a month of his return home, Robert Martin was dead. Another victim of the war at this time was Mrs Prudence Wadden, the mother of fifteen children and the wife of Plymouth's popular MP Mr John Wadden.

Robert Trelawny, the town's most passionate royalist champion, whose home at Ham had been sequestered and lay plundered, burnt and desolate, also died in 1644. Trelawny had petitioned parliament for his release on several occasions, but was always refused. His wife Anne had passed away the year before and now at the age of forty-five, doleful and unhappy he succumbed to illness brought on by imprisonment. Robert Trelawny lies in an unmarked grave, forgotten by most, though he never forgot his home town. In his will he bequeathed £200 towards the continued building of Charles' Church.

Many others of lesser fame were also dying; in October 136 people were buried in St Andrew's, followed by 107 more in November. Plympton interred twenty-six people in an eight-week period. A local royalist, Walter Hele of Merrafield Plympton, had been persecuted and forced to flee from his home early in the war. When the cavalier army occupied the area, Hele returned to his looted home. Now as plague ripped through the community he was struck down and died. Walter Hele was buried at St Mary's on October 5th. Smallpox, typhus, influenza and other diseases were spread through Plymouth by overcrowding and poor sanitation, killing many. December proved to be the worst month of all, when recorded burials in St Andrew's ran up to 140, forty-two of them soldiers, but the town continued to remain firm, though not necessarily united.

One, whose life came to a sudden end on December 23rd and was not mourned by the people of Plymouth, was Sir Alexander Carew. After his trial, during which he fervently denied the charge of treason, Carew was temporarily reprieved. This came about by his wife's intervention and it kept him alive for the next year. At this time Sir Alexander was held in the Tower of London, while Jane Carew did her best to have him released. Her final petition was read in the Commons of November 23rd and Carew's existence on earth was extended for a further month. Jane, unhappy and distressed, had informed Westminster that her husband's mind was distracted and that he was unwell. Consequently the lieutenant of the Tower was ordered to visit Alexander Carew and acquaint the House of Commons on the state of his mind.

Two days later the Commons granted Sir Alexander Carew no more than the four weeks already given so he could put his estate in order for the sake of his wife and children. Finally on December 23rd 1644 Sir Alexander's time ran out. At 10 a.m. Carew, escorted by several officers and two companies of militia, made his way to Tower Hill, where the scaffold stood. Having carefully climbed the steps to the execution platform, Carew, weak after his confinement, briefly conversed with one of the ministers present.

Sir Alexander spoke quietly and told the priest that he blamed no one for his predicament, he then went on to explain: *"All that you can lay to my charge is but intention, and no man knowest my intentions better than myself, put me to what tortures you please. Sir this is clear that when I came ashore at Plymouth, I asked them whether they would believe me what I said, they told me no. I am in that condition that whatsoever I say is not to be believed, and therefore I have leave to hold my peace".*[26]

Alexander Carew then faced the crowd, spoke a few words and requested all to listen while he read the 23rd psalm. Once he had finished, the prisoner turned to face his executioner, who with axe in hand, asked the baronet to forgive him. Handing the axeman some coins Carew replied: *"I forgive thee, leave my clothes, take my head and do handsomely".* Sir Alexander knelt before the block and repeated the last words his mother had uttered: *"Lord though thou killest me, yet I will put my trust in thee".*[27]

The executioner lifted his axe and brought it down, severing Carew's head cleanly. His body was then taken by cart and buried at Hackney. The so-called traitor was dead, a fitting end to one whose attempt at treason, if treason it was, could have lost Plymouth to the enemy and changed the entire course of the war.

One of Plymouth's greatest heroes of the war, Philip Francis the popular mayor and militia captain, who had fought so gallantly in a number of engagements and a man who had received the thanks of many, including William Lenthall speaker of the House of Commons, recently crossed swords with two despicable embezzlers. Charles Vaughan, the town's treasurer and Thomas Gewen, his deputy and brother-in-law, had persecuted Francis for months over a set of pearls. Both men reported to parliament that Francis had refused to hand over a string of pearls, which had been sequestered from Lord Marlborough. The two men also declared that after hearing news of Waller's defeat at Devizes, Philip Francis had sided with Sir Alexander Carew.

The pearls had been seized by the deputy lieutenants of Plymouth and given to Francis for safekeeping. Late in February 1644, Colonel Gould, Mr John Champnes and Thomas Gewen requested the pearls be given over. Concerned by the motives of the treasury agents, Philip Francis declared he would hand the item back only if he received a written order to do so. For his impertinence the old mayor was imprisoned for two months, during which time his home was searched and his servants questioned. Once the pearls had been located they were taken away and sent to Charles Vaughan, who was in London at that time with Peter Keckwich.

Vaughan kept the pearls for over six weeks, but it was only after Francis' release from prison that their existence was brought to parliament's attention. Vaughan and Keckwich were ordered to report to the House of Commons immediately, where they were questioned. Vaughan endeavoured to pass the blame for not handing the pearls over sooner to others. He even tried to involve the Earl of Warwick. None of Vaughan's statements were given credence, and the fact that some of the pearls had mysteriously disappeared from the string, but could not be proved, helped destroy his integrity. Philip Francis was acquitted of any scandal and Colonel Gould was dead, so no blame could be attached to such a hero, even though he may have been involved somewhere along the line.

Despite the garrison's loyalty to parliament, many found the Puritan way of life extremely austere. Lord Robartes himself was a devout Puritan who continued Colonel Gould's policy of punishing blasphemers. Many officers were penalised by Robartes for swearing and gambling, consequently rumours of discontent were constantly spread around the blockaded port. John Ellison, captain of the *Providence,* a ship often seen in Plymouth waters, was a true parliamentarian, but like many, he was also strongly opposed to rigid Puritanism.

Ellison frequently objected to the way Lord Robartes punished his subordinates for minor transgressions. When John Syms, the radical cleric, heard Ellison berating the governor one day, he spoke out against the captain. An argument broke out and the two men almost came to blows; surprisingly a number of Ellison's officers took Syms' side and the captain was forced to back down. The next day Ellison had great difficulty in maintaining discipline on board his ship. John Syms encouraged the crew to obey their captain, but many of the junior officers had already signed a petition against Ellison, which Syms sent to the Earl of Warwick, thereby weakening the captain's authority even further.

The incident eventually came before the naval commissioners in early December, and John Syms appeared in London to give his own evidence and protect those who had helped him. The members of the board listened to all the evidence, but with their own naval backgrounds and a dislike for the harsh ways of Puritanism, they came out sympathetically towards Ellison. Not so lucky were those crewmen who went against their captain, many were arrested and imprisoned in the Marshalsea. Syms was more fortunate and found himself released without punishment.

With sordid rumours and open criticism circulating, and a lack of regular pay, discontentment intensified. When the House of Commons cleared Philip Francis, suspicion of foul play and corruption hovered over the heads of Charles Vaughan and Thomas Gewen. As father-in-law to Nicholas Rowe, who would soon become secretary to the Plymouth war committee, Gewen soon found himself embroiled in another scandal, involving Rowe. Rowe was rumoured to have been in correspondence with Sir Richard Grenville, but this was never proved. Also Gewen's eldest son was reported to have attempted to coerce one of the officers of the garrison. Rowe allegedly persuaded Captain Thomas Staynor to desert parliament and go with him into the royalist lines. One of his father-in-law's servants was to bring horses to a point outside the outer line and the two men would ride away from Plymouth. Such stories were invented and spread with relish by dissatisfied soldiers and civilians, but they faded away just as rapidly as they had appeared.

Greatly concerned over arms shortages, Mayor Justinian Peard and Lord Robartes wrote constantly to parliament requesting weapons with which to continue the town's defiant stance against tyranny. Westminster responded on October 14th with an order for 300 carbines, 300 sets of pistols, 180 back, breast and pots and 200 muskets. These were delivered to the committee for Plymouth for use of the town. Unfortunately they would not arrive quickly enough and Robartes would be forced to send further communiqués to the capital. Cash for the port was also being collected from the confiscated estates and possessions of royalist delinquents, such as Sir James Palmer.

Despite everything, Grenville's fractional blockade continued and Plymouth could enjoy its third Christmas of the war still undefeated, but Robartes was far from happy. In a letter to William Lenthall dated November 16th 1644 he declared in part: *'I desire the ammunition I asked for should be sent with all speed and also that money be supplied for the garrison. Had not a ship of fish and some lyncloth been taken, which for the instant necessity of this garrison we were forced to sell, I do not know how dangerous our condition had been.*

Here is now but one ship belonging to the state. I conceive that very good service might be done if there were six or eight small ships such as the Providence *here, the enemy making use of this season for his supplies'.*[28]

After King Charles left Plymouth in mid-September, he marched through Devon, Somerset and into Dorset, recapturing Barnstaple and Ilfracombe along the way. Eventually he reached Newbury and relieved Donnington Castle in October, while William Waller, the Earl of Essex, the Earl of Manchester and Oliver Cromwell squabbled amongst themselves as to what should be done. With Prince Rupert on his way, Charles remained in and around Newbury. While he waited, the king received news that a small army of loyal Scots under the Earl of Montrose, had won a number of engagements which culminated in the capture of Aberdeen. On the down side, the royalists had surrendered Newcastle to Alexander Leslie's Scottish army, almost the entire north was now lost to parliament and their allies.

Shortly after the departure of 1,500 royalist cavalry from Newbury for the relief of Banbury, the parliamentarians moved north from Basingstoke to attack the king's foot. On the 27th of October the roundheads advanced into battle, but the fighting did not go as arranged. The plan, a two-pronged movement, was badly coordinated and after three hours of combat, during which parliament suffered heavy casualties, nightfall brought an end to the useless slaughter. In the darkness the king left his ordnance at Donnington Castle and withdrew his foot towards Bath, where he joined forces with Prince Rupert. When the two armies met, King Charles marched back to Oxford. In the second week of November the king believed himself strong enough to fetch his artillery from Donnington, which was again under siege. Regardless of strong parliamentary forces, the cavaliers were able to move in, limber up their cannon and march back to Oxford without hindrance.

On December 9th the House of Commons voted to change the way its military leaders were fighting the war. Instead of the armies being led by inept politicians, it was decided a man could only serve Westminster or the military, not both. Those members in the field were to resign their commissions and retain their political seats. The only exception to this new law would be Oliver Cromwell; such was Cromwell's success in the field and in parliament that he could not be spared from either. Fortunately two of Oliver Cromwell's most troublesome opponents, Manchester and Essex were not so lucky, both would be forced to resign from the army in April 1645. This Bill, that should have been passed at the beginning of the war, would be known as the Self Denying Ordinance.

(22) Page 220: Letter from Lord Robartes, Governor of Plymouth to the Committee of Both Kingdoms, September 18th 1644; State Papers 21/16 pp 248,249; by kind permission of the National Archives, London.
(23) Page 222: Letter from Lord Robartes, Governor of Plymouth to the Committee of Both Kingdoms, September 18th 1644; State Papers 21/16 pp 248,249; by kind permission of the National Archives, London.
(24) Page 223: Letter from Lord Robartes, Governor of Plymouth to the Committee of Both Kingdoms, September 26th 1644; State Papers 21/17 p 7; by kind permission of the National Archives, London.
(25) Page 226: Letter from Lord Robartes, Governor of Plymouth to the Committee of Both Kingdoms, October 4th 1644; State Papers 21/17 p 25; by kind Permission of the National Archives, London.
(26) Page 229: The speech and confession of Sir Alexander Carew, Baronet, who was beheaded on Tower Hill on Monday December 23, 1644, Thomason Tracts E (22) 6; by kind permission of the British Library.
(27) Page 229: The speech and confession of Sir Alexander Carew, Baronet, who was beheaded on Tower Hill on Monday December 23, 1644, Thomason Tracts E (22) 6; by kind permission of the British Library.
(28) Page 232: Letter from Lord Robartes, Governor of Plymouth to the Committee of Both Kingdoms; Oxford Bodleian Library, MS Nalson 3 Fols 292-293, by kind permission of the Bodleian Library, Oxford.

Chapter 11

The Royalists' Last Chance

King Charles believed Devon and Cornwall to be almost totally secured for his cause. Cornwall was fully under the royal banner, while in Devon Sir Edward Seymour held Dartmouth and Sir John Berkeley controlled most of the county from Exeter. Totnes, although rebellious in the past, now contributed money freely to the royalists, as a consequence Berkeley wrote to the king on November 1st asking that a pardon be granted the town for its earlier support for the rebels. Sir Edmund Fortescue, under orders since his exchange late in 1643 to rebuild the old fort near Salcombe, continued in his task. Only Plymouth remained defiant, but the king was confident that his aggressive general Sir Richard Grenville would find a way to crack the town's impudence.

1645 began with Sir Richard planning an early major assault against his nemesis. By family prestige, promises and threats, Grenville had miraculously increased the size of his army to almost 6,000 horse and foot, all well armed. The infantry were divided into four new Cornish regiments, commanded by colonels Richard Arundell, John Arundell, Lewis Tremayne and Grenville himself. Colonel Philip Champernowne commanded Prince Maurice's old regiment, replacing his father Colonel Henry Champernowne who had died in December 1644, possibly from a bad wound he received at Lostwithiel. Though greatly reduced in numbers, Champernowne's regiment included many Devonshire royalists. The Cornish militia remained west of the Tamar, occupying various strategic points, while those Devonshire cavaliers, who rallied to Grenville's call, helped man the batteries and fortifications east of the Plym or north of the town. To keep his army together, Sir Richard knew he would have to pay his soldiers on time, thus he made every effort to do so and succeeded.

Eventually Grenville was ready to use this new army and he expected high dividends for all his hard work. Satisfied with their commander's plans for the forthcoming assault, the royalist colonels massed their troops north of Plymouth on January 8th. To soften up the opposition, a number of hidden long-range cannon were unmasked at Compton. Then, out of the blue, dark clouds loomed overhead and rain began to pour, turning narrow country lanes and roads into thick, slippery mud, a serious obstacle to an army preparing to attack. The torrential downpour continued into the next day and did not cease until late that evening, when the royalist foot finally appeared and sloshed into their assigned positions. The objectives of Grenville's attack were to be four of the major forts on the outer line, Maudlyn, Holiwell, Pennycomequick and Little Pennycomequick. Sir Richard's elaborate plan was to send 2,000 foot in first, followed by two supporting lines each made up of 1,500 men. It was to be an ambitious all or nothing thrust and, if successful, the roundhead line would be ruptured at several points, leaving the town at his mercy.

The battle began around 2 a.m. on Friday the 10th of January with the royalist ordnance opening up against the earthworks dotted along the high ground above Lipson Creek and along the upper reaches of Pennycomequick.

Counter cannon fire was soon taken up by the defenders who, hampered by the darkness, aimed at the smoke and flame belched out by the enemy guns. Minutes later Grenville's regiments stumbled along the Maudlyn Ridge towards their assigned targets, preceded by a thin line of skirmishers. When they were close, the main bodies formed up and charged forward, hitting the four forts almost simultaneously. The fighting that followed would prove, like many night encounters, confused, noisy and barbarous. Parliamentary reinforcements grabbed their weapons and rushed to meet the threat with their usual élan and the battle swayed back and forth amidst the muddy fortifications. Pikes were useless in such a melee, therefore musket, sword, pieces of wood, stones and fists were the order of the night. Roundhead and royalist beat each other senseless, while the guns went silent.

Outnumbered, the gallant defenders of Maudlyn Fort, aided by the timely arrival of Colonel John Birch and eight companies of his Kentish regiment, beat off the attack on their post, but only just. In the process they killed sixty of the enemy and wounded many more. At the high point of the attack one of the fort's cannon, loaded with scrap metal, fired point blank and caused over a score of the enemy to fall dead and dying before its smoking barrel. Many citizens, who came out into the streets to listen to the carnage, could distinctly hear the screams of the men fighting for their lives.

The situation at the Pennycomequick Work was the same, the cavaliers pressed forward up the hill from Stonehouse Creek and over into the earthwork. Captain Richard Clarke fought his guns well and received a wound during the action. To bolster the garrisons of the main forts, a number of seamen served the cannon, many of these were killed, helping to blunt Grenville's multi-pronged attack. One of the gunners, John Pine, a local man, died defending his post in the Pennycomequick Work, leaving behind a wife and three little children.

Having successfully thrown back the enemy at Maudlyn, Colonel John Birch wondered why no sound was audible off to his left, at the Little Pennycomequick Work. Gathering up as many men as he could find, Birch marched down the connecting road and made his way toward the ominously silent fort. Approaching within pistol shot of the work, the roundhead scouts were suddenly challenged by a sentinel and commanded to identify themselves. Concerned, but grateful at the alertness of the guards, Birch yelled out that they were friends, parliamentarians. His words were greeted by a scattered, inaccurate volley of musketry, which so surprised the roundheads that they charged forward. Aware the enemy must have overrun the earthwork, Birch knew that unless the bastion was recaptured immediately the entire line would be threatened.

The Kentish regiment preferred to go forward with their fiery commander urging them on. The only advantage for Birch was the fact that the enemy had fired their muskets and it would take time for them to reload. Should the roundheads have withdrawn the cavaliers could have reinforced their position and expanded the breach. Fortunately John Birch was not a man to give his enemy time; before the royalists realised what was happening, the Kentishmen leapt over the low wall and were in amongst them. Hand-to-hand combat now dominated Little Pennycomequick Work, as both sides fought for control.

Soon other parliamentary troops arrived from the direction of Pennycomequick and the town. Attacked on three different sides, the outnumbered cavaliers broke and fled, leaving twenty-three men killed and sixty-three wounded and captured. This bought an end to the fighting. Amongst the prisoners taken by Birch's men was Colonel John Arundell, one of Grenville's senior officers. Later Arundell's sword was presented to Colonel Birch for his gallantry. Out of respect for his opponent, Birch wore this sword thereafter.

One of the town's more dynamic and candid personalities, John Birch was a twenty-nine-year-old Lancastrian who had moved to Bristol in 1633 to start up a small business. During the siege of Bristol, Birch served the garrison as a captain, unfortunately when the city surrendered he lost everything. Later Birch found himself with Sir William Waller and saw action at Arundell, where he was seriously wounded. Once recovered, the charismatic captain rejoined Waller's army and fought at the battles of Cheriton and Winchester. By June 1644 John Birch had risen to the rank of lieutenant colonel, but later his regiment was taken over by Sir Arthur Haselring and converted to dragoons. As a replacement, Birch was given a new regiment from Kent, and transferred to Plymouth.

During his unsettled stay in the southwest, Birch saw what many others failed to see, that John Robartes was not a capable military commander. He had misled the Earl of Essex and failed miserably to support or extricate the Saltash garrison back in October, allowing Grenville to overwhelm the place at his leisure. Never afraid to voice an opinion, Colonel Birch and several other officers, openly criticised the governor. Within two weeks of his arrival in Plymouth, John Birch left his regiment and travelled to London. In the capital Birch blasted Robartes' command ability to the authorities, but what he was really after was compensation for his earlier losses. Many in the House of Commons thought the fiery Birch extremely brusque, and on the 16th of October, he was ordered back to Plymouth.

Colonel Birch rode out of London a week later and almost into the battle of Newbury. Deciding to delay his trip and observe, Birch enjoyed the spectacle and after the battle he led a detachment of roundhead horse in pursuit of a royalist coach. Overtaking the vehicle, John Birch found he had captured Lord Patrick Ruthven's wife. Later the buoyant captain, whose eccentric exploit was, surprisingly, frowned upon by his superiors, returned to Plymouth.

Shortly after his failure to break through the outer line of Plymouth's defences, Grenville pulled his army back to its camps, having lost 300 killed, wounded and missing. Many wounded cavaliers later died of their injuries, as did a number of the defenders. An old legend relating to the bombardment of Maudlyn Fort just prior to January 10th is interesting. It names a man called Smith who, whilst on duty at Maudlyn, had his head blown away by an enemy cannonball. Smith's body was wrapped in sackcloth, thrown over a horse and taken back down the hill towards the town for burial. At the same time one of his relatives was on the way to the fort with his dinner and met the body on the way down. On January 6th a soldier named Richard Smith was interred in St Andrew's, it is interesting to think this man could be the Smith of the story, which was told many, many years after the event by one of his descendants.

The morning after the battle, the soldiers cleared up the debris of battle and noted large amounts of blood staining Little Pennycomequick; abundant evidence of the ferocity of the fighting there. Although Birch's Kent regiment saved the day, many other units had fought equally well, especially the gunners and a detachment of sailors. In a letter written after the engagement and addressed to the naval commission in London, William Thomas, captain of the frigate *Warwick* and also the commander of the seamen stationed in Plymouth, stated the town needed supplies and stressed that if the port fell, parliament might as well lose London.

After the carnage of battle had been cleared away and the status quo restored, the town's defence committee searched around for a scapegoat. The outer line had almost been ruptured in several places, someone would have to pay. Benjamin Close, a soldier, was arrested and accused of passing vital information concerning the town's defences over to the enemy. Consequently found guilty, Close was sentenced to death. For some unknown reason Ben Close was kept confined until February 21st, then he was taken out to a point near the gallows at Mount Gould and shot to death. According to John Syms, Close refused to confess to his crime and declared to the assembled people who had turned up for his execution: *'Take heed of breaking the sabbath, as he had given in to that sin and that drunkenness was a sin and they should take heed as a man who gives into drunkenness will fall into the sins of lying and swearing'.*[29]

Sir Richard Grenville also sought out someone to blame for his failures, and he pointed the finger at Colonel Philip Champernowne. Grenville believed Plymouth had fought itself out and urged his subordinates into a second attack, but no one was willing to face the formidable earthworks a second time. Frustrated, Sir Richard settled down and sent out his provosts to bring in more so-called volunteers to make up for his losses. To bolster his army further, Grenville requested reinforcements from Cornwall and Dartmouth. Eventually he got what he wanted and was soon in a position to plan a new attack against the defences.

Early in January, Mayor Justinian Peard had written to parliament voicing his concerns for Plymouth, due once again to the restrictive royalist blockade. Peard asked for money to pay the troops, provisions to feed the people and ammunition to allow the defenders to push back the enemy and gain a breathing space. The mayor went on to explain that the garrison was in high spirits and was resolute in its support of parliament. When this news reached London, the city's mayor, council and merchants asked the House of Commons to support the port in its hour of need. Westminster responded by organising a small naval squadron and filled the vessels with munitions and provisions.

Meanwhile the Plymouth defence committee took steps to collect and distribute the money when it arrived. The men who made up the committee at this stage were Justinian Peard, Harcourt Leighton, John Cawse, Thomas Ceely, Francis Godolphin and Lieutenant Colonel Christopher Savery, a Totnes man. Originally Sir John Bampfield and Colonel Kerr were on the list, but other duties demanded their attention and both had to be replaced. The treasurer for Plymouth at this time was Timothy Alsop, while the military commissariat was in the hands of Samuel Slade and Richard Clapp. Robert Chislett was the town's provost marshal, but Lord Robartes still retained overall command as governor.

By the spring of 1645, the town's defences were due for extensive repairs; bad weather and an almost constant battering had taken their toll. Throughout February and March work on all the fortifications was undertaken; Pennycomequick and Maudlyn were strengthened. Old rotting palisades were replaced, stonework reinforced and collapsing earthen walls shored up. Parts of the inner line were also in need of refurbishment; trenches were cleaned out and deepened, Frankfort Gate was repaired and the town wall bolstered. Two new half-moon works were begun at Gasgoine Gate and the drawbridge mended. With money in short supply, wages to pay workmen and soldiers were subsidised in part by coal and wood, ideal alternative for the cold weather.

It was not just the fortifications that needed repairing, weapons, shoes, uniforms, drums and flags were always in need of restoration. On February 20th, Commissary Clapp received the huge sum of £117 6s 2d for boots, shrouds and the mending of shoes. On the 24th, Thomas Quick was paid £7 15s for fixing arms and Richard Manning received £3 8s for similar work. Three days later two other gunsmiths, William Tutley and Thomas Bickford, were given £6 and £3 10s respectively.[30]

Meanwhile Sir Richard Grenville's plans for a second offensive were well under way, only this time the attack was to be directed against How Stert, on the eastern side of the Cattewater. This narrow peninsula, now known as Mount Batten in honour of Captain William Batten, had since August been turned into a strong fortification by gangs of sailors taken from ships anchored at Plymouth. Batten himself poured £500 of his own money into the project; this new fort would allow the parliamentarians to use the peninsula as a base for raids against the enemy at Plymstock and in the South Hams. With such a threat to his main region of supply, Grenville knew he must act quickly. If he could push the enemy off the peninsula before they could consolidate, the royalists would have a strong position from which to launch amphibious raids against the town's eastern forts. Should he fail, the parliamentarians could threaten Grenville's isolated left flank.

As a prelude to his attack east of the Plym, Sir Richard hoped to draw roundhead attention away from Mount Batten by a diversion. Early on the 6th of February, a substantial body of cavalier horse and foot was assembled above Townsend Hill. These men taunted the roundheads to come out of their forts and fight. As expected part of the garrison obliged. The parliamentarians opened their barriers and marched down and along the Maudlyn Ridge. For several hours the two sides skirmished heavily, but no serious fighting occurred and the few guns firing from Maudlyn and Holiwell did little, if any damage. Eventually the engagement fizzled out and both sides withdrew, taking their few casualties with them.

The same day a parliamentary force, consisting mainly of seamen landed from warships in the harbour and joined those sailors already on Mount Batten. Possibly aware of Grenville's plans, the naval detachment charged uphill and attacked a body of royalists camped close to the ruins of Fort Stamford. These men belonged to Colonel Philip Champernowne's Devonshire foot regiment and they fled at the approach of the seamen. Pursuing the enemy, the parliamentarians followed them as far as the Plymstock Work. Colonel Champernowne received a bad wound in the thigh during the fighting; an injury that would keep him away from his men for many weeks. The roundheads marched back to Mount Batten with a small number of prisoners.

An incident occurred during this time, of which there are two separate versions, both involve Captain John Clobery. The first mentions a Captain George Clobery, John's brother, who was shot in the head by the roundheads during an engagement and captured. The second, a more dramatic account, describes the event differently. Stationed with the royalist forces at Plympton, Captain George Clobery received a report that a party of parliamentarians were observed heading for Trennimans Jump. Mounting his troop, Clobery rode out in pursuit, but the headstrong captain urged his horse ahead of his men and soon a gap had opened between them.

Two roundhead soldiers out scouting, saw Clobery and set up an ambush. Without warning both men fired simultaneously at Captain Clobery and he fell desperately wounded. The two men then reputedly tied his feet together with match chord and using his horse, they dragged the prisoner back to their own lines, bashing Clobery's head against rocks and trees en route. When informed of the prisoner's identity and of his wounds, Captain John Clobery, a younger brother of the captive, serving in the Plymouth garrison, made his way out to where he lay. John Clobery of Bradstone near Tavistock, although only in his early twenties was a veteran of the Thirty Years' War. However he had never seen anything to compare with the gross mistreatment of his poor brother. John Clobery remained at his brother's side, hoping to nurse him back to health, but George failed to respond and died a short time later. Captain George Clobery was buried in St Andrew's on February 11th. It was reported that the two men who had abused Captain Clobery so badly were later hanged.[31]

On the dark night of Monday February 17th, Colonel Champernowne's regiment, now under Lieutenant Colonel Mohun, and a detachment of royalist horse, roughly 300 men in total, silently approached the ruins of old Fort Stamford from the direction of Radford House. Once the cavaliers reached the hill top, silence and speed became essential. The men sweated and exhausted themselves all through the night, hauling up wooden planks and filling wicker baskets with earth. Eventually these were lashed together to form a crude earthwork fortification, which according to parliamentary reports was twelve feet thick and between four and five feet high.

During the very early morning hours, parliamentary guards near Mount Batten, were alerted by the noise from the direction of Stamford. Relaying their concerns to their superiors, several cannon in forts along the west bank were ordered to fire at long range in order to dissuade the enemy. By first light the Mount Batten guards were shocked to find an enemy fort had been thrown up during the darkness, sited less than half a mile from their own position. Despite its imposing facade the royalist work was weak, there were no cannon in place and the troops behind its walls were weary, having spent the entire night building. With no guns, no sleep and little immediate support the cavaliers were apprehensive as to what would happen at daybreak. Had they been granted a further twenty-four hours, the Plymouth men would have been hard put to successfully attack the new fort. Lord Robartes refused Grenville the time he needed by immediately preparing an assaulting force.

When word reached the governor of the enemy's presence above Mount Batten, he made immediate plans to counter the reoccupation of Stamford. Detachments were selected from the forts along the Cattewater and a body of several hundred men was assembled. Included in this force were part of Captain John St Aubyn's cavalry troop, several other troops of horse, sailors and infantry, almost 500 men all told. Once assembled, this task force was marched to the riverbank, where a number of lighters were hired to ferry the troops and horses across to the east bank. Meanwhile a number of guns in the roundhead forts and on ships anchored in the Cattewater, continually fired up at the enemy earthwork, softening up its walls and greatly annoying the defenders.

The assaulting force crossed the Cattewater and landed unopposed on the beach north of Fort Stamford, where the men disembarked and scrambled over the rocks to the top. To cover the landings and to prevent Grenville from reinforcing his troops in

Stamford, Robartes ordered his gunners in the Pennycomequick Fort to open up a steady fire at the enemy to the north. The stage was now set for another parliamentary victory. Enemy lookouts must have noticed the transfer of so many soldiers across the Cattewater, but due to the lay of the land, the royalists were unable to go to Champernowne's support in time.

Having disembarked, a small advance guard moved out ahead of the main roundhead force and immediately ran into a mounted body of the enemy. Outnumbered, the parliamentarians fell back and rejoined the main force. To cover their avenue of escape, should the battle go against them, the roundheads left a detachment of musketeers lining a hedge close to the landing point, while the rest set off after the horse. By 1 p.m. some 400 roundheads were preparing to move against Stamford. Preceding the main force was a small body of horse under Captain Mathew Cousins, which moved forward to press back the enemy cavalry. After a brief clash the cavalier horse fled, pursued by Cousins. The attention of Lieutenant Colonel Mohun, and those cavaliers in the new earthwork had been focused on Mount Batten and they failed to comprehend a serious attack from the north.

It was near mid-afternoon on the 18th when the roundhead foot was finally ready and the two sides clashed. The sight of the determined parliamentary foot and the fatigue of the defenders helped win this battle for the Plymouth men before it began. The cavalier horse quickly galloped away from the fort and rode hard for Plymstock, many not stopping until they reached Plympton. Picking up the momentum, the Plymouth foot moved directly against the fort, withholding the urge to fire their matchlocks until well within range. As the parliamentarians closed in, royalist musketeers put match to powder and fired. This initial burst of fire knocked down a number of roundheads, but without artillery support the volley lacked potency and failed to stop the attack.

The parliamentary musketeers now halted, and fired, filling the area briefly with billowing white smoke. This was quickly dispersed by a gust of wind, allowing the royalists to see their opponents only yards away. Stronger in both manpower and resolve, the parliamentarians were soon swarming up over the low, makeshift wall and smashing their way through the discouraged defenders, many of whom were local men. Lieutenant Colonel Mohun and Major Hele tried to raise their troops but failed. The royalists put up only weak resistance before breaking. Many distressed cavaliers fled from the earthwork and ran down the steep hillside towards Hooe.

Minutes before the roundheads overran Stamford and stuck their banners in its earthen walls, a royalist officer set the magazine alight, blowing up most of the gunpowder to prevent its capture. Except for the dead and dying and a very large number of bewildered prisoners, the garrison had disappeared, abandoning weapons and accoutrements in their effort to escape. Many headed for Radford, where another cavalier force was stationed, others were pursued almost a mile by the victorious roundhead horse. During the chase more prisoners were taken, but as darkness descended the cavalry returned, herding their captives back up the slope towards the smouldering ruins of Fort Stamford.

All told twelve officers, including Lieutenant Colonel Mohun and Major Lewis Hele, were captured along with almost 100 common soldiers, 300 arms, six barrels of powder and a stash of other military equipment. Some fifty cavaliers were killed and wounded during the attack, while parliamentarian losses were reported at one man killed; this figure does not tally with those buried in St Andrew's who died of wounds. Between February 19th and the 21st, eight roundheads and three cavaliers were interred. Of those royalists taken during the battle, three were to die in prison either from wounds or disease, George Smale was buried on March 15th, Henry Gill on the 22nd and Lewis Baker on April 3rd. One of Mohun's officers, Captain William Hill, also died of his injuries and was laid to rest on the 21st of February.[32]

The second battle of Fort Stamford lasted only minutes before turning into a rout, one can only surmise that this was due to the inferior quality of troops in the fort. With both sides lacking artillery, the royalists should have made more of a fight of it. Despite other forces in the area, Lieutenant Colonel Mohun found himself alone and when the first troops fled from the fort their action seemed to signal a mass desertion. The officers, unable to stem the tide, fought on for a while longer before surrendering, thereby chalking up Grenville's second major defeat of the year.

The engagement had been witnessed from a distance by naval personnel on board ships, by those men stationed at Mount Batten, and by Mayor Peard and many of the townsfolk who had lined the seashore. Justinian Peard later sent a report of the affair to parliament and announced February 21st as a day of thanksgiving to honour the victory. Throughout the night of the 18th the victorious roundheads remained in the fort, lest the enemy return. Fortunately the cavaliers had had enough and they were happy to slink away and reform in safety. To prevent a surprise attack, Robartes sent over several more detachments of cavalry. These were the troops of Captain Nicholas Roope and Captain Wool. On the day after the Haltnersday fight, as the battle became known, fresh supplies were sent across to the men at Stamford and Mount Batten. A week later Lord Robartes wrote to the House of Lords announcing the victory. The Lords responded immediately by ordering the Lord Admiral of England to return the thanks of the House to the seamen at Plymouth for their good service.

When the prisoners from Fort Stamford were brought into Plymouth, three of the officers, Lieutenant George Battishill, Lieutenant Aishford and Captain Maynard were identified as being ex-roundheads. All had fought for parliament in the past, but had turned their coats; it was their misfortune to have been at Fort Stamford. Battishill, who lived with his wife and family at Plymstock, served in the company of Captain Anthony Stert. When marched through the town, Battishill, Aishford and Maynard were recognised; they were immediately separated from the rest and taken before a court martial. The military authorities quickly found them guilty of treason and two days later, on the 21st, they were marched out to Mount Gould. The three unfortunate officers were hanged and their bodies buried nearby. John Syms, who witnessed the executions, wrote that none of the accused showed signs of remorse and their courageous bearing greatly moved the crowd.

A period of quiet now settled over Plymouth, no more major assaults, only minor raids and skirmishing broke the monotony of the soldier's lot. This was due in part to the way the war had swayed against the king in other parts of the country. On March 4th the royalist high command reorganised their forces in the southwest and Prince Charles arrived at Bristol to take supreme command of the western counties. It was hoped the presence of the king's eldest son would rally and unite all his supporters in the area, and help them combine to capture Plymouth, Taunton and Lyme Regis, the only obstacles to complete royalist domination of the southwestern peninsula.

Amongst the more prominent of the prince's new military

advisors were Sir Ralph Hopton, Governor of Bristol, Sir Edward Hyde, Sir John Culpepper and Arthur Capel. The active army commanders under the new association's orders, Sir Richard Grenville, Sir John Berkeley and later George Goring, were independent and very protective of their own troops and territory. None could get along with the other, as a consequence petty arguments and poor cooperation would hasten the destruction of royalism in the west.

Goring was possibly the best of the trio, his past record being the most impressive. Upon his return to England in 1643, Goring took command of the cavalier horse in Yorkshire. At Seacroft Moor, on March 30th, he claimed his first victory when he attacked and defeated Sir Thomas Fairfax. On May 21st, Fairfax got his own back when he trounced Goring at Wakefield. George Goring was present at Marsten Moor and fought reasonably well, but his successes in the field were always countered by indiscipline. Goring's troopers often indulged in plunder and drunkenness, which greatly hindered the king's cause. When George Goring came west the behaviour of his men would force many neutrals to side with parliament, more out of fear than loyalty. Preceding Goring's arrival, Prince Charles had named Grenville commander of all royalist troops in the new western association. Unfortunately the king later cancelled his son's choice of senior officer in favour of Goring. By this solitary act, Charles Stuart showed his distrust of the prince's judgement and made a mockery of his so-called independent command.

On March 29th Plymouth witnessed the funeral of magistrate and ex-mayor John Cawse, who died only six months after leaving office. Alexander Grosse travelled to Plymouth specifically for the service and conducted the sermon in St Andrew's. Mr Robert Gubbs, whose appointment was confirmed by Lord Robartes on March 25th, took John Cawse's place on the defence committee. Gubbs, a Gloucester man, whose wife Thomasin had died in Plymouth only six weeks previous, was well respected and he promised to serve to the best of his ability. However Gubbs retained his position for only a short period, by April he was out.

After Cawse's funeral, Alexander Grosse decided to remain in Plymouth and serve the garrison's spiritual needs, as if there weren't enough ecclesiastics in the town already. From Christow in Devon, Grosse had first come to Plymouth in 1623. As a Puritan minister,

Grosse had been offered, but refused to be lecturer of St Andrew's. By the outbreak of war, Alexander Grosse was in Bideford, where he remained until travelling to Plymouth. Others who performed divine services to the garrison were Stephen Midhope, Christopher Lawrie, George Shugge, John Wills, chaplain to Colonel Rouse's regiment and Francis Porter, a man highly-respected by the troops he served, George Hughes, vicar of St Andrew's, a familiar face to all in Plymouth, and the stern, if unpopular John Syms, who plied his trade at the outworks and aboard the naval vessels. All the clergy were well paid by the corporation for their services, and many added to their income by conveying messages through the lines, or by renting out property, such as stables, to the army.

With the Mount Batten area secure and the royalists licking their wounds, the defenders of Plymouth continued the constant repairs necessary on the miles of fortifications. In addition several new forts were begun, one northwest of Maudlyn and named appropriately Little Maudlyn, and another between Prince Rock Fort and the Laira Point Work covering the Plym estuary and christened Fort Gould. The trench system, where it existed, was cleaned up and new timbers and stone added for extra strength. Parliamentary ships also brought in money regularly for the garrison, and the corporation found itself in its best financial position for years. Unfortunately the outgoings still outweighed the incomings. Monthly expenses averaged approximately £3,000 for wages and everything to do with defence, far exceeding the amount brought in by ship.

On February 16th, word reached Captain William Batten that a royalist force, under Sir Lewis Dyve and George Goring had captured Weymouth. The warships *Warwick,* twenty guns under Captain William Thomas, and the *Providence,* eighteen guns under Captain Ellison, then anchored at Plymouth, were ordered to sail at once. Batten planned to head for Melcombe, where the roundheads from Weymouth had taken refuge and fortified themselves. Both ships however were low on victuals and ammunition, and would need almost a week to resupply. Rather than wait, Batten went alone with one vessel, the *Expedition*. Two days later he arrived at Melcombe and immediately landed part of the ship's complement as a reinforcement. Later, after only a brief blockade in which treachery almost gave the royalists victory, the cavaliers withdrew back to Dorchester. Batten's presence with an eighteen-gun warship had spoilt the royalist attempt at holding Weymouth.

Shortly after Captain Batten had sailed away from Plymouth, Sir Richard Grenville marched away from the port with part of his army. Grenville's reluctant abandonment of the siege stemmed from the arrival in the west of George Goring, who after his failure at Weymouth had marched to Exeter and joined forces with Sir John Berkeley. Though Devonshire was not yet under Goring's authority, the man began throwing his weight about almost immediately. Establishing himself in the county town, George Goring high-handedly issued orders for Berkeley and Grenville to unite and attack the roundhead garrison at Taunton. Grenville, equally egotistical, refused to obey Goring. Later when the king endorsed Goring's orders, Sir Richard claimed his troops would not leave Plymouth, for fear of an attack upon their rear. Eventually, on March 15th, Sir Richard and the better part of his army grudgingly left their camps and marched to Exeter.

To maintain a partial blockade of Plymouth and protect his rear, Grenville left behind 2,000 foot and 400 horse under Colonel John Digby, who by now had partially recovered from his wounds. Unable to man a continuous line, Digby concentrated his army at a number of key points. Large detachments were centred at Plymstock and Plympton, while smaller, more mobile units were retained at Hoptons Work, Keame House and a new fort at Pennycross. Before leaving the area, Grenville dashed off a note to Sir Edward Seymour at Dartmouth, advising him to keep alert.

The town of Taunton in Somerset had been half-heartedly besieged on and off for months prior to Grenville's arrival, but Colonel Robert Blake managed to repulse every royalist assault and hold on. By late March cavaliers from Bristol and Bridgewater were also moving against Taunton. These were reinforced by part of Goring's army, while he himself rode up and down the Dorset-Wiltshire county line, watching for roundhead reinforcements, supposedly on their way under Waller. Despite the whining of his Cornish foot, Grenville, disobeying Goring's latest order to join him against Waller, arrived at Taunton and settled his army before the town, he would never return to Plymouth.

The departure of Grenville with three-fifths of his army, allowed the Plymouth garrison to breathe a little easier. Enemy numbers had been more than halved, giving Robartes a wonderful opportunity to launch a coordinated counteroffensive and drive the cavaliers away from the town. Unfortunately nothing was done, John Robartes believed his army too weak for offensive operations. In fact the governor was content to vegetate behind his formidable defences and allow the enemy to remain east of the Plym despoiling the South Hams. Digby exhibited similar behaviour, he knew he was not strong enough to attack Plymouth, and with the rest of Devon under the king's banner, he was happy to keep the situation a static stalemate. This remained the picture around the port throughout the summer months, the only excitement being the occasional raids for plunder or prisoners.

On March 23rd a roundhead troop, edging too close to a royalist detachment near the ruins of Fort Stamford, found themselves pressed back to their own lines. A week later, on April 1st, a mounted parliamentarian detail hit an unsuspecting royalist patrol at Compton. After a brief clatter of sabres, the roundheads withdrew with two prisoners and three horses. The parliamentarians failed to find a wounded cavalier who had secreted himself beneath a hedge, and when the patrol left the man made his way back to his own lines. On the same day Captain Thomas Plunkett arrived in Sutton Pool with three prizes; several more vessels from Lyme Regis followed him in two days later. On board Plunkett's ship was an officer from Sir William Waller's army, who was immediately taken to see Lord Robartes. Once face-to-face with the governor, the officer announced the news that Shrewsbury and Scarborough Castle had been taken by parliamentary forces.

Occasionally the severity of the skirmishing intensified; during the night of April 11th a mixed detachment of roundheads crossed over to How Stert. Next morning the eighty musketeers followed their horse up the hill and fell upon a force of royalists; the outnumbered cavaliers were routed losing an officer and five horses. Suddenly reinforcements came up from the direction of Plymstock. These fresh troops instilled renewed courage into the retreating royalists and the situation turned completely around. The cavaliers formed up and counterattacked, forcing the parliamentarians to flee. Two corporals and one common soldier were killed before the roundheads reached their own lines.

With many horses dying or simply being worn out by harsh service, replacements in an area almost destitute of good remounts were difficult to obtain. To keep the cavalry in the saddle, many troopers were encouraged to rustle royalist mounts, the only source of supply available. To stimulate such raids, the town council paid cash for as many remounts as these rustlers could bring in. On April 21st, Cornet

Francis Rolle and a small mounted detachment managed to capture five enemy horses during a dash north of Plymouth. Four of the mounts were given over to Captain St Aubyn as replacements for his cavalry company. On May 13th, Lieutenant Hunt Greenwood, St Aubyn's second in command, was paid £8 for eight horses he had captured from the royalists. Captain Onesimus Penrose and Cornet Edward Beare also received cash rewards for similar captures.[33]

When the month of May arrived, it brought with it the Self-Denying Ordinance, which took the trusted, well-loved, but almost inert Lord Robartes away from Plymouth. Despite a petition, signed by thousands of soldiers and civilians for his retention as governor, parliament had spoken and Robartes was recalled to Westminster. On the 30th of the month his name would be added to the committee for western affairs. Sir John Bampfield, who left Plymouth on the 29th of May, would join Robartes later in the capital. The Earl of Warwick had laid down his commission a month earlier, thus taking away three of the most popular men who had served the port throughout the war. Command of the town and its fortifications now devolved upon the committee of defence, with Colonel Kerr once again in charge of the army. Brought into existence on May 10th 1645 by order of parliament, this five-man directorate consisted of Colonel Kerr, Justinian Peard, Thomas Ceely, Colonel John Crocker and John Beare. These men were authorised to proclaim martial law, if it became necessary.

One man who was glad to see the back of Lord Robartes was Colonel John Birch; since coming to Plymouth, Birch had been openly critical of the way the governor and some of his armchair colonels were fighting the war, especially after part of his regiment had been captured needlessly at Saltash the previous October, and he was not alone. Colonel Birch's candid opinions, and his own popularity amongst his officers, soon had others echoing similar sentiments. When Robartes heard the whispers, he confronted Colonel Birch. Infuriated by his subordinate's angry defiance, the governor sent the colonel and his misfits to London under guard to explain their attitude to the House of Commons. Fortunately for the colonel and his confederates, they arrived in the capital at the time the Government was arranging the new Self-Denying Ordinance, which more or less agreed with their own views. Consequently by the time Birch and his associates were on their way back to Plymouth,

Robartes was on his way up to London.

Much to the relief of the town, Westminster agreed to allow Colonel Birch and his veteran Kentish regiment to remain as part of the garrison for a further four months, and funds were sent down for the unit's upkeep. The town's joy at this news was to be short lived; when Lyme Regis came under siege in June, the Kent regiment was ordered to take ship and sail. Only the sick and wounded were left behind.

As spring wore on and the roads dried, skirmishing increased; with the royalists on the decline, the scope of parliamentary raids from Plymouth expanded. Warleigh, Oreston and Shaugh were visited in May; occasionally though Colonel Digby struck back. On May 6th, a cavalier detachment raided Mr Symons' property at Thornhill, taking a small herd of sheep before returning to their own lines. Suddenly a parliamentary troop thundered down from the direction of Fort Maudlyn and struck the rustlers near Efford Hill. The unsuspecting royalists lost their sheep and scattered, losing several men as prisoners.

Throughout the war the practice of prisoner exchange between locally opposing forces was a common practice. Unable to cope with large numbers of captives, Plymouth was forced to transport many prisoners to London, or exchange them. As 1645 wore on, Robert Chislett, the provost marshal of Plymouth's prisons, grew concerned. Already overstretched by the influx of hundreds of refugees, the defence committee found itself straining to find extra food for the prisoners. Captain Chislett did receive money to purchase food for those held in the old castle and the Marshalsea, but they continued to die. Many were buried in St Andrew's, where the records list twenty-five cavaliers interred between February and May.

Royalist prisoners held in Plymouth were far more fortunate than their counterparts incarcerated in Lydford. Stories continued to circulate of the horrors of this nefarious hellhole. A parliamentary trooper named Martin Edwards, captured during Balfour's retreat from Lostwithiel, was sent to Exeter gaol for almost four months. Later he was transferred to Lydford where he died within eight weeks. Others succumbed to the miseries of mistreatment, and eventually parliament heard the tales of murder and brutality. On May 14th, the House of Commons ordered the committee of the west to arrange relief for those prisoners held at Lydford, the House urged the same committee to arrange the speedy exchange of Colonel Alexander Popham's officers, who were being detained at Lydford under atrocious conditions.

A week later, the Commons approved the exchange of Colonel Richard Fielding held by parliament, for Lieutenant Colonel Bassett, Major Francis Champneys, Captain Powell and Captain Richard Ellingsworth, all suffering at Lydford. The House of Lords agreed to the exchange on May 28th, and arrangements were made. Unfortunately Captain Ellingsworth was found to be too ill to travel far and was brought into Plymouth. Taken to the home of Dorothy Collins, a widow, Ellingsworth spent his final days in relative comfort and Mrs Collins nursed the captain until he died on July 11th. Richard Ellingsworth was buried in St Andrew's on the 13th and 7s was paid out by the corporation for a coffin.[34]

On May 6th, a sizable exchange of prisoners took place at Plymouth; fifty royalists were marched out under guard to a point near Hoptons Work. Here they were given over for an equal number of roundheads brought up from Launceston. Many of these men were sick and had to be hospitalised, and all were destitute. One of the officers who arrived from this exchange was a Captain William Halsey. Once recovered from his ordeal, Halsey was given £2 by Colonel Kerr for his journey to London. Another who gained his freedom at this time, though not from the same gaol, was the long-suffering Sir John Northcote.

Since his capture at Exeter in September 1643, parliament had tried in vain to secure Northcote's exchange. On the 25th of January 1645, Prince Rupert wrote to Westminster offering Northcote for Lord Brereton. Rupert's proposal was read in the Commons, but nothing came of the offer. Finally, almost three months later, parliament agreed to exchange Brereton for Northcote, providing Sir John was released first. Eventually the two men were exchanged, and on the 7th of May Sir John Northcote was permitted to take his seat once again as a member of the House of Commons.

The final day of May saw a body of soldiers march through the streets of Plymouth with drums beating a slow rhythm. These men proclaimed the ordinance for strict observance of the Sabbath day, and announced the ordinance would be enforced. With many military men in the town against such rigid religious discipline, a number of the clergy felt themselves threatened. Their anxiety increased when Lord Robartes left in May. John Syms who had a run in with Captain John Ellison of the *Providence* back in 1644, had bumped into him again in Plymouth on the dark night of February 24th. Recognising his antagonist, Ellison pursued Syms, calling him names and hitting him. Those who witnessed the incident did nothing to stop the irate naval officer. Eventually Syms got away and Ellison was not punished; evidence of a lack of sympathy many felt for the rigid Puritanism dominating the town.

With news of further parliamentary victories over the king's forces, confidence in the town rose higher. Roundhead detachments continued to raid enemy outposts, and as more and more prisoners were brought in the impudence of the raiders grew. On June 7th, though, parliamentary enthusiasm received an abrupt check. A detachment of cavalry was transported over to How Stert by boat, once ashore the men headed for Plymstock Church. The vanguard, consisting of part of Captain St Aubyn's cavalry under Lieutenant Hunt Greenwood, attacked a royalist force camped around the graveyard, forcing the cavaliers to flee and leave behind two men dead and several bewildered prisoners. Now everything went wrong, a much larger detachment of royalist horse suddenly emerged from the countryside and counterattacked. Greenwood fell back toward his main body, which had halted near an abandoned royalist fort known as the Plymstock Work.

The roundhead cavalry unexpectedly broke and sprinted for their boats, Lieutenant Greenwood showing a disgraceful example by racing away faster than most of his men. Captains William Wooton and John Treife held momentarily before the rout became general. Half a dozen parliamentarians were killed during the action and forty captured, some of them wounded. When the survivors arrived back in Plymouth, and the whole shameful episode recounted, a court of inquiry was convened. Captain Treife was blamed for the debacle and hauled over the coals. Treife appealed to be tried by the high court of parliament and gave his oath to go to Westminster. The captain made his way to the capital and spent a week waiting to be heard. Frustrated, Treife told his prosecutors that he believed they were delaying his case on purpose, hoping to damage his defence. Eventually the House of Lords ordered Treife's prosecutors to bring to the House the charge against the officer and the proceedings. Eventually Captain John Treife was found not guilty and released.

Back at Plymouth, the navy continued to bring money down from

London. On April 4th two ships, the *Happy Endurance* and the *Globe,* under Captain Richard Willoughby, dropped anchor in Plymouth. Besides valuable stores, Willoughby also carried £4,000 for the town's beleaguered treasury. The money was welcomed, but it lasted barely a month; once the bills and the garrison were paid the coffers were once again barren. To make up the deficiency, the council was forced to rely on loans from the citizens and many of the officers. Colonel Birch spent £2 7s and 8d on his own regiment, while two local men paid £47 to supply boots for the soldiers. Even Captain Batten gave from his own pocket, as did Captain Henry Hatsell and others, including a number of local widows.[35]

On May 10th King Charles named George Goring top royalist general of the western army, with Grenville and Berkeley subordinate to him. Berkeley was to take over from Colonel Digby and assume command of the royalist forces blockading Plymouth, but John Berkeley seethed internally, as both he and Grenville despised Goring's appointment. Along with most of Prince Charles' advisors, Berkeley and Grenville resented such a crucial position being held by such an irresponsible officer.

Once Berkeley settled in at Plymouth he did nothing to improve the royalist position, though he was a far less contemptible character than Grenville had been. Like Digby, Sir John felt himself much too weak for offensive operations, preferring to maintain the partial blockade of the port. As each month passed the royalists grew weaker, the parliamentarians stronger. Eventually the garrison found itself in a position to aid other parliamentary armies, and five hundred men soon found themselves on their way to join Colonel Rowland Laugharne's army at Milford Haven.

While most royalist troops around Plymouth now remained east of the River Plym, the threat to the main outer line north of the town diminished considerably. The chief gunners of the five major forts found they had an excess of artillerymen; many of these men stood around for most of the day grumbling about their infrequent pay. As a consequence those gunners who were no longer needed were discharged. In late May, early June, a number of cannoneers from Pennycomequick, Maudlyn, Holiwell, Laira Point Work, New Work and Mount Gould found themselves paid off and out of work.

Meanwhile money continued to arrive; the *Eliza* blew in on June 5th with £2,000 which lasted no more than a week. A further £2,000, brought in by Captain John Stansby on July 4th, petered out nine days later. Not only was the corporation forced to feed and clothe its gallant defenders and its citizens, but by 1645, many Cornish and Devonshire royalists, under threat of being pressed into the king's service, had fled into Plymouth to seek refuge behind her guns. These asylum seekers were joined by country folk, whose homes had been pillaged by marauding bands of cavaliers. Accordingly, the money coming in drained away much faster than ever before.

Although Devon still remained predominantly royalist, the war was clearly turning against their cause over the rest of the country. 1645 had opened with victory for the Scottish cavaliers at Inverlochy and their subsequent capture of Dundee, before they fled back into the mountains to avoid pursuit. South of the border, the pendulum swung the other way; Prince Rupert attacked Abingdon but was beaten off. George Goring saw his army thrown back at Christchurch, and Devizes fell to Cromwell and Waller. In February Shrewsbury was lost by sheer incompetence, and a valuable recruiting centre for royalist Welsh levies was gone forever. Although successful most of the time, the parliamentarians did occasionally meet with a setback. Prince Rupert and his brother Maurice managed to beat Edward Massey at Ledbury. A peace meeting at Uxbridge failed when both sides refused to back down and weeks of hope were dashed, the war would continue.

In late April the committee of both kingdoms (England and Scotland) ordered Cromwell and part of the newly-raised New Model Army to cut communications between Prince Rupert on the Welsh border, and King Charles at Oxford. For a week the roundheads beat up numerous royalist detachments, but were eventually repulsed when they attacked Farringdon. Events now began to move more rapidly; Fairfax was commanded to relieve Taunton and Cromwell was to join him. With the main parliamentary army gone, the king saw his opportunity to leave Oxford. With Prince Rupert and 10,000 men, he marched out of his capital on May 8th heading north in an effort to regain some of his lost territory.

With the king gone, Fairfax was suddenly recalled by Westminster and ordered to besiege Oxford in an effort to draw him back. Meanwhile the royalist march into the Midlands had forced Sir William Brereton to break off his siege of Chester. As a result of

Brereton's withdrawal, a large detachment of cavalier horse rode away from Chester and joined the king's army. The situation now turned around, with Fairfax threatening Oxford, the western royalists begged Charles Stuart to return to his capital. Despite Rupert's strenuous objections, the king revised his plan and marched eastwards, heading for Leicester, which he stormed and plundered on May 30th.

To entice Fairfax away from Oxford, the royalist army shifted to Daventry, only thirty miles north of Charles' capital. Here, while their men rested, the royalist commanders spent the days bickering. Thomas Fairfax, on the other hand, wasted no time, moving swiftly he broke off the siege of Oxford and marched rapidly northwards. By June 12th, and before the royalists knew what was happening, Fairfax was less than six miles away. The king reacted promptly and withdrew his army to Market Harborough, then, against his nephew's advice, he ordered his army to attack. Fairfax, who had been joined by Cromwell, was also ready to attack. What followed on the 14th was the great battle of Naseby, which ended in complete defeat for the royalist army. Almost all of the king's foot, amounting to some 5,000 men, with the artillery and baggage were captured and the horse dispersed. So rapid had been the roundhead victory that casualties were light, the king retreated to Hereford and Fairfax retook Leicester.

In the southwest the major campaign of the late spring, early summer, centred on Taunton and Lyme Regis. Sir Richard Grenville had been wounded during the early part of the siege, and Sir John Berkeley was ordered up from Exeter to replace him. Upon Berkeley's appointment, Grenville's officers refused to obey his orders, enabling Berkeley to achieve nothing at Taunton. Eventually Sir John was sent down to Plymouth and George Goring took his place in front of Taunton.

After the defeat at Naseby, royalist morale everywhere was damaged beyond repair. Once he recovered from his wound, Grenville was sent to Lyme, where no sooner had he set up his headquarters than Sir Thomas Fairfax and the New Model Army marched into Somerset on July 8th. His appearance in the county forced Grenville to fall back almost as far as Exeter. To prevent the parliamentarians from reaching the Bristol Channel and cutting off reinforcements from south Wales, Goring shifted his army to Langport. Poor generalship by Goring allowed the roundheads to cross the River Yeo unopposed, and on July 10th the New Model Army, including the Plymouth horse, smashed the royalists at the battle of Langport. In this, its second swift, decisive battle in less than a month, Fairfax's army captured 2,000 prisoners. The surviving cavaliers fled towards Bridgewater, which fell after a two-week siege.

Notes

(29) Page 239: John Syms, A daybook of special passages and mercies, British Library, Add 35297; by kind permission of the British Library, London.
(30) Page 241: State papers 28/128 PT2, National Archives; by kind permission of the National Archives, London.
(31) Page 242: The story of Captain John Clobery is to be found in Prince's Worthies accession 373 held at the West Devon Record Office Plymouth and is included by their kind permission.
(32) Page 245: St Andrew's Church burial records, held at the West Devon Record Office.
(33) Page 251: Siege Accounts of Plymouth, held in the Worth Collection, accession 1/644-5; by kind permission of the West Devon Record Office.
(34) Page 253: Siege Accounts of Plymouth, held in the Worth Collection, accession 1/644-5; by kind permission of the West Devon Record Office.
(35) Page 255:Siege Accounts of Plymouth, held in the Worth Collection, accession 1/644-5; by kind permission of the West Devon Record Office.

Chapter 12

Winter of Discontent

The summer months of 1645 were chaotic in certain parts of England, but around Plymouth the situation remained static, broken only by the occasional artillery exchange or an adventurous raid. The majority of the latter involved cavalry, usually out searching for fresh horses. The raiders often went as far as Elburton, Ermington, Cornwood, Brixham, Yealmpton, Wembury, Shaugh, Sheepstor and Goodameavy. Most contact between the opposing forces occurred close to the town, usually around Hoptons Work, Efford, Warleigh, Tamerton and Plymstock. Casualties were usually light and the results negligible, but such encounters did have an effect upon morale.

On June 5th the Plymouth defence committee received a letter from parliament, advising its members to exchange a number of royalist prisoners held in the town for an equal number of Scottish ship-masters taken at sea and confined at Falmouth. The Scots were reported to be in a terrible condition and desperate for release. In early September, five Scotsmen from Falmouth were brought to Plymouth and exchanged, as were others from Lydford and five more from Dartmouth. In November more Scots arrived from Penryn, but the exchange system was painfully slow and disorganised, and the numbers exchanged were always small. One exchanged soldier who was not so lucky was Walter Yeoland. A local man, Yeoland was captured by the enemy and imprisoned in Lydford. Eventually exchanged, Walter Yeoland soon died as a result of his injuries and appalling treatment and was buried at St Andrew's on July 10th, his death left a wife, Margery, to survive on charity and three weeks' pay.

On May 10th the Plymouth horse, commanded by Colonel Nicholas Boscowan, and a number of other individual cavalry detachments, were ordered by the committee for both kingdoms to join the party sent into the southwest under Colonel Ralph Weldon of Fairfax's command. Boscowan, the son of Hugh Boscowan, a knight of Cornwall, had raised a small troop of horse from his own tenants in the early days of the war, and joined the parliamentary forces as a captain. Rising in rank after seeing plenty of action, Boscowan, a promising officer only twenty-one years of age, had risen to the rank of colonel. Since December 1644 Boscowan's regiment had been filtering out of Plymouth in small groups, now they were merged with other units under colonels John Fitz James and Edward Cooke. The aim of this force was to aggravate the royalist troops in Bridgewater. When Taunton came under siege, these combined cavalry detachments made numerous raids against the besieging cavaliers.

With the parliamentary threat from Somerset, and Plymouth still defiant, Prince Charles' council in Cornwall agreed with Goring and Grenville to raise a new army. From the troops blockading Plymouth, 1,000 men were transferred to Goring's army. To replace them, Grenville, in his role as royalist High Sheriff of Devon, was to call out the posse comitatus and send the men to Berkeley at Plymouth. Sir Richard himself rode to Cornwall in a forlorn attempt to ignite the Cornish flame of royalism and raise new regiments for the prince. With Grenville and Goring on good terms for once, the situation for a revival looked promising. However within weeks, royalist hopes had rapidly disintegrated. Having learnt that Goring had spoken badly of him, Grenville refused to cooperate with his commanding officer ever again. A lack of arms, money, enthusiasm, unity and able leadership were destroying any chance Prince Charles had of raising a fresh army. To make matters worse, Bridgewater surrendered to parliament on July 23rd.

Around Plymouth little changed, the offensive power of the garrison was never fully brought to bear against an enemy even more lifeless. This may have been due in part to the fact that the garrison troops were so used to being on the defensive they didn't know any better. Several units had been in Plymouth since the beginning of the war, and these troops felt safe behind their fortifications. Why go out now and risk being killed with the end of the war in sight? By using interior lines and concentrating their manpower, the quick raid was still the favoured mode of warfare for the roundhead commanders in Plymouth.

On July 26th, a parliamentarian force did move out and attack the cavaliers near Hoptons Work. The enemy was easily forced back, and when the roundheads returned they brought in a captured officer. On August 14th, another mounted detachment went further and attacked the royalist guard at Plymbridge. So surprised were the royalists that all but five were captured, the rest fleeing across the bridge. On the same day a minor raid from Mount Batten brought in three prisoners and four horses. The following month a much larger force, numbering around 300, went over to Staddon in search of horses. Within forty-eight hours the expedition returned with many remounts, having encountered no opposition. Berkeley's outnumbered little army was far too weak and spread out to stop such a large raiding party.

By the late summer Sir Thomas Fairfax was ready to invade the county of Devon. Having captured Bath and Sherborne, the New Model Army laid siege to Bristol. Prince Rupert, badly outnumbered, put up such a poor defence that the town was overwhelmed on September 10th. The following day the royalists surrendered and Fairfax snapped the last link between the king at Oxford and Prince Charles in the west. Now with his rear clear of enemy forces, Thomas Fairfax turned southwestwards.

Meanwhile the lack of military activity in and around Plymouth allowed internal bickering to simmer and boil over. One day Abraham Jennings, a local merchant, was arrested by order of Colonel Kerr and confined to his father's home for over two months without trial. Possibly Jennings had crossed the governor somewhere along the line. Another incarcerated without a hearing was Kettleby Woodhouse, a man who had charge of repairing the Lower Lipson Fort. Woodhouse received numerous amounts of money with which he claimed he paid the workmen's wages and bought materials for work on the Lower Lipson Fort, but his name appears far too often in the accounts, especially considering the Lower Lipson Work was only a minor fortification.[36] Both Jennings and Woodhouse were ordered by the House of Lords to appear before parliament and explain the reason for their imprisonment. The town authorities were also commanded to send up the evidence against the two men.

A third incident of discontentment quickly followed, this time involving a local hero, John Hancock, the sergeant who had discovered Sir Alexander Carew's treachery and aided in his subsequent arrest. Driven from his home earlier in the war by the enemy, Hancock brought his family into Plymouth and joined the garrison as a soldier serving on St Nicholas Island. For his diligence in the Carew incident, Hancock was promoted to ensign and allowed to live on the island with his family. Later Sir John Bampfield and Captain Henry Hatsell, Hancock's immediate superiors, forced him from his home and kept his pay back. The reason for their actions has not come to light, but it could have been that they were sceptical of Carew's guilt and blamed Hancock for his arrest and execution.

Eventually John Hancock petitioned parliament for restoration of his rights. On June 27th the House of Lords read Hancock's appeal and ordered that he be restored to his home on the island, be restored to his rank of ensign and that his arrears of pay be handed over. The House of Commons was asked to concur to the Lords' recommendations. By September the Commons had not replied and the Lords was forced to repeat its request. Another month passed and still no answer came back.

After half a dozen times of being asked, the Commons finally responded on December 7th: *'Ordered that the committee of Plymouth, Poole and Lyme, do pay unto Mr John Hancock, two hundred pounds, in satisfaction of his arrears. Recompense of his services performed in the parliament; and in full discharge of his demands or desires, concerning any place in the isle of St Nicholas near Plymouth, or the fort there'.*[37]

Activity around Plymouth increased during the months of August and September, with raid and counter-raid spreading through the countryside to the north and east of the port. On the 7th of August a cavalry detail from the town rode out to the village of Shaugh, returning the next morning with four good horses. A week later a party of cavalier horse was able to creep in closer to Plymouth than many believed possible. Two local men out chopping wood were killed and six reapers and several washerwomen were captured, along with a small herd of sheep. Before a rescue could be organised the royalists had vanished.

Four weeks later, on September 5th, a roundhead detachment rode out to Cornwood and brought in two prisoners, a Mr Adam Williams and a Mr Baskerville. The following week a detail came into town with seven horses in tow. On the 14th seven merchant ships were escorted into Plymouth Sound, all captured en route to Ireland. The prizes contained everything from pilchards to ammunition and were a great boost to the garrison. During the final week of September, raiders from Plymouth went out as far as Looe in Cornwall and Walkhampton on Dartmoor and brought in pigs, cows, bullocks, horses, pilchards and prisoners.

Three vital changes now took place in Plymouth, on September 17th Justinian Peard gave up the mayoralty chair to Bartholomew Nicholl, who took over civic responsibility twelve days later. Nicholl, another well-to-do merchant, had previously been the Plymouth receiver (1633-4), overseer of the poor (1644), and a close friend of the deceased royalist Robert Trelawny. The second change took place in the enemy camp, where Sir John Berkeley was sent back to Exeter, leaving Colonel John Digby once again in command. Digby was given a small reinforcement to tighten his partial blockade, but there was nowhere near enough royalist troops available to be effective.

The third and most important change took place at the top, when on September 29th parliament assigned the military command in Plymouth to one of Fairfax's most trusted officers, Colonel Ralph Weldon. Being tied up with operations elsewhere, Weldon would not replace Kerr until January 1646. The commander of St Nicholas Island and Plymouth Fort was also changed; Henry Hatsell being replaced by Captain Arthur Upton, while Mount Wise remained under Captain Arthur Gay. Ralph Weldon, the son of Anthony Weldon of Kent, had commanded a regiment from his home county and served with the New Model Army and saw action at Taunton and Bridgewater, he was also present during the capture of Bristol and in the storming of Tiverton.

On the 4th of October, Captain William Batten, commanding the parliamentary navy since the Earl of Warwick's departure, arrived in Plymouth with £3,000 for the garrison. This money lasted almost a month, but it did not prevent the defence committee from petitioning London for additional supplies and more troops. A secondary, though far from reliable source of income for the town, was still the donation; loyal citizens continued to contribute to the cause. One such person was Lady Alice Buller, the widow of Sir Richard Buller, who had recently been voted a pension of £4 per week by parliament for the loss of her estate. Despite her lack of substance, Lady Alice, who resided in Plymouth, continued to advance money for the defence committee whenever it was needed.

The fourth winter of the war was by now on its way, and until Fairfax arrived, or unless Colonel Kerr could achieve a stunning victory over Digby, which seemed unlikely, the town would have to wait and continue to bear the hardship. Ironically Sir Thomas Fairfax had already made up his mind to leave Plymouth until the following spring. Satisfied her condition was stable, and the garrison unswerving in its loyalty, he believed the port to be in no danger of being lost. Meanwhile Prince Charles had ordered all royalist troops not needed at Dartmouth, Exeter and from around Plymouth, to concentrate at Tiverton, on the east bank of the River Exe. Grenville, whose Cornish levies refused to serve under anyone but Sir Richard, moved slowly to reinforce Goring at Tiverton. Berkeley could spare no one from Exeter, neither could Digby at Plymouth, nor Sir Edward Seymour at Dartmouth. One of the few units to actually obey the prince was Piers Edgcumbe's little regiment. Leaving a small detachment to protect his house, Colonel Edgcumbe led his regiment to Launceston, where he received orders from the prince to halt.

George Goring failed to comprehend the strength and determination of Fairfax's New Model Army. Rather than concentrate his scattered forces, as he had been ordered, he broke up his army at Tiverton. The majority of troops were sent westwards to Lord Wentworth in Cornwall, the rest Goring took to Exeter as reinforcements for the garrison, leaving only a small detachment to guard the Exe at Tiverton. The royalist towns of Devon now prepared themselves for parliament's advance. The apprehensive civilians of Dartmouth and Exeter awoke one morning to find engineers demolishing a number of houses to clear avenues for artillery. Sir Alan Apsley strengthened Barnstaple, and minor forts at Exmouth, Ilfracombe and Salcombe were reinforced. Private homes, such as Powderham Castle, Ince House, Canon Teign and Fulford House, were prepared for siege. The royalists would have done better to abandon most of these insignificant points and consolidate their forces to take on Fairfax in strength.

Outnumbered and disillusioned, Tiverton's 300 or so defenders under Sir Gilbert Talbot, surrendered to Fairfax on October 19th after only weak resistance. Exeter was the next logical target in line, or so it seemed. Fearing a confrontation, Goring pulled out of the county town and withdrew towards Totnes on the River Dart, so as to protect the landward approaches to Dartmouth, leaving Berkeley to cope as best he could. In Totnes the cavalier horse behaved badly, stealing and beating up the locals, despite being promised £150 by the town council if law and order were preserved.

Meanwhile Sir Richard Grenville, having left Cornwall once again, edged his way cautiously towards Okehampton where he halted and threw up fortifications rather than continue on to reinforce either Berkeley or Goring. Grenville and his moaning Cornishmen, plus a few hundred militia totalling no more than 500 men, remained stationary and totally useless. The royalist war machine in the southwest was breaking down. Fortunately for those cavaliers in Exeter, but unfortunately for Plymouth, sickness, caused by disease, and the approaching winter, which turned roads into mire, bogged down artillery and wagons, forced Fairfax to put his army into winter quarters.

On October 20th the New Model Army set up its main camps around Ottery St Mary. Keeping Fairfax company at Ottery were Sir Samuel Rolle, Sir John Bampfield, Francis Buller and Anthony Nicholl. No doubt these prominent gentlemen had arrived to find out if Sir Thomas planned to relieve Plymouth, the general however, refused to be hurried. A number of short, sharp thrusts and quick victories had given the parliamentarians half a dozen strategic strongholds around Exeter, but they still remained a fair distance from the city itself. Fairfax would soon be in a position to choke off supplies and sever communications between Exeter and the surrounding countryside. Despite the New Model Army's cautious manoeuvrings, a close siege of the city was not yet on Fairfax's mind, neither was the relief of Plymouth. Illness and exaggerated reports of Grenville's strength kept Sir Thomas in east Devon.

Late in November, Grenville, rather than lead an advance across the moors to harass Fairfax, abandoned his earthworks at Okehampton and withdrew back into Cornwall. A short time before Grenville's retreat, George Goring had had enough, coming to terms with the dire predicament of the royalist cause, he abandoned his troops, as he had done at Portsmouth in 1642. Riding to Dartmouth, Goring took a ship for France, and command of his cavalry, quartered in and around Bovey Tracy, went to Lord Wentworth. With Grenville's small army now spread out along the west bank of the Tamar, guarding fords and bridges and achieving absolutely nothing,

Prince Charles set up his headquarters in Tavistock. From here he issued orders that all available troops, including trained bandsmen, were to concentrate at Tavistock.

The news of Fairfax's sluggish advance and of royalist misfortunes in the southwest increased daily and was conveyed to the people of Plymouth by ship. A second more dangerous source of news was the mounted messenger. These daring volunteers took their lives in their hands as they rode through hostile territory to bring in the latest intelligence, often receiving a small fee for their services. On July 23rd two officers were sent out of Plymouth for information and news, Captain James Pearce went to Fairfax and Major Gabriel Barnes to Colonel Edward Massey. On November 21st Robert Man was paid £2 for riding into Fairfax's camp at Ottery St Mary.[38] Priests also took to delivering messages, though the work was hazardous, couriers were liable to be robbed, beaten or killed by roving enemy patrols, or even unfriendly country folk who were heartily sick of the war.

During the later stages of the conflict there were a great many furious people in the county, all up in arms at the way George Goring and his men had treated them. Nor were parliamentarians thought of any better. The poor citizens of the rural southwest had much to complain about. Their homes, livestock and crops had been plundered for years by troops from both sides, causing great distress and resentment for military personnel, whichever banner they fought under.

By the summer of 1645 many were at their wits' end, local men met and began forming themselves into armed groups, which became known as clubmen. These clubmen first appeared in Somerset and Dorset early in 1645, with the intention of keeping the countryside free from devastation by peaceful means. In June 5,000 clubmen had assembled near Castle Cary, to protest against Goring's destructive cavalry. Both sides suddenly realised the potential of such a force and each bargained for their support. As the New Model Army was more disciplined, the clubmen generally sided with parliament.

As Goring's army fell back into Devon in July, their spoliation of the county began. As a consequence the local clubmen gathered and began resisting the cavaliers. Occasionally such encounters flared into pitched battles that ended predictably, with the better-trained royalists dispersing the unruly country boys. Finding themselves under increasing pressure and with no sign of Fairfax, the clubmen eventually broke up and scattered to their homes. A number of the more stubborn stayed together and made their way to Plymouth, the only parliamentary stronghold in the county. The majority walked down to the port, but one group from Kingsbridge came in by boat.

On October 18th a large body of clubmen, numbering 180, came into the roundhead lines at Mount Batten, many of these men were from the South Hams and most of the group joined the garrison. The following month another band of clubmen marched into Mount Batten, this time they brought a royalist prisoner with them. Clubmen were not the only armed men coming into Plymouth, on October 20th thirty dissatisfied cavaliers rode into town with their arms. While the royalist hierarchy continued to squabble amongst themselves, the unfortunate soldiers occupying the wet, muddy fortifications dotted around Plymouth, lost more and more of their enthusiasm for the king's cause. As roundhead detachments from the garrison rode further and further afield, resistance to their raids grew weaker and weaker.

On the 16th of October a parliamentary cavalry unit rode out as far as Staverton and captured a captain, a lieutenant, three other troopers, ten horses and three cases of pistols, besides killing a Dutch officer. Later in the month, with the royalists needing to concentrate against Fairfax, many of Digby's troops were ordered away to reinforce other armies. Such constant reductions forced Colonel Digby to evacuate outposts such as Ham House and Kinterbury and reduce others. These were temporary measures and later both Ham and Kinterbury would be reoccupied. At one stage four companies of royalists were ordered to leave Plymouth, several going north to Tavistock, the rest out to Plympton.

One morning Captain Mathew Cousins spotted a body of cavaliers between Pennycross Work and Hoptons Work. Cousins launched his horsemen into a charge, which pressed the enemy downhill. After a brief clash of sabres and pistols, in which one of Cousins' men lost a horse, the royalists broke and fled westwards towards Saltash passage, not stopping until they had reached the river. A boat was rapidly procured and the cavaliers managed to escape. Two or three who were captured at Hoptons Work were escorted back to Plymouth.

The news in town was not all good, despite the rush of

parliamentary victories throughout England. Mayor Nicholls wrote to Lord Robartes at the House of Lords, voicing his anger at Fairfax for camping at Ottery St Mary and thereby indirectly aiding Digby's continual blockade of the town, he also complained of a shortage of money. Nicholls' petition explained the situation in Plymouth, how the town had withstood siege and had continued, through perseverance, to sustain a partial trade with the outside world. The mayor's letter also described the low spirit of an exhausted citizenry, who could no longer billet the soldiers as they had previously done. The petition was signed not only by Mayor Nicholls but also by committee members, army officers, Governor Kerr, councillors and sequestration officials. Nicholls' epistle and its signatories show evident signs of war weariness, and an eagerness for quick relief that with Fairfax so close, must have been exasperating.

Lord John Robartes, still considered Plymouth's champion, spoke up for his old friends in the House of Lords, extolling the town's loyalty and pressing for its immediate support. Robartes later went to the House of Commons and acquainted the members there with Plymouth's appeal. In response the House of Commons voted to send £10,000 to help Plymouth through the winter months. Also both houses voted on whether Fairfax should be ordered to continue his advance toward the Tamar. The Lords voted yes, the Commons no and so the New Model Army remained in camp, recruiting and endeavouring to overcome the disease that was killing hundreds of its soldiers. Fairfax's continual inactivity irritated Rolle and Bampfield who were still with the army and they wrote to Westminster, complaining that the Devonshire countryside around Ottery St Mary could not sustain the army for long. Rolle hoped supplies would be brought in from outside the county, or that Fairfax would shift his troops and soon.

Sir Samuel Rolle of Heanton Sackville near Petrockstow, had been born around 1588, his first wife died in 1614 and Rolle later married the daughter of Sir Thomas Wyse, who owned Mount Wise in Plymouth. Sam Rolle studied law and in 1640 sat as MP for Truro, a year later he was MP for Devon. At the outbreak of war Rolle commanded a Devonshire regiment and was present at Stratton, but his military career was nothing compared to his political influence during the struggle, despite Rolle's powerful authority Fairfax could not be moved.

The situation in Plymouth was improving steadily, despite low morale and an even lower treasury. Raids by detachments from the garrison increased as autumn faded. Late in October, Captain Mathew Cousins, married only two weeks, was again active with his cavalry troop. This time his men captured an ensign and two other royalists and brought in sixteen oxen and two horses for the use of the garrison. On the final day of the month, a rumour reached Plymouth that the small royalist fort at Pennycross had been abandoned. A detail was mounted and sent out to destroy the fortification before the enemy reoccupied the place. The Plymouth men arrived at Pennycross and pulled down the fort before going on to burn Ham House, at one time the beautiful home of the Trelawny family, now a deserted royalist outpost.

Several royalist prisoners taken in the recent skirmishing around Plymouth turned out to have been deserters from the garrison. One Joseph Hillyer was hanged on November 12th, the next day another, Samuel Mingo, met the same fate. On the 17th of November twenty-three bullocks were brought into the town from Buckfastleigh. The same day twenty troopers rode out towards Hoptons Work and routed a small enemy detachment, killing several men and capturing a prisoner. Two days later fifteen roundheads rode out and attacked a house where seven royalists had barricaded themselves. Promised quarter if they surrendered, the cavaliers threw out their arms and gave up. Having travelled a mile or two back to Plymouth, the roundheads stopped and dismounted. The prisoners were suddenly stripped and cruelly murdered; several fell on their knees and begged for mercy but none was shown. When news of the incident reached the town, it did not go down well with the high command or the church.

Towards the end of the year the old royalist earthwork near Widey House, known as Hoptons Work, became the scene of almost daily skirmishing. On November 28th a party of horse and foot moved out of Plymouth and headed for Knackersknowle Hill, where a detachment of royalist cavalry had been spotted. When the parliamentarian advance was observed, the cavaliers took up position in the earthwork. Outnumbered, the royalists quickly abandoned the fort and fled, but not before losing two men and a cannon to the roundheads. The next day a parliamentary patrol caught an enemy convoy on its way from Cornwall to the royalist garrison at Dartmouth The drovers panicked and scattered, leaving all thirty-six bullocks to be captured, as well as four prisoners.

On the 23rd of November, Joseph Shute, Rector of Meavy Church, was brought into Plymouth as a prisoner. A Cambridgeshire man, now in his sixties, Shute had been abused by roundhead troopers from the garrison on several occasions during the war. Plundered of his money and possessions, which had been secreted, but found, Joseph Shute was not a happy man. On the other hand, John Syms, whose son had recently arrived in Plymouth, was buoyant. As a bonus Syms' wife Elizabeth joined him on November 29th, when she was escorted into town by a troop of horse that had been out on patrol. More good news for Syms followed shortly, when six fat bullocks belonging to John Nosworthy were confiscated and brought into Plymouth. Nosworthy was an old enemy of Syms who, in 1643, had been a royalist constable, and one of the men assigned to carry Prince Maurice's proclamations into the countryside and force the clergy to read them from their pulpits. Joseph Shute agreed to obey the prince, John Syms declined, and Nosworthy abused him verbally, calling Syms rogue, knave, rascal, ass and fool,[39] but he still refused.

With an ever-decreasing army, Colonel John Digby knew he was never going to launch a full-scale assault, so he changed his tactics. Learning of Ralph Weldon's appointment as Governor of Plymouth, Digby, for some mysterious reason, believed Colonel James Kerr would be infuriated at being superseded and liable to turn his coat, so on December 30th he sent him a private letter: *'Sir I am troubled to understand that through ingratitude of those you serve, you are likely to be rewarded. With dishonour of having a person of much inferior merit put over your head, an injustice insupportable to any man of spirit and which may offer you a justifiable passion, of doing a very eminent service to your native king and country, and which if you will embrace, to deliver up the town and works of Plymouth. I shall engage myself on my honour and the faith of a gentleman you shall be rewarded with £10,000 and have the command, if you please, of a regiment of 500 horse with what honour yourself can desire. Sir be not scrupulous in taking the advice of an enemy that desires heartily on these terms to become your true friend'.*[40]

Colonel Kerr showed Digby's communication to the town council, then immediately penned a reply: *'Sir, your notion to treason I have seen and it is below my spirit for personal injury to take rational revenge and for a punctilio of honour to take advice from hell and betray my trust. I am sorry that one so ingenious as yourself should abuse your natural parts only to do mischief, yet I have reason to wonder much at your persuasion to treachery because I have had the experience of the endeavours of your family to corrupt others also. I remember the gunpowder plot, the letter which your brother (Sir George Digby) wrote to the Lord Robartes in this place for the same purpose and his negotiations with General Browne at Abingdon, surely these principles came from Spain but you should have told me also that Spanish proverb. To love the treason, but hate the traitor'.*[41]

For his loyalty James Kerr was presented with a gift of £500, and the House of Commons put his name forward to the committee of the army, for a post of honour upon his replacement by Colonel Weldon.

With December came plummeting royalist morale, the misery in Digby's camps multiplied as sickness and desertion took their toll. Despite the cold weather, roundhead cavalry still rode out in search of weak, isolated enemy patrols. On the 11th Cornet George Charleston led a detachment out and brought in ten enemy horses. Two days later another unit brought in thirteen mounts. On December 21st a roundhead troop escorted in five cavaliers, one of whom was a lieutenant. Three days after Christmas day, another roundhead detachment rode as far as Whitchurch and captured five men from Major John Polewele's troop. A soldier named Thomas Reede, taken during one of these raids, was found to have been a deserter from the garrison; on December 17th he was taken out and hanged for his treachery.

By late December minor raids turned into bolder much stronger thrusts by the parliamentarian forces in Plymouth. The high command finally believed itself strong enough to strike more aggressively at Digby's shrinking army. On Saturday December 27th a body of 500 foot and 120 horse, under Colonel John Crocker, mostly from the local trained bands, left their fortifications and headed in a northwesterly direction, towards a royalist fort known as the Kinterbury Work. This substantial earth fortification, reinforced by wooden boards, had been constructed near Kinterbury House (today Barne Barton) and overlooked Kinterbury Creek. Approaching the earthwork unobserved, the roundhead vanguard, almost entirely horse, made a sudden charge and overran the fort before the enemy knew what was happening. Overcome by the swiftness of the assault, the small garrison threw down its arms and surrendered. The parliamentarians took seventeen prisoners and plenty of equipment without loss.

Securing their prisoners, the parliamentarian column moved on to St Budeaux Church, which was manned by a much larger detachment of royalists. Here men from two small regiments, Sir James Smith's horse and Sir Charles Trevannion's foot, believed themselves secure in and around the church. Offered the chance to surrender, the cavaliers boldly refused, so the roundheads moved into positions opposite the south and west sides of the church. When the fighting began it was both hot and fierce and lasted over ninety minutes, with the old church taking a terrible pounding. Eventually superior numbers began to tell, the parliamentary foot, having worked their way close to the church killed an ensign up in the tower and rushed the main door. Sensing defeat those inside fired several shots before calling for quarter, having suffered twelve killed and many wounded. Colonel Crocker granted the defenders mercy and they opened the door and filed out.

Six roundheads had lost their lives in the fighting, amongst them the gallant Major Haines, while more than a score lay in the fields wounded. Captain Lieutenant John Vaughan, of Colonel Sir Edmond Fowell's regiment, and Lieutenant Keckwich were amongst the injured. Vaughan had been shot in the thigh as he rushed the church door and thus became the last parliamentary casualty of the day. Total prisoners taken during the two engagements numbered thirty-three royalist cavalrymen and their mounts and forty-six foot, amongst them two majors, two captains, two lieutenants, two cornets, two ensigns, six sergeants and eight corporals.

Packing up their spoils, the parliamentarians marched back to Plymouth, where the dejected captives were thrown into the old castle, still being used as a prison. Those unfortunate to be captured at St Budeaux now added to the misery of those already incarcerated. Overcrowded prisons had always been a major concern to the town authorities throughout the war. To relieve the burden prisoner exchanges still occasionally took place. Two days after the twin engagements, a small roundhead force returned to Kinterbury, dismantled the fort and took away the planking.

A report of the St Budeaux fight was sent to the House of Commons by the Plymouth defence committee, while the dead were buried with due courtesy. Major Haine's funeral, organised by Captain James Pearce, the same officer who had bravely ridden to Sir Thomas Fairfax back in July, was an expensive affair and was attended by most of his fellow officers. Haines had been a gallant and pious soldier, much admired and respected by many, from the governor down to the ordinary trooper; all mourned his passing. The coffin and stone for the major must have been specially constructed, as the entire funeral cost £38,[42] a considerable sum in those days.

Following their easy victory over the enemy at St Budeaux, a body of twenty-five parliamentarians crossed the Cattewater and threw up a rough fort right under the noses of the royalist guard at Oreston. Reinforcements were quickly dispatched, and an assault made against an enemy earthwork known as Fort Arundell. Enthusiasm did not make up for lack of numbers, and the roundheads were forced to withdraw back across the water. During the assault Tobias Markes became one of the last soldiers from the Plymouth garrison to be killed, leaving his wife Dorothy to grieve over another wasted life. The close proximity of Fairfax and his New Model Army did not encourage the townsmen to diminish their vigilance, on the contrary, guards at the outer works were as alert as ever. The forts were continually maintained, gun platforms repaired, walls strengthened and trenches cleared.

Many of Plymouth's high-ranking army officers made an appearance in the capital during 1645 for one reason or another. Besides Colonel Birch, three other colonels, Anthony Rouse, Michael Searle and Elizeus Leighton spent some time in London. In November, Colonel Rouse, who earlier in the war had a run in with the Earl of Stamford, took a petition up from Plymouth and presented it to the House of Lords. Rouse's petition called for rapid action by both Houses, for money and supplies for the town, and demanded relief by land from the enemy. The appeal also called for Sir Thomas Fairfax to be ordered to relieve Plymouth with all speed.

Colonel Michael Searle, dissatisfied by the way he had been treated since Colonel Kerr's arrival, and considering his past record, sent his own petition to parliament in October. In his defence, Searle professed that he had served parliament faithfully at Plymouth and other places, with little pay and often having to use his own money to procure supplies for his soldiers. Searle was claiming £1,300 back pay, and a further £578 for supplies he had been forced to purchase. When he arrived in London the colonel was arrested, possibly due to the inflated amount he was demanding. Studying his record, the Lords reconsidered and Michael Searle was released. Later the Lords ordered that Colonel Searle should have the protection of the House and be recompensed by the auditors for the amount they believed he was due.

Colonel Leighton had arrived in Plymouth in 1643 as a major of cavalry and served the garrison ably. Rising to colonel, Leighton was another disatisfied officer owed money. In April 1645 the town treasury paid him £30 towards his arrears and allowed him to proceed to London. Leighton was in the capital to urge parliament to promote him to the command of all the cavalry in Plymouth. Colonel Leighton's request was considered, but the war was going so well for parliament, that such overtures were pushed to the back of the agenda.

In Hereford, since his defeat at Naseby, King Charles was totally distressed by the worsening situation. Then one morning his anguish suddenly disappeared, to be replaced by apprehension. New Welsh regiments could be raised and troops were expected from Ireland by way of Chester and the southwest, while Cornwall, most of Devon and parts of Wales remained royalist. Oxford was secure and Montrose's outnumbered little army continued to run rings around the Covenanter forces in Scotland.

This hopeful, illusory picture vanished as rapidly as it had appeared, when on May 9th Montrose was defeated by Sir John Hurry at Auldern. The king shifted into south Wales, while Prince Rupert took command at Bristol and met with disaster. In the north the remaining royalists suffered one defeat after another. Carlisle surrendered before the end of July, as did Scarborough. The king now saw Scotland as his only hope and Montrose eagerly awaited his arrival. Meantime the new Welsh levies were beaten on Colby Moor, forcing the royalists to abandon Haverfordwest and retreat to Castle Carew.

Reaching Lichfield, north of Birmingham, King Charles received word from Montrose that he had come down from the highlands and hammered the Covenanter army under William Baillie at Alford. Montrose then moved against Perth, frightening that city before falling back. The Covenanters had by now raised a second army and both forces turned on Montrose. With such odds against him, the king's man in the highlands should have been trapped and annihilated, it was not to be. On August 16th the royalists inflicted another embarrassing defeat on the Covenanter armies, and two days later James Graham, the dauntless Marquis of Montrose, led his triumphant little army into Glasgow.

The king was overjoyed at the news from Scotland and he pressed on from Lichfield to Rotherham, only to learn later that the large Scottish army in England, under Alexander Leslie, was marching towards him. Switching his route the king headed back down to Oxford, then aimed for Wales via Worcester. On the way the royalists were able to relieve Hereford, not by battle, but because the parliamentarian besiegers were short of supplies, which forced them to withdraw to Gloucester.

Bristol surrendered in September, and the king's trust in his nephew vanished completely. Charles Stuart, camped in south Wales, now sought to escape before the parliamentary noose tightened even further around his neck. Marching once again for the north in a last ditch effort to join Montrose, the king detached a force for the relief of Chester, but it failed and his tiny army found itself unable to reach Scotland. Now the king sought out a friendly garrison town outside of Oxford and while he searched, the Marquis of Montrose met with defeat at Philiphaugh on September 13th.

Camping at Newark, the royalist army disintegrated due to desertion and internal disputes. The cavalry was already gone, some into Yorkshire others towards Oxford. The foot, numbering less than 2,000, shrank in size more and more each day and the artillery was non-existent. More disasters followed as parliament began mopping up operations. Monmouth, Chepstow and Carmarthen were captured, but Chester, the last route between the Irish ports and Wales, still held out. On December 8th, Hereford, having been reinvested, was taken by of all people Colonel John Birch. The king's cause was in its final death throes; soon it would be all over.

One who would not see parliament's final victory was William Strode, worn out and having exhausted himself on behalf of the cause, the elder statesman had died in his rooms at Westminster on September 8th. William Strode was laid to rest near his old friend John Pym in Westminster Abbey.

(36) Page 261: Siege Accounts of Plymouth, held in the Worth Collection, accession 1/644-5; by kind permission of the West Devon Record Office.
(37) Page 262: House of Commons Journal.
(38) Page 266: Siege Accounts of Plymouth, held in the Worth Collection, accession 1/644-5; by kind permission of the West Devon Record Office.
(39) Page 270: John Syms, A daybook of special passages and mercies, British Library, Add 35297; by kind permission of the British Library, London.
(40) Page 270: Letter from Colonel John Digby to Colonel James Kerr, to be found in A Compleat History of the life and raigne of King Charles (London 1658) by William Sanderson.
(41) Page 270: Letter from Colonel James Kerr to Colonel John Digby, to be found in A Compleat History of the life and raigne of King Charles (London 1658) by William Sanderson.
(42) Page 273: Siege Accounts of Plymouth, held in the Worth Collection, accession 1/644-5; by kind permission of the West Devon Record Office.

Chapter 13

The War Ends

During the fighting around Exeter, in late December, early January, Ashton, only six miles from the city, was captured and occupied by parliamentary forces. Ashton's owner, the unfortunate Sir George Chudleigh, later rode into Sir Thomas Fairfax's camp and surrendered himself, hoping for leniency after his family's misguided change of loyalty to the king. Chudleigh though had little to worry about, Sir Thomas treated him with the utmost courtesy, after all he had more pressing matters on his mind. The slow encirclement of royalist Exeter continued through the dreary winter months. Colonel Kerr at one point wrote to Fairfax, warning him of a possible advance on Ashburton by 5,500 cavaliers, who were attempting to blunt parliamentary developments along the west bank of the Exe. To coincide with this manoeuvre was a planned charge out of Exeter's gates by 2,000 royalists. These movements never took place, as cavalier organisation rapidly broke down.

Prince Charles still counted on his most loyal troops to stop the relentless roundhead advance. His presence at Tavistock helped raise a large army, but the majority of men who came in were mostly of poor quality, untrained and undisciplined. The prince however was not dispirited, and he quickly detached 800 of his new soldiers and sent them to Okehampton as a forward observation post. From here they could raid the parliamentary positions around Exeter and block any surprise attack on Tavistock from across the moors.

On January 8th the Plymouth horse, despite the recent death of it's twenty-two-year-old commander Colonel Nicholas Boscowan, attacked and beat up a detachment of Sir Allen Apsley's royalist horse, also a Devon regiment, near Barnstaple, a town then under partial roundhead blockade. The following day saw a more important blow to the prince's hopes. Early in the morning, while Sir Hardress Waller skirmished with cavaliers near Okehampton as a diversion, two regiments of parliamentary foot and one of horse left Crediton. This force, under the infamous Oliver Cromwell, advanced quickly down on Bovey Tracy, fifteen miles distant. Here Lord Wentworth and his unruly cavalry were encamped, guarding a crossing point of the River Bovey that connected the village with Ashburton, Totnes and Dartmouth.

Poorly-posted guards failed to notice the approach of Cromwell's horse and were taken completely by surprise. The few troopers who remained at their posts were quickly overpowered and captured, while the rest vanished into the countryside. Roundhead cavalry now swarmed around a house being used by the royalist officers. One quick-witted cavalier gathered up a handful of coins, which were being used as gambling stakes, and tossed them out of the window. As the parliamentarians dismounted and fought each other for a share of the money, the royalists disappeared through a back door. These men escaped across the river, some going as far as Ashburton, where a second detachment of Wentworth's horse was quartered. The remainder of the Bovey Tracy garrison, who at the moment of attack were settling down to a meal, found themselves in a bad situation. Without their officers they could do nothing and the majority surrendered. All told Wentworth lost four colonels, three lieutenant colonels, five majors, eleven captains, 140 troopers, 400 horses, 300 arms and seven colours including a royal standard. Casualties were light during the attack, as the speed of Cromwell's advance gave little chance for organised resistance.

Some 120 cavaliers managed to escape across the river and took refuge inside Ellington Church, from where they sent word to Lord Wentworth for help. The morning after the Bovey Tracy fiasco, Cromwell's foot advanced against the church, forcing the defenders to abandon their strongpoint and withdraw. Almost simultaneously, Sir Hardress Waller's operations in north Devon and around Okehampton, put pressure on Prince Charles at all points. Ashburton, Sir John Northcote's parliamentary seat, was also easily captured at this time, the cavaliers fleeing disheartened, their foot in one direction, their horse in another.

By midday of January 11th the roundheads were ready to move against Dartmouth by way of Totnes. The community of Totnes was fortunate that the royalist regiment stationed there withdrew at Cromwell's approach, thus preventing the town from becoming a battlefield. The parliamentarians occupied Totnes later in the day without a shot being fired, which greatly pleased most of the local merchants. However a group of royalist sympathisers, who resided in and around the town, were not so enamoured by Cromwell's visit. One of the more ardent was John Seymour, the brother of Sir Edward Seymour of Berry Pomeroy. The Seymour family had staked a great deal on the king, now they feared retribution and ruin.

With such dynamic leaders as Fairfax and Cromwell leading the well-trained New Model Army and the royalists lacking organisation, discipline and solidarity, Prince Charles cancelled his planned push across Dartmoor. He decided to leave Exeter and Dartmouth to their fate and retreat into Cornwall with the rest of his army. Dartmouth, occupied by the royalists since Prince Maurice captured the place back in October 1643, had been heavily-strengthened by its gifted and popular governor Sir Edward Seymour. Advantageous as a haven for royalist shipping and a base for privateers, Fairfax marked Dartmouth as his primary objective in Devon.

Unfortunately at the time of Fairfax's approach Seymour was in Exeter on business, leaving Sir Hugh Pollard in charge during his absence. To defend Dartmouth, Pollard, who had been a prisoner of parliament until the spring of 1644, and Sir Henry Cary commanded approximately 1,000 soldiers, nowhere near enough to fully garrison the port and its irregular chain of defences. Once the royal standard had been raised over Dartmouth, the cavaliers built up existing fortifications and erected new works at Gallants Bower, half a mile south of Dartmouth Castle atop the hill overlooking the Dart. Mount Ridley, another new fortification, had been thrown up above Kingswear Castle, across the river from the main line, which helped to protect the seaward approach to the town. Pollard himself commanded the troops on the west bank of the Dart, while Cary took charge of those along the east bank.

On the 17th of January, 400 cavalrymen, under Major Ducroc, arrived in Dartmouth from Torrington as a reinforcement for the garrison. It was to Pollard's great misfortune that he quarrelled with Ducroc, for the major saddled up and left, taking his horsemen back to Torrington. By the middle of the second week of January,

Fairfax's vanguard approached the royalist outposts, but no major attack went in. Four days after the general himself arrived, William Batten brought a squadron into the Dart ready to cooperate in an attack upon the town. The assault finally came late on Sunday January 18th. Due to the atrocious state of the roads, the parliamentarians had no artillery available. As Fairfax's infantry assembled, the men had to keep low, while royalist ordnance blasted death into the trees above their heads. Once the inaccuracy of the barrage was noted, the roundheads rushed forward, capturing many guns and prisoners whose morale they found to be almost non-existent.

Within a short space of time, Dartmouth's defences had fallen one after another; the defenders putting up little resistance. Mount Boone, the West Gate, Tunstal Church, Bayard's Cove Castle and two ships lying in the river were all captured before nightfall. Deputy Governor Pollard attempted to escape across the river to Kingswear, but he was wounded and captured in flight. A month after the fall of Dartmouth, General Fairfax would write to parliament, recommending Hugh Pollard for fair treatment, as he had been equally fair with the people in and around Dartmouth.

The morning after the breakthroughs on the west bank, a mixed detachment of dragoons, musketeers and sailors from Batten's squadron, crossed the Dart and moved against Kingswear Castle. Expecting a tough fight, the parliamentarian officers were surprised when Sir Henry Cary mildly surrendered. On Tuesday the 20th, the main castle and Gallants Bower fell, bringing resistance in Dartmouth to an end. The port had been the most-important royalist storehouse and shipping base in the South Hams, now it was gone. Three days later captured enemy flags were presented to parliament, a number of high-ranking royalists taken at Dartmouth were also on their way to London to receive their paroles

A messenger brought word of Dartmouth's capture into Plymouth, while other couriers, who had arrived on the 16th, announced the news that the enemy were withdrawing from Tavistock and falling back across the Tamar. Dispatch riders had been able to ride into Plymouth almost at will for a week before the capture of Dartmouth, the reason for this was the departure on January 12th of Colonel Digby and his army. With Fairfax so close, Digby had found his army crumbling. Each day desertions from his camps increased and he was powerless to stop them. Dispirited cavaliers came into Plymouth and surrendered or rode away to their homes. However there were still a considerable number of die-hards whose only desire was to fight on.

Skirmishing around Plymouth continued right up until the cavaliers broke camp and marched away. A detachment from the town went out early on Saturday the 3rd of January, and lay siege to the small royal garrison occupying Hoptons Work. The parliamentarians remained close to the enemy until Sunday, when Digby, having managed to round up enough of a relieving force, appeared and the roundheads withdrew. The following week a roundhead cavalry troop rode out to Meavy, upon their return they brought with them a Mr Philip Giles, several bullocks belonging to William Crymes and a few horses. Two days later, a mounted parliamentary patrol galloped towards Longbridge and charged the royalist guard. After a desperate little fight, the cavaliers fled, leaving one man captured, several killed and the rest scattered.

Finally on the 12th of January, Colonel John Digby had had enough, aware that Fairfax could sweep down and attack him at any moment, he hastily broke camp and marched away, leaving behind a large quantity of supplies and guns. Seven pieces of ordnance and 200 arms were left at Plympton, other guns were abandoned at Longbridge, Plymstock and Fort Arundell. As Digby's army sullenly withdrew into Cornwall, a royalist officer and a woman came into Plymouth to inform the town of their departure. Kerr did not pursue, believing the enemy too strong in horse.

The only irritation to Plymouth now was the small royal garrison across the water at Mount Edgcumbe House, but its existence as such could be counted in days, hours if attacked. The situation within the town was now most favourable, the death rate had receded greatly and troops from Plymouth, whose garrison numbered 2,500, excluding the trained bands, were able to march out and assist the New Model Army. Captain Nicholas Roope and his Dartmouth company left the town they had helped defend for three years on January 26th. Sadly the captain had to leave one relative behind, Gilbert Roope, who died back in April 1644. Captain Roope returned to a completely different Dartmouth than the one he had left at the beginning of the war. His home at Warfleet had been completely destroyed and his small fleet of merchant ships lost. Five hundred soldiers from Plymouth were also ordered to Dartmouth to be used as a garrison, so Fairfax would not have to weaken his own army.

The House of Lords appreciated Roope's service to parliament and recommended to the House of Commons that he be made Governor of Dartmouth.

Sir Shilston Calmady's regiment departed Plymouth on the same day as Roope's company ending a long period of sustained defence, unfortunately he would not return. On February 4th Sir Shilston's troops were involved in a minor skirmish with royalist soldiers near Membury in east Devon and Calmady was killed near a gateway, becoming one of only a handful of roundhead casualties. Shilston Calmady was buried in the churchyard on the same day, alongside one other soldier killed during the skirmish.

Absent from Plymouth at this time was the town's new governor, Colonel Ralph Weldon, who, shortly after Digby's departure and the surrender of Dartmouth, had marched down towards Salcombe. The story of Salcombe (or rather Fort Charles), involves a Devonshire royalist, Sir Edmund Fortescue, whose military career was both unfortunate and inglorious. Fortescue had been captured at Modbury in December 1642, and after his exchange he was assigned by Prince Maurice to rebuild the old dilapidated Tudor Castle, lying on rocks at the end of a flooded causeway. Fortescue had authority to seek assistance from the royalist Sheriff of Devon and the governors of the various garrisons in the South Hams. Shortly after his arrival, Fortescue rechristened the old bulwark Fort Charles and began restoration work immediately. Well over £4,000 would be spent on rebuilding and rearming the old work, and by the end of 1645 Fort Charles looked capable of withstanding a moderate siege. Behind its walls were Sir Edmund Fortescue, Sir Christopher Luckner, a surgeon, a chaplain and fifty-two other ranks.

Several minor attacks had been directed at Fort Charles during its reconstruction, but with royalist domination of the county throughout most of the war, such petty raids were not taken too seriously. The first intimation of a major offensive came with the New Model Army's operations against Dartmouth. Upon reaching the area, a small force of roundheads, under Colonel Richard Ingoldsby, was detached by Fairfax from the main army and sent to operate against Salcombe. This tiny port had always been a favourite hideaway for royalist privateers and needed to be closed; consequently the siege of Fort Charles began properly on January 15th 1646. At first the artillery available to the parliamentarians was not of a large enough calibre to batter down the walls, but with the departure of Digby from Plymouth, Colonel Weldon was able to haul up a number of heavier guns to reinforce Ingoldsby.

On the outskirts of Aveton Gifford, the royalist vicar William Lane, tried to build a crude fortification on high ground overlooking the long bridge. Lane and his half-hearted supporters hoped to stop Weldon's artillery train, but at the approach of the roundhead column, Lane and his confederates abandoned their unfinished work and fled. To reach Fort Charles there were but two options, by boat or at low tide across a narrow causeway, therefore a besieging army could not assault the castle without suffering heavy loses. The only way to force Fortescue into submission would be starvation and cannonade, both of which could take months. With no other alternative, the parliamentarians settled down to better their gun emplacements and open up a series of bombardments, aimed at smashing the castle walls. On March 24th, after nine weeks of long-distant artillery fire, Colonel Weldon, commanding the roundhead batteries, sent in a demand for surrender, Fortescue refused and the siege continued.

Back on the Devon-Cornwall border, Prince Charles had given Sir Ralph Hopton command of all royalist troops on January 5th. Slighted by the prince's choice, even though he himself had recommended Hopton for the position, Sir Richard Grenville resigned. Grenville was to have commanded the foot and Wentworth the horse; for his unwillingness to serve under Hopton, Sir Richard was summoned to Launceston. Charles Stuart tried to make Grenville withdraw his resignation, but all his entreaties failed to budge his stubborn subordinate. In the end Richard Grenville was arrested and imprisoned on St Michael's Mount.

While the prince made his changes in Cornwall, the last remaining royalist strongholds in Devon were falling to parliament. On January 25th Powderham Castle was captured and Fairfax found himself a step closer to completing his encirclement of Exeter. Two days later Sir John Berkeley refused an offer to surrender, and for a brief moment it looked as though Fairfax would assault the city. Reinforcements were called down from Bristol, and several thousand Devonshire roundheads and clubmen came forward to offer their services to Sir Thomas. Despite extra troops the parliamentary commander decided against wasting lives and destroying property unnecessarily. Instead Fairfax left Sir Hardress Waller with a sizeable force to keep pressure on the city, and with the rest of the army he marched northwestwards towards Torrington, where, it was reported Hopton had concentrated a large force to relieve Exeter. On February 16th the battle of Torrington took place, and Sir Ralph Hopton watched as his army was pushed back across the Tamar for the last time.

Those surviving royalists still with the colours withdrew to the old battleground at Stratton, where they rested. Nine days after Torrington, a substantial body of roundhead cavalry galloped down to the Tamar and splashed across the river near Stratton; amongst them were the Plymouth horse. On a hilltop guarding the area were 500 cavalier horse; Hopton and his foot having pulled back deeper into Cornwall. When the parliamentarians advanced, the demoralised enemy broke and fled, scattering to rejoin the rest of the army consolidating near Bodmin. Hopton was now forced to divide his command, part went to Lostwithiel and the rest were sent to protect the approaches to Liskeard and Bodmin. A strong detachment of horse and foot was also left at Launceston.

On Wednesday February 25th, Fairfax detached 1,500 men to watch Barnstaple and marched south from Stratton towards Launceston, which was hastily evacuated at his approach, except for a small rearguard. For several hours the parliamentary vanguard fought with the defenders, forcing them back slowly through the town. Eventually the cavaliers disengaged and retreated. Fearing capture, the garrison at Saltash evacuated the town on the 28th, leaving behind three cannon as they hurried westwards to join the main army.

From Launceston the New Model Army turned to the southwest, aiming for Bodmin, which fell on March 2nd. On the same day, in an effort to avoid capture, Prince Charles deserted his remaining troops and boarded a ship bound for the Scilly Isles. Hopton found himself alone, abandoned by his superior to sort out the mess himself. Since evacuating Bodmin, Sir Ralph had been camped at St Columb, but here disintegration of the army set in as never before. Many men wished to surrender and return to a normal life, but Hopton still had a faint glimmer of hope.

As Fairfax edged towards St Columb, Hopton gloomily fell back towards Truro; royalist Cornwall was shrinking by the hour. Between the roundhead crossing of the Tamar and the capture of Bodmin, a Cornish clergyman, Mr Hugh Peters, alone and in disguise, arrived in Plymouth. Fairfax had given Peters secret instructions to meet and talk with local royalists in eastern Cornwall and to those within Plymouth. Sir Thomas feared an uprising in his rear while he concentrated on capturing Hopton's army, and he hoped Peters could achieve some kind of promise from the cavaliers not to intervene.

Meeting with Governor Weldon, or as he was still absent overseeing the siege of Fort Charles, with Mayor Nicholls and informing him of his mission, Hugh Peters next met discreetly with Miss Philippa Coryton, daughter of a Cornish royalist. Miss Coryton had covert orders from her father, Colonel Piers Edgcumbe and several other prominent cavaliers to make a deal with the roundhead authorities. Miss Coryton asked Peters that if the royalists of east Cornwall could prevent an uprising in support of a possible breakout by Hopton, would Sir Thomas Fairfax show leniency to those concerned. Hugh Peters guaranteed Philippa Coryton that her father and his colleagues would receive fair treatment if they kept the lid on eastern Cornwall if Hopton should attempt a break through the parliamentary net.

As proof of his word Peters offered to take Colonel Edgcumbe, Mr William Coryton, Lieutenant Colonel William Scawen and Mr Thomas Lower to meet with General Fairfax. They agreed and accompanied the clergyman to Bodmin. When they arrived on March 4th Sir Thomas confirmed the offer made by his agent; if the eastern Cornish remained passive, property and persons would not be molested. Pleased with the outcome of the meeting, Colonel Edgcumbe agreed to do his best, he also surrendered Mount Edgcumbe House to parliament. Later a petition was organised by Edgcumbe and other Cornishmen, proclaiming their regiments to be disbanded and requesting to come under the protection of parliament.

As a consequence of the meeting in Bodmin, Fairfax sent a communication to the House of Commons on March 6th. The letter recommended Colonel Edgcumbe, Major Nicholas Sawle, Mr Thomas Lower, Mr Glanville, Mr Coryton, Mr William Trevise, Lieutenant Colonel William Scawen, Major Richard Edgcumbe and Mr Ambrose Manaton to the favour of parliament, as persons whose interests and endeavours have been very useful in reducing the west.

Since Colonel Robert Martin's raid back in May 1644, Mount Edgcumbe had remained relatively quiet, and many of the troops assigned to the house were dispatched to other fields of operations. The defences previously thrown up with great energy, then partly-destroyed by the roundheads, were never repaired and with Fairfax's offer of leniency, Piers Edgcumbe took his house and family out of the war. Edgcumbe's reward for his submission was permission to retain his home and live there in peace; he was one of the more fortunate of the royalist gentry. Officially Colonel Edgcumbe surrendered on March 9th to Colonel Robert Hammond, leaving only Ince House under enemy control in eastern Cornwall. Ince House's fate was sealed, though and within a few weeks it too would be given up.

In the meantime Fairfax's vanguard was closing in on Hopton's army around Truro. On March 11th part of the Plymouth horse, under Lieutenant Somaster, whist out on a reconnaissance, ran into a party of cavaliers near St Columb. After a brief clash of swords the outclassed royalists withdrew; such minor encounters occurred daily, with Hopton's demoralised troops usually coming off second best. A lack of enthusiasm amongst Sir Ralph's soldiers showed a frightening increase in the moral destruction of his army.

The end finally came, having received a communiqué from Sir Thomas Fairfax requesting him to spare any further loss of life, Hopton knew the game was up. Urged by most of his subordinates, Sir Ralph Hopton surrendered his army on Thursday March 12th. No doubt such action was necessary, as secret letters taken from a royalist ship captured at Padstow, revealed that Irish troops were being sent over to support the king. Fairfax made this information available to the Cornish people, who vented their fury upon the royalists. Hopton did not surrender all his troops, several hundred of the more disciplined were dispatched to St Michael's Mount and 800 others to Pendennis. A number of royalist die-hards accompanied the soldiers, while Hopton remained behind to help the rest of his army disband. Three days after the surrender, the western royalist army demobilised. Colonel Philip Champernowne's regiment was included in the break up; the colonel himself and a servant were given passes issued by Fairfax to travel home to Modbury.

With Hopton's surrender the New Model Army shifted to Launceston, the Plymouth horse being quartered at Bodmin. Fairfax now made plans to rescue the few remaining outposts under royalist control. Setting out for Plymouth on March 21st, Sir Thomas Fairfax and his competent lieutenant, Oliver Cromwell, rode into the town to a tumultuous welcome. Citizens and soldiers cheered loudly as the two officers inspected the ominously-silent fortifications, where almost every stretch of wall could tell a story of heroism. The town cannons fired a three hundred-gun salute in a dazzling crescendo of victory, and the corporation splashed out £20 for a banquet to honour parliament's most gifted soldiers. Governor Weldon returned to Plymouth from the Fort Charles siege to attend the dinner, as did the mayor, many of the town councillors and a multitude of other leading notables. Having thanked the corporation and the people of Plymouth for their effort, loyalty and kindness, Tom Fairfax and his party left for Exeter.

As March drew to a close, and the roundhead stranglehold on Exeter tightened, Sir John Berkeley, isolated and abandoned, awaited the inevitable. His best troops had long gone, sent away previously to reinforce Hopton, all he could do now was sit behind his extensive fortifications. On the last day of the month Fairfax sent in a demand for surrender. Weary and with no other recourse open, Sir John agreed to surrender Exeter. The next nine days were spent negotiating terms. Growing impatient Sir Thomas rode away to Barnstaple, which still held out for the king and would do so until April 12th. During his absence Berkeley signed the articles of capitulation on April 13th and it was almost over. Leaving sufficient troops to stamp out the last strongholds of royalism in Devon and Cornwall, Fairfax took the rest of his army out of the southwest towards Oxford; with him went the Plymouth horse.

Shortly before Hopton's surrender, Colonel Weldon took a body of troops over the Tamar on a raid, which he hoped would secure the submission of Ince House, home of the absent royalist Sir Henry Killigrew. The fortified manor lay only a short distance from Saltash and was occupied by approximately sixty musketeers. On March 8th, sixty of Weldon's soldiers advanced upon the house and sent in a request for surrender, it was rejected. Firing from both sides sparked off a brief, bloodless engagement. Weldon reinforced his vanguard and opened up with a small cannon. Realising he had absolutely no chance the royalist commander raised the white flag and his men were permitted to march away unhindered, leaving behind them four cannon and ninety muskets.

Colonel Ralph Weldon was an intensely busy man during the final months of the war. Besides his main responsibility as Governor of Plymouth, Weldon also commanded the parliamentary batteries bombarding Fort Charles. By the middle of March, Fortescue still defiantly held out, hoping, no doubt, for a miracle. Much of Weldon's time was spent mopping up around Plymouth and arresting known royalist sympathisers. On the 12th a party of parliamentary horse rode into the village of Stokenham, six miles east of Kingsbridge. Here they attacked and ransacked the home of William Randall, a well-known royalist. The roundhead troopers kept firing into the house until Randall finally gave himself up. During the haphazard discharge of parliamentary carbines and pistols, Randall's daughter had been mortally wounded. When William Randall emerged from the house, he was arrested and taken away.

Later Modbury received a visit from a party of parliamentary horse, dismounting at the top of the village the troopers stabled their mounts in St George's Church, a popular affront used by roundheads everywhere to show their contempt for papists. Portlemouth, Marlborough and Kingsbridge were also visited by roundhead detachments, and nearly all suffered retribution of some kind. Unlike other parts of England, where the war had passed by and entire towns had been pillaged and partially destroyed, Fairfax's discipline and the weariness of war saved much of Devon and Cornwall from a similar fate.

By the end of April Fort Charles was the only slice of royalist real estate remaining in Devon; the war now drifted away from the Westcountry and Fortescue's valiant little band were marooned and forgotten. With no hope of relief and with food running out, Edmund Fortescue and his officers finally agreed to surrender. On May 9th, upon articles agreed upon by himself on the one side and Major James Pearce and Captain Hall on the other, Fortescue marched out of Fort Charles and retired to his home at Fallapit, and the war in Devonshire came to an end.

The final act was also being played out over the rest of the country. Chester had surrendered on February 3rd, leaving Falmouth as the only port open to the royalists. In March Plymouth's old governor, Jacob Astley, now Lord Astley, left Bridgenorth with 2,000 men and made a forlorn effort to reach Oxford. Finding the enemy concentrating against him, Astley changed direction. On the 21st the greatly-outnumbered cavalier force was surrounded at Stow-in-the-Wold and thrashed. A few of the cavalry escaped but the infantry surrendered. A month later Sir Henry Killigrew handed over St Michael's Mount. Fearing capture King Charles disguised himself and left his capital on April 27th.

Making his way north, Charles Stuart gave himself up to the Scottish army besieging Newark on May 5th, and the town surrendered the following day. Prince Rupert and his brother Maurice rode out of Oxford on June 22nd and the remnants of the garrison broke up and went home. Several defiant bastions of royalism still flew the king's flag, Pendennis Castle in Cornwall, where Colonel John Digby and many other intransigent cavaliers had taken refuge, would hold out until the middle of August, and Raglan and Harlech Castles in Wales. The Scots would later escort the king to Newcastle where he remained, as antagonistic as ever, until early 1647. Charles' temperament failed to adhere him to his own people, and on February 3rd the king and the city of Newcastle would be given over to parliament.

Despite the overwhelming victories of the New Model Army and the king's capture, the aftereffects of the civil war continued for many years. Plymouth, like many towns throughout England, was forced to maintain a strong military garrison. Parliament feared a royalist revival, and for good reasons. Large numbers of prominent cavaliers had fled abroad during the last months of the war, and many of these corresponded surreptitiously with those who remained in England. Later a secret society, named the Sealed Knot, would come into existence and unite leading royalists. Plot and counterplot were whispered words that bounced around the corridors of Westminster, causing a reaction of fear and persecution. With the king a prisoner, Westminster constantly anticipated an attempted coup to release him.

To maintain its precarious position, parliament ousted many suspected royalists from office and replaced them with staunch parliamentarians. The clergy also suffered, many at Westminster believed the rural Devonshire churches harboured clandestine royalists, and 128 Episcopalian ministers were ejected from churches within the county before 1646 was out. During the Restoration, in blatant retribution, 132 Puritan ministers would in turn be expelled from their diocese. A number of these would find themselves imprisoned for their wartime alliance to parliament.

A year after the end of the war, discontent amongst the soldiers in the Plymouth garrison broke out once again, this time, as before, it was caused by the irregularity of pay. Colonel Weldon wrote an abundance of letters to parliament complaining of the deteriorating situation, but received no answer. Unable to get no more than a token response, Weldon resigned on July 30th 1647. Three days later the garrison mutinied and were joined in angry protest by the impoverished people of the town. Parliament finally woke up and £4,000 was earmarked for Colonel Weldon's use, but his resignation was not accepted, and Ralph Weldon remained in unhappy command at Plymouth until 1649. Eventually the garrison and the burden to pay for it, would be reduced, part of the command sailing away for service in Ireland.

Plymouth suffered badly throughout the war, and her sacrifice was unsurpassed. When the war ended, many in the town were left destitute; war widows and orphans roamed the streets begging. Old soldiers with missing limbs and terrible wounds, made worse by poor surgery, flooded the streets, unable to work or feed their families. Eventually parliament would recognise its obligations to these soldiers, and in 1647 a pension system was initiated. To claim a pension, a soldier or his dependants would have a petition drawn up and signed by a person of note, such as his old commanding officer or company captain and send it to the county quarter sessions. The petition would be read and a pension awarded or not, depending on the circumstances.

The cost of the war to Plymouth cannot be truly ascertained, her trade had been dramatically reduced during the four years of conflict, her markets for inland produce curtailed, expansion stunted and thousands of pounds had been poured away on military expenditure. Though the town itself had suffered little damage from the effects of war, the population was so decimated it would take years for the birth rate to catch up. From January 1643 to April 1645, burials in St Andrew's alone numbered over 3,000, inclusive of death from battle, disease and executions. Of this number, 460 were soldiers, including thirty-two officers. These figures do not take into consideration the many hundreds killed and buried on site at Lipson, Fort Stamford, Maudlyn and a dozen other battlefield locations around the town. Other internments in pits and churchyards dotted around Plymouth, and those seamen who died on board their ships, must bring the total number of deaths in the town to above 6,000; over a third of them soldiers.

It would take Plymouth years to recover, and in the meantime the aftereffects continued to depress the populace. The army remained in occupation for years, trade and growth perked up a little, but it would be many years before the pre-war population and trade was surpassed. The years of Cromwell's military dictatorship proved oppressive and ruthless, and where strict Puritans were in control, communities faced harsh treatment for breaking even minor laws. In 1659, John Old, an innkeeper, was arrested in Plymouth for allowing men to drink on his premises on the 8th of January, the Lord's day. Another, John Wood, was taken into custody for walking along the Hoe at sermon time. George Cragg was arrested for permitting friends to drink at his home at sermon time, and a number of vagrants found themselves scooped up and in gaol for begging in the town at sermon time.

When Oliver Cromwell died on September 3rd 1658, and his weak son Richard took over, people realised it was time for change. Richard Cromwell was not his father, Oliver had fought three civil wars, and cut off a king's head to retain total control of Government, when he passed away, the system quickly fell apart. With mistrust and smouldering resentment hanging over parliament, and no one fit to replace Cromwell, General George Monck, supported by many others, invited Charles Stuart to return and take his father's place as King of England, but not with the power the monarchy previously held. Consequently Charles II entered London on May 29th 1660 and the Restoration was born.

The reverberations of war now echoed back to haunt many, only now, those who had fought against the king would find themselves on the receiving end of vengeance. Plymouthians immediately shook off their strict Puritan shackles and whole-heartedly embraced the Restoration. The town council spent a generous amount of money on a huge royal parade and several expensive gifts for the king. No doubt the old parliamentarians hoped their show of newborn loyalty would adhere them to King Charles.

One of the most shameful acts endorsed by the new king upon his assumption of the throne was the exhumation of the bodies of deceased parliamentary leaders from Westminster. Primarily Oliver Cromwell, John Pym, William Strode and Colonel Nicholas Boscowan, commander of the Plymouth horse, who had died in September 1645, aged only twenty-two. The remains of these men were disinterred, piled together on a cart and transported across to St Margaret's Churchyard. Here they were crudely thrown into a common pit, however Cromwell was not so fortunate, his rotting remains were beheaded and the corpse left hanging at Tyburn.

This was only the beginning of the new king's reprisals, those who signed his father's death warrant were to be sought out, as would many members of parliament who fought against the royalist cause. Army officers and clergymen who had opposed and humiliated his father were marked for retribution. Those who remained loyal to the king's memory and helped in his son's restoration would reap generous rewards. In Devon and Cornwall many would benefit and many more would suffer. General George Monck, a successful parliamentary officer, who saw action in Ireland and Scotland, was made Duke of Albemarle. On the other side of the coin, John Carew, brother of the executed Sir Alexander, and one of those who signed the king's death warrant in 1649, received the headsman's axe by order of the new king in 1660.

In the town of Plymouth, William Jennings, a nasty, spiteful little character, according to James Yonge, though a close friend of Philip Francis, was elected mayor in 1662. A merchant throughout the war, Jennings, the son of Abraham Jennings, the man who had been arrested and held under house arrest by Colonel Kerr, suddenly found he was a good king's man. During William Jennings' mayoralty many parliamentarians suffered at his hands. Samuel Northcote (Mayor of Plymouth 1658-9), and his son were imprisoned in London as non-conformists. In August 1662, three magistrates, the Plymouth town clerk and ten councillors were ejected; all refused to declare it unlawful, upon any pretext, to take up arms against the king. In 1683 Jennings received his reward, he along with seven of the town's twelve magistrates were kicked out of office by the king for attempting to exclude councillors from choosing their fellow councillors; Jennings died five years later aged seventy-one.

The new king's lasting legacy to Plymouth was the royal citadel, built upon the eastern half of the Hoe and dominating both the sea and the old town. Charles saw Plymouth's importance as a port and the need for stronger, more modern defences. Consequently he ordered the engineer Sir Bernard De Gomme to design a citadel that would rise above the sea front and give protection to both the harbour and the town beyond. Work on the new fortress began early in 1666, but its construction meant the destruction of Plymouth's older fort and the final abandonment of the old castle. Legend has it that almost every person able to walk in Plymouth carried a stone of some size up to the new bastion, so as to claim their place in its history.

Very little is left to remind us of the siege; a few names have been retained, Mount Gould, Fort Stamford and Mount Batten, but most of the old town has been knocked down, covered up or altered so completely one has difficulty finding anything original. All the major outer forts have vanished without a trace, as have the town walls, gates, trenches, old wells and most of the buildings that stood at the time. A person can however, trace the line of the outer forts, by walking from Eldad Hill along North Road and up to the old fire station. Follow Longfield Road around to Mount Gould Road you will come across the area where the Sabbath day battle began in December 1643.

Ancient names have also gone or been distorted; Maudlyn has been corrupted to Mutley. Warleigh House, Mount Edgcumbe, Cann House and Saltram remain, but are nothing like they must have appeared during the war. Of the others, Radford, Widey, Mannadon, Venn, Mount Wise, Whitleigh Hall, Kinterbury, Keame, Efford Hall and Place House have all disappeared. Plymouth Fort is also gone, as is most of the old castle. Vapron Road retains its legend as the position of the royalist artillery during the king's siege. Most of the churches still stand, St Andrew's, St Budeaux, Maker and the shell of Charles' Church. If a person looks hard enough, evidence of the war does exist, part of Fort Stamford's supporting breastworks are visible, as is the blockhouse at Mount Edgcumbe. Wearde Quay at Saltash, an earth bank is remaining evidence of a royalist battery. Several stone blockhouses around Plymouth's foreshore still exist, though these were of earlier construction, they were used during the civil war.

Relics from the war years have often been discovered all over Plymouth, burial pits were found at Laira and Furzehill, cannonballs and musket balls were dug up at Plympton, near Maudlyn, Stamford, Hooe and along Torr Lane. North Road, Mount Gould and Efford have given up clay pipes and lead shot dating from the period. Part of an old cannon has been unearthed on the site where St Gabriel's Church now stands, and the remains of an old ship was dredged up out of the Cattewater, reputedly sunk by royalist cannon fire during the war.

In 1882, a man standing on Burrows Hill Plymstock, found an old cannon dating from the civil war period. This ancient object stood upright in the soil and was being used by grazing cattle as a scratching post. In later years the cannon was dug out and mounted as a monument. Part of the inner town defence line, constructed during the early days of the conflict, was unearthed during construction work below Beaumont Park. During excavations, a part of Resolution Fort was exposed and studied, fortunately this tiny portion of the line has been preserved. Silver, hastily buried during the war, has been found at Plymstock, supposedly belonging to the Harris family. In 1813 a hoard of silver coins from the siege period was also dug up at Oreston.

There is only one monument in Plymouth dedicated to those who fought and died during the civil war. This was erected in 1891 in what is today Freedom Park, but was then called Two Fields. The monument stands to the west of Lipson Fort and the area around it was turned into an enclosed park. In 1652 Anne Pryn left 10s in her will as an annuity each year for the mayor and commonalty of Plymouth. This generous donation was to be used for the preaching of a sermon every year forever on the third day of December, in remembrance of the town's deliverance from the enemy. Each year after the battle, the bells of St Andrew's rang out in celebration and a dedication was held in the fields, now a simple service is performed at the monument on each December 3rd.

Of the people who fought the war around Plymouth, almost all have faded into history, their names forgotten. Many thousands will never be known, but over the years a few have come to light from army lists, account books, pension petitions, burial records, siege tracts, diaries and letters. I think it only right to include some of these people in this work, otherwise their deeds will be lost forever.

Chapter 14

The Forgotten Roll

For Parliament

Philip Francis, whose heroic career during the war was overshadowed, but not diminished by his reputed involvement with the mysterious string of pearls, lost both his father and his first wife within eight months of each other. Margaret died on April 27th 1643, and his father, Philip Francis senior, died on December 23rd aged sixty-nine, and was buried in the south aisle of St Andrew's. Undaunted by his loss he remained steadfast and continued to serve the garrison to the best of his ability. After the war Philip Francis remained a pillar of the Plymouth community, indeed his popularity was such that it brought him a second term as mayor in 1651. Residing at a house in Vauxhall Street, Francis continued his mercantile business and found time to serve as a JP and remarry. His second wife Katherine died on May 17th 1655, and three years later, on the 29th of August 1658, Captain Francis followed her to the grave. Upon his death Philip Francis continued the example of the town's well off by bequeathing money for the poor people of Plymouth, and his house to his son, another Philip Francis.

Colonel John Birch, the outspoken opponent of Lord Robartes left Plymouth with his regiment in July 1645. After a colourful final year that took him into action many times, the war came to an end. Birch put down his sword and took on a new role as MP for Leominster. He sat again for the same constituency in 1654, 1656 and 1660, later he sat for Penryn (1661-78), and Weobly in 1679, 1680 and 1689. After an interesting career, both military and political,

Colonel John Birch finally passed away on May 14th 1691.

Birch's much-maligned superior, John Lord Robartes, returned to Westminster after the Self-Denying Ordinance took away his commission. After the war Robartes returned to his family and estate in Cornwall, where due to the feelings of his neighbours, he remained inconspicuous. At the Restoration Lord Robartes, who eagerly backed the return of Charles II, befriended George Monck, the man chiefly responsible for the king's homecoming. For his support Robartes was given a place in the new king's Government. After a brief, but unhappy stint as Lord Deputy of Ireland, Robartes became Lord Privy Seal in 1661. Eight years later King Charles appointed Robartes Lord Lieutenant of Ireland, however this posting was not for him and within twelve months Robartes was back in England. On June 23rd John Lord Robartes was made Viscount Bodmin and Earl of Radnor; on October 25th his status rose even higher when he became Lord President of the king's new Privy Council. Robartes retained his high position until 1681. John Robartes died at his Chelsea home on July 17th 1685, and his body was taken back to Lanhydrock for burial.

Robert Rich, the popular Earl of Warwick, was another who lost his military status due to the Self-Denying Ordinance. On April 19th 1645, parliament handed over the running of the navy to five lords and twelve commoners, but the high regard Westminster held for Warwick led his name to be placed at the top of the new committee. After the war Warwick was affiliated with a group that tried, and failed, to work out an acceptable settlement for the king. When most of the parliamentary navy, anchored in the Downs, mutinied in 1648, Warwick was reappointed lord high admiral. Though he struggled to persuade the seamen to remain loyal to parliament, he failed, and a large part of the fleet set sail to join Prince Charles in Holland. Despite nullifying royalist efforts to use their newly-acquired fleet, Warwick's loyalty to parliament was suddenly questioned in a popular pamphlet of the day. Rather than risk his good name being dragged through the mud, Robert Rich planned his retirement from the navy. Before he could leave though parliament stepped in and replaced him on February 23rd 1649. Despite the Commonwealth's mistreatment of Warwick, the old earl faithfully supported his friend Cromwell on almost all matters, indeed his grandson Robert married Oliver

Cromwell's daughter Frances. During the first civil war Warwick's eldest son, also called Robert, had sided with King Charles, though he never bore arms against parliament. On April 19th 1658 the seventy-one-year-old Earl of Warwick died and was buried at Felsted Essex. Of all who knew him Cromwell missed Robert Rich more than most.

After the war William Batten, Warwick's second in command and a man very popular with mariners, continued on in the navy. During the trouble between parliament and the army, and the latter's open disrespect for the captive king, the navy refused to comply with the army's demands and a rift opened up between the two services. Batten received orders from parliament to attend the House on September 17th 1647. Obeying the call William Batten tendered his resignation, but not due to dissatisfaction. He added that should the House need his services again, he would return. Batten's replacement was immediately unacceptable to the officers and seamen of the fleet and many wrote to Batten begging for him to return. Considering his popularity, William Batten rejoined the fleet in the Downs but found himself in the midst of a mutiny, which ended with eleven ships sailing away to join Prince Charles in Holland. When he was introduced to the Prince of Wales, William Batten was offered a knighthood if he would stay and take command of the royal navy. The old parliamentarian refused the prince's generous proposal, he could never fight against his old friend Warwick, instead he asked permission to return to England and Charles Stuart granted his request. Upon returning home, William Batten fades from history until the Restoration, when he once again took up the office of naval surveyor. In later years he became well-acquainted with Samuel Pepys the diarist, and served as MP for Rochester. Unlike his friend Warwick, who had three wives, Batten married only twice and had two children. After a painful illness, William Batten died on October 5th 1667, and was buried at Walthamstow. Mount Batten in Plymouth was named in his honour.

Christopher Martyn, owner of Chaddlewood, served the Plymouth garrison ably as a company officer and major of the local trained band regiment. After the war he represented Plympton St Maurice as MP for the years 1646, 1659 and 1660. He was also elected JP for the county of Devon for the years 1647 and 1654. On December 15th 1650 Martyn married Jane Snelling and lived until 1678, when all his property passed to his son John.

Captain Arthur Upton was a member of the Devonshire parliamentary commission in 1643, and commander of St Nicholas Island later in the war. He married Colonel William Gould's sister Elizabeth, and after the war served two terms as JP. Arthur Upton, always a radical, died in 1662 not yet fifty years of age.

Sir John Bampfield was made a freeman of Plymouth in September 1644 for his unceasing efforts on behalf of the town. In 1647 he found himself in London during the violence between the army and the city apprentices. Bampfield lived less than five years after the war ended, dying in 1650; he lies buried on his estate at Poltimore.

Colonel James Kerr continued his association with Plymouth on and off for several years after the war, then he disappears from history.

After his exchange in 1645, Sir John Northcote served as a JP and held his Ashburton seat in parliament until 1648 when the army excluded him. But he returned to Westminster in 1654. Until his death in June 1676, Northcote sat as MP for Bere Alston (1654 and 1656), and Barnstaple (1667). Sir John lies buried at Newton-St-Cyers.

Upon the cessation of hostilities, Sir Francis Drake was appointed High Sheriff of Devon early in 1646, and in June he represented Bere Alston as MP. Although absent most of the time from his Plymouth horse regiment, Drake was present at its disbandment in October 1646. With the Restoration Sir Francis received a royal pardon from the new king on August 12th 1661. Elected MP for Newport in the same year, Drake was already ill and on January 6th 1662 he died at the age of forty-four.

Sir Francis' younger brother Thomas, after his treachery and fortunate discharge from parliamentary service, stayed away from the Plymouth area for several years. When he eventually returned to his family home at Buckland sometime in 1647, he kept away from public life. Tom Drake always regretted his disloyalty to parliament, and in June 1653 he petitioned parliament, but for what reason I have found no evidence. Receiving no answer, Drake travelled to London personally and during the journey he died suddenly at the age of thirty-three.

Colonel Sir Edmond Fowell was one of many officers who held high rank but left the fighting to their younger subordinates. Baptized at Ugborough on August 15th 1593, Fowell was knighted at

Greenwich eighteen years later and became heir to his brother Arthur's estate in 1612 after he accidentally drowned. Sir Edmund married Margaret Pawlett in 1614, and sat in the Long Parliament as MP for Ashburton and for Devon. During the war he commanded a small regiment in Plymouth of no more than a few hundred troops, and was president of the Devonshire committee for sequestrations. Two years after the war, Fowell retired from politics, but attended the 1660 parliament in order to add his name to the vote for Restoration of the Monarchy. Sir Edmond was created baronet in April 1661, and died in October 1674; Sir Edmond Fowell is buried in the village of Ugborough.

Henry Hatsell, a captain of the town, who served part of his duty on St Nicholas Island, began as an ensign under another gallant soldier Captain Arthur Gay early in the war. Hatsell was soon promoted to lieutenant and then captain, but this was as far as he went; duty on the island would prove tame compared to life on the outer line, and promotion a long time coming. After the war, Henry Hatsell and his wife Elizabeth purchased Saltram House, and in 1656 he was appointed commissioner of the navy at Plymouth, and MP for the town two years later. Not forgetting his military experiences, Hatsell retained command of a troop of militia. At the Restoration, Hatsell, also a JP, lost his position and settled down at Saltram. Despite a reputation as a possible future insurrectionist, Henry Hatsell remained passive until his death.

John St Aubyn, born at Crowan in Cornwall around 1610, was another who profited by the war, though during the conflict he was fairly obscure. He is often called colonel, though one of the military quartermasters in Plymouth, Richard Clapp, refers to him as captain of a cavalry troop. I tend to agree with Clapp, who was in constant contact with St Aubyn's officers during the latter part of the war. Another reason for the choice is, the only officer mentioned as belonging to Captain St Aubyn's command is a Lieutenant Hunt Greenwood, there was also a cornet named Rowe. John St Aubyn had a brother Thomas, a colonel who commanded a regiment in the king's army. During the second civil war John St Aubyn greatly aided Sir Hardress Waller in putting down the revolt of the Cornish royalists. As a consequence he probably received his colonelcy during this period. St Aubyn, an acquaintance of Sir Richard Buller, was one of the elite groups of Cornishmen who sided with parliament. In 1643 St Aubyn was appointed Sheriff of Cornwall, or more accurately that part of the county which came under parliamentary control. On April 6th 1635 John and his wife Catherine stood in St Andrew's Church and had their son John baptized. St Aubyn's mediocre army career was confined mostly to Plymouth, but after the war he rose in prominence. In 1648 St Aubyn was commissioner for east Cornwall, the following year he found himself military governor of St Michael's Mount. Seventeen years later he was again made Sheriff of Cornwall, and in 1679 he was elected MP for Mitchell. John St Aubyn eventually purchased the mount and lived there, but one evening in 1684, whilst returning across the causeway linking the mount with the mainland, he went off course and drowned. King Charles created his son John baronet in 1671, and the family's fortune rose steadily after that.

Justinian Peard, the popular mayor, continued in his property speculations at home and abroad and served Plymouth a second term as its mayor (1656-7). Sadly his first wife died in January 1669, but before the year was out he had remarried, unfortunately within ten days of his new marriage Justinian Peard was dead.

One who suffered tragically for his loyalty to parliament was George Hughes, vicar of St Andrew's for eighteen glorious years. At the Restoration he and his son Obadiah were arrested and escorted by a body of musketeers across to St Nicholas Island, then being used as a political prison. Here they were incarcerated and kept in disgraceful circumstances, but neither man was charged. Eventually, after friends raised and paid the extortionate sum of £2,000, George and his son were released, but the elderly priest was ordered never to set foot in Plymouth again. George Hughes moved to Kingsbridge and remained there until his death, shortly after his release.

Another martyr to pay the ultimate price was Abraham Cheare, a man who served the town with musket and Bible. Cheare, who had been born in Plymouth in 1626, served in the town militia during the war, but was dissatisfied that he remained nothing but a common foot soldier throughout. In 1648 he took up religion and became the first minister of George Street Baptist Church. At the Restoration Cheare was sentenced to three months' imprisonment in Exeter for nonconformity. In August 1662 he refused to take the oath of allegiance required by all men over the age of eighteen years and again went to prison. This time it was for three years, and he was only released then due to the intervention of his sister. Abraham

Cheare refused to be intimidated and went back to preaching. Consequently he was confined to a gloomy dungeon under the Plymouth Guildhall for four weeks, and then taken across to St Nicholas Island. Here he found himself in good company, General John Lambert and Colonel Robert Lilburn, two of Cromwell's officers were also incarcerated on the island. So too were George Hughes, his son and Thomas Martyn, as well as many other so-called enemies of Charles II. Cheare spent what remained of his life on the island, finally dying after a long illness on March 5th 1668.

The passionate Puritan minister, John Syms, who was forced to flee from his home on Dartmoor and seek refuge in Plymouth, kept a daybook during and after the war. His account of events, although informative and biased, gives a different perception of characters and events during the conflict. Syms himself left Plymouth in 1646, and in August the following year he found himself appointed to the Church of St George the Martyr at Dean Prior, where he replaced the royalist Robert Herrick. After a brief stay he moved on to the parish of Buckland. Of his four children, the two eldest died, Mary aged twenty-one and Nathaniel aged thirteen. John Syms lost his office at the Restoration and moved to Water in the parish of Ashburton. Later he shifted to West Ogwell, where in 1672 he received permission to preach in Ashburton. Within four years the fiery, controversial minister from Sheepstor was dead.

Thomas Halsey, was the cavalry major who married in St Andrew's Church back in December 1643. Being one of the more active officers in the garrison, Halsey had been involved in the fighting from the beginning of the war until its end. Thomas and his wife Joane had five children, Thomas born October 19th 1645, followed by John, James, Mary and Joane. Sadly Major Halsey was dead by the late 1650s as was his wife. The administration of the Halsey estate was granted to William Braddon, guardian of the children and an old comrade in arms of Halsey's.

Captain William Braddon, the officer who took on Colonel Arundell and mortally wounded him back in 1644, left Plymouth and served in Colonel Sir Francis Drake's Plymouth horse regiment. Drake's command was amalgamated with other units to form Major General Edward Massey's infamous brigade. In December 1650 William Braddon purchased the manor of Treworgie in north Cornwall and served as captain of the Cornish militia (1655-6), a justice of the peace, and MP for Camelford (1658). In the years following the war he married Anne and they had four children, three sons and a daughter. Braddon rebuilt the manor house and at the Restoration he refused to donate money towards a gift for the new king. His eldest son William died in 1668, followed ten years later by his wife. William Braddon lived on at Treworgie until his death in late January 1694, and the old captain was finally laid to rest on January 31st.

Captain William Braddon was buried in the church of St Gennys, and his memorial stone is still there on the chancel wall, it reads: *'Here lyeth the body of William Braddon of this parish esquire, who departed this life ye 31st day of January Anno Domini 1694'.*

Mortuus alloquitur viatores

In war and peace I bore command
Both gowne and sword I wore,
Yet now am here lay'd in cold clay,
As those I rul'd before.

Vain is ye pomp and splendour, sure,
Which in this world men have,
For't leaves ym, wn they come to dye,
And to be lay'd in grave.

Strive not for earthly grandeur, yn,
Which is so poor a thing,
But seek for grace wch, will at last,
Immortal glory bring.

Another loyal officer who served Plymouth and went on to greater glory during the Restoration was Captain John Clobery. Clobery was a cavalry officer whose elder brother George was killed fighting for the king near Plymouth. Later Clobery left the garrison with the rest of the cavalry and served in Massey's brigade with William Braddon. In 1650 he was elected MP for Launceston and was later found fighting in Scotland as a lieutenant colonel under General George Monck. At the Restoration Colonel Clobery was knighted by the new king and presented with an ample pension. In 1662 he married Anne, a widow and the pair set up home in Winchester.

Five years later, with a threat of war with the Dutch looming, John Clobery raised a troop of horse. He went on to represent Winchester in parliament and became a leading figure in the city's governance. In his final years Sir John suffered greatly from an incurable illness, and in January 1687 he died aged sixty-three. The gallant soldier was buried in Winchester Cathedral and four years after his death his widow paid a large sum of money for a monument to be constructed to her loving husband.

For the King

Sir Ralph Hopton, the man who first united the Cornish royalists and organised them into an elite fighting machine, was rewarded on September 4th 1643 by the king with the title Lord Hopton of Stratton. Throughout that winter Hopton fought against his old friend Waller, and the following summer he joined the king as he advanced westwards after Essex. Late in the war, Lord Hopton was back in the Westcountry, only this time royalist fortunes were on the decline. As the situation deteriorated Hopton found himself abandoned by Prince Charles and the other leading royalists, and forced into a corner by Fairfax's New Model Army. Unable to break out Sir Ralph Hopton was forced to surrender the remnants of his army at Truro on March 11th 1646. After signing the surrender document, Hopton took ship for the Scilly Isles, where he tarried only a short time before continuing on to Jersey, one of the last bastions of royalism. Prince Charles and his advisors, many of whom were those who so hastily abandoned the royal cause, welcomed Hopton to the Channel Islands. Hopton spent the final years of his life living in Wesel, trying to recover his property in England. Parliament refused all his requests, and in September 1652 Hopton died in the city of Bruges, a sad and weary man.

Dartmouth was Prince Maurice's high-water mark of the war, and Plymouth his turning point. After failing to capture Plymouth, the prince moved on and also failed to take Lyme Regis; failure followed him to Taunton and at Bridgewater he received a bloody nose, though he was present with the king during the Lostwithiel campaign. Maurice gave a fair showing at the second battle of Newbury, but he was growing dissatisfied. Resigning his post in the west, Prince Maurice was quickly promoted major general of Worcestershire, Shropshire, Herefordshire and Monmouthshire.

Unfortunately the prince's luck was no better here, sent west to relieve Chester early in 1645, he achieved his goal, but then, while he was away from the town, the parliamentarians returned and forced Chester's surrender. Maurice served the king at Leicester and Naseby, and he was with his brother Rupert in the city of Oxford when the end came on June 22nd 1646. Four days later parliament passed a vote that the king's nephews should leave England within ten days. Rupert went first and his brother followed. Used to nothing but warfare, Maurice served the Prince of Orange, then campaigned in Flanders where he was joined temporarily by his brother in 1648. The next year Maurice decided to take part in his brother's plans to raise a small fleet and sail to the West Indies in search of adventure. The brothers met on the coast of Africa and Rupert made Maurice vice admiral. As the small flotilla sailed across the Atlantic, a heavy storm blew up, and on September 14th 1652 Rupert lost three of his four ships, and his brother.

Sir Richard Grenville, after grudgingly leaving his headquarters outside Plymouth in March 1645, marched up to Somerset, furious at having to serve under Goring. During the royalist siege of Taunton, Grenville was wounded, but once recovered he was sent down to take command of the cavalier forces besieging Lyme Regis. The summer of 1645 brought internal dissention and disaster to the royal cause in the southwest. While Sir Richard argued with his superior, Prince Charles retreated first into Devon and then into Cornwall. Open hostility amongst the royalist leaders escalated to new levels, while the army's morale sank to new depths. Too young and inexperienced in military matters, Prince Charles took advice from others even less capable of uniting his generals. On January 19th 1646 the prince, fed up with his high-handed, disobedient subordinate, had Grenville arrested for insubordination. Sir Richard spent several days at Launceston prison before being transferred to St Michael's Mount. Somehow he escaped from the island and took a ship for France, where his son Richard joined him. Later father and son made their way into exile in Italy. During his self-banishment, Grenville and his old antagonist Sir Edward Hyde, the royalist Earl of Clarendon, continued the bickering that had begun during the final months of the war. After a brief discreet visit to England, and a spell in a Brussels prison, Sir Richard found himself almost destitute. He died on October 21st 1659, still at odds with his old comrades in arms.

In 1651 Piers Edgcumbe, whose home had lain tantalizingly close to the roundhead garrisons at Mount Wise House and St Nicholas Island, was forced to pay one tenth the value of his estate. Due to Edgcumbe undervaluing his property, the imposed fine of £1,275 16s and 8d was increased. Always a loyal royalist Edgcumbe saw his son Richard knighted by King Charles II, and was himself appointed Sheriff of Cornwall in 1661. Five years later, on January 6th 1666, Piers Edgcumbe died and was buried at Calstock.

Still only in his mid-forties by the end of the war, Sir Edward Seymour lost his governorship of Dartmouth when Fairfax overran the place in January 1646. Trapped in Exeter, Seymour was captured at the city's surrender three months later. Possibly due to his earlier escape from a parliamentary prison, Sir Edward was held in Exeter as a prisoner until 1652. Upon his release Seymour was carefully watched, as many believed him to be part of a group that sought the restoration of Charles II. Parliament's suspicions were well founded, Sir Edward was indeed in touch with the exiled monarch. In 1658 he took ship and visited his exiled king in France, handing over a £1,000 gift for his majesty's use. Seymour's home at Berry Pomeroy had been looted several times by roundhead troops, but not destroyed and his father was permitted to live there in peace throughout much of the war. In 1659 Sir Edward's father died and he succeeded to the baronacy. Sir Edward bided his time and at the Restoration he managed to recoup part of his loses. He was also appointed Deputy Lieutenant for Devon, Vice Admiral of the same county, MP for Totnes, colonel general of all trained bands raised in Devon and captain and governor of the castles and blockhouses; titles lavished upon a most loyal subject by a grateful monarch. He died on December 7th 1688 at the age of seventy and was buried at his home.

After his gallant, though fruitless defence of Fort Charles, Sir Edmund Fortescue returned to his home at Fallapit before travelling abroad. Fortescue died early in 1647 at Delft and was buried there, leaving behind a son, Edmund, who would become third baronet in 1664, and three daughters.

For his royalism Sir Thomas Hele, who commanded a small cavalry regiment for the king, was forced to pay a yearly composition of £280 in order to retain his Flete House Estate. Hele had a son, Thomas, by his first wife Penelope, and two others, Samuel and Henry, by his second wife Elizabeth. At the Restoration he was elected MP for Plympton, the same seat he sat for back in 1640. Sir Thomas died in 1670 and was buried near his second wife at Holbeton.

The passionate royalist William Lane, Vicar of Aveton Gifford Church and rabble rouser, who spent much of the war hiding, or running like his opposite number John Syms, though his adversaries were roundheads rather than royalists. Educated at the University of Oxford, Lane had been Rector of Ringmore before coming to Aveton Gifford. At the time Plymouth announced her intention of siding with parliament, William Lane was in the midst of shifting his belongings from one church to the other. Due to his passionate contempt for parliament the Devonshire parliamentarians, who named him 'That derisive Bishop Lane' marked him for retribution. During raids by roundhead soldiers, the elderly cleric was often forced to hide and listen as soldiers looted his church and smashed up his furniture. After the war William Lane lost his position to Francis Barnard and fled to France. Later he returned home and lived quietly with his wife and five children. To solve a grievance between himself and Barnard, William Lane, now in his early sixties personally took a petition to London. Surprisingly parliament came out on his side and promised to replace the zealous Barnard. During his walk back between Honiton and Exeter, Lane, weary from the heat, drank foul water and became ill. Due to his age and the rigours of a hard life William Lane never recovered and died, he was buried in Alphington Church on August 31st 1654, aged sixty-three.

Many of the thousands of soldiers who died will never be known, however a number of the more prominent officers who served the garrison can be listed, these were: Colonel Elizeus Leighton, Colonel John Crocker, Colonel William Gould deceased, Colonel Sir Shilston Calmady deceased, Colonel William Ruthven, Lieutenant Colonel Robert Martin deceased, Lieutenant Colonel Michael Searle, Lieutenant Colonel Robert Moore, Lieutenant Colonel Thomas Fitch, Major Thomas Halsey, Major Gabriel Barnes, Major Worthyvale, Major Robert Symonds and Major James Pearce.

The captains and lieutenants are too numerous to list but I have selected a small number of the more active; Captain Nicholas Roope, Captain Arthur Gay, Captain Richard Laugharne, Captain William Wootton, Captain Humphrey Burton deceased, Captain Richard Evans, Captain Richard Burthogge, Captain Richard Corbett deceased, Captain Richard Sandall deceased, Captain John Wansey deceased, Captain James Anderson deceased, Captain Samuel Rawlinson deceased, Captain Henry Gosnal deceased, Captain George Keckwich, Captain William Braddon, Captain Haines deceased, Captain William Owen, Lieutenant Foxworthy, Lieutenant John Chaffin, Lieutenant Richard Showers and Lieutenant Philip Beaumont deceased. Those marked deceased died during the war.

The suffering of the wounded soldiers who survived the primitive surgery of the time did not end with the king's surrender. Many endured their agony for the rest of their lives and were forced to beg for a living. Of the few pension petitions that exist, several of these unfortunates can be brought to life once again.

The multi-wounded William Chapman, a Plymouth husbandman who fought at Braddock Down and Fort Stamford, was so badly crippled by injuries sustained during both engagements, he was unable to walk. In 1648 Chapman petitioned parliament for a pension and his appeal was signed by three of the town's wartime mayors, Francis, Peard and Nicholls. Parliament approved Chapman's petition and when the sickly veteran died in 1652 his wife Anne continued to receive his annuity.

Walter Hurrell, a mariner, lost his right arm during the Sabbath day fight (Freedom Fields) fought on December 3rd 1643. In 1655 Hurrell was awarded a pension of £4 p.a.

Another who fought at what became known in later years as the battle of Freedom Fields was Michael Bloye. Unfortunately Bloye was killed in the fighting, leaving a wife Elizabeth and three small children impoverished. After the war she petitioned for a pension; Philip Francis signed her appeal and Mrs Bloye received an allowance. Philip Francis gladly put his name to many of the petitions sent in to the county quarter sessions after the war.

Katherine Collier of the town sought his moniker when in 1649 she petitioned for her dead husband Thomas, who had served under Francis and been killed during an engagement, leaving her with two children and no means of support.

Stephen Webb who served with Captain Arthur Gay received two shoulder wounds during the war; the second, received in a skirmish at Warleigh House, forced Webb to retire from the army. With a wife and six children to support Stephen Webb was forced to petition parliament for a pension.

John Fox from Ugborough, a trooper under Captain Pearce, had a bad fall from his horse and as a consequence he was disabled. In 1647 Fox was forced to appeal for a pension, happily he received an annual pension of 40 shillings.

William Clark, a trooper under Lieutenant Colonel Searle, was killed in a skirmish leaving a wife and five children; Mrs Clark was awarded a pension after the war, as was Stephen Tuckerman.

Tuckerman had been a trained bandsman under Major Christopher Martyn, and was wounded through both arms during the war. Lieutenant John Pearce signed his petition.

William Collyn, a soldier from Captain Hughes' company, was so badly wounded in the face he lost both eyes and he joined the growing list, petitioning parliament for a pension.

Royalist veterans were forced to wait until the Restoration for their allowances. Captain William Pomeroy, a Plymouth man who rode away to serve his king, was wounded several times during the war. Later he served in the king's navy on the frigate *Dolphin* and died on board ship. In 1665 Pomeroy's wife Anne petitioned King Charles' parliament on behalf of herself and her children, she was awarded £6 13s 4d.

William Browne, a Plympton royalist, who served as a gunner under Colonel John Digby, was wounded and captured at the same battle that Digby had received his eye wound. During his extensive confinement at the Marshalsea, Browne's health deteriorated. After the war Browne's condition grew worse, and by 1662 he was so ill he could not attend the quarter sessions to plead for his case.

Probably one of the saddest cases was that of Grace Battishill, whose husband George had served as an ensign under Captain Anthony Stert in Colonel Philip Champernowne's regiment. Captured during the second battle of Fort Stamford, known as the Haltnersday fight, Battishill was taken to Plymouth, recognised as a turncoat and hanged. Grace Battishill's home was later plundered, and with no income she was forced out of her house, to live on charity. Philip Champernowne, Sir Thomas Hele, John Harris, and Anthony Stert gladly signed Mrs Battishill's petition, and stated that her husband had been a true royalist. In 1662 her long suffering was alleviated by a pension of £6 13s 4d.

Sources

Accounts of John Halsey.

Accounts of Philip Francis.

Accounts of Richard Clapp.

Accounts of William Braddon.

Army lists of the Roundheads and Cavaliers, edited by Edward Peacock FSA.

Annals of the Seymours, by H. St Maur, West Country Studies Library, Exeter.

Around and About Saltash, by Philip E. Porter.

Bath Central Library, Bath.

Barnstaple and the Northern Part of Devonshire During the Great Civil War, by R. W. Cotton.

Battles and Generals of the Civil War, 1642-1657, by Colonel H. C. B. Rogers.

Belum Civille by Ralph Hopton.

Buller papers, edited by R. N. Worth, Plymouth City Library.

Burial Registers for St Andrew's Church, St Budeaux Church, Plympton St Marys, Charles' Church, Plymstock Church, West Devon Record Office.

Calendar of State Papers Domestic, 1625-1649, Plymouth City Library.

Churchwardens' Accounts for St Andrew's Church, St Budeaux Church, Charles' Church and St George's Church Modbury, West Devon Record Office, Plymouth.

Committee on Compounding.

Cornish Worthies, by Walter K. Tregellas.

Cornwall in the Great Civil War and Interregnum, by Mary Coate.

Corwall Record Office, Truro.

Devon and Cornwall Notes and Queries, Plymouth City Library.

Devon and Exeter in the Civil War, by Eugene Andriette.

Devon Quarter Sessions Order Book, Devon Record Office, Exeter.

Devon Worthies, 2 Vols, by John Prince, West Devon Record Office, Plymouth.

Diary of the Marches kept by the Royal Army During the Great Civil War, by Richard Symonds.

Dictionary of National Biography, Plymouth City Library.

Dorchester Reference Library, Dorchester.

Dorset in the Civil War, 1625-1666, by Tim Goodwin.

Duke of Portland MSS, Bodleian Library Oxford.

Exeter and the Civil War, by Mark Stoyle.

The Family and Heirs of Sir Francis Drake, 2 Vols, by Lady Elliot Drake.

From Deliverance to Destruction, by Mark Stoyle.

The Great Rebellion, 1642-1660, by Ivan Roots.

Historical Management Associates Ltd., Stuart Peachy and Alan Turton.

Histories of Launceston and Dunheved, by R. and O. Peter.

A History of the Parish of Aveton Gifford, by Rev C. C. Shaw.

A History of Plymouth, by C. W. Bracken.

A History of Kingsbridge and Salcombe, by Anne Born.

A History of Plymouth, by Llewellyn Jewitt.

History of the Great Civil War, by Samuel Rawson Gardiner.

House of Commons Journal, Exeter City Library.

House of Lords, Journal Exeter City Library.

John Syms, A Daybook of Some Special Passages and Mercies, Add 35297; the British Library.

The King's General in the West, by Rev Roger Granville.

The Life of Sir William Waller, by John Adair.

Location and Locality, by Mark Stoyle.

New Light on Old Plymouth, by James Barber.

Officers and Regiments of the Royalist Army, by Stuart Reid.

Old Cornwall, Plymouth City Library.

Place Names of Plymouth, Dartmoor and the Tamar Valley, by Bill Best Harris.

Plymouth City Council, Archaeology.

Prince of Cavaliers, by Frank Knight.

Recovery and Restoration in an English County, 1646-1670, by Stephen K. Roberts.

The Regimental History of Cromwell's Army, by Sir Charles Firth.

Reports of the Devonshire Association, Plymouth City Library.

Roundhead to Royalist, A Biography of Colonel John Birch, by E. Heath-Agnew.

Royal Institute of Cornwall, Plymouth City Library.

Royalist Officers in England and Wales, by P. R. Newman.

Seymour family papers, Devon Record Office.

Sherborne Castle Estates.

Siege Accounts for Plymouth, West Devon Record Office.

Siege Accounts for Plymouth, Published by R. N. Worth in Transactions of the Devonshire Association, XVII, pages 215-239, Plymouth City Library.

Sir Bevil Grenville and His Times, by John Stuckley.

Sir Richard Grenville of the Civil War, by Amos Miller.

Somerset and Dorset Notes and Queries.

Somerset in the Civil War, by David Underdown.

Sufferage of the Clergy, by John Walker.

Transactions of the Plymouth Institute, Plymouth City Library.

Thomason Tracts.

Visitations of the County of Cornwall, by J. L. Vivian.

Visitations of the County of Devon, by J. L. Vivian.

Western Antiquary, Plymouth City Library.

Winchester Cathedral, its Monuments and Memorials, by John Vaughan.

Index of Names

General Index